MCAT

**Organic Chemistry
Review Notes**

© 2010 by Kaplan, Inc.

Published by Kaplan Publishing, a division of Kaplan, Inc.
1 Liberty Plaza, 24th Floor
New York, NY 10006

In Partnership with Kaplan's National MCAT Team, 1440 Broadway, 8th Floor New York, NY 10018

Printed in the United States of America

10 9 8 7 6 5 4 3

ISBN: 978-1-60714-825-8

Kaplan Publishing books are available at special quantity discounts to use for sales promotions, employee premiums, or educational purposes. Please email our Special Sales Department to order or for more information at kaplanpublishing@kaplan.com, or write to Kaplan Publishing, 1 Liberty Plaza, 24th Floor, New York, NY 10006.

Contributors

The Kaplan MCAT Review Notes Series was created by a dedicated team of professionals who worked a combined total of over 11,000 hours.

This text would not exist without the tireless work of Cait Clancy, Henry Conant, Ed Crawford, PhD, Suneetha Desiraju, Marilyn Engle, Christopher Falzone, PhD, Jennifer Farthing, Sheryl Gordon, Walter Hartwig, PhD, Jeannie Ho, Jessica Kim, Jeff Koetje, MD, John Linick, Keith Lubeley, Amjed Mustafa, Joanna Myllo, Glen Pearlstein, MD, Dominique Polfliet, Ira Rothstein, PhD, Matthew Wilkinson, and Sze Yan.

Special thanks to Jesse Barrett, Susan E. Barry, Jason Baserman, Jessica Brookman, Geri Burgert, Deana Casamento, Da Chang, David Elson, Robin Garmise, Rita Garthaffner, Chip Hurlburt, Colette Mazunik, Danielle Mazza, Stephanie McCann, Diane McGarvey, Maureen McMahon, Jason Miller, Jason Moss, Maria Nicholas, Walt Niedner, Jeff Olson, Rochelle Rothstein, MD, Lisa Pallatroni, John Polstein, Ron Sharpe, Brian Shorter, Glen Stohr, Martha Torres, Bob Verini, and the countless others who made this project possible.

Using This Book

This book is designed to help you review the science topics covered on the MCAT. It represents one of the content review resources available to you in the Kaplan program.

Additional review is available through the live and on-demand lessons, the library of available practice tests and explanations-on-demand that accompany them, and your flashcards and QuickSheets.

Please understand that content review, no matter how thorough, is not sufficient preparation for the MCAT! The MCAT Biological Sciences and Physical Sciences sections test your reading, reasoning, and problem-solving skills, as well as your science knowledge. Don't assume that simply memorizing the contents of this book will earn you high science scores—it won't. If you want your best shot at great science scores, you must also improve your reading and test-taking skills through the lessons, testing sessions, and the Kaplan and AAMC practice tests in the Training Library. So resist the temptation to reread this book at the expense of taking practice tests! Rather, strike a balance between content review and critical reasoning practice.

At the end of each chapter, you'll find MCAT-style review questions and open-ended questions for study group discussion. These are designed to help you assess your understanding of the chapter you just read.

The last chapter of this book is a special section devoted to what we call the High-Yield Problem Solving Guide. Although not presented exactly in the style of the MCAT, these questions tackle the most frequently tested topics found on the test. For each type of problem, the guide will provide you with a stepwise technique for solving the question and key directional points on how to solve specifically for the MCAT.

Consult the Syllabus in your MCAT Lesson Book for specific reading/practice assignments. Reading the appropriate chapters will greatly enhance your understanding of the lesson material. A glossary and index are included in the back of each review book for easy reference.

This is your book, so write in the margin, highlight the key points—do whatever is necessary to help you get that higher score. It should be your trusty companion as Test Day approaches.

Sincerely,
The Kaplan MCAT Team

About Scientific American

As the world's premier science and technology magazine, and the oldest continuously published magazine in the United States, *Scientific American* is committed to bringing the most important developments in modern science, medicine, and technology to 3.5 million readers worldwide in an understandable, credible, and provocative format.

Founded in 1845 and on the "cutting edge" ever since, *Scientific American* boasts over 140 Nobel laureate authors, including Albert Einstein, Francis Crick, Stanley Prusiner, and Richard Axel. *Scientific American* is a forum where scientific theories and discoveries are explained to a broader audience.

Scientific American published its first foreign edition in 1890 and, in 1979, was the first Western magazine published in the People's Republic of China. Today, *Scientific American* is published in 17 foreign language editions with a total circulation of more than 1 million worldwide. *Scientific American* is also a leading online destination (www.ScientificAmerican.com), providing the latest science news and exclusive features to more than 2 million unique visitors monthly.

The knowledge that fills our pages has the power to inspire—to spark new ideas, paradigms, and visions for the future. As science races forward, *Scientific American* continues to cover the promising strides, inevitable setbacks and challenges, and new medical discoveries as they unfold.

Guide To Margin Notes

Our Review Notes are designed with ample white space for you to take notes while you work your way through the Kaplan MCAT program. Periodically, you'll come across some of our own comments in the margins. We call these sidebars "margin notes" (pretty clever, right?).

The following is a legend of the five main types of margin notes you'll find in the science Review Notes.

Real World: These notes are designed to illustrate how a concept discussed in the text relates to the practice of medicine and the world at large. Since you are a premed (if not, you're reading the wrong book), we felt that these correlations would both be of interest to you and help solidify your understanding of some key concepts.

Key Concept: These are synopses of the concepts discussed on a page. Typically, we reserve this type of margin note for pages where lots of important and complex information is presented.

Bridge: We use "Bridges" to alert you to the conceptual links that occur between chapters or disciplines.

MCAT Expertise: These are designed to illuminate some of the conceptual patterns that the test maker tends to focus on when writing MCAT questions.

Mnemonics: Sometimes they rhyme, and sometimes they don't. But we hope that they will all help you recall information quickly on Test Day.

Star Rating

In the current version of our review notes, you'll find a new feature: The Kaplan MCAT Star Rating. We have developed a system to help you focus your studies. The star rating uses a 6 star scale. Two factors are considered when determining the rating for each topic: the "learnability" of the topic – or how easy it is to master – and the frequency with which it appears on the MCAT exam. For example, a topic which presents relatively little difficulty to master and appears with relatively high frequency on the MCAT would receive a higher star rating (e.g., 5 or 6 stars) than a topic which is very difficult to master and appears less frequently on the test. The combination of these two factors represented by the star rating will help you prioritize and direct your MCAT studies.

Contents

Chapter 1: Nomenclature 1
    Practice Questions 19
Chapter 2: Isomers 23
    Practice Questions 41
Chapter 3: Bonding. 45
    Practice Questions 55
Chapter 4: Alkanes, Alkyl Halides, and Substitution Reactions. 59
    Practice Questions 73
Chapter 5: Alkenes, Alkynes, and Elimination Reactions. 77
    Practice Questions 95
Chapter 6: Aromatic Compounds. 99
    Practice Questions 109
Chapter 7: Alcohols and Ethers 113
    Practice Questions 129
Chapter 8: Aldehydes and Ketones 133
    Practice Questions 149
Chapter 9: Carboxylic Acids 155
    Practice Questions 167
Chapter 10: Carboxylic Acid Derivatives 171
    Practice Questions 188
Chapter 11: Amines and Nitrogen-Containing Compounds 193
    Practice Questions 204
Chapter 12: Purification and Separation. 209
    Practice Questions 228
Chapter 13: Spectroscopy 233
    Practice Questions 249
Chapter 14: Carbohydrates 253
    Practice Questions 266
Chapter 15: Amino Acids, Peptides, and Proteins 271
    Practice Questions 290
Chapter 16: High-Yield Problem Solving Guide for Organic Chemistry 295
Glossary. 345
Index 353

Nomenclature

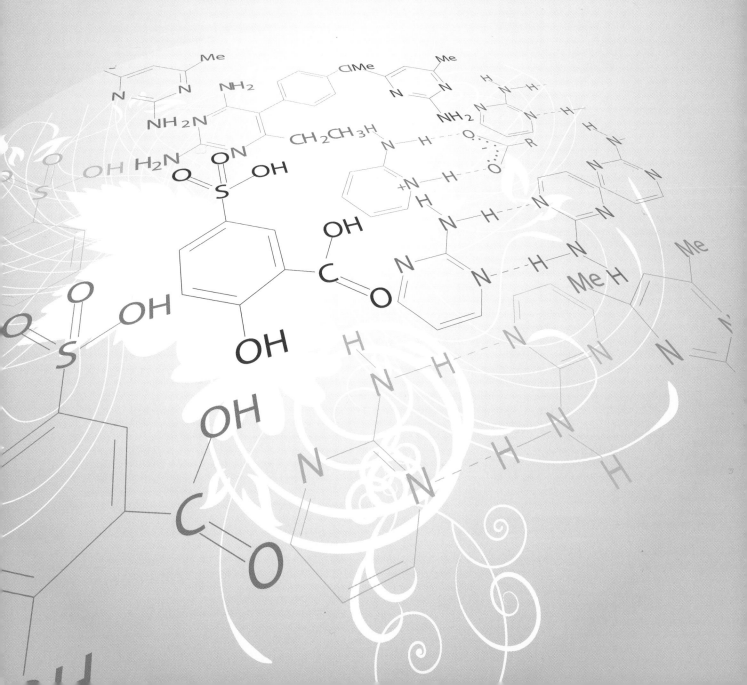

Early in my undergraduate career, I was warned, as I'm sure all of you were, about the dangers of Organic Chemistry. We've heard that the course is designed to weed out unworthy premeds, that it's both a GPA and a spirit breaker for optimistic future doctors. With these horror stories being passed down from generation to generation, it's no surprise that I, too, feared Organic Chemistry long before even setting foot in the classroom. While my expectations of fire, brimstone, and failing grades never actually came to pass, it did turn out to be one of the most challenging classes of my college career.

After surviving both Organic Chemistry I and II, I still didn't really understand the material. I could answer most of the questions with fairly decent accuracy and get good grades (owing to the strong curve), but I never really felt all that confident in the material. It wasn't until I started preparing for the MCAT that I actually began to comprehend what was happening in these reactions. You see, Organic Chemistry on the MCAT is a lot different from what it was in your Organic Chemistry classes. You will no longer be tested on your ability to memorize scattered reactions; instead, you will be tested on your understanding of the fundamental characteristics that drive reactions.

In fact, Organic Chemistry is a lot like chess—just as every piece on the board is capable of different motions, so is each element. It's actually a bit simpler than chess, because there are really only two different actions the atom can take in a reaction: Does it attack a nucleus with its excess electrons (negative charge), or does it get attacked as a result of its electron deficiency (positive charge)? You can decide between these two actions by considering a few important questions: How electronegative is the atom? Can it resonate its electrons? Are other atoms inductively pulling its electron density away? Learning the game of Organic Chemistry is much like learning any other game—if we want to play correctly, we need to know the rules.

Before we jump into examining reactions and solving problems, let's lay out the rules for naming organic compounds. Attempting to solve chemistry problems without knowing nomenclature is like trying to read *A Tale of Two Cities* without knowing English. Whereas the rules of English can sometimes seem unpredictable and inexact, the International Union of Pure and Applied Chemistry (IUPAC) established a precise and comprehensive language for Organic Chemistry. This means that learning IUPAC nomenclature will be infinitely easier than learning English—and, hey, you've already done that!

The MCAT occasionally employs a second dialect, known as a chemical's "common name." These names are based on the traditional names that were used before the IUPAC system (and, like reading Shakespeare, can sometimes seem like a completely different language), but they follow certain trends as well. There are only a handful of common names that you'll need to know on Test Day, and we'll point them out throughout the course of this book.

With a solid understanding of organic nomenclature, you should be able to both draw out the structure of any IUPAC name and give the IUPAC name for any structure you are given. We will provide you with the tools to learn the language of Organic Chemistry, though as with any language, fluency can only come with practice.

Alkanes

STRAIGHT-CHAIN ALKANES

Alkanes are the bare bones of the Organic Chemistry world; they are the simplest of the organic molecules, just a chain of carbons connected by single bonds with hydrogen atoms attached. Alkanes include commonly used fuels such as propane, butane, and octane.

The four simplest straight-chain alkanes are these:

CH_4	CH_3CH_3	$CH_3CH_2CH_3$	$CH_3CH_2CH_2CH_3$
methane	ethane	propane	butane

The general formula for alkanes is C_nH_{2n+2} (where n is an integer).

When the carbon chain contains five or more carbons, the naming gets a little simpler. Just use the Greek root for the number of carbons followed by the ending –**ane**.

C_5H_{12} = **pent**ane C_9H_{20} = **non**ane

C_6H_{14} = **hex**ane $C_{10}H_{22}$ = **dec**ane

C_7H_{16} = **hept**ane $C_{11}H_{24}$ = **undec**ane

C_8H_{18} = **oct**ane $C_{12}H_{26}$ = **dodec**ane

BRANCHED-CHAIN ALKANES

Whenever we have a chain of carbon atoms with smaller carbon chains branching off it, IUPAC gives us an organized system of naming the compound in five easy steps.

Step 1: Find the Longest Chain in the Compound

Finding the longest possible chain might sound easy, but be careful. Sometimes a molecule will be drawn so the backbone is actually composed of what looks like a side branch. Figure 1.1 shows a branched-chain alkane with its backbone.

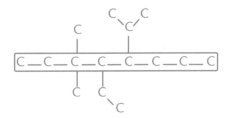

Figure 1.1

If there are two or more chains of equal length, the most substituted chain (the one with the most stuff attached to it) gets priority.

Step 2: Number the Chain

Number the chain such that most substituents get the lowest numbers possible. If you're not sure, just number it both ways and find the sum of each chain (see Figure 1.2). And then, well... it's like golf: The lowest wins.

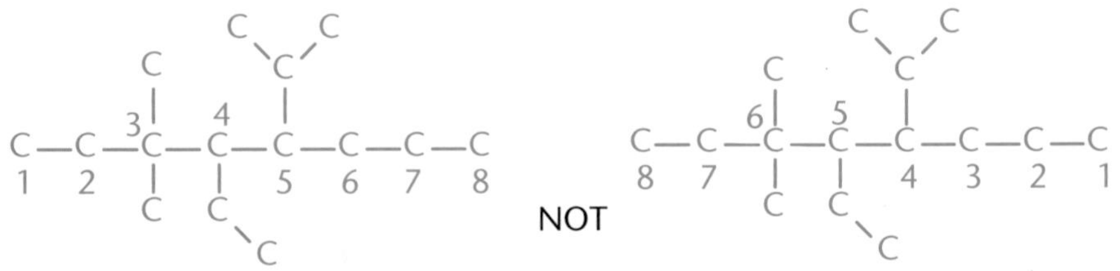

Figure 1.2

Step 3: Name the Substituents

Carbon chain **substituents** are named according to their Greek number root followed by the suffix **–yl**. This term is placed at the beginning of the compound, followed by the name of the longest side chain. Here are examples of some common substituents are.

CH_3–	CH_3CH_2–	$CH_3CH_2CH_2$–
methyl	ethyl	*n*-propyl

The prefix ***n-***, as we see in *n*-propyl above, simply stands for "normal." The normal designation indicates that the substituent is a straight-chain alkane that attaches to the backbone at one end of its chain. Sometimes the *n*- will be left out, but it's safe for you to assume that a molecule is normal, unless specified otherwise.

So what do abnormal substituents look like? The most common examples of alkane side chains that are not normal are shown in Figure 1.3.

MCAT Expertise

While this is an important rule, the MCAT is not looking to trick you—although they do reserve the right to do so! Most often, you will have smaller chains and not have to work too hard to find the longest carbon chain.

MCAT Expertise

Memorize these structures!

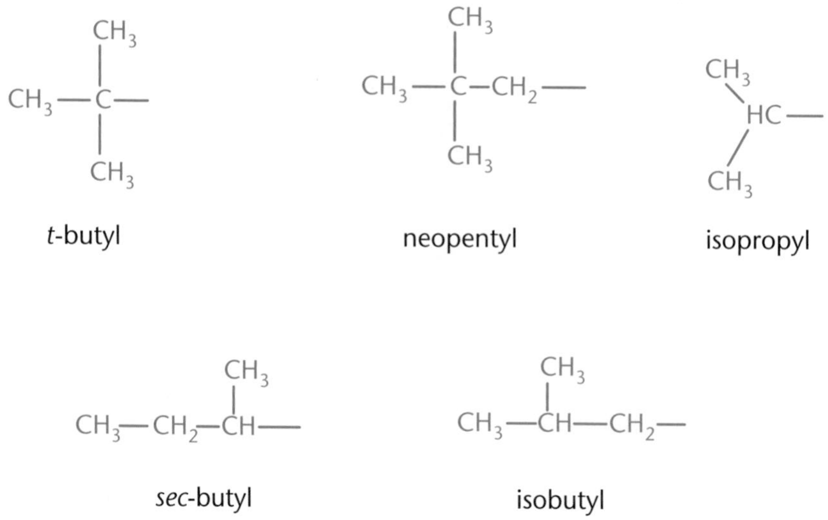

t-butyl neopentyl isopropyl

sec-butyl isobutyl

Figure 1.3

If there are multiple identical substituents, then we use the roots **di–**, **tri–**, **tetra–**, and so on.

Step 4: Assign a Number to Each Substituent.

Each substituent is assigned a number to designate its place on the principal chain. If the prefixes di–, tri–, and tetra– are used, we still assign a number for each group, even if those groups are attached to the same carbon. Don't worry if this sounds confusing; we will piece it all together in the next step.

Step 5: Complete the Name.

Names will always begin with the substituents listed in *alphabetical order,* with each substituent name preceded by its assigned number. Here's the tricky part. Numerical prefixes such as **di–**, **tri–**, and so on, as well as the hyphenated prefixes (***tert–*** [or ***t–***], ***sec–***, and ***n–***) are ignored in alphabetizing. In contrast to this, nonhyphenated roots that *are* part of the name, such as **iso–**, **neo–**, or **cyclo–**, *are* alphabetized. We then separate numbers from numbers with commas, and we separate numbers from words with hyphens. Remember that the end of every name will be the name of the backbone chain. Figure 1.4 shows an example.

MCAT Expertise

The MCAT is not a "picky" exam, so you probably won't be asked to choose between two answers that differ only in their alphabetization, but the rule about the prefixes may come in handy.

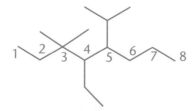

4-ethyl-5-isopropyl-3,3-dimethyl octane

Figure 1.4

CYCLOALKANES

Alkanes can also form rings; these are named by the number of carbon atoms in the ring with the prefix **cyclo–** (see Figure 1.5).

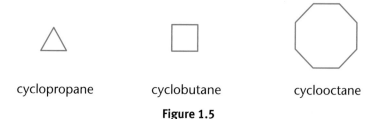

cyclopropane   cyclobutane   cyclooctane

Figure 1.5

The general formula for **cycloalkanes** is C_nH_{2n}. For every ring in the structure, there will be two fewer hydrogens than in the straight-chain counterpart. Let's think about what happens to those two hydrogens. We know that straight-chain hydrocarbons must end with $-CH_3$ groups, and we form a ring by connecting the two ends of the chain. Each carbon must lose a hydrogen to make an additional bond with the other carbon. This loss of hydrogens is also called a "degree of unsaturation." For example, an alkane with two rings present will have the general formula C_nH_{2n-2}, or two degrees of unsaturation.

As long as the ring itself is the longest carbon chain, substituted cycloalkanes will be named as derivatives of the parent ring. *The ring is numbered starting at the point of greatest substitution.* Once again, this means that the carbon with the most stuff attached to it will be assigned the number 1. Afterward, the goal is to give the lowest series of numbers as described in rule 2. If the ring structure is *not* part of the largest carbon chain, it will be listed as a substituent. Figure 1.6 shows two examples.

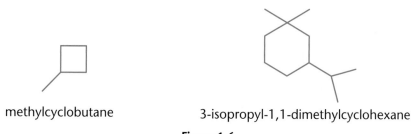

methylcyclobutane   3-isopropyl-1,1-dimethylcyclohexane

Figure 1.6

More Complicated Molecules ★★★★★★

All other molecules can be named using this five-step process, although as the molecules get more complicated, we will have more considerations to incorporate. The biggest difference between simple alkanes and these more complicated molecules

> **Key Concept**
>
> The general formula for both cycloalkanes and straight-chain alkenes is C_nH_{2n}.

> **Key Concept**
>
> Rings are numbered starting at the point of greatest substitution, and as always, try to get the lowest possible numbers.

> **MCAT Expertise**
>
> The MCAT is a multiple-choice exam. Therefore, it will be more advantageous for you to identify nomenclature errors quickly than to write out the exact name of a giant structure. Remember, speed is going to be one of your greatest assets on the MCAT.

is this: (You'd better be ready because this is huge!) *When counting out the longest chain of carbons, it MUST include the highest-priority functional group, this group must receive the lowest possible number, and the compound's name must end with the suffix of this group.* What do we mean by priority? Whereas Rolexes and celebrity escorts usually bestow priority upon people trying to get into fancy clubs, molecules just need to be more oxidized than all of their neighbors. We'll return to the concept of oxidation later, but for now, let's begin discussing **alkenes**.

Multiple Bonds ★★★★★★

ALKENES

Alkenes (sometimes referred to by their common name, **olefins**) are compounds that contain carbon–carbon double bonds. You'll use the same root as an alkane of equivalent length, but instead of ending with –**ane**, alkenes end with –**ene**.

The general formula for an alkene is C_nH_{2n}. Similar to cyclic alkanes, each double bond leads to two fewer hydrogens on the molecule, or one degree of unsaturation. For example, if we were to have a molecule with one ring and three double bonds, the molecule would have eight fewer hydrogens than its corresponding straight-chain alkane and, thus, four degrees of unsaturation.

As stated before, we need to incorporate the highest priority group when selecting the longest chain and assigning numbers. If there are multiple double bonds, select the chain that contains the greatest number of double bonds, and give the carbons the lowest numbers possible.

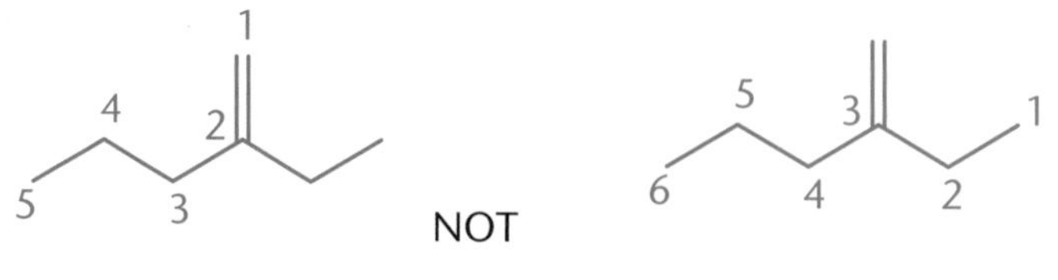

NOT

Figure 1.7

Our old rules still apply, so if there are multiple double bonds, they must be named using the numerical prefixes (di–, tri–, etc.) and each bond must receive a number. Also, you may need to name the configurational isomer (*cis/trans*, *Z/E*). This topic will be discussed further in Chapter 2. Substituents are named in the same manner as they are for alkanes, and their positions are specified by their respective numbers.

Frequently, an alkene group must be named as a substituent. In these cases, the systematic names may be used, but the common names are more popular. **Vinyl** derivatives are monosubstituted ethylenes (**ethenyl–**), which is actually just a carbon–carbon double bond as a substituent. You will likely see **allyl** derivatives on the MCAT; these are propylenes attached to a backbone at the C–3 position (**2-propenyl–**), meaning the double bond is at the end of the chain and the single-bonded carbon is attached to the rest of the chain. **Methylene–** refers to the =CH$_2$ group, where the substituent is only one carbon that is double bonded to the rest of the molecule. Examples of all three of these are shown in Figure 1.8.

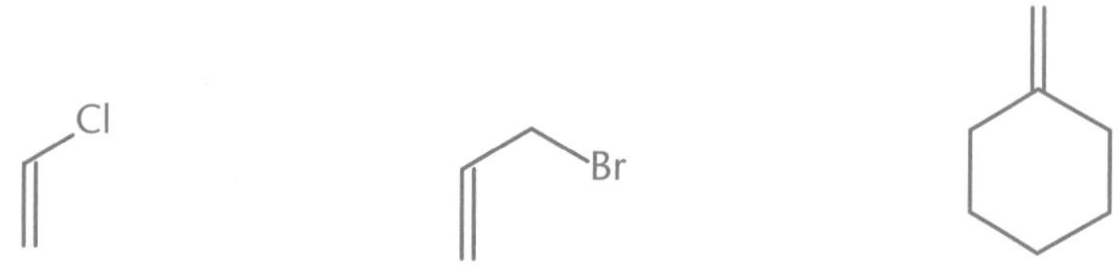

Bridge

A carbon backbone with alternating single and double bonds is called a conjugated system. Conjugation gives the molecule notable stability because its electrons can be delocalized, a phenomenon that has important consequences for our later discussion of aromatic compounds in Chapter 6.

chloroethene
(vinyl chloride)

3-bromo-1-propene
(allyl bromide)

methylene cyclohexane

Figure 1.8

CYCLOALKENES

Cycloalkenes (rings containing one or more double bonds) are named like cycloalkanes but with the suffix **–ene** rather than **–ane** (see Figure 1.9). If there is only one double bond and no other substituents, the ring does not have to be numbered.

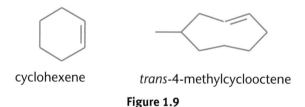

cyclohexene

trans-4-methylcyclooctene

Figure 1.9

ALKYNES

Alkynes are compounds with carbon–carbon triple bonds. The nomenclature rules are the same, but the suffix **–yne** replaces **–ane** from the parent alkane. If necessary, a number indicates the position of the triple bond. No matter how the triple bonds are depicted, they are always linear. Figure 1.10 shows some examples. (*Common name alert:* Two triple-bonded carbons are known by the common name **acetylene**. The IUPAC name **ethyne** is almost never used.)

Key Concept

The general formula for an alkyne is C$_n$H$_{2n-2}$. An alkyne has two degrees of unsaturation because it has two pi bonds.

ethyne
(acetylene)

4-methylhex-2-yne

cyclononyne

Figure 1.10

Although this is not likely to come up on the MCAT, when there are both double and triple bonds in a molecule, the molecule's name ends in "*y-root*-en-*x*-yne," where the first number y describes the position of the double bond, the second number x describes the position of the triple bond, and *root* is the prefix representing the length of the principal carbon chain. These numbers must be chosen so that the sum of x and y is as small as possible, and (as stated before) the double bond is given the lowest number where there is a choice.

Substituted Alkanes ★★★★★★

HALOALKANES

Compounds that contain a **halogen** (F, Cl, Br, or I) substituent are named **haloalkanes**. The substituents are numbered as alkyl groups; thus, the lowest number is determined alphabetically. Notice that the presence of the halide does not dramatically affect the numbering of the chain; we still proceed so that substituents receive the lowest possible numbers. Figure 1.11 shows two examples.

2-chloro-3-iodopentane

1-chloro-2-methylcyclohexane

Figure 1.11

Alternatively, you may see some haloalkanes on the MCAT named as **alkyl halides**. Remember that the MCAT is a multiple-choice exam, so it is far more important for you to see a name and know what the structure should look like than to decide whether to name the molecule as a haloalkane or an alkyl halide. For example, chloroethane is called **ethyl chloride** using the alkyl halide-naming convention. Two more examples are shown in Figure 1.12.

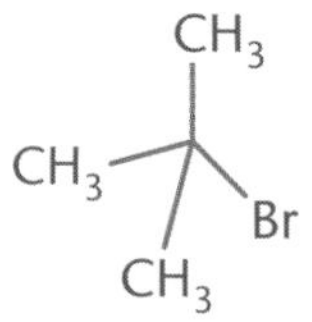

2-bromo-2-methylpropane
(*t*-butyl bromide)

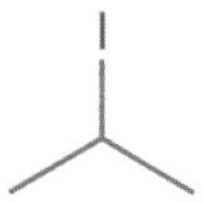

2-iodopropane
(isopropyl iodide)

Figure 1.12

ALCOHOLS

According to the IUPAC system, **alcohols** are named by replacing the **–e** of the corresponding alkane with **–ol**. The chain is numbered so that the carbon attached to the hydroxyl group (–OH) receives the lowest number possible. Even when there is a double bond in the molecule, the –OH group still takes precedence and is given the lowest number. Figure 1.13 shows some exmples.

Key Concept

–OH has priority over double and triple bonds when numbering the chain.

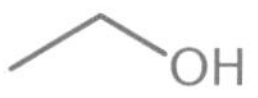

ethanol

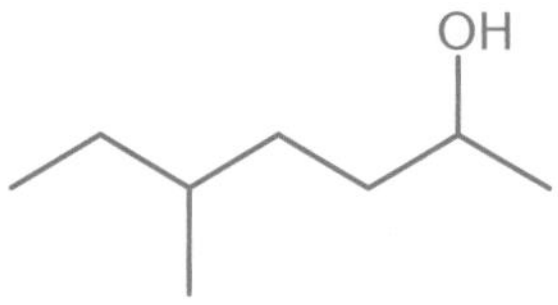

5-methyl-2-heptanol

hept-6-en-1-ol

Figure 1.13

Common name alert: A common system of nomenclature exists for simple alcohols in which the name of the alkyl group is simply followed by the word *alcohol*. For example, ethanol may be named **ethyl alcohol**, or 2-propanol may be named **isopropyl alcohol**.

Molecules with two hydroxyl groups are called **diols** (or **glycols**) and are named with the suffix **–diol**. Two numbers are necessary to distinguish the two functional groups. For example, ethane-1,2-diol is an ethane molecule with an –OH group attached to each carbon, and it is known by its common name **ethylene glycol**. Diols with hydroxyl groups on adjacent carbons are referred to as **vicinal**, and diols with hydroxyl groups on the same carbon are **geminal**. Geminal diols (also called **hydrates**) are not commonly observed because they spontaneously lose water (dehydrate) to produce carbonyl compounds (containing C=O, as we will see in Chapter 8).

Mnemonic

Vicinal diols are in the *vicinity* of each other—that is, from adjacent carbons.

Mnemonic

Geminal diols (like the astrological sign Gemini) are *twins* of each other—that is, from the same carbon.

ETHERS

Following the system from our friends at IUPAC, ethers are named as derivatives of alkanes; once again, the largest alkyl group is chosen as the backbone. The backbone chain is numbered to give the carbon bound to the oxygen the lowest position. The ether functionality is specified by an **alkoxy–** prefix, indicating the presence of an ether (–oxy–) and the corresponding smaller alkyl group (alk–). To make sense of this language, imagine an ether that has its oxygen connected with an ethyl group on one side and a methyl group on the other. The methyl group is named as a substituent and termed a **methoxy**, and the ethane is simply named (because it is the larger group): hence, **methoxyethane**.

Common name alert: Common names for ethers are frequently used. They are derived by naming the two alkyl groups in alphabetical order and adding the word *ether*. The generic term *ether* refers to diethyl ether, a commonly used solvent and one of the original anesthetics. For cyclic ethers, the numbering of the ring begins at the oxygen and proceeds to provide the lowest numbers for the substituents (same way we always do). Three-membered rings are called **oxiranes** by IUPAC, but they are almost always referred to as **epoxides**.

MCAT Expertise

On the MCAT, you will see ethers named in IUPAC as frequently as they are named by common names, so know them both well.

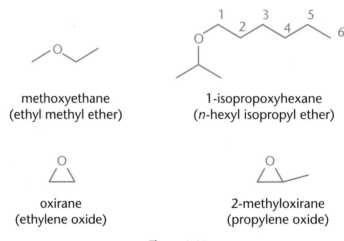

methoxyethane
(ethyl methyl ether)

1-isopropoxyhexane
(*n*-hexyl isopropyl ether)

oxirane
(ethylene oxide)

2-methyloxirane
(propylene oxide)

Figure 1.14

tetrahydrofuran
(THF)

Figure 1.15

ALDEHYDES AND KETONES

Before jumping into the differences between aldehydes and ketones, let's first talk about what makes them *similar*. Both of these compounds have a **carbonyl**, which is a carbon double-bonded to an oxygen. What makes them *different* is simply the placement of the carbonyl within the molecule. In **aldehydes**, the carbonyl is located at the end of the chain. Because the functional group is terminal, it will always receive the number 1, so we do not need to state the number in its name. The only thing we have to do is replace the **–e**, from the parent alkane, and replace it with **–al**, and we've named our aldehyde (see Figure 1.16).

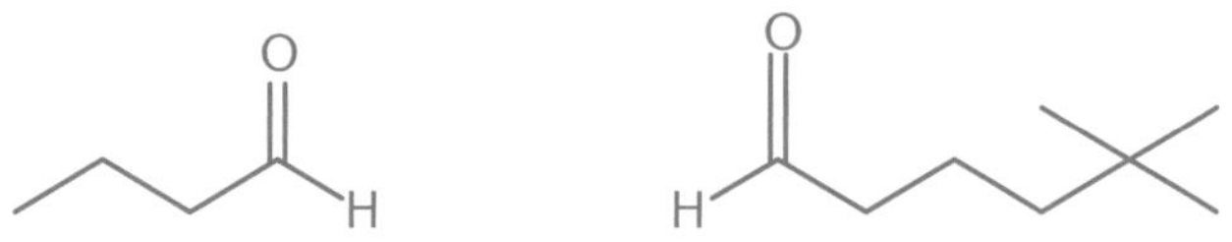

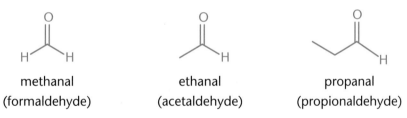

butanal   5,5-dimethylhexanal

Figure 1.16

Common name alert: The common names **formaldehyde**, **acetaldehyde**, and **propionaldehyde** are used almost exclusively instead of their respective IUPAC names **methanal**, **ethanal**, and **propanal** (see Figure 1.17).

methanal   ethanal   propanal
(formaldehyde)   (acetaldehyde)   (propionaldehyde)

Figure 1.17

MCAT Expertise

Common name alert: On the MCAT, the common names *formic acid*, *acetic acid*, and *propanoic acid* are used almost exclusively. *Make sure you know these!*

Ketones are similar to aldehydes, except that the carbonyl is located somewhere in the middle of the carbon chain. As such, a number must be assigned to the carbonyl, and the suffix **–one** is used instead of the **–e** of the parent alkane (see Figure 1.18). As always, our goal in assigning numbers is to give the highest-priority functional group (in this case, the carbonyl) the lowest possible number.

Common name alert: To determine the common name of a ketone, simply list the alkyl groups in alphabetical order followed by the word *ketone*.

In a more complex molecule containing a group with higher priority, the carbonyl group (yes, whether it's a ketone *or* an aldehyde) is named as a substituent with the prefix **oxo–** (because of the oxygen).

MCAT Expertise

On the MCAT, *formaldehyde*, *acetaldehyde*, and *acetone* are used almost exclusively. *Make sure you know these!*

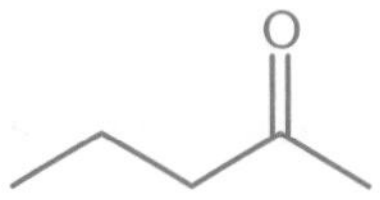

2-pentanone 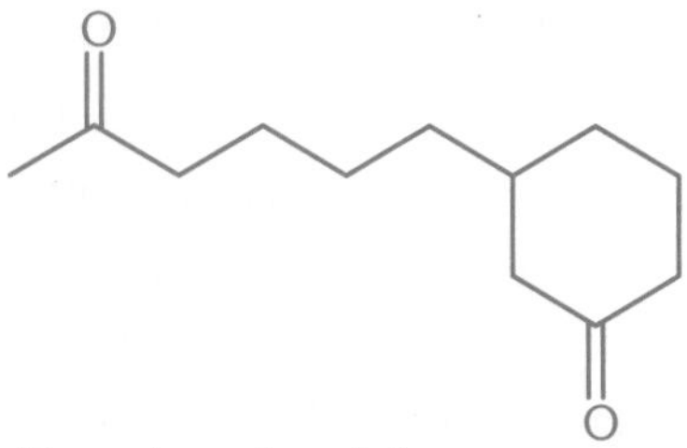   3-(5-oxohexyl)cyclohexanone

2-propanone   3-butene-2-one
(dimethyl ketone)   (methyl vinyl ketone)

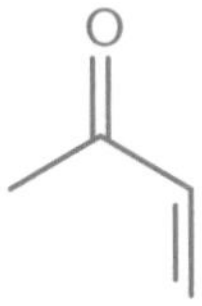

(acetone)

Figure 1.18

Key Concept

Carbons adjacent to a carbonyl are named α carbons; the carbons next to that are named β carbons. All of the hydrogens attached to those carbons have the same name as the carbon to which they are bound.

On the MCAT, you will probably come across an alternative to the numeric designations discussed thus far, a convention that names all of the carbons relative to the carbonyl group. In this convention, we call the carbon atom adjacent to the carbonyl alpha (α), and the carbon atoms successively along the chain are named beta (β), gamma (γ), delta (δ), etc. These Greek letter names apply on both sides of the carbonyl, which means the carbons on either side of a ketone are called α carbons. This system is encountered with dicarbonyl compounds with halocarbonyl compounds, or when referring to α-hydrogen acidity, as we will do often when we start reviewing aldehydes and ketones (Chapter 8).

CARBOXYLIC ACIDS

Like aldehydes, **carboxylic acids** are terminal functional groups, and the carbonyl will always receive the number 1 when the chain is numbered. Carboxylic acids contain a carbonyl *and* an –OH group, making them quite oxidized. In fact, they are the most oxidized functional group, with three bonds to oxygen. The only carbon that is more oxidized is carbon dioxide, which has four bonds to oxygen. Carboxylic acids are the highest-priority functional group, so every other functional group on a carboxylic acid will be named as a substituent. Figure 1.19 shows some examples.

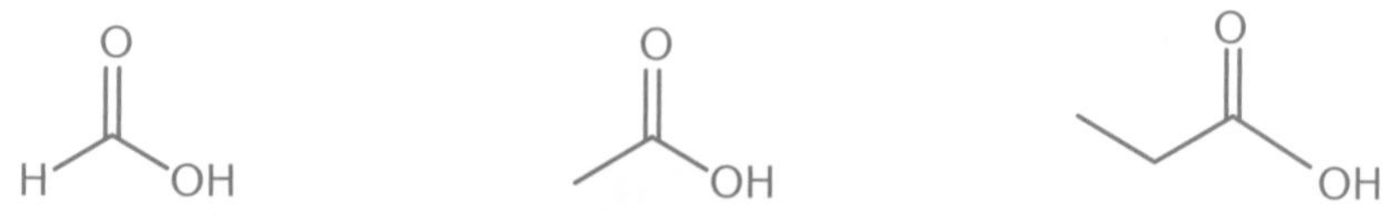

methanoic acid
(formic acid)

ethanoic acid
(acetic acid)

propanoic acid
(propionic acid)

Figure 1.19

AMINES

When naming **amines**, which are nitrogen-containing compounds, the longest chain attached to the nitrogen atom is used as the backbone. When dealing with simple compounds, you simply name the alkane and replace the final –e with –**amine**. More complex molecules, with higher-priority functional groups, are named using the prefix **amino**– (see Figure 1.20).

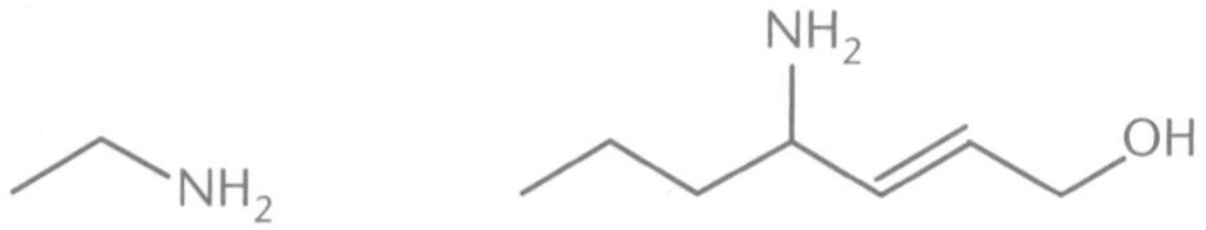

ethanamine

4-aminohept-2-en-1-ol

Figure 1.20

When additional groups are attached to the nitrogen atom, we can designate their position by using the prefix N– (see Figure 1.21).

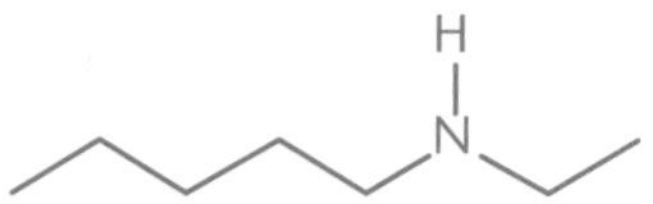

N-ethylpentanamine
(ethylpentylamine)

Figure 1.21

Summary of Functional Groups ★★★★★★

Table 1.1 lists all the major functional groups you need to know for the MCAT. Both prefixes and suffixes are given. If the functional group is the highest-priority group on the molecule, the suffix is used. If the functional group does *not* hold the highest priority, it is named as a substituent, and the prefix is used.

Table 1.1. Major Functional Groups

Functional Group	Structure	IUPAC Prefix	IUPAC Suffix
Carboxylic acid	$R-\overset{\displaystyle O}{\underset{\displaystyle OH}{C}}$	carboxy-	-oic acid
Ester	$R-\overset{\displaystyle O}{\underset{\displaystyle OR}{C}}$	alkoxycarbonyl-	-oate
Acyl halide	$R-\overset{\displaystyle O}{\underset{\displaystyle X}{C}}$	halocarbonyl-	-oyl halide
Amide	$R-\overset{\displaystyle O}{\underset{\displaystyle NH_2}{C}}$	amido-	-amide
Nitrile/Cyanide	$RC\equiv N$	cyano-	-nitrile
Aldehyde	$R-\overset{\displaystyle O}{\underset{\displaystyle H}{C}}$	oxo-	-al
Ketone	$R-\overset{\displaystyle O}{\underset{\displaystyle R}{C}}$	oxo-	-one
Alcohol	ROH	hydroxy-	-ol
Thiol	RSH	sulfhydryl-	-thiol
Amine	RNH_2	amino-	-amine
Imine	$R_2C=NR'$	imino-	-imine
Ether	ROR	alkoxy-	-ether
Sulfide	R_2S	alkylthio-	
Halide	-I, -Br, -Cl, -F	halo-	
Nitro	RNO_2	nitro-	
Azide	RN_3	azido-	
Diazo	RN_2	diazo-	

Key Concept

The more oxidized a functional group is, the higher its priority. Table 1.1 lists the functional groups in order of priority, with the highest priority being at the top.

Conclusion

This chapter may not have transformed you into a Grand Chemistry Master, but it does contain all of the nomenclature knowledge that you will need for the MCAT. We also got our first look at the various functional groups that may be present in a molecule. Often, the ability to recognize functional groups (from either the structure or the name) will get you halfway to the correct answer. That's why knowing the rules of nomenclature is such a vital skill and the first topic we introduce you to in this review. A strong foundation in organic nomenclature is requisite for every one of the topics to follow and, ultimately, for success on Test Day. Learning a new language is tough, and although the ability to speak it fluently would be nice, it may not be necessary. Remember that the MCAT is a multiple-choice exam, and any nomenclature that is tested will either be stated in the question stem or in the answer choices. The ability to recognize names will often prove to be nearly as useful as the ability to recall them from memory. If learning other languages had a similar multiple-choice shortcut, far more of us would spend our summers traveling the world.

CONCEPTS TO REMEMBER

☐ Identify the backbone (longest chain of carbons).

☐ Number the chain, keeping numbers for the substituents as low as possible.

☐ Name substituents.

☐ Assign numbers.

☐ Put the whole name together, remembering to alphabetize substituents.

☐ Multiple bonds should be on the main carbon backbone whenever possible.

☐ –OH is a high-priority functional group, placed above multiple bonds in numbering. More oxidized groups have even higher priority.

☐ Haloalkanes, ethers, and ketones are often given common names (e.g., methyl chloride, ethyl methyl ether, diethyl ketone).

☐ Aldehydes and carboxylic acids are terminal functional groups. If present, they define C–1 of the carbon chain.

☐ Remember to specify the isomer, if relevant (such as *cis* or *trans*, *R* or *S*, etc.).

Practice Questions

1. What is the IUPAC name of the following compound?

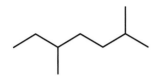

   A. 2,5-Dimethylheptane
   B. 2-Ethyl-5-methylhexane
   C. 3,6-Dimethylheptane
   D. 5-Ethyl-2-methylhexane

2. What is the name of the following compound?

   A. 1-Ethyl-3,4-dimethylcycloheptane
   B. 2-Ethyl-4,5-dimethylcyclohexane
   C. 1-Ethyl-3,4-dimethylcyclohexane
   D. 4-Ethyl-1,2-dimethylcyclohexane

3. What is the name of the following compound?

   A. 2-Bromo-5-butyl-4,4-dichloro-3-iodo-
      3-methyloctane
   B. 7-Bromo-4-butyl-5,5-dichloro-6-iodo-
      6-methyloctane
   C. 2-Bromo-4,4-dichloro-3-iodo-3-methyl-
      5-propylnonane
   D. 2-Bromo-5-butyl-4,4-dichloro-3-iodo-
      3-methylnonane

4. What is the name of the following compound?

   A. *trans*-3-Ethyl-4-hexen-2-ol
   B. *trans*-4-Ethyl-2-hexen-5-ol
   C. *trans*-3-Ethanol-2-hexene
   D. *trans*-4-Ethanol-2-hexene

5. What is the correct structure for *cis*-1-ethoxy-2-methoxycyclopentane?

A.

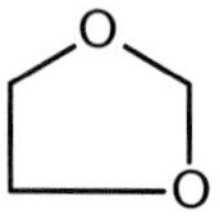

B.

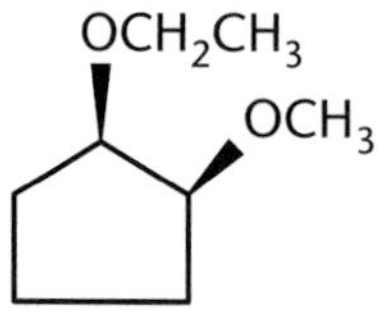

C.

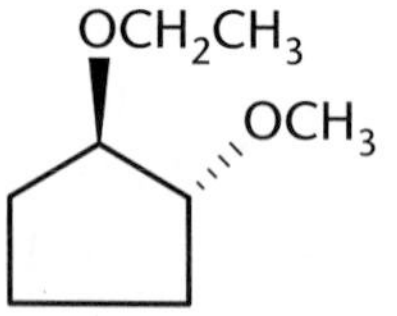

D.

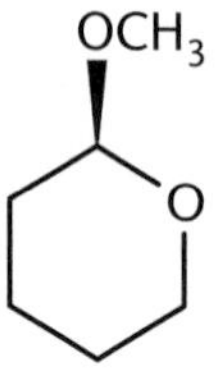

6. Which of the following are considered terminal functional groups?

A. Aldehydes
B. Ketones
C. Carboxylic acids
D. Both (A) and (C)

7. In the figure below, what is the correct name for the molecule shown in the Haworth projection?

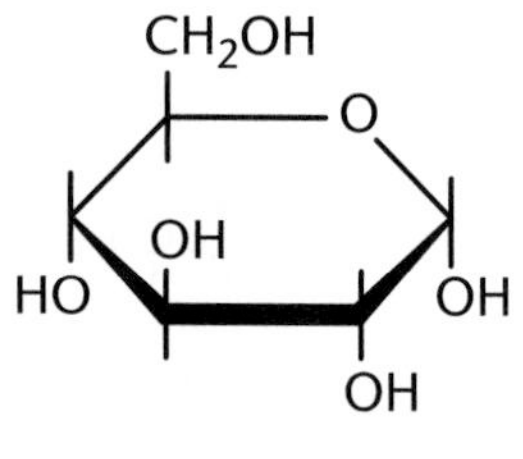

A. α-D-Glucose
B. β-D-Glucose
C. β-L-Glucose
D. σ-L-Glucose

8. The IUPAC name for the structure below ends with what suffix?

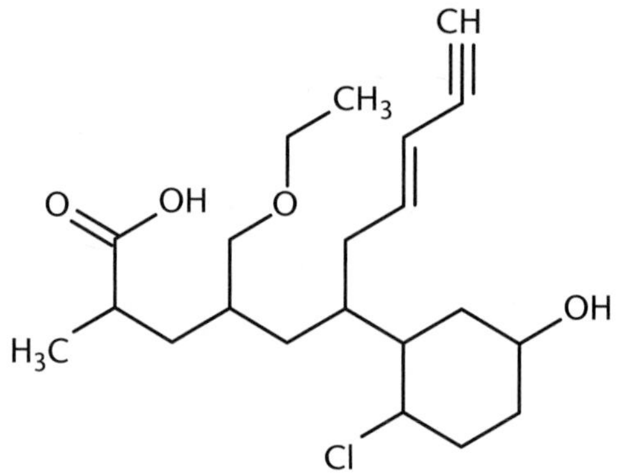

A. –ol
B. –ide
C. –oic acid
D. –yne

Small Group Questions

1. Pyruvic acid is also known as acetylformic acid. Draw the structure of pyruvate, one of the end products of glycolysis.

2. NAD$^+$ is a coenzyme that releases high-energy electrons in the electron transport chain. It is known as nicotinamide adenine dinucleotide, as well as diphosphopyridine nucleotide. Using what you know about naming conventions, what functional groups would you expect this molecule to have?

Explanations to Practice Questions

1. A

The first task in naming alkanes is identifying the longest carbon chain. In this case, the longest chain has seven carbons, so the parent alkane ends in –heptane. Choices (B) and (D) can be eliminated. Making sure that the carbons are numbered so that the substituents' position numbers are as small as possible, let's identify those substituents. This compound has two methyl groups at carbons 2 and 5, so the correct IUPAC name is 2,5-dimethylheptane. Choice (C) is wrong because the position numbers of the substituents are not minimized.

2. D

Substituted cycloalkanes are named as derivatives of their parent cycloalkane, which in this case is cyclohexane. Thus, choice (A) can be ruled out immediately. Then the substituents are listed in alphabetical order, and the carbons are numbered so as to give the lowest sum of substituent numbers. This cyclohexane has an ethyl and two methyl substituents; it is therefore an ethyl dimethyl cyclohexane. All of the remaining answer choices recognize this; they differ only in the numbers assigned. To give the lowest sum of substituent numbers, the two methyl substituents must be numbered 1 and 2, and the ethyl substituent must be numbered 4. The correct name for this compound is thus 4-ethyl-1,2-dimethylcyclohexane.

3. C

This question requires the application of the same set of rules used in question 1. The longest backbone has nine carbons, so the compound is a nonane. Thus, choices (A) and (B) can be ruled out immediately. The substituent groups are, in alphabetical order, bromo, chloro, iodo, methyl, and propyl. These substituents must be given the lowest possible position numbers on the hydrocarbon backbone. The resulting name is 2-bromo-4,4-dichloro-3-iodo-3-methyl-5-propylnonane.

4. A

The first step is to locate the longest carbon chain containing the functional groups (C=C and OH). The backbone has six carbons (–hex–). Because the alcohol group has higher priority than the double bond, it dictates the ending (–ol) and is given the lower position (2). The alkene is named according to the position of the double bond on the backbone followed by *ene* (or *en* if it's not the highest-priority substituent). Thus, the chain is called 4–hexen–2–ol. There is also an ethyl group at C–3, so we can conclude that answer choice (A), *trans*-3-ethyl-4-hexen-2-ol, is correct.

5. B

A cyclopentane is a cyclic alkane with five carbons. A *cis* cyclic compound has both of its top-priority substituents on the same side of the ring. Only choices (B) and (C) have two substituents, so (A) and (D) can be ruled out. In fact, choice (C) is a *trans* compound, so the correct answer must be (B). *Ethoxy* and *methoxy* represent ether substituents, and as shown in choice (B), they must be on adjacent carbons on the same side of the molecule. Thus, the structure of *cis*-1-ethoxy-2-methoxycyclopentane is given by choice (B).

6. D

Aldehyde and carboxylic acid functional groups are characterized by their positions at terminal ends of carbon backbones. As a result, the carbons to which they are attached are named C–1. Ketones (B) are internal by definition, as there must be a carbon on either side of the carbonyl. Choice (D) is correct.

7. A

Starting from the anomeric carbon (hemiacetal), we see that the anomeric –OH group is pointing downward and is positioned *trans*- to the –CH$_2$OH group. Therefore, it is an α-sugar, which rules out answer choices (B), (C), and (D). *Sigma* (D) is not a term used to classify sugars.

8. C

Among the functional groups presented, carboxylic acids have the highest priority, so their parent compounds end with an –oic acid suffix. Answer (A) denotes an alcohol, (B) a halide, and (D) an alkyne, all of which have lower priorities than carboxylic acids.

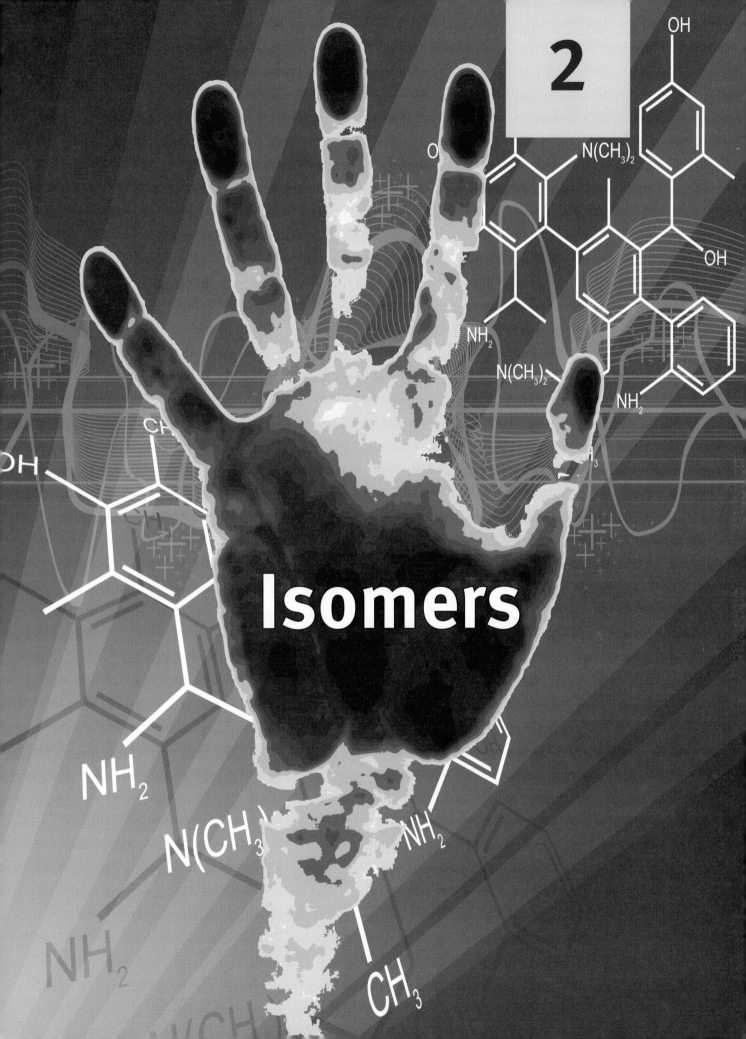

The more time we spend with chemistry, the more we may start to imagine that molecules have their own personalities and that many of our human characteristics can be projected onto them. For instance, many of the relationships that describe similarities among humans can be ascribed to members of the molecular world. We can imagine that isomers are much like siblings. After all, siblings come from the same formula: mom + dad = child, although as I'm sure you've noticed, each child has his or her own specific characteristics. It's the same way with isomers. Isomers have the same molecular formula, but their differences can be as substantial as those between you and your weird brother who ate bugs on the playground. Keep in mind that isomers describe a relationship; there is no such thing as a single isomer. Just as you need at least two children for them to be siblings, two molecules can be isomers to each other, but no molecule can simply be an isomer by itself. Throughout this chapter, we will learn how to identify these relationships and describe the similarities and differences between isomers.

Key Concept

Isomers = same molecular formula, different structure.

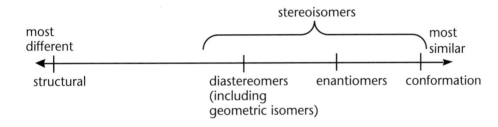

Structural Isomerism ★★☆☆☆

Remember your weird bug-eating brother who seems as if he might even be of a different species? Well, you two are the structural isomers of the social world. Structural isomers are the least similar of all isomers.

In fact, the only thing that **structural isomers** (also called **constitutional isomers**) do share is their molecular formula, meaning that their molecular weights must also be the same. Otherwise, these are completely different molecules, with different chemical and physical properties. This would probably be a good time to make sure we hammer down these concepts, because it is prime MCAT material. **Physical properties** are characteristics such as melting point, boiling point, and solubility. **Chemical properties** determine how the molecule reacts with other molecules. For example, five different structures exist for compounds with the formula C_6H_{14}.

Key Concept

Physical properties: MP, BP, solubility.
Chemical properties: How it reacts.

Bridge

Physical properties are determined by intermolecular forces; we'll talk more about those in Chapter 3.

Key Concept

Structural isomers can possess different functional groups as well as bonding patterns.

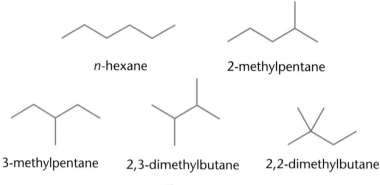

n-hexane   2-methylpentane

3-methylpentane   2,3-dimethylbutane   2,2-dimethylbutane

Figure 2.1

Although all of the molecules look totally different, they share the same number of carbon and hydrogen atoms.

Stereoisomerism ★★★★★★

Now, we get into the real fun of isomerism. Like structural isomers, **stereoisomers** have the same chemical formula. However, they also have the same atomic connectivity. The only difference among stereoisomers is how the atoms are arranged in space. Other isomers (geometric isomers, enantiomers, diastereomers, *meso* compounds, and conformational isomers) all fall under the category of stereoisomers (see Figure 2.2).

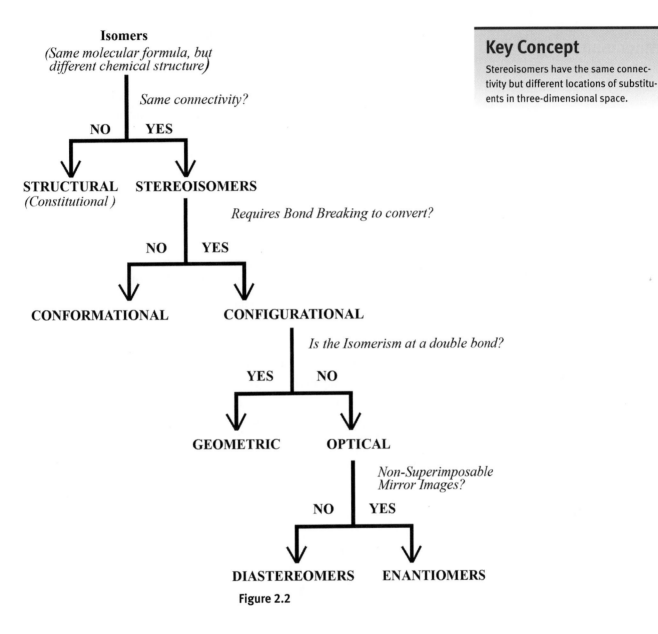

Figure 2.2

GEOMETRIC ISOMERS

Geometric isomers are compounds that differ in the position of substituents attached to a double bond or a cycloalkane. In simple compounds with only one substituent on either side of the double bond (hydrogen doesn't count as a substituent), we use the terms *cis* or **trans**. If two substituents are on the same side, the double bond is called *cis*. If they are on opposite sides, it is a *trans* double bond. For more complicated compounds with polysubstituted double bonds, an alternative method of naming is employed. First, the highest-priority substituent attached to each double-bonded carbon has to be determined. Using the nomenclature convention, the higher the atomic number, the higher the priority, and if the atomic numbers are equal, priority is de-

Mnemonic

Z = "z"ame side; *E* = "e" opposite side.

termined by the substituents attached to these atoms. The alkene is named (**Z**) (from German *zusammen*, meaning "together") if the two highest-priority substituents on each carbon are on the same side of the double bond and (**E**) (from German *entgegen*, meaning "opposite") if they are on opposite sides (see Figure 2.3). Don't worry if you aren't fluent in German; this is one of the few times we will use it in Organic Chemistry. If you did have the time to learn a language, Greek or Latin would be far more useful, but who has time to learn a language when they're studying for the MCAT?

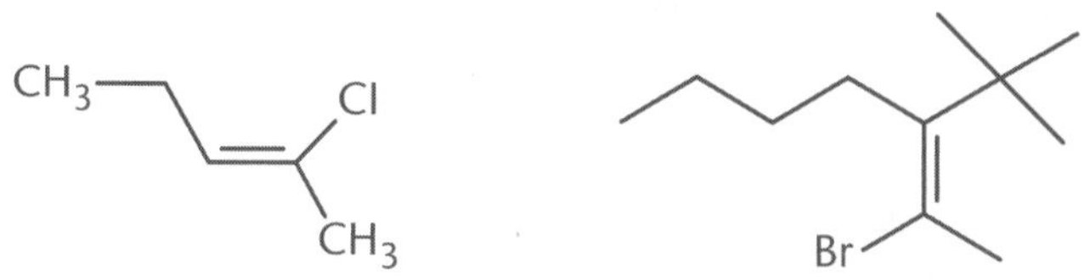

(*Z*)-2-chloro-2-pentene   (*E*)-2-bromo-3-*t*-butyl-2-heptene

Figure 2.3

CHIRALITY

An object that is not superimposable upon its mirror image is **chiral**. An example of chirality that you've undoubtedly seen before are your right and left hands (see Figure 2.4). Although essentially identical, they differ in their ability to fit into a right-handed glove. They are mirror images of each other yet cannot be superimposed. Achiral objects have mirror images that *can* be superimposed; for example, a fork is identical to its mirror image and therefore achiral.

Key Concept

Chirality = handedness.

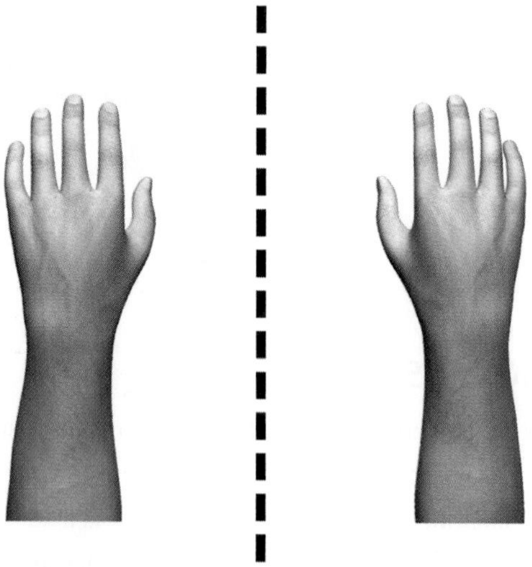

nonsuperimposable mirror images

Figure 2.4

MCAT Expertise

Whenever you see a carbon with four different substituents, *think chirality!*

On the MCAT, we will see this concept tested whenever there is a carbon with *four different* substituents. These carbons, known as **chiral centers**, lack a plane of symmetry. For example, the C–1 carbon atom in 1-bromo-1-chloroethane has four different substituents. The molecule is chiral because it is not superimposable on its mirror image (see Figure 2.5). The nonsuperimposable mirror images of chiral objects are called their **enantiomers**, a specific type of stereoisomer.

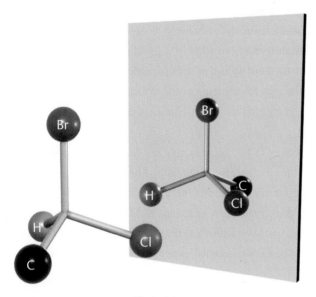

Figure 2.5

Alternatively, a carbon atom with only *three different* substituents, such as 1,1-dibromoethane, has a plane of symmetry and is therefore **achiral** (not chiral). A simple 180° rotation around a vertical axis allows the compound to be superimposed upon its mirror image. Rotating a molecule in space does not change its chirality (see Figure 2.6).

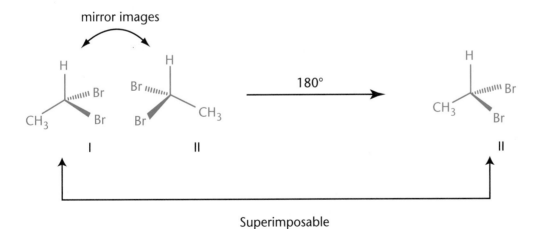

Figure 2.6

Relative and Absolute Configuration

The **configuration** is the spatial arrangement of the atoms or groups of a stereoisomer (enantiomers are configurational isomers). The **relative configuration** of a chiral molecule is its configuration in relation to another chiral molecule (often through chemical interconversion). We will use this to determine whether molecules are enantiomers, diastereomers, or simply the same molecule. On the other hand, the **absolute configuration** of a chiral molecule describes the exact spatial arrangement of these atoms or groups, independent of other molecules. Next, we will go through the set sequence to determine the absolute configuration of a molecule at a single chiral, or stereogenic, center.

Key Concept

When assigning priority, look *only* at the first atom attached to the chiral carbon, not at the group as a whole. The higher the atomic number of this first atom, the higher the priority—this same system is used to determine *Z* and *E* isomers.

Step 1:

Assign priority to the four substituents, looking only at the atoms directly attached to the chiral center. Once again, higher atomic number takes precedence over lower atomic number. If the atomic numbers are equal, priority is determined by the combination of the atoms attached to these atoms. If you come across a tie, just keep looking to the next atoms until you find a winner. If there is a double bond, it is counted as two bonds. Figure 2.7 shows an example.

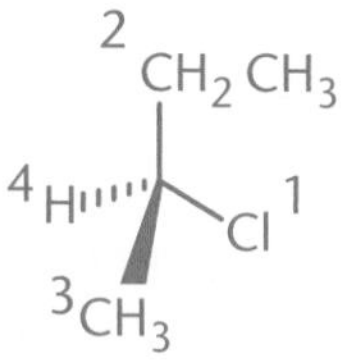

Figure 2.7

Step 2:

Orient the molecule in space so that the atom with the lowest priority (it will usually be hydrogen) is at the back of the molecule. Another way to think of this is to arrange your point of view so that your line of sight proceeds down the bond from the asymmetric carbon atom (the chiral center) to the substituent with lowest priority. The three substituents with higher priority should then radiate out from the central carbon, either coming out of the page or on the plane of the page (see Figure 2.8).

Step 2 (Modified Version):

If you find it difficult to rotate three-dimensional structures in your mind, we have a trick to get around this step. All you need to do is switch the lowest-priority group and the group at the back of the molecule (the substituent projecting *into* the page). This will give us the results of the standard step 2, with one big difference. We now have the *opposite* configuration. So if we use this modified step, we need to remember to switch our final answer (either *R* to *S*, or *S* to *R*. Don't worry, we'll get there next).

Practice Questions

1. Which of the following do not show optical activity?

    A. (*R*)-2-Butanol

    B. (*S*)-2-Butanol

    C. A solution containing 1 M (*R*)-2-butanol and 2 M (*S*)-2-butanol

    D. A solution containing 2 M (*R*)-2-butanol and 2 M (*S*)-2-butanol

2. How many stereoisomers exist for the following aldehyde?

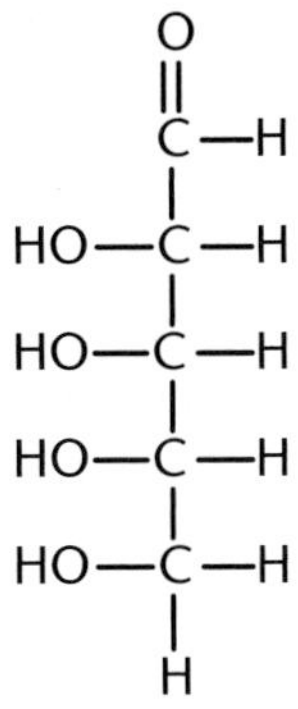

    A. 2

    B. 4

    C. 8

    D. 16

3. Which of the following compounds is optically inactive?

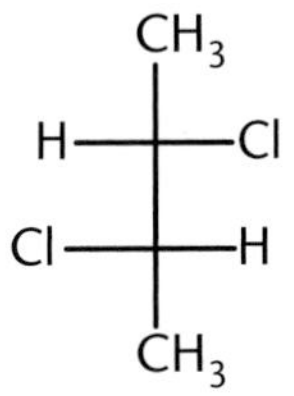

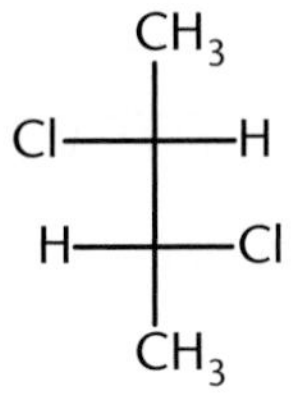

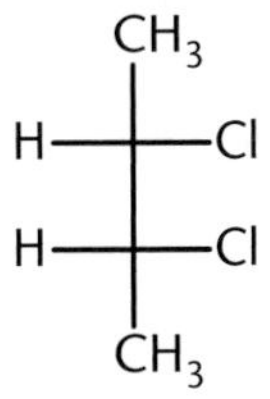

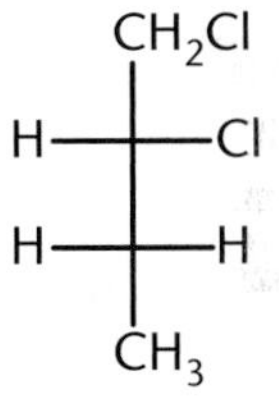

4. Cholesterol, shown below, contains how many chiral centers?

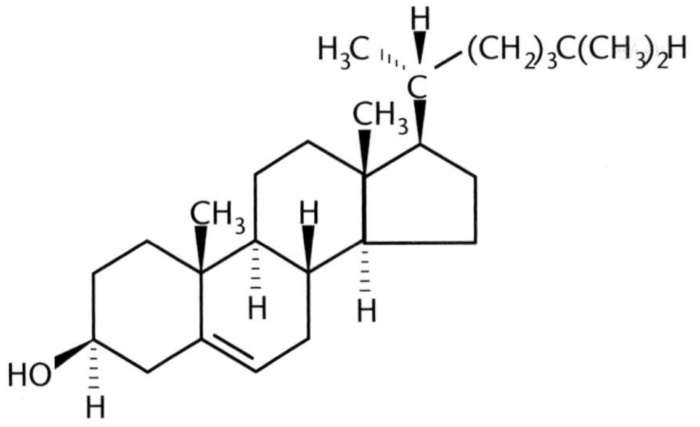

cholesterol

    A. 5

    B. 7

    C. 8

    D. 9

5. Which isomer of the following compound is the most stable?

A.

B.

C.
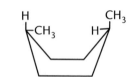

D.   They are all equally stable.

6. The following reaction results in

$$H-O \overset{CH_3}{\underset{CH_2CH_3}{\rule{0pt}{0pt}\!-\!\!-\!\!-\!H}} + CH_3\overset{O}{\overset{\|}{C}}Cl \longrightarrow HCl + \overset{O}{\overset{\|}{C}}O \overset{CH_3}{\underset{CH_2CH_3}{\rule{0pt}{0pt}\!-\!\!-\!\!-\!H}}$$

A. retention of relative configuration and a change in the absolute configuration.

B. a change in the relative and absolute configurations.

C. retention of the relative and absolute configurations.

D. retention of the absolute configuration and a change in the relative configuration.

7. The following is a pair of what structures?

I

II

A. Enantiomers

B. Diastereomers

C. *meso* compounds

D. Structural isomers

Small Group Questions

1. Compare the energies (with respect to torsional strain) of the different conformational isomers of 2-dimethyl propane (neopentane) using Newman projections.

2. How are diastereomers used to separate racemic mixtures into their enantiomers?

Explanations to Practice Questions

1. D

Choice (D) is a racemic mixture of 2-butanol because it consists of equimolar amounts of (R)-2-butanol and (S)-2-butanol. The (R)-2-butanol molecule rotates the plane of polarized light in one direction, and the (S)-2-butanol molecule rotates it by the same angle but in the opposite direction. For every (R)-2-butanol molecule, there is an (S)-2-butanol molecule; as a result, each rotation is canceled out. No net rotation of polarized light is observed. Choice (A) is wrong because all the molecules of the (R)-2-butanol solution rotate the plane of light in the same direction, so rotations do not cancel and optical activity is observed. For the same reason, the (S)-2-butanol solution (B) also shows optical activity. Thus, choices (A) and (B) are incorrect. Choice (C) has more (S)-2-butanol molecules than (R)-2-butanol molecules. The entire rotation produced by the (R)-2-butanol molecules is canceled by half of the (S)-2-butanol molecules; the rotation produced by the other half of (S)-2-butanol molecules contributes to the optical activity observed in this solution. Thus, choice (C) is incorrect.

2. C

The maximum number of stereoisomers of a compound equals 2^n, where n is the number of chiral carbons in the compound. Here, there are three chiral carbon atoms ($n = 3$), marked by asterisks in the following figure:

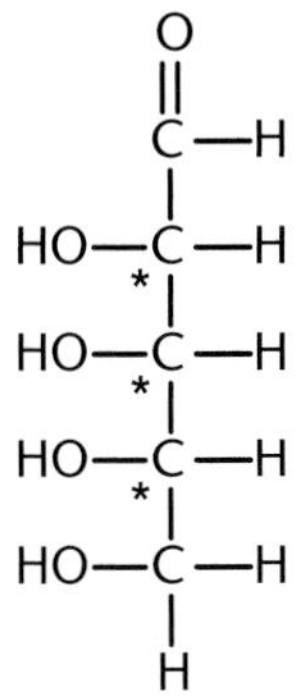

Thus, the number of stereoisomers it can form is $2^n = 2^3 = 8$. Hence, the correct choice is (C).

3. C

The answer choice is an example of a *meso* compound: a compound that contains chiral centers but is superimposable on its mirror image. A *meso* compound can also be recognized by the fact that one half of the compound is the mirror image of the other half:

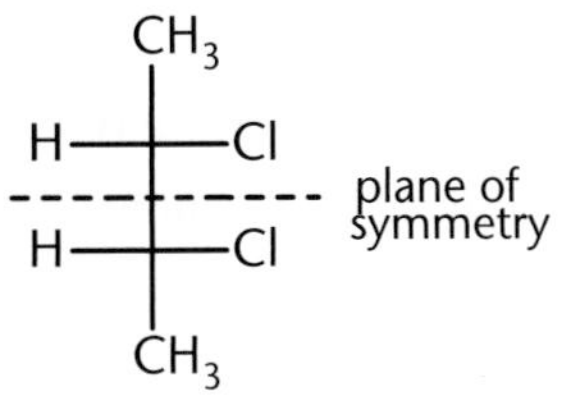

Owing to this internal plane of symmetry, the molecule is achiral and, hence, optically inactive. Choices (A) and (B) are enantiomers of each other and will certainly show optical activity on their own. Choice (D), because it contains a chiral carbon and no internal plane of symmetry, is optically active as well.

4. C

To be considered a chiral center, a carbon must have four different substituents. There are eight stereocenters in this molecule, which are marked below with asterisks.

cholestrol

The other carbons are not chiral for various reasons. Many are bonded to two hydrogens; others participate in double bonds, which count as two bonds to the same thing.

5. B

Choice (B) is a chair conformation in which the two equatorial methyl groups are *trans* to each other. Because the axial methyl hydrogens do not compete for the same space as the hydrogens attached to the ring, this conformation ensures the least amount of steric strain. Choice (A) would be less stable than choice (B) because the diaxial methyl group hydrogens are closer to the hydrogens on the ring, causing greater steric strain. Choice (C) is wrong because it is in the more unstable boat conformation. Choice (D) is incorrect because we can definitively order these structures from most to least stable.

6. C

The relative configuration is retained because the bonds of the stereocenter are not broken. The cleaved bond is between a substituent of the stereocenter (the O atom) and another atom attached to the substituent (the H attached to the O). The absolute configuration is also retained, because the $(R)/(S)$ designation is the same for the reactant and the product.

7. A

The correct answer is choice (A), enantiomers. If you look at the two structures, you can see that they are mirror images of each other. To make our analysis a bit easier, we can rotate structure II by 180° to give structure III. Structures I and III are nonsuperimposable mirror images, which means they are enantiomers.

Choice (B) is incorrect because diastereomers are stereoisomers, which are not mirror images of each other. Choice (C) is incorrect because for a compound to be designated as a *meso* compound, it must have a plane of symmetry, and neither of these do. Choice (D) is wrong because structural isomers are compounds with the same molecular formula but different atomic connections. These compounds do have the same atomic connections. The only difference is that they differ in their spatial arrangement of atoms. As a result, they are in the class of stereoisomers, not structural isomers.

3

Bonding

Practice Questions

1. Within one principal quantum level, which orbital has the least energy?

   A. s
   B. p
   C. d
   D. f

2. Which of the following compounds possesses at least one σ bond?

   A. CH_4
   B. C_2H_2
   C. C_2H_4
   D. All of the above

3. In a double-bonded carbon atom (C=C)

   A. hybridization occurs between the s-orbital and one p-orbital.
   B. hybridization occurs between the s-orbital and two p-orbitals.
   C. hybridization occurs between the s-orbital and three p-orbitals.
   D. no hybridization occurs between the s-and p-orbitals.

4. The hybridization of the carbon atom and the nitrogen atom in the ion CN^- are

   A. sp^3 and sp^3, respectively.
   B. sp^3 and sp, respectively.
   C. sp and sp^3, respectively.
   D. sp and sp, respectively.

5. Which of the following hybridizations does the Be atom in BeH_2 assume?

   A. sp
   B. sp^2
   C. sp^3
   D. None of the above

6. Two atomic orbitals combine to form

   I. a bonding molecular orbital.

   II. an antibonding molecular orbital.

   III. new atomic orbitals.

   A. I only
   B. I, II, and III
   C. III only
   D. I and II only

7. Molecular orbitals can contain a maximum of

   A. one electron.
   B. two electrons.
   C. four electrons.
   D. $2n^2$ electrons, where n is the principal quantum number of the combining atomic orbitals.

8. π bonds are formed by which of the following orbitals?

   A. Two s-orbitals
   B. Two p-orbitals
   C. One s- and one p-orbital
   D. All of the above

9. How many σ bonds and π bonds are present in the following compound?

A. Six σ bonds and one π bond
B. Six σ bonds and two π bonds
C. Seven σ bonds and one π bond
D. Seven σ bonds and two π bonds

10. The four C–H bonds of CH_4 point toward the vertices of a tetrahedron. This indicates that the hybridization of a carbon atom is

A. *sp*.
B. *sp²*.
C. *sp³*.
D. None of the above.

Small Group Questions

1. Why is a single bond stronger than a pi bond?

2. Draw an orbital diagram for allene ($H_2C=C=CH_2$). What is the hybridization of all three carbons? What is the shape of the molecule? What other (more common) molecule is reminiscent of allene?

Explanations to Practice Questions

1. A

The energies of the subshells within a principal quantum number are as follows: $s < p < d < f$.

2. D

σ bonds are formed when orbitals overlap end to end. All single bonds are σ bonds; double and triple bonds each contain one σ bond in addition to their π bonds. The compounds CH_4, C_2H_2, and C_2H_4 (choices (A), (B), and (C), respectively) all contain at least one single bond, so the correct answer is (D).

3. B

In a double-bonded carbon, sp^2 hybridization occurs—that is, one s-orbital hybridizes with two p-orbitals to form three sp^2 hybrid orbitals. Therefore, the correct choice is (B). The third p-orbital of the carbon atom remains unhybridized and takes part in the formation of the π bond of the double bond.

4. D

The carbon atom and the nitrogen atoms are connected by a triple bond in CN^-.

$$:N\equiv C:^-$$

A triple-bonded atom is sp hybridized; one s-orbital hybridizes with one p-orbital to form two sp-hybridized orbitals. The two remaining unhybridized p-orbitals take part in the formation of two π bonds. The correct choice, therefore, is (D).

5. A

BeH_2 is a linear molecule, which means that the angle between the two Be–H bonds is $180°$. Because sp-orbitals are oriented at an angle of $180°$, the Be atom is sp-hybridized. Therefore, the correct choice is (A).

6. D

When atomic orbitals combine to form molecular orbitals, the number of molecular orbitals obtained equals the number of atomic orbitals that take part in the process. Half of the molecular orbitals formed are bonding molecular orbitals, and the other half are antibonding molecular orbitals. In this case, two atomic orbitals combine to form one low-energy bonding molecular orbital and one high-energy antibonding molecular orbital. New atomic orbitals do not form, so answer choices (B) and (C) can be eliminated. The correct choice is (D).

7. B

Like atomic orbitals, molecular orbitals each can contain a maximum of two electrons with opposite spins.

8. B

π bonds are formed by the parallel overlap of unhybridized p-orbitals. The electron density is concentrated above and below the bonding axis. A σ bond, on the other hand, can be formed by the head-to-head overlap of two s-orbitals, two p-orbitals, or one s- and one p-orbital. Here, the density of the electrons is concentrated between the two nuclei of the bonding atoms.

9. A

Each single bond has one σ bond, and each double bond has one σ bond and one π bond. In this question, there are five single bonds (five σ bonds) and one double bond (one σ bond and one π bond), which gives a total of six σ bonds and one π bond. Thus, the correct choice is (A).

10. C

The four bonds point to the vertices of a tetrahedron, which means that the angle between two bonds is $109.5°$, which is characteristic of sp^3 orbitals. Hence, the carbon atom of CH_4 is sp^3 hybridized. The correct choice, therefore, is (C).

Alkanes, Alkyl Halides, and Substitution Reactions

In Chapter 3, we talked about the backbone of Organic Chemistry: bonding. In this chapter, we will begin discussing the simplest type of molecules with a carbon backbone: alkanes. They are our basic organic molecules, containing only carbon and hydrogen. As fully **saturated hydrocarbons**, they have no double bonds, and thus each carbon is *saturated* with the maximum number of hydrogens it can hold. This is reflected in the general formula for alkanes, which you probably recall from Chapter 1 to be C_nH_{2n+2}.

In our modern world, it is incredibly difficult, if not downright impossible, to go a single day without using alkanes. If you've ever cooked with a gas grill (propane), driven a car (octane), or sparked up a lighter (butane), you've used alkanes. As you can see from these examples, most alkanes are combustible liquids and gases. The first four alkanes (methane, ethane, propane, and butane) are probably the most familiar to you, as they are used primarily for heating and cooking. Longer alkanes tend to exist as liquids and are used as fuels in internal combustion engines (such as the one in your car), diesel engines, and jet engines. As alkanes increase even further in length, they are used as oils, waxes, and tars. We are almost guaranteed to come into contact with alkanes in the real world, but how will we see alkanes on Test Day? This chapter will cover all the information you'll need to know about alkanes and their much more reactive derivatives, alkyl halides (alkanes with a halogen in place of hydrogen).

Nomenclature ★★★☆☆☆

Bridge

Refer to Chapter 1 for the general rules of nomenclature for alkanes.

As we mentioned in Chapter 1, there are a couple of common names for alkanes that you will frequently encounter on the MCAT, including those shown in Figure 4.1.

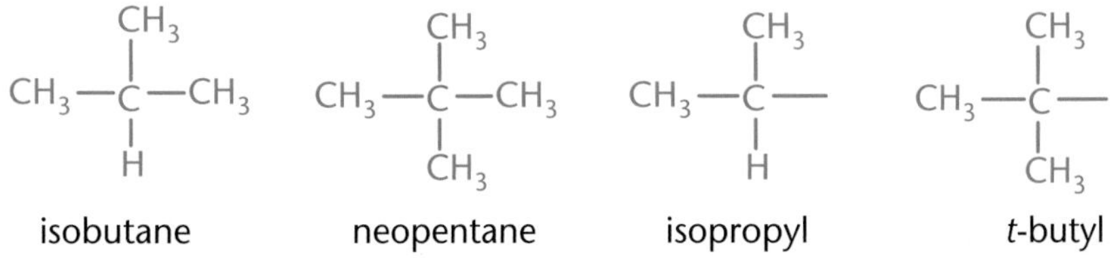

isobutane   neopentane   isopropyl   t-butyl

Figure 4.1

We classify carbons by the number of other carbon atoms to which they are directly bonded. A **primary** carbon atom (written as **1°**) is bonded to only one other carbon atom. A **secondary** (**2°**) carbon is bonded to two, a **tertiary** (**3°**) to three, and a **quaternary** (**4°**) to four other carbon atoms (see Figure 4.2). In addition, we also classify the hydrogen atoms attached to 1°, 2°, or 3° carbon atoms as 1°, 2°, and 3°, respectively. In fact, the hydrogens attached to carbons will always carry the same name as their parent carbon atom.

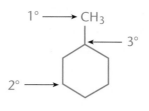

Figure 4.2

Physical Properties

The physical properties of alkanes (melting point, boiling point, density, etc.) are all prime information to be tested on the MCAT. The nice thing about physical properties is that they vary in a predictable manner. As the molecular weight increases, so do the melting point, boiling point, and density. This is logical; the heavier the molecule is, the harder it should be for the molecule to break away from others and enter the higher-energy gas phase. That's why, at room temperature, straight-chain compounds of up to 4 carbons are found in the gaseous state, chains of 5 to 16 carbons exist as liquids, and the longer-chain compounds are waxes and harder solids. Branched molecules follow a similar trend, but they have slightly lower boiling points than their straight-chain isomers. This is because greater branching reduces the surface area of the molecule available for interactions with neighboring molecules. The weakened intermolecular attractive forces (van der Waals forces) result in a decreased boiling point. Whereas the boiling point follows a perfectly predictable trend, the trend for melting points tends to be a little funky. Generally, the melting point does follow the same trend—after all, with greater branching, the molecules cannot stack up as close to each other as they would prefer. Imagine trying to stack up whole trees instead of just logs. Tough, right? But for a given number of carbons, what really matters is how symmetrical the molecule is. Think about the trees again: It would be much easier to stack symmetrical trees than irregular ones. Therefore, the more symmetrical a molecule, the higher the melting point.

Reactions

Alkanes are very stable molecules; they don't react easily with other compounds—that is, unless we agitate them into reacting. As we've seen with fuels, they can sit on shelves for years without concern, but as soon as they are exposed to a spark and some oxygen . . . fire in the hole!

COMBUSTION

Combustion is the reaction of alkanes with molecular oxygen to form carbon dioxide, water, and heat. The combustion reaction has been a favorite among humans for a long time, although its mechanism isn't as simple as striking a match. The reaction is believed to proceed through a radical process, and because it is complex, the mechanism is not within the scope of the MCAT. What *is* within the scope of the MCAT is the equation for combustion:

$$C_3H_8 + 5\ O_2 \rightarrow 3\ CO_2 + 4\ H_2O + heat$$

One problem that arises is that combustion is often incomplete. This dangerous incompletion results in significant quantities of carbon monoxide instead of carbon dioxide. This carbon monoxide production is a major cause of air pollution.

FREE RADICAL HALOGENATION

One of the frequently encountered alkane reactions on the MCAT is **halogenation**, in which one or more hydrogen atoms are replaced with a halogen atom (Cl, Br, or I) via a **free-radical substitution** mechanism. These reactions involve three steps, but the second step can occur multiple times before the final step occurs.

Initiation

Diatomic halogens are homolytically cleaved (the two electrons of the sigma bond are split equally) by either heat or ultraviolet light, resulting in the formation of two free radicals. Free radicals are neutral species with unpaired electrons (such as Cl• or $R_3C•$). They are extremely reactive and readily attack alkanes, or pretty much anything that gets near them. Free radicals act in the same manner as political radicals (easily roused citizens who will readily take part in a rally or demonstration).

$$\text{Initiation:}\quad X_2 \xrightarrow[\text{or }\Delta]{h\nu} 2X•$$

Propagation

A propagation step is one in which a radical produces another radical that can continue the reaction. A free radical reacts with an alkane, removing a hydrogen atom to form HX and creating an alkyl radical. The alkyl radical can then react with X_2 to form an alkyl halide, generating X•. We can always identify a propagation step because it is the only step that both begins and ends with a radical. Note that the product of the first propagation step is the starting material of the second, and the product of the second is the starting material for the first step (a chain reaction). Just as with the propagation of a species, the end goal is to make more of the same thing.

$$\text{Propagation:}\quad X• + RH \rightarrow HX + R•$$
$$R• + X_2 \rightarrow RX + X•$$

Real World

Nitrogen in the air is often oxidized accidentally in the internal combustion engine, whereas nitrous oxide injection systems can be purposely (and illegally) installed to increase the engine power of a car. Unfortunately, various nitrogen oxides are major contributors to air pollution.

Bridge

Foods high in antioxidants reportedly help remove the free radicals naturally produced within the body from oxidative phosphorylation.

Termination

Propagation will continue until two free radicals combine with one another to form a stable molecule, ending the reaction.

$$\text{Termination:} \quad 2X\bullet \rightarrow X_2$$
$$X\bullet + R\bullet \rightarrow RX$$
$$2R\bullet \rightarrow R_2$$

Larger alkanes have many hydrogens available for the free radical to attack. Bromine radicals react fairly slowly and primarily attack the hydrogens on the carbon atom that can form the most stable free radical (i.e., the most substituted carbon atom). This is a good general rule to get down now: *The more stable the intermediate is, the more likely the reaction is to occur.*

$$\bullet CR_3 > \bullet CR_2H > \bullet CRH_2 > \bullet CH_3$$
$$3° > 2° > 1° > \text{methyl}$$

Thus, a tertiary radical is the most likely to be formed in a free radical bromination reaction (see Figure 4.3).

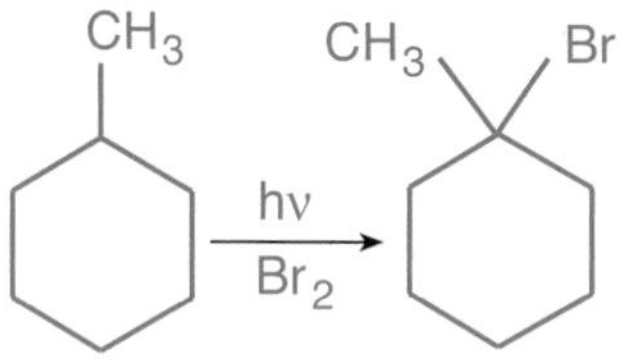

Figure 4.3

Free-radical chlorination is a more rapid process and thus depends not only on the stability of the intermediate but also on the number of hydrogens present. Free-radical chlorination reactions are more likely to replace primary hydrogens if they are the most abundant type of hydrogen present, despite the relative instability of primary radicals. Because of this decreased selectivity, free-radical chlorination reactions yield mixtures of products and are useful only when just one type of hydrogen is present.

MCAT Expertise

Always think of carbocations and free radicals as electron-deficient because both species have fewer than the eight electrons needed to be complete. In this way, we can remember the trends of stability of both of these species: 3° > 2° > 1° > methyl.

PYROLYSIS

Pyrolysis occurs when a molecule is broken down by heat. You can remember the name of this reaction by breaking it down into components: *Pyro* indicates that the reaction needs heat (just as a pyromaniac needs to light things on fire), and *lysis* is a term we use to talk about breaking molecules (or cell membranes, in the case of cell death). Pyrolysis, also known as **cracking**, is most commonly used to reduce the average molecular weight of heavy oils and increase the production of the more desirable volatile compounds. In the pyrolysis of alkanes, the C–C bonds are

MCAT Expertise

When a reaction involves UV light, you will almost always see a free radical. When a reaction involves heat, you should consider the possibility of free radicals and elimination reactions (which do not involve radicals and will be discussed in Chapter 5).

cleaved, producing smaller-chain alkyl radicals. These radicals can recombine to form a variety of alkanes, as shown in Figure 4.4.

$$CH_3CH_2CH_3 \xrightarrow{\Delta} CH_3\bullet + \bullet CH_2CH_3$$

$$2\ CH_3\bullet \longrightarrow CH_3CH_3$$

$$2\ \bullet CH_2CH_3 \longrightarrow CH_3CH_2CH_2CH_3$$

Figure 4.4

Alternatively, in a process called **disproportionation**, a radical transfers a hydrogen atom to another radical, producing an alkane and an alkene, as shown in Figure 4.5.

$$CH_3\bullet + \bullet CH_2CH_3 \rightarrow CH_4 + CH_2 = CH_2$$

Figure 4.5

Substitution Reactions of Alkyl Halides ★★★★★★

Alkyl halides and other substituted carbon atoms can take part in nucleophilic substitution reactions. **Nucleophiles** ("nucleus lovers") are electron-rich species that are attracted to positively charged or positively polarized atoms (known as **electrophiles**, or "electron lovers"). Alkyl halides are some of the most common substrates you will see undergoing nucleophilic substitution reactions on the MCAT. In these reactions, and with every reaction you see on the MCAT, the first thing we need to do is identify the nucleophile and the electrophile.

NUCLEOPHILES

Basicity

When comparing two nucleophiles, if both have the same attacking atom (for example, oxygen), nucleophilicity is roughly correlated to basicity. This seems logical: After all, the stronger the base is, the more likely it is to attract a positively charged proton. (Aha! Our Brønsted-Lowry definition of a base!) Because nucleophilic strength also measures how much the atom wants to find a positive charge, these two traits strongly correlate. For example, nucleophilic strength decreases in this order:

$$RO^- > HO^- > RCO_2^- > ROH > H_2O$$

> **Key Concept**
>
> A rule of thumb is that basicity and nucleophilicity are directly related because both imply that the compound wants to donate electrons, but the solvent may stabilize these species and alter that trend. In aprotic solvents, the trend stays intact.

Size and Polarizability

If the attacking atoms differ, or if the conditions differ, nucleophilic ability doesn't necessarily correlate with basicity. For example, in a **protic** solvent (solvents with protons in solution, such as water or alcohols), large atoms tend to be better nucleophiles because they can shed the solvating protons surrounding them and are more polarizable. Let's think about this: If we had a small, incredibly electronegative atom such as fluoride in a protic solvent, what would happen? Would it even make it to the electrophile? Probably not. It would probably pick up a proton out of solution the second it could. But what if we had a big old iodide atom? Well, it's not nearly as electronegative, so it would be less likely to pick up a proton the second it hit the solution. Furthermore, it's so big that it can be polarized, meaning the electrons can shift around, making some areas more negative than others, giving it a much better chance to make it to the electrophile while it is still negative enough to attack. Hence, nucleophilic strength decreases in this order:

$$CN^- > I^- > RO^- > HO^- > Br^- > Cl^- > F^- > H_2O$$

In **aprotic** (without protons) solvents, however, the nucleophiles don't have fancy proton coats surrounding them; they are not solvated. In this situation, nucleophilic strength *is* related to basicity. For example, in the aprotic solvent dimethylsulfoxide, the order of nucleophillic strength is the same as base strength:

$$F^- > Cl^- > Br^- > I^-$$

Note that this is the opposite of the trend in protic solvents.

LEAVING GROUPS

The ease with which nucleophilic substitution takes place also depends on how good a leaving group is present. Good leaving groups are easy to detect: The best leaving groups are those that are weak bases or, if you like, stable anions or neutral species. That is, they can easily accommodate an electron pair. Good leaving groups (weak bases) are the conjugate bases of strong acids. In the case of the halogens, this is the opposite of base strength (the pK_a of HI is -10.4, whereas the pK_a of HF is 3.1):

$$I^- > Br^- > Cl^- > F^-$$

S$_N$1 REACTIONS

S$_N$1 is the designation for a **unimolecular nucleophilic substitution** reaction. The term *unimolecular* tells us that the rate of the reaction depends on only one species, the **substrate** (the original molecule) itself. The rate-determining step is the dissociation of this species to form a stable, *positively charged* ion called a **carbocation.**

> ## Key Concept
> When it comes to nucleophilicity, *size matters* in protic solvents (those capable of hydrogen bonding, or donating protons). The smaller atoms can easily be surrounded by the solvent to decrease its ability to act as a nucleophile, and a larger atom thus becomes more nucleophilic in comparison.

> ## Key Concept
> Weak bases make good leaving groups because they are able to spread out electron density, making the species more neutral or more stable.

Mechanism of S$_N$1 Reactions

S$_N$1 reactions involve two steps: the dissociation of a molecule into a carbocation and a good leaving group, followed by the combination of the carbocation with a nucleophile (see Figure 4.6).

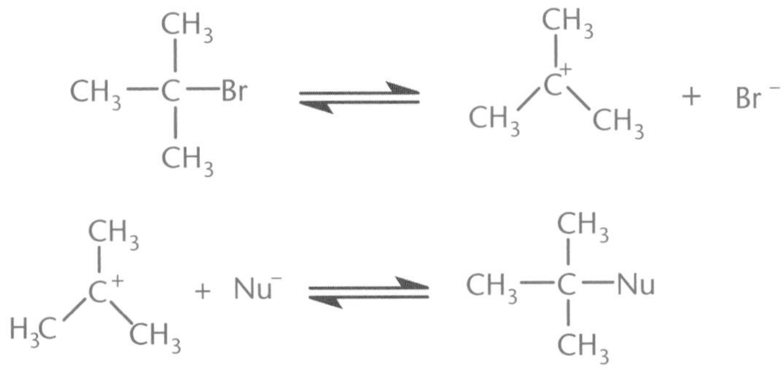

Figure 4.6

The first step of this mechanism is interesting. Notice that carbon is happily located with the other nonmetals on the right side of the periodic table, a place where atoms don't like to have positive charges. As such, it takes a little bit of coaxing to get carbon to become a carbocation. This can be accomplished using polar protic solvents with lone electron pairs, because the electron-rich groups can solvate the carbocation and help stabilize it. Carbocations are also stabilized by charge delocalization. The more highly substituted the cation is, the more stable it will be. This means the order of stability is as follows:

tertiary > secondary > primary > methyl

If we want to get a particular product from an S$_N$1 reaction, we need to make sure that the original substituent is a better leaving group than the nucleophile; otherwise, the reverse reaction will outcompete the forward reaction. This is an important factor, because it means that S$_N$1 reactions *do not* require strong nucleophiles, however, the more reactive the nucleophile the more likely an S$_N$2 reaction will result. Since the carbocation is *such* a strong electrophile, it will basically pick up anything that comes near it with lone electrons.

Rate of S$_N$1 Reactions

Like a relay race team, the rate at which a reaction occurs depends on its slowest step. Such a step is termed the **rate-limiting** or **rate-determining step** of the reaction, because it limits the speed of the reaction. In an S$_N$1 reaction, the slowest step is the dissociation of the molecule to form the carbocation, which we said was energetically unfavorable. In other words, the formation of a carbocation is the rate-limiting step. The only reactant in this step is the original molecule (substrate), so the rate of the entire reaction, under a given set of conditions, depends only on the

MCAT Expertise

The carbocation intermediate is the hallmark of the S$_N$1 reaction, and our understanding of the intermediate will be essential in determining all of the facts surrounding the reaction, including the rate and the products.

> **Key Concept**
>
> The kinetics of unimolecular reactions are first order.

concentration of this original molecule, rate = k[RX] (a so-called first-order reaction). The rate does not depend on the concentration or the nature of the nucleophile because it is not involved in the rate-determining step.

The rate of an S_N1 reaction can be increased by anything that accelerates the formation of the carbocation. The most important factors that we have already discussed are summarized below.

Structural Factors

Highly substituted alkyl halides allow for distribution of the positive charge over a greater number of carbon atoms and, thus, form the most stable carbocations.

Solvent Effects

Highly polar solvents are better at surrounding and isolating ions than less polar solvents. Polar protic solvents, such as water, work best because solvation stabilizes the intermediate state.

Nature of the Leaving Group

Weak bases dissociate more easily from the alkyl chain and thus make better leaving groups, increasing the rate of carbocation formation.

> **Key Concept**
>
> The pentacoordinate (five-coordinate) transition state, where one bond is forming and the other is breaking, is the hallmark of the S_N2 reaction. The increased crowding around that central atom will guide the rate and products of the reaction.

S_N2 REACTIONS

Under certain conditions, the formation of a carbocation is unlikely, if not downright impossible. Even under such conditions, substitution reactions can still proceed, but they must occur by a different mechanism that avoids the carbocation altogether. Enter S_N2: An **S_N2 (bimolecular nucleophilic substitution)** reaction involves a strong nucleophile pushing its way into a compound, while simultaneously displacing the leaving group in one concerted step (see Figure 4.7). Because this reaction has only one step, it must be the rate-determining step. The reaction is called bimolecular because the rate-determining step involves two molecules, as we will soon discuss.

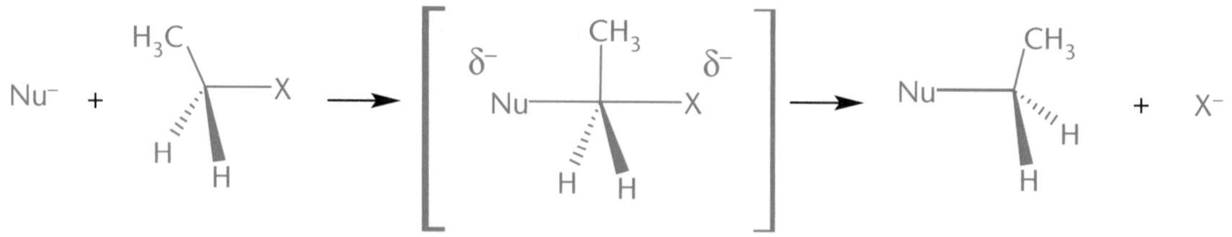

Figure 4.7

Mechanism of S_N2 Reactions

In S_N2 reactions, the nucleophile actively displaces the leaving group in an in-line attack. This is sometimes called a *backside attack*. For this to occur, the nucleophile must be strong, and the substrate cannot be sterically hindered. This tells us something important about the reactivity of substrates: Primary substrates are the most likely to undergo S_N2 reactions, followed by secondary, whereas tertiary substrates are just too crowded to participate in this mechanism. Notice that this is the opposite of the trend for S_N1 reactions. The nucleophile attacks the reactant from the backside of the leaving group, forming a **trigonal bipyramidal** transition state (sp^2). As the reaction progresses, the bond to the nucleophile strengthens, while the bond to the leaving group weakens. The leaving group is displaced as the bond to the nucleophile becomes complete.

Rate of S_N2 Reactions

The single step of an S_N2 reaction involves *two* reacting species: the substrate (the molecule with a leaving group, often an alkyl halide or a tosylate) and the nucleophile. Therefore, the concentrations of both have a role in determining the rate of an S_N2 reaction; the two species must meet in solution, and raising the concentration of either will make such a meeting more likely. Because the rate of the S_N2 reaction depends on the concentration of two reactants, it follows **second-order kinetics** (rate = k[Nu] [RX]).

S_N1 Versus S_N2 ★★★★☆

Now, we come to the real stuff the MCAT loves to test: What conditions favor one mechanism over the other? As you try to decide which mechanism or mechanisms are occurring, be sure to consider such factors as sterics, nucleophilic strength, leaving group ability, reaction conditions, and solvent effects.

Stereochemsitry of Substitution Reactions ★★★★☆

S_N1 STEREOCHEMISTRY

The S_N1 mechanism involves a carbocation intermediate in which the carbon only has three groups bound to it. With only three substituents, the molecule takes on a planar shape, with 120° between each of the bonds. That means that the carbons are sp^2 hybridized. Because the molecule is planar (and therefore achiral), the nucleophile can attack either the top *or* the bottom of the compound. This means that as long as the end product has four different groups, we can have two different products, depending on whether the nucleophile attacks from the top or the bottom (see Figure 4.8).

Key Concept

An intermediate is distinct from a transition state. An intermediate is a well-defined species with a finite lifetime and must be at a relative minimum energy for this to occur. On the other hand, a transition state is a theoretical structure used to define a mechanism. The transition state represents a maximum (in energy) between two minima on a reaction coordinate.

Key Concept

The kinetics of S_N2 reactions are second order.

MCAT Expertise

The comparison of molecules and which mechanism will be favored by particular reactants under particular conditions is a common topic on the MCAT.

Key Concept

S_N1 leads to loss of stereochemistry; S_N2 leads to a *relative* inversion of stereochemistry owing to backside attack. Be careful, though, because the *absolute* configuration may remain the same if the leaving group and the nucleophile do not maintain the same priority.

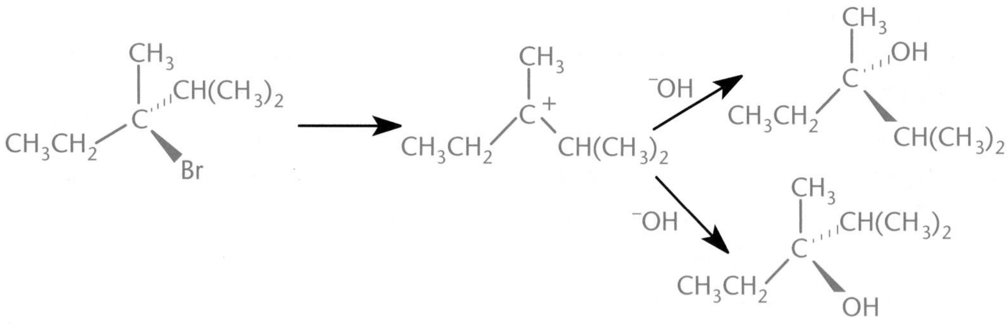

Figure 4.8

Bridge

Refer to Chapter 2 for further discussion of optical activity.

So, if the original compound was optically active, the product will be a racemic mixture and, thus, no longer optically active.

S$_N$2 STEREOCHEMISTRY

In the S$_N$2 mechanism, the nucleophile must attack the backside of the molecule, because the leaving group leaves from the other side. If a chiral molecule undergoes an S$_N$2 reaction, the molecule will flip, and an inversion of configuration will take place (see Figure 4.9). We've all had the unpleasant experience of trying to use an umbrella on a blustery day. When the wind blows your umbrella inside out, the original configuration of the umbrella is inverted. Your umbrella has been S$_N$2-ed!

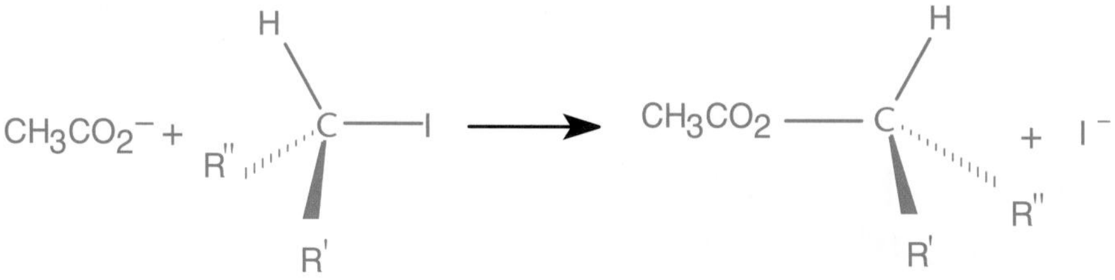

Figure 4.9

One important thing to be aware of is that this inversion of stereochemistry will lead to an inversion of the *absolute* configuration only if the leaving group and the nucleophile have the same priority (*R* will be changed to *S*, and vice versa). If the nucleophile and the leaving group have *different* priorities, even though the molecule will still flip, the designation will *not* be changed.

Table 4.1 summarizes S$_N$1 and S$_N$2 reactions.

If this reaction is carried out in a nucleophilic solvent, the cyclic halonium ion can be attacked by solvent molecules before the halogen ion gets a chance to do so. For example, if the reaction is run with water as a solvent, this can produce a halo alcohol.

Addition of H₂O

Water can be added to alkenes under acidic conditions (most commonly H_2SO_4). The first step? Once again, the double bond is protonated according to Markovnikov's rule, forming the most stable carbocation. This carbocation then reacts with water, yielding a protonated alcohol, which then loses a proton to become an alcohol (see Figure 5.8). We have to perform this reaction at low temperatures because at high temperatures, the reverse reaction, acid-catalyzed dehydration, is heavily favored. Remember, if heat is part of the reaction, look for the formation of a double bond. Adding water will break the double bond, so we'll need low temperatures. Hydration of the double bond can also be achieved under mild conditions with oxymercuration-reduction. As with acid-catalyzed hydration, which is consider harsh, Markovnikov regiochemistry is observed.

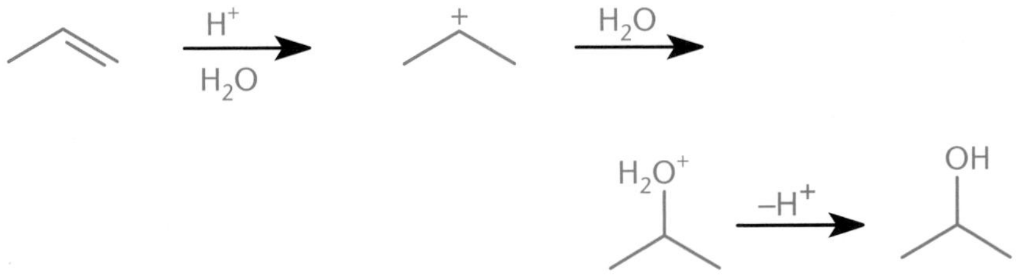

Figure 5.8

Free Radical Additions

There's another way to add HX to alkenes: through a mechanism that uses free-radical intermediates. This reaction occurs in the presence of peroxides, oxygen, or ultraviolet light. Free-radical additions disobey the Markovnikov rule because X• adds first to the double bond, producing the most stable free radical. As you can see in Figure 5.9, this means that the halogen will end up on the least substituted carbon. This is in contrast to standard electrophilic additions, where H⁺ adds first to produce the most stable carbocation. The important thing to realize here is that both of these mechanisms are in place to create the most stable intermediate. This reaction is useful for HBr, but it is not practical for HCl or HI, because they are energetically unfavorable.

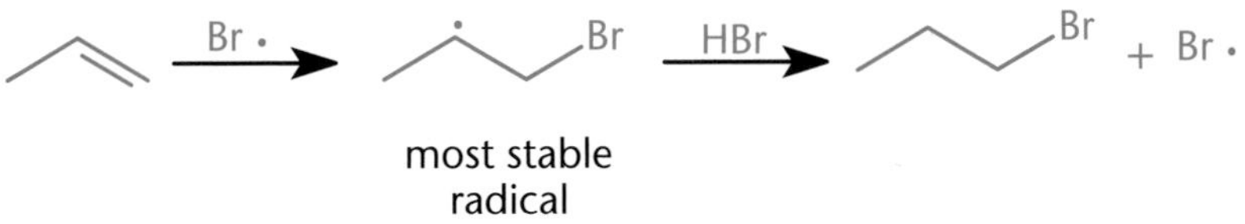

most stable
radical

Figure 5.9

MCAT Expertise

When peroxides or UV light are present, expect free radical reactions that do not follow Markovnikov's rule.

Key Concept

In anti-Markovnikov reactions, we can see that the most stable radical forms on the most substituted carbon (just as the most stable carbocation formed before), but because the halogen adds first, it ends up on the least substituted carbon. Remember, the most stable intermediate and least energetic transition state will *always* determine the favored products.

Hydroboration

Diborane (B_2H_6; often written as *borane*: BH_3) adds readily to double bonds. The boron atom (owing to its incomplete octet) is a Lewis acid and attaches to the less sterically hindered carbon atom. At the same time, a hydride is transferred to the adjacent carbon (a concerted mechanism). The second step is an oxidation-hydrolysis with peroxide and aqueous base that directly transfers water to the bond with boron, producing an alcohol with overall anti-Markovnikov, *syn* orientation (see Figure 5.10).

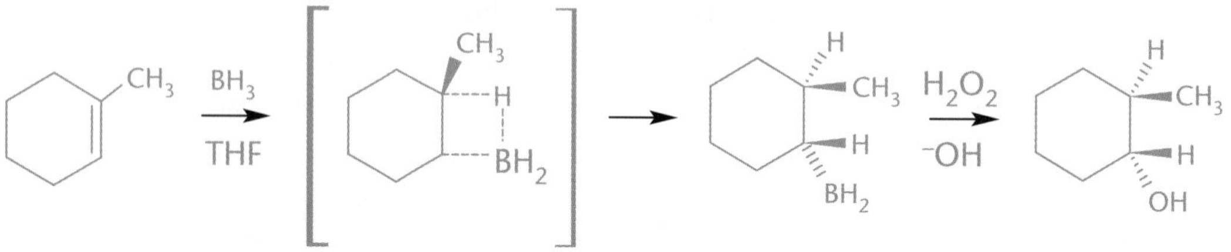

Figure 5.10

Oxidation

Oxidation is *prime* MCAT material, and luckily there's a useful trick to figure out if we're looking at an oxidation reaction. As a general rule, if a reagent has a whole bunch of oxygen in it, chances are that it's an oxidizing agent. In this chapter, we will discuss only a few of these reagents, but we will introduce you to the rest of the oxidizing reagents that you'll need to know on Test Day as we discuss aldehydes, ketones, and carboxylic acids later in this text.

Potassium Permanganate

Alkenes can be oxidized with $KMnO_4$ (potassium permanganate), although depending on the reaction conditions, we can end up with drastically different products (see Figure 5.11). If we make our conditions as mild as possible, using cold, dilute, basic $KMnO_4$, the product simply has –OH groups added to each side of the double bond. Such products are called 1,2 diols (vicinal diols), or glycols, and they have *syn* orientation.

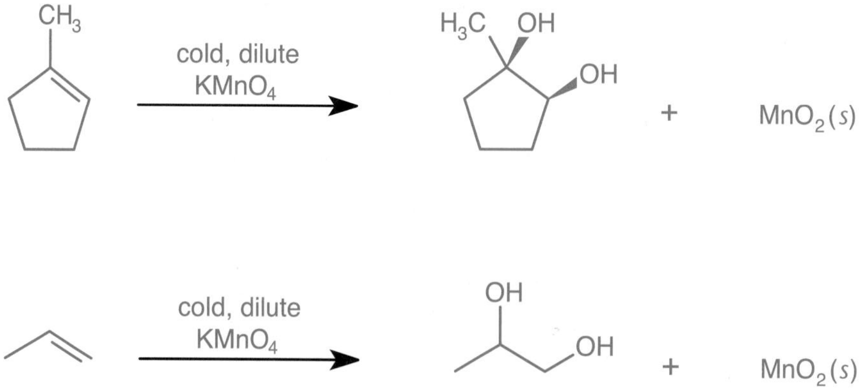

> **Key Concept**
>
> Cold, basic, and dilute conditions should always make you think of a mild or weak reaction (adding alcohols to a double bond). Hot, acidic conditions should make you think of rigorous or strong reactions (breaking the double bond altogether and forming carboxylic acids).

Figure 5.11

Alternatively, we can kick it up a notch and use a hot, basic solution of potassium permanganate, followed by an acid wash (see Figure 5.12). When we do this, nonterminal alkenes are cleaved to form two molar equivalents of carboxylic acid, and terminal alkenes are cleaved to form a carboxylic acid and carbon dioxide. If the nonterminal double-bonded carbon is disubstituted, a ketone will be formed. Under these intense conditions, we simply chop the double bond in half and make those cleaved carbons as oxidized as possible.

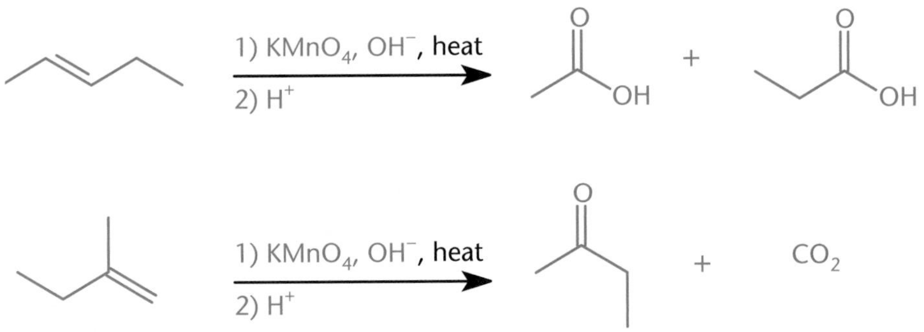

Figure 5.12

Ozonolysis

Ozonolysis is another strong oxidative process, but it can be made more selective than hot, acidic $KMnO_4$. Although it still cleaves the double bond in half, it only oxidizes the carbon to an aldehyde (or a ketone if the starting molecule is disubstituted) under reducing conditions (Zn/H^+ or $(CH_3)_2S$; see Figure 5.13). Ozonolysis under oxidizing conditions (H_2O_2) yields the same products as hot, acidic $KMnO_4$.

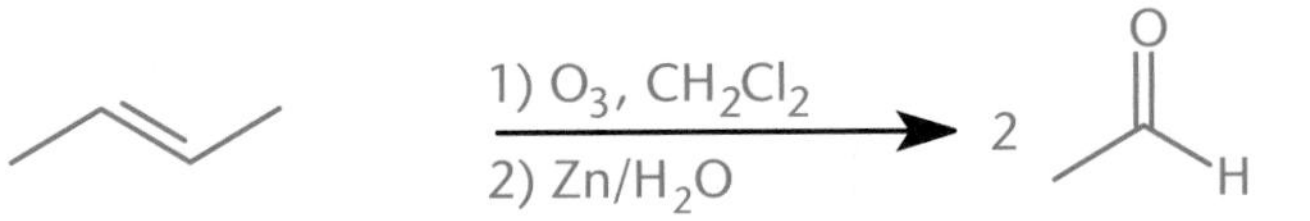

Figure 5.13

We can also obtain alcohols from this reaction; all we need to do is reduce the aldehyde or ketone products with a mild reducing agent, such as sodium borohydride ($NaBH_4$), or the more potent $LiAlH_4$ (see Figure 5.14).

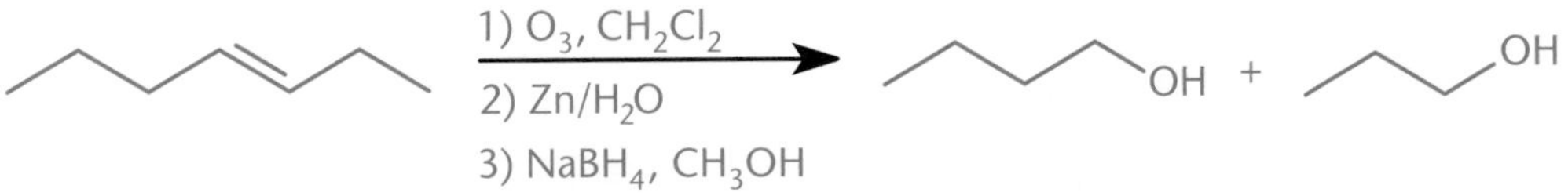

Figure 5.14

Peroxycarboxylic Acids

Alkenes can also be oxidized with peroxycarboxylic acids, which are strong oxidizing agents. Peroxyacetic acid (CH_3CO_3H) and *m*-chloroperoxybenzoic acid (MCPBA) are commonly used. The unique thing about this reaction is that the products are **epoxides** (also called **oxiranes**). This reaction is an example of syn addition:

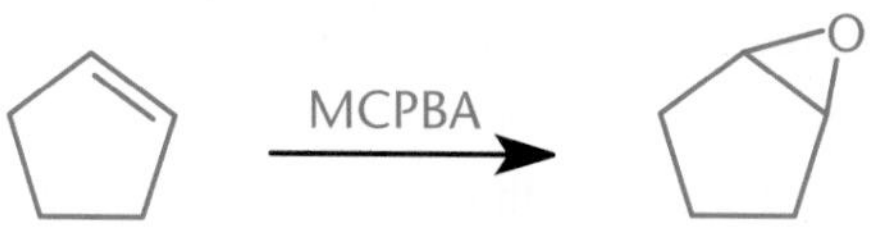

Figure 5.15

Polymerization

Polymerization is the creation of long, high-molecular-weight chains **(polymers)** composed of repeating subunits (called **monomers**). Polymerization usually occurs through a radical mechanism, although anionic and even cationic polymerizations are commonly observed. A typical example is the formation of polyethylene from ethylene (ethene) that requires high temperatures and pressures (this is the reaction used to make those grocery store plastic bags), shown in Figure 5.16.

Key Concept

When heat is present, consider the possibility of a radical mechanism.

$$CH_2{=}CH_2 \xrightarrow[\text{high pressure}]{R\cdot,\ \text{heat}} RCH_2CH_2(CH_2CH_2)_nCH_2CH_2R$$

Figure 5.16

MCAT Expertise

Alkynes will not be directly tested and will probably show up even less than alkenes on the MCAT. However, notice that alkynes undergo many reactions that are similar to those of alkenes, because they both have pi bonds.

Alkynes ★★★★☆☆

Alkynes are hydrocarbons that possess one or more carbon–carbon triple bonds. All triple bonds form straight lines with 180° between carbons as a result of the *sp* hybridization.

NOMENCLATURE

To name alkynes, use the suffix **–yne** and specify the position of the triple bond when it is necessary (see Figure 5.17). A common exception to the IUPAC rules is ethyne, which is almost exclusively called **acetylene**. Frequently, compounds are named as derivatives of acetylene.

$CH_3CH_2CH_2CH(Cl)C{\equiv}CCH_3$	$CH{\equiv}CH$	$CH_3C{\equiv}CH$
4-chloro-2-heptyne	ethyne (acetylene)	propyne (methylacetylene)

Figure 5.17

PHYSICAL PROPERTIES

As we'd expect, the physical properties of the alkynes are similar to those of analogous alkenes and alkanes. In general, similar to alkanes and alkenes, the shorter-chain compounds are gases, but alkynes boil at somewhat higher temperatures than their corresponding alkenes. Internal alkynes, like alkenes, boil at higher temperatures than terminal alkynes.

Asymmetrical distribution of electron density causes alkynes to have dipole moments larger than those of alkenes but still small in magnitude. Thus, we can assume that solutions of alkynes will be slightly polar, or at least more polar than a solution of alkenes.

One unique property to remember is that terminal alkynes are fairly acidic (at least for a carbon atom); they have pK_a's of approximately 25. This means that terminal alkynes can stabilize a negative charge fairly well, something that is uncommon for carbon atoms. As stated earlier, this stabilization stems from the 50 percent s-character. Recall that s-electrons have some probability of being found at the nucleus (negative electrons are happier in the positive nucleus). This property is exploited in some of the reactions of alkynes, which we will discuss soon.

> **MCAT Expertise**
>
> The acidity of the hydrogen on a terminal alkyne is the one major difference from all other hydrocarbon molecules. If anything about alkynes shows up on the MCAT, it will likely be in a question about acidity or a synthesis passage involving the reactions below.

SYNTHESIS

One way to make triple bonds is through two rounds of elimination of a geminal (remember twins, from the same carbon) or vicinal (neighbors in the vicinity) dihalide.

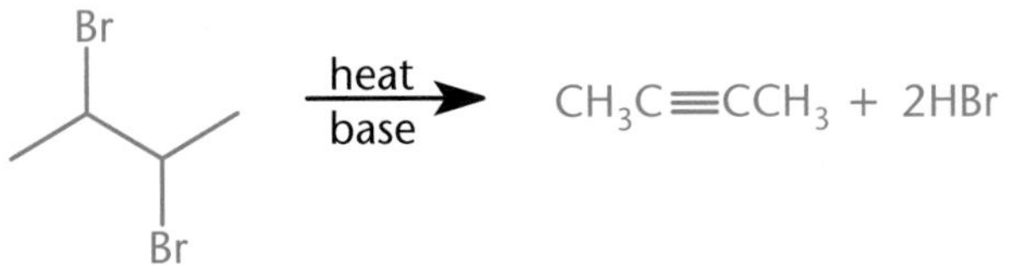

Figure 5.18

As you can see in Figure 5.19, this reaction requires high temperatures and a strong base, and so it's not always practical. A more useful method adds an already existing triple bond into a new carbon skeleton. To do this, a terminal triple bond is converted into a nucleophile by removing its acidic proton with a strong base ($NaNH_2$ or n-BuLi), producing an *acetylide ion*. Remember that terminal alkynes are fairly acidic, so this is a reasonable process. Once formed, the ion will perform nucleophilic displacements on primary alkyl halides at room temperature, as shown in Figure 5.19.

Figure 5.19

REACTIONS

Reductions

Alkynes, just like alkenes, can be hydrogenated (reduced) with a catalyst to produce alkanes. If we want alkenes as our final product, we need to stop the reduction after addition of just one equivalent of H_2. This partial hydrogenation can take place in two ways (see Figure 5.20). The first uses **Lindlar's catalyst**, which is palladium on barium sulfate ($BaSO_4$) with quinoline, a heterocyclic aromatic poison that stops the reaction at the alkene stage. Because the reaction occurs on a metal surface, the alkene product is the *cis*-isomer (just like the other reduction reactions we discussed using metal catalysts). The second method uses sodium in liquid ammonia at temperatures below –33°C (the boiling point of ammonia) and produces the *trans*-isomer of the alkene via a free-radical mechanism.

MCAT Expertise

In Organic Chemistry, think about reduction as adding bonds to hydrogen and oxidation as adding bonds to oxygen.

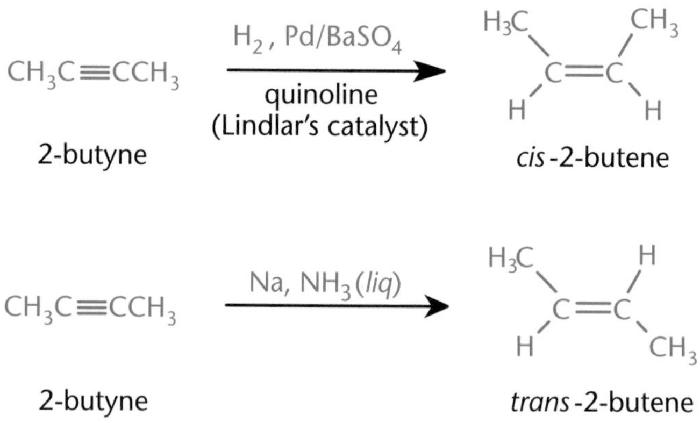
CH3C≡CCH3
H2, Pd/BaSO4
quinoline
(Lindlar's catalyst)
H3C
CH3
C=C
H
H
2-butyne
cis-2-butene
CH3C≡CCH3
Na, NH3(liq)
H3C
H
C=C
H
CH3
2-butyne
trans-2-butene

Figure 5.20

Addition

Electrophilic

Electrophilic addition to alkynes occurs in the same manner as it does to alkenes. The products form according to Markovnikov's rule. Addition can be stopped at the intermediate alkene stage or carried further. Of course, if we want to go all the way to the alkane stage, we will need two equivalents of reactants (see Figure 5.21).

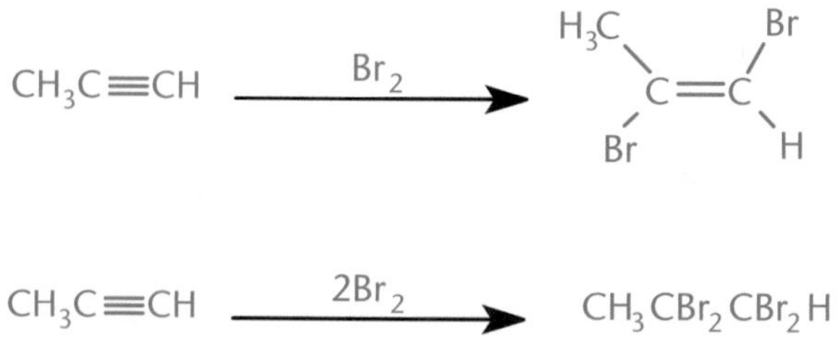
CH3C≡CH
Br2
H3C
Br
C=C
Br
H
CH3C≡CH
2Br2
CH3CBr2CBr2H

Figure 5.21

Free Radical

Radicals add to triple bonds just as they do to double bonds, with anti-Markovnikov orientation (see Figure 5.22). Be aware that the reaction product is usually the *trans*-isomer. This is because the intermediate vinyl radical can isomerize to its more stable form.

Key Concept

As always, the most stable electron-deficient species forms. In this reaction, we get an anti-Markovnikov product.

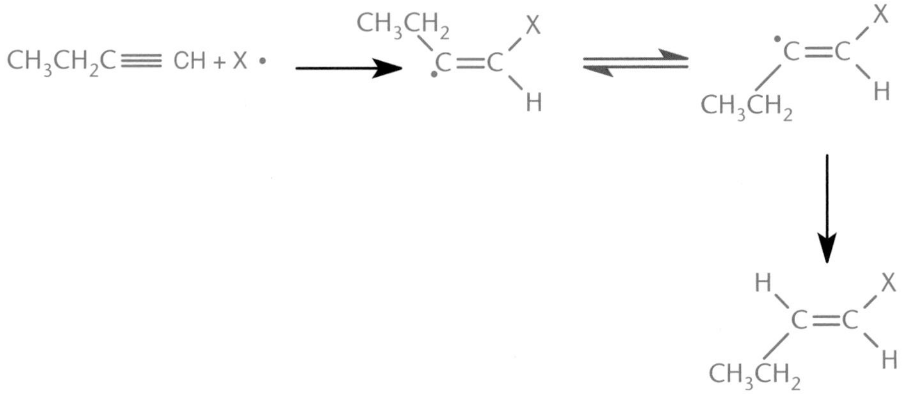

Figure 5.22

Hydroboration

As we'd expect, the addition of boron to triple bonds occurs by the same method as addition of boron to double bonds. Addition is *syn,* and the boron atom adds first. Notice that in the intermediate below, the boron is bound to three different substituents. If we follow the reaction with an acetic acid wash, the boron atom can be removed, and each substituent will have a proton from acetic acid in its place. This produces a *cis*-alkene, as shown in Figure 5.23.

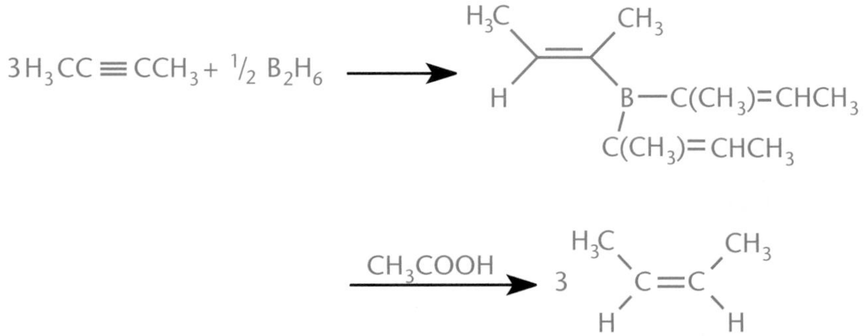

Figure 5.23

If we're dealing with terminal alkynes, a disubstituted borane is used to prevent further boration of the vinylic intermediate to an alkane. The vinylic borane intermediate can be oxidatively cleaved with hydrogen peroxide (H_2O_2), creating an intermediate vinyl alcohol (an enol), which tautomerizes to the more stable carbonyl compound (via keto-enol tautomerism; see Figure 5.24).

Bridge

Keto-enol tautomerism will be discussed in Chapter 8.

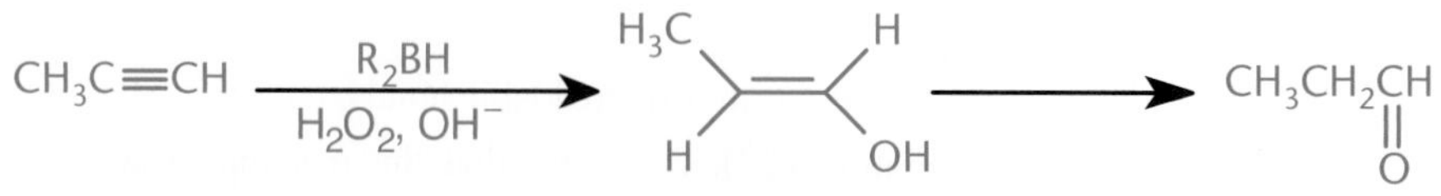

$$CH_3C\equiv CH \xrightarrow[\text{H}_2\text{O}_2,\ \text{OH}^-]{\text{R}_2\text{BH}} \quad \begin{array}{c} H_3C \\ \diagup \\ H \end{array} \!\!=\!\! \begin{array}{c} H \\ \diagdown \\ OH \end{array} \quad \longrightarrow \quad CH_3CH_2CH\!\!=\!\!O$$

Figure 5.24

Oxidation

Just like their alkene counterparts, alkynes can be oxidatively cleaved with either hot, basic potassium permangenate, $KMnO_4$ (followed by acidification) or with ozone (see Figure 5.25). Notice that both alkenes and alkynes will give the same product when reacted with hot, acidic $KMnO_4$. The difference here is with ozone. Remember that when alkenes react with ozone under reducing conditions (Zn/CH_3COOH), they yield aldehydes or ketones. However, under oxidizing conditions (H_2O_2) carboxylic acids are obtained instead of aldehydes. When alkynes are reacted with ozone, they yield carboxylic acids or CO_2. Note that triple bonds (with two π bonds) will add two oxygens to each carbon. Terminal alkynes produce CO_2.

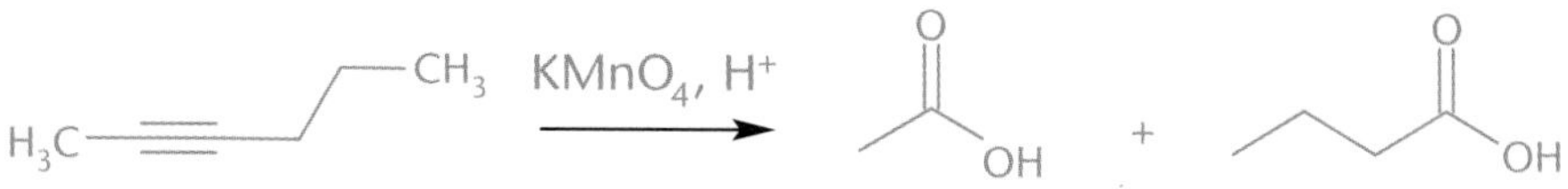

Figure 5.25

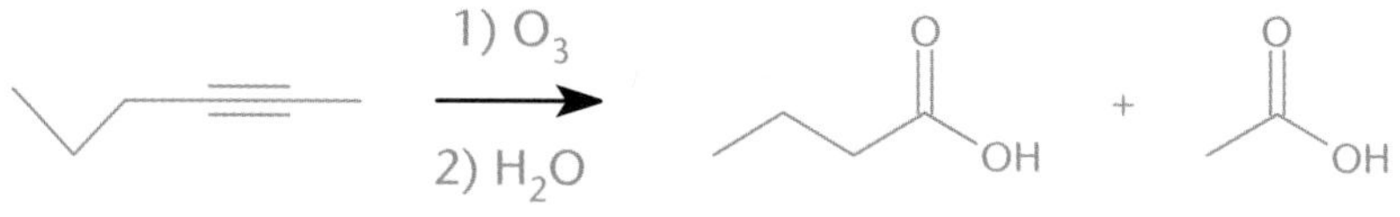

Figure 5.26

Conclusion

It's true that the carbon atom is capable of an astonishingly wide variety of forms and uses. Nevertheless, the alkene and alkyne varieties have similar names, similar structures, and, as you have learned from this chapter, many of the same properties. We saw that alkenes and alkynes can be synthesized by elimination reactions and that, just as in the substitution reactions discussed in Chapter 4, there are two mechanisms of elimination that take place selectively under certain conditions. Unlike the stable alkanes of Chapter 4, alkenes and alkynes can undergo additions, oxidations, and reductions.

We arrive now at one of the greatest lessons in your preparation for the MCAT. Simply put, you should focus on key differences and similarities. This will hold true for all topics and all subjects on the MCAT. The test makers know that memorizing Organic Chemistry in its entirety is an impossible, and ultimately useless, task. By focusing on key concepts, the MCAT gives you the chance to prove that you *understand* Organic Chemistry. It is far more important for you to know the rules of chemistry and understand what the possible products could be than it is to memorize the exact products of every reaction. This is going to be a lot different from your Organic Chemistry class in college and, in all likelihood, much easier.

CONCEPTS TO REMEMBER

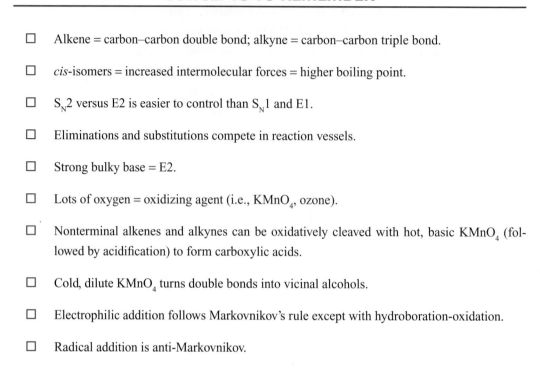

☐ Alkene = carbon–carbon double bond; alkyne = carbon–carbon triple bond.

☐ *cis*-isomers = increased intermolecular forces = higher boiling point.

☐ S_N2 versus E2 is easier to control than S_N1 and E1.

☐ Eliminations and substitutions compete in reaction vessels.

☐ Strong bulky base = E2.

☐ Lots of oxygen = oxidizing agent (i.e., $KMnO_4$, ozone).

☐ Nonterminal alkenes and alkynes can be oxidatively cleaved with hot, basic $KMnO_4$ (followed by acidification) to form carboxylic acids.

☐ Cold, dilute $KMnO_4$ turns double bonds into vicinal alcohols.

☐ Electrophilic addition follows Markovnikov's rule except with hydroboration-oxidation.

☐ Radical addition is anti-Markovnikov.

Practice Questions

1. What is the major product of the reaction below?

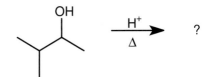

H⁺ / Δ → ?

   A. 3-methyl-1-butene
   B. 2-methyl-3-butene
   C. 3-methyl-2-butene
   D. 2-methyl-2-butene

2.

—C—Cl CH_3O^-, CH_3OH / $-HCl$ →

The above reaction takes place mostly by which of the following mechanisms?

   A. S_N1
   B. S_N2
   C. E1
   D. E2

3. Which of the following products would be formed if 2-methyl-2-butene were reacted with hot, basic $KMnO_4$?

   A. 1 mole of acetic acid and 1 mole of propanoic acid
   B. 2 moles of pentanoic acid
   C. 1 mole of acetic acid and 1 mole of acetone
   D. 2 moles of acetic acid and 1 mole of CO_2

4. What are the products of the following reaction?

1) O_3/CH_2Cl_2
2) Zn, H_2O → ?

   A. (structure) —OH + (structure)
   B. (structure) + CH_3OH
   C. (structure) + CO_2
   D. (structure) + (structure)

5. What are the products of the following reaction?

$$CH_3 - C \equiv C - \underset{CH_3}{\overset{CH_3}{CH}}$$

1) hot $KMnO_4$, OH^-
2) H^+ → ?

   A. (structure) + (structure)
   B. (structure) + HO (structure)
   C. (structure) OH + HO (structure)
   D. (structure)

6.

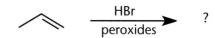

HBr / peroxides → ?

Which of the following represents the product obtained in the above reaction?

A.  Br

B. (structure)

C. (structure) Br

D. (structure) Br

7. What is the major product of the reaction shown below?

$$\text{(alkyne)} \xrightarrow[\substack{\text{Lindlar's} \\ \text{catalyst}}]{H_2} \text{?}$$

A. (Z)-2-pentene
B. Pentane
C. (E)-2-pentene
D. No reaction

8. Given the reaction shown below, what is the major product, not counting stereoisomers?

$$\text{(cyclohexadiene)} \xrightarrow[-78°C]{Br_2} \text{?}$$

A. (structure) Br, Br

B. (structure) Br, Br

C. (structure) Br, Br

D. (structure) Br, Br

9. Which of the reagents shown below will furnish 2-butanone starting with either 2-butyne or 1-butyne?

$$\text{(butyne)} \xrightarrow{?} \text{(2-butanone)} \xleftarrow{?} \text{(butyne)}$$

A. H_3O^+/H_2O
B. BH_3/THF, followed by $H_2O_2/NaOH$
C. Acidic $KMnO_4$, heat
D. H_2SO_4, $HgSO_4$, and H_2O

Small Group Questions

1. What makes I^- such a good leaving group? Why is tosylate a good leaving group as well?

2. Why is E1 least likely to occur of all four substitution and elimination reactions?

Explanations to Practice Questions

1. D

Heating an alcohol generally leads to loss of a water molecule. Multiple products (in this case, two) can be obtained depending on which H atom joins the –OH group to form water. The most stable product will be the most substituted alkene, which in this case is 2-methyl-2-butene.

2. D

Because this reaction converts a tertiary haloalkane into an alkene, it's an elimination. Strong bases favor E2, and weak bases favor E1. Because methoxide is a strong base, elimination occurs by the E2 mechanism in this situation. Choice (D) is the correct response.

3. C

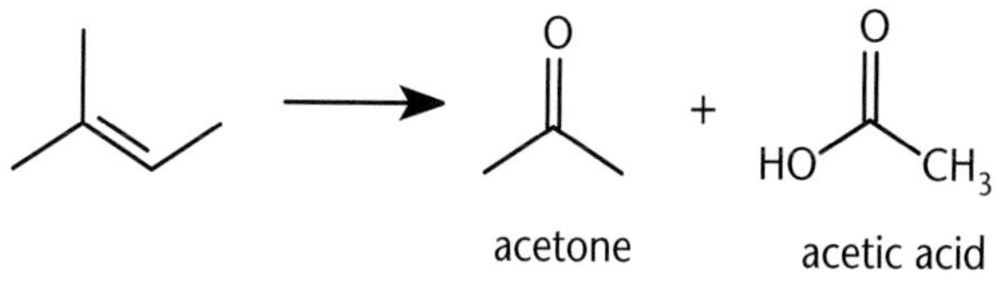

acetone   acetic acid

The double bond of 2-methyl-2-butene is cleaved by hot, basic potassium permanganate to form acetone and acetic acid. Cleavage of a primary double-bonded carbon yields a carboxylic acid (in this case, acetic acid), but cleavage of a secondary double-bonded carbon results in a ketone (here, acetone).

4. D

Ozonolysis of an alkene and subsequent treatment with zinc and water produces carbonyl compounds. After cleavage, any or all sides with secondary carbons become ketones, and the remaining side(s) with primary carbons become aldehydes.

5. C

Treating alkynes with hot, basic $KMnO_4$ leads to triple-bond cleavage and the formation of carboxylic acids.

6. A

In the presence of peroxides, the addition of HBr to the double bond takes place in an anti-Markovnikov manner in a series of free-radical reactions initiated by peroxides.

1. $ROOR \xrightarrow{h\nu} 2RO\bullet$
2. $HBr + RO\bullet \longrightarrow ROH + Br\bullet$
3. $CH_3CH = CH_2 + Br\bullet \longrightarrow CH_3-C\bullet H-CH_2Br$
4. $CH_3-C\bullet H-CH_2Br + HBr \longrightarrow CH_3-CH_2-CH_2 Br + Br\bullet$

In step 3, $CH_3-H_2-CH_2Br$ is formed instead of $CH_3-CHBr-H_2$ because the more substituted free radical is more stable than the less substituted one. Thus, the correct choice is (A). Note that in the absence of peroxides, HBr adds to the double bond in a Markovnikov manner and would result in the figure shown in answer (C).

7. A

Hydrogenation with Lindlar's catalyst will partially reduce triple bonds to yield alkenes; thus, answers (B) and (D) are incorrect. The addition of hydrogen occurs in a *syn* fashion (i.e., both hydrogen atoms are added on the same side). This means that the alkene's highest-priority substituents will both be pushed to the same side of the double bond, which is referred to as *Z* geometry.

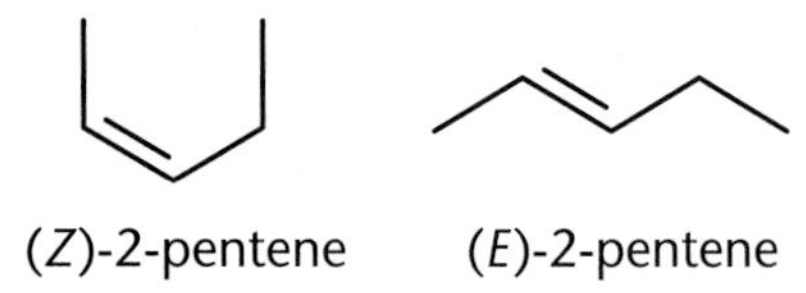

(*Z*)-2-pentene   (*E*)-2-pentene

8. B

The products depend on the reaction conditions. At low temperatures (−78°C), the major product resulting from the addition of bromine across a diene is the kinetically favored product (1,2-addition). Thus answer choice (B) is correct. Answer (C), the thermodynamically favored product (more highly substituted alkene) results from a 1,4-addition and is the major product at higher temperatures. Answer (A) is incorrect because bromine wouldn't add twice to the same carbon. Answer (D) is also incorrect because the addition of bromine would break the double bond.

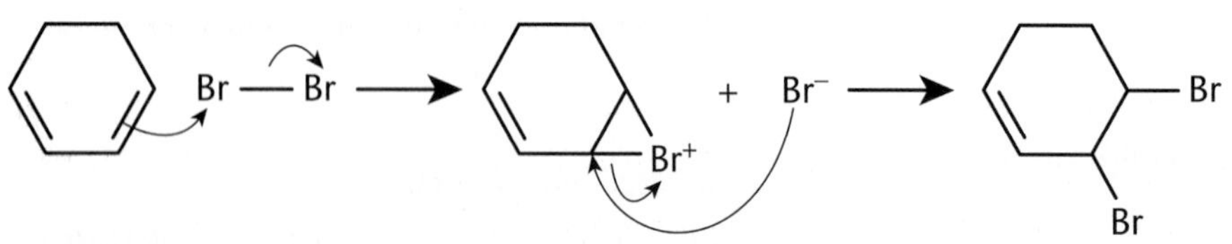

9. D

Answers (A) and (B) add across the triple bond to yield aldehydes when reacted with terminal alkynes and ketones when reacted with internal alkynes, so they are incorrect. Answer (C) is also incorrect because acidic $KMnO_4$ will cleave triple bonds with concurrent oxidation, giving carboxylic acids (and carbon dioxide with terminal alkynes).

7

Alcohols and Ethers

Alcohols and ethers are probably the two most popular chemicals that you'll encounter in Organic Chemistry, among scientists and laypeople alike. Ethanol, for one, has been popular with humans for more than ten thousand years. It's not just humans, either: Many animals are known to seek out rotten fruits that have fermented enough to contain moderate levels of alcohol. Note that when we talk about consuming alcohol, we are referring exclusively to ethanol. In fact, consuming other alcohols can have drastically negative effects. Methanol, for example, can cause blindness when ingested, an effect that many home distillers during Prohibition learned the hard way.

Ether, on the other hand, is young by comparison (only around 500 years old), but it should be a favorite of the aspiring surgeon. Ether became well known in the 1800s, when it was introduced as one of the first anesthetics for early surgeries. Once again, not just any ether was used as an anesthetic but specifically diethyl ether.

Alcohols ★★★★★★

Alcohols have the general formula ROH. The functional group is –**OH**, and it is referred to as a **hydroxyl** group. One way to think of alcohol is as a water molecule substituent that loses a proton when it attaches to an alkyl group, restoring its neutrality.

NOMENCLATURE

Alcohols are named in the IUPAC system by replacing the –e ending of the root alkane with the ending –ol. The carbon atom attached to the hydroxyl group must be included in the longest chain and receives the lowest possible number. Some examples are shown in Figure 7.1.

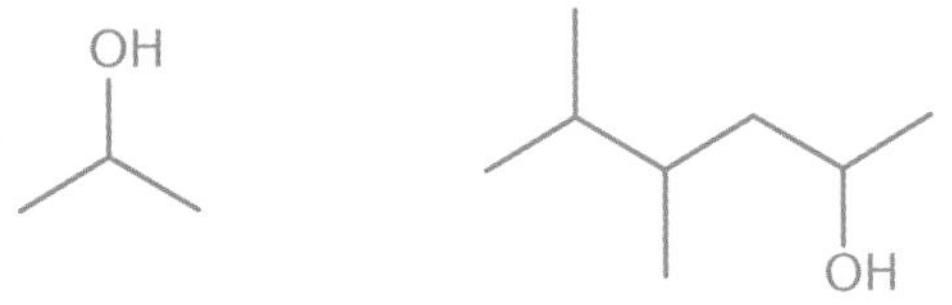

2-propanol   4,5-dimethyl-2-hexanol

Figure 7.1

Alternatively, the alkyl group can be named as a derivative, followed by the word *alcohol*, as in Figure 7.2.

ethyl alcohol   isobutyl alcohol

Figure 7.2

> **MCAT Expertise**
>
> Alcohols are an important group of compounds. They will be seen on the MCAT as protic solvents, reactants, products, and a prime example of hydrogen bonding.

> **Key Concept**
>
> The –OH group has high priority, so its C must be in the carbon backbone with the lowest number possible.

We will also see (as we did in Chapter 6) that alcohols can be attached to aromatic rings (see Figure 7.3). These compounds are called phenols and have the general formula ArOH.

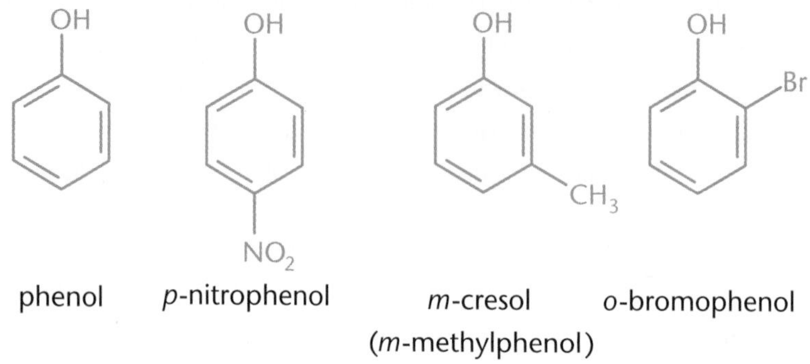

phenol   *p*-nitrophenol   *m*-cresol (*m*-methylphenol)   *o*-bromophenol

Figure 7.3

PHYSICAL PROPERTIES

The boiling points of alcohols are significantly higher than those of analogous hydrocarbons, owing to intermolecular **hydrogen bonding** (see Figure 7.4).

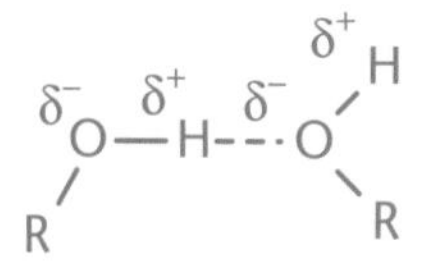

Figure 7.4

Molecules with more than one hydroxyl group show greater degrees of hydrogen bonding, as is evident from the boiling points in Figure 7.5.

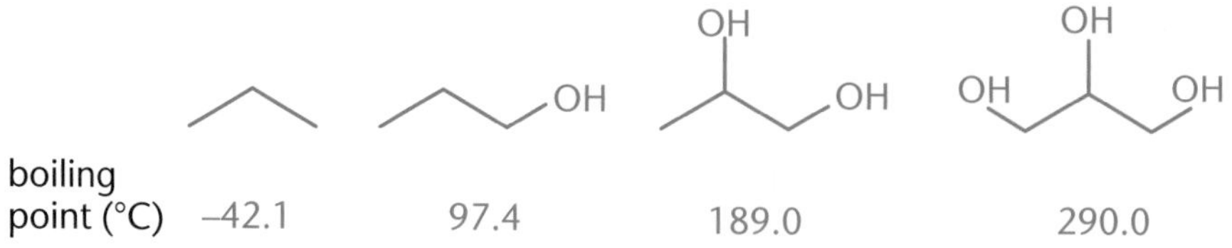

boiling point (°C)   −42.1   97.4   189.0   290.0

Figure 7.5

Hydrogen bonding occurs when hydrogen atoms are attached to highly electronegative atoms: namely nitrogen, oxygen, and fluorine. Hydrogen bonding exists as a result of the extreme polarity of these bonds. Thus, we can expect that HF will have particularly strong hydrogen bonds because the high electronegativity of fluorine causes the HF bond to be highly polarized.

The hydroxyl hydrogen atom is weakly acidic, and alcohols can dissociate into protons and alkoxy ions in the same way that water dissociates into protons and hydroxide ions. Table 7.1 gives pK_a values of several compounds.

Table 7.1

Dissociation		pK$_a$
H_2O	$\rightleftharpoons$ $HO^- + H^+$	15.7
CH_3OH	$\rightleftharpoons$ $CH_3O^- + H^+$	15.5
C_2H_5OH	$\rightleftharpoons$ $C_2H_5O^- + H^+$	15.9
i-PrOH	$\rightleftharpoons$ i-PrO$^- + H^+$	17.1
t-BuOH	$\rightleftharpoons$ t-BuO$^- + H^+$	18.0
CF_3CH_2OH	$\rightleftharpoons$ $CF_3CH_2O^- + H^+$	12.4
PhOH	$\rightleftharpoons$ $PhO^- + H^+$	≈10.0

Looking at Table 7.1, we can see that the hydroxyl hydrogens of phenols are more acidic than those of alcohols. This is because the aromatic nature of the ring allows for the distribution of negative charge throughout the ring, thus stabilizing the anion. As a result, phenols form intermolecular hydrogen bonds and have relatively high melting and boiling points. Phenol is slightly soluble in water (presumably owing to hydrogen bonding), as are some of its derivatives. Because phenols are much more acidic than aliphatic (nonaromatic) alcohols, they can form salts with inorganic bases such as NaOH.

The presence of other substituents on the ring has significant effects on the acidity, boiling points, and melting points of phenols. As with other aromatic compounds, electron-withdrawing substituents increase acidity, and electron-donating groups decrease acidity.

Another interesting trend that you probably noticed from Table 7.1 is that for aliphatic alcohols, the more alkyl groups that are present, the less acidic the molecule is. This is the opposite of the trend for carbocations. Logically enough, it's all based on the same concept. Because alkyl groups donate electron density (as we discussed in Chapter 6), they help *stabilize* a *positive* charge but will *destabilize* a *negative* charge.

REVIEW

Key Reaction Mechanisms for Alcohols and Ethers

As you read about the synthesis and reactions of alcohols and ethers, you'll see the same basic reaction mechanisms occurring over and over. Rather than memorizing each reaction individually, try to think of them in broad categories. Focus on how the basic mechanism works and how a particular reaction exemplifies it. The Big Three mechanisms for alcohols and ethers are these:

Bridge

pK$_a$ = −logK$_a$. Strong acids have high K$_a$'s and small pK$_a$'s. Thus, phenol, which has the smallest pK$_a$, is the most acidic of the alcohols listed.

Key Concept

Charges like to be spread out as much as possible. Acidity decreases as more alkyl groups (electron donating) are attached because they destabilize the alkoxide anion. Resonance or electron-withdrawing groups stabilize the alkoxy anion, making the alcohol more acidic.

1. *Nucleophilic substitution: S_N1, S_N2*

   Example: $CH_3Br + OH^- \longrightarrow CH_3OH + Br^-$

   See Chapter 4 for an in-depth review of nucleophilic substitution.

2. *Electrophilic addition to a double bond*

   Example: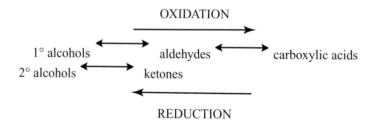

   This and other reactions that add H_2O to double bonds were covered in Chapter 5.

3. *Nucleophilic addition to a carbonyl*

   This mechanism is discussed in great detail in Chapters 8 to 10.

   Example: CH_3MgBr +

   Also, when thinking about alcohols, you should keep in mind their place on the oxidation-reduction continuum:

   OXIDATION

   1° alcohols   aldehydes   carboxylic acids
   2° alcohols   ketones

   REDUCTION

As you read about the individual reactions in which alcohols participate, try to fit them into this three-reaction framework. It will work for most of the reactions you will see on Test Day.

SYNTHESIS

Alcohols can be prepared from a variety of compounds. Ethanol can be produced from the fermentation of sugars, as we mentioned in the introduction with the example of rotting fruits. Methanol, on the other hand, is obtained from the destructive distillation of wood and is, therefore, called wood alcohol. As we said, methanol is toxic and can cause blindness if ingested. Ethanol can be metabolized by the body, but is also toxic if consumed in large quantities.

Addition Reactions

In Chapter 5, we discussed the addition of water to double bonds, an addition reaction that prepared alcohols. Alcohols can also be prepared from the addition of organometallic compounds to carbonyl groups; we'll get to this in Chapter 10.

Substitution Reactions

Both S_N1 and S_N2 reactions can be used to produce alcohols under the proper conditions, as discussed in Chapter 4.

Reduction Reactions

Alcohols can be prepared from the reduction of aldehydes, ketones, carboxylic acids, or esters. Lithium aluminum hydride ($LiAlH_4$, or LAH) and sodium boro-hydride ($NaBH_4$) are the two most common reducing reagents, and they each work a little bit differently (see Figure 7.6). LAH is the powerful one, and it will reduce just about anything (even esters, amides, and carboxylic acids) all the way to an alcohol. $NaBH_4$ is weaker, so although it, too, will reduce aldehydes, ketones, or acyl chlorides, it cannot reduce esters, carboxylic acids, or amides.

MCAT Expertise

Oxidation and reduction reactions are an important tool to the organic chemist and will be important for you to know on the MCAT. Remember: Reducing agents have a lot of Hs ($NaBH_4$ and $LiAlH_4$), and oxidizing agents have a lot of Os ($KMnO_4$ and CrO_3).

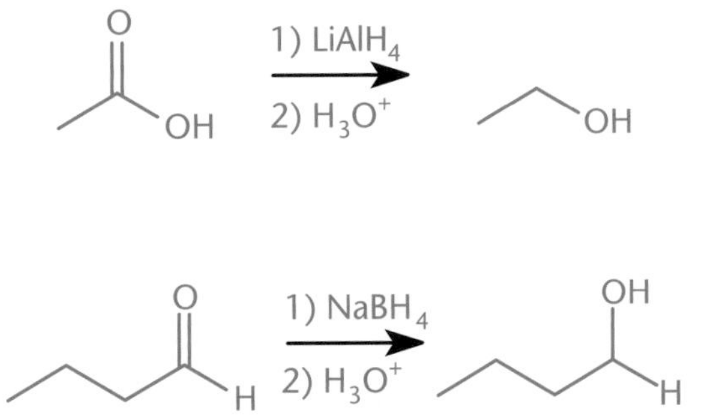

Figure 7.6

Phenol Synthesis

Phenols may be synthesized from arylsulfonic acids with hot NaOH. However, this reaction is useful only for phenol or its alkylated derivatives, as most other functional groups are destroyed by the harsh reaction conditions. A more versatile method of synthesizing phenols is by the hydrolysis of diazonium salts, shown in Figure 7.7.

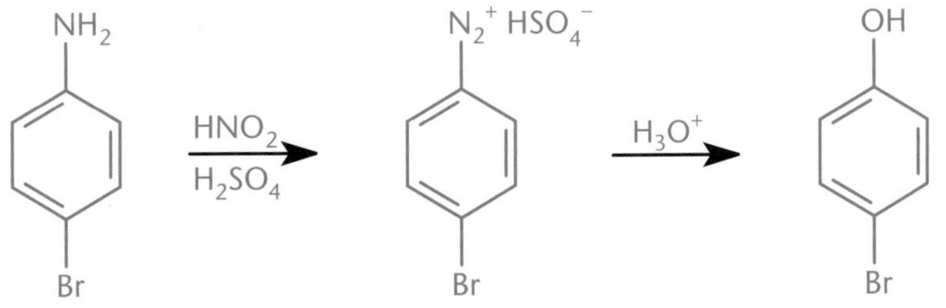

Figure 7.7

REACTIONS

Elimination Reactions

Alcohols can be dehydrated in a strongly acidic solution (usually H_2SO_4) to produce alkenes. The mechanism of this dehydration reaction is E1 for secondary and tertiary alcohols but E2 for primary alcohols. We need an acidic solution so that the –OH group can be protonated and converted to a good leaving group

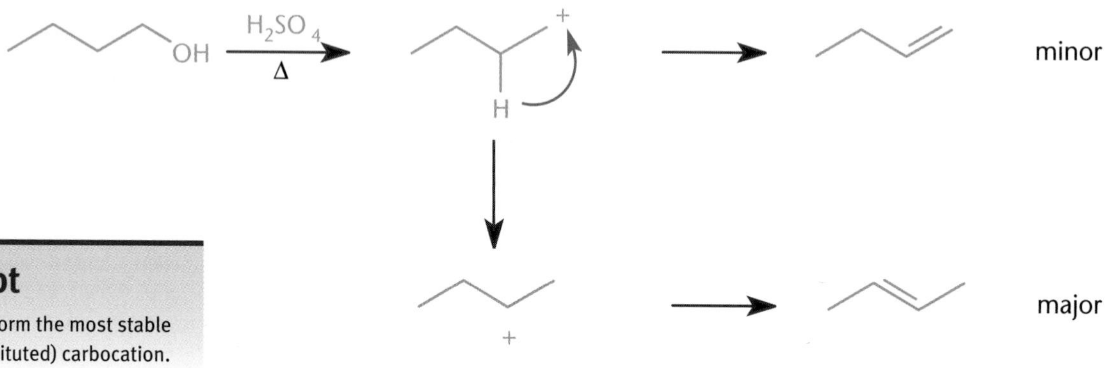

Figure 7.8

Notice in Figure 7.8 that two products are obtained, with the more stable alkene as the major product. This occurs via movement of a proton to produce the more stable 2° carbocation. This type of rearrangement, hydride shift, is commonly encountered with carbocations.

A milder method employs $POCl_3$ (phosphorus oxychloride), which follows an E2 mechanism for primary and secondary alcohols. Again, it converts the –OH group into a good leaving group.

Substitution Reactions

The displacement of hydroxyl groups in substitution reactions is rare because the hydroxide ion is a poor leaving group. If such a transformation is desired, the hydroxyl group must be made into a good leaving group. As we said before, protonating the alcohol makes water a good leaving group for S_N1 reactions. Even better, the alcohol can be converted into a tosylate (*p*-toluenesulfonate) group, which is an excellent leaving group for S_N2 reactions (see Figures 7.9a and 7.9b).

> **Key Concept**
> It's like the electrophilic addition of H_2O to a double bond, only this time it's in reverse—elimination.

> **Key Concept**
> In E1, you want to form the most stable (that is, most substituted) carbocation.

> **Key Concept**
> Alcohols can participate in S_N1/S_N2 reactions but only if you turn the –OH into a better leaving group by one of the following methods:
> —Protonate it
> —Convert to a tosylate.
> —Form an inorganic ester.

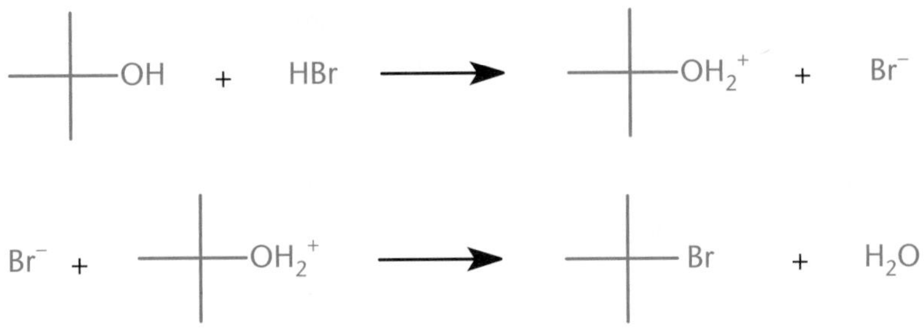

Figure 7.9a

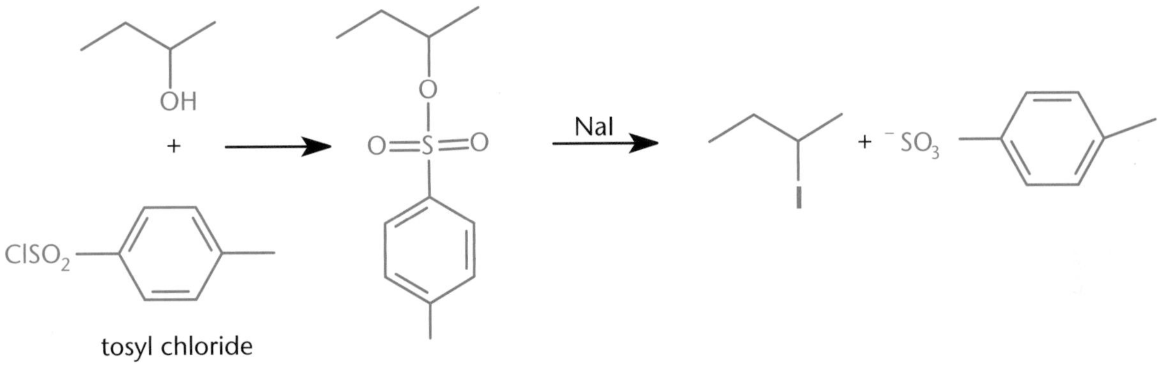

tosyl chloride

Figure 7.9b

Another useful reaction is the conversion of alcohols to alkyl halides. A common method involves the formation of inorganic esters, which readily undergo S_N2 reactions. Alcohols react with thionyl chloride to produce an intermediate inorganic ester (a chlorosulfite) and pyridine. The chloride ion, through an S_N2 mechanism, attacks the backside of the carbon bearing the oxygen (from the alcohol) and the chlorosulfite group. The reaction generates SO_2 and Cl^-, forming the desired alkyl chloride with inversion of configuration. Take a look at the mechanism outlined in Figure 7.10.

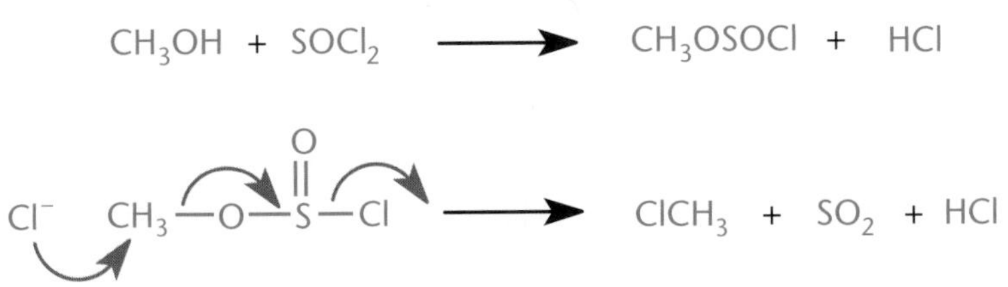

$$CH_3OH + SOCl_2 \longrightarrow CH_3OSOCl + HCl$$

Figure 7.10

An analogous reaction to this, where the alcohol is treated with PBr_3 (in pyridine) instead of thionyl chloride, produces alkyl bromides. In both cases, as with tosylates, the poor alcohol leaving group is converted to a good leaving group.

MCAT Expertise

Phenols are good substrates for the EAS reactions from Chapter 6. Remember that the lone pair from the oxygen makes it an electron-donating substituent. Therefore, the –OH will be activating and *ortho*/*para* directing.

Mnemonic

When you see a transition metal (such as Cr or Mn) with lots of oxygen ($Na_2Cr_2O_7$, CrO_3, or $KMnO_4$), think *oxidation*.

Phenols readily undergo electrophilic aromatic substitution reactions because the lone pairs on the oxygen donate electron density to the ring. This means the –OH group is strongly activating and, thus, an *ortho*/*para*-directing ring substituent (see Chapter 6).

Oxidation Reactions

The oxidation of alcohols generally involves some form of chromium (VI) as the oxidizing agent, which is reduced to chromium (III) during the reaction. Every oxidizing agent we discuss here is a strong oxidizing agent (will convert a primary alcohol into a carboxylic acid) except for one, **PCC**. PCC (**pyridinium chlorochromate**, $C_5H_6NCrO_3Cl$) is the only "mild" (anhydrous) oxidant you need to know on the MCAT. This means it only *partially* oxidizes primary alcohols; thus, it stops after it has been converted to an aldehyde. It does this because it lacks water to hydrate the aldehyde (aldehydes are easily hydrated). When aldehydes are hydrated (gem diols or 1,1-diols), they can be oxidized to carboxylic acids. PCC will also form ketones from 2° alcohols, so the only difference between PCC and all of the other oxidizing agents is how they react with 1° alcohols. Tertiary alcohols are already as oxidized as they can be and so do not react with *any* of the oxidizing agents.

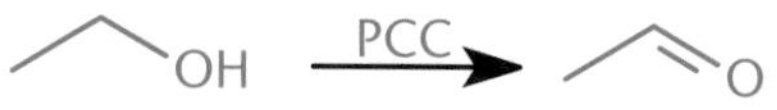

Figure 7.11

Another reagent used to *fully* oxidize primary and secondary alcohols is alkali (either sodium or potassium) dichromate salt. This means it will oxidize 1° alcohols to carboxylic acids and secondary alcohols to ketones.

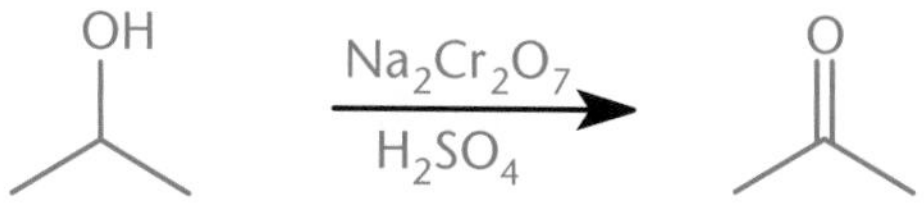

Figure 7.12

An even stronger oxidant is chromium trioxide, CrO_3. This is often dissolved with dilute sulfuric acid in acetone, a reaction called **Jones's oxidation**. This, too, oxidizes primary alcohols to carboxylic acids and secondary alcohols to ketones.

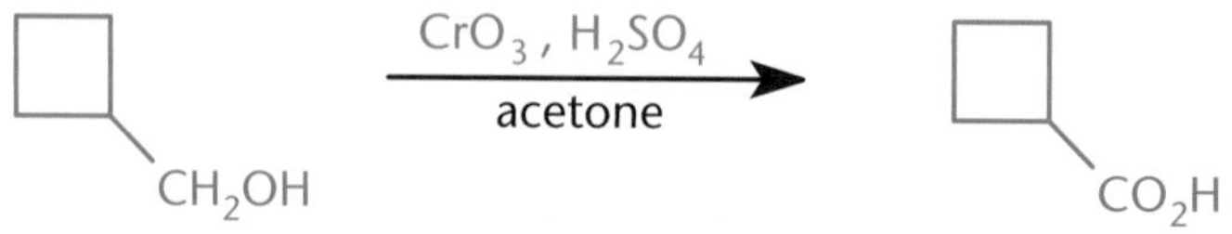

Figure 7.13

Treatment of phenols with oxidizing reagents produces compounds called **quinones** (2,5-cyclohexadiene-1,4-diones).

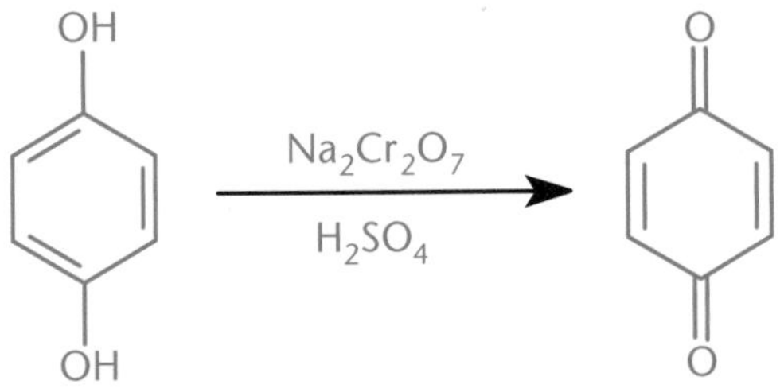

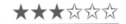

1,4-benzenediol

p-benzoquinone

Figure 7.14

Ethers ★★★☆☆☆

An ether is a compound with two alkyl (or aryl) groups bonded to an oxygen atom. The general formula for ethers is ROR. Ethers can be thought of as disubstituted water molecules. As we mentioned at the beginning of this chapter, the most familiar ether is diethyl ether. Although it is no longer used as a medical anesthetic, it is still often used in the laboratory.

> **Key Concept**
>
> Ethers, like alcohols, are important solvents, *but* ethers are aprotic and unreactive.

NOMENCLATURE

As explained in Chapter 1, ethers are named according to IUPAC rules as alkoxyalkanes, with the smaller chain as the prefix and the larger chain as the suffix. There is also a common system of nomenclature in which ethers are named as alkyl alkyl ethers, with the substituents alphabetized. For example, *methoxyethane* would be named *ethyl methyl ether* (see Figure 7.15).

methoxyethane
(ethyl methyl ether)

ethoxybenzene
(ethyl phenyl ether)

Figure 7.15

Exceptions to these rules occur for cyclic ethers, as there aren't two different alkyl groups attached to them. Many common names exist for these cyclic compounds (see Figure 7.16).

> **Key Concept**
>
> Remember that smaller rings have more angle strain, making them less stable and more reactive.

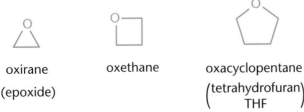

oxirane
(epoxide)

oxethane

oxacyclopentane
(tetrahydrofuran THF)

Figure 7.16

PHYSICAL PROPERTIES

An important distinction to note about ethers is that they do not undergo hydrogen bonding. Think about it; ethers have no hydrogen atoms bonded to the oxygen atoms, so they can't possibly participate in hydrogen bonding. Ethers therefore boil at relatively low temperatures compared with alcohols; in fact, they boil at approximately the same temperatures as alkanes of comparable molecular weight.

Key Concept

Note that the *lack* of hydrogen bonding is significant when determining the physical properties of ethers.

Ethers are only slightly polar and, therefore, only slightly soluble in water. They are inert to most organic reagents and as such, they are frequently used as solvents.

SYNTHESIS

The Williamson ether synthesis, an important reaction for the MCAT, produces ethers from the reaction of metal alkoxides with primary alkyl halides or tosylates. The alkoxides behave as nucleophiles and displace the halide or tosylate via an S_N2 reaction, producing an ether. There's nothing new here; this is a reaction you should already know. Note that it is in competition with E2.

Key Concept

Look, it's S_N2 again! Therefore, you need a strong nucleophile (alkoxides are good) and an unhindered substrate (not bulky or highly substituted).

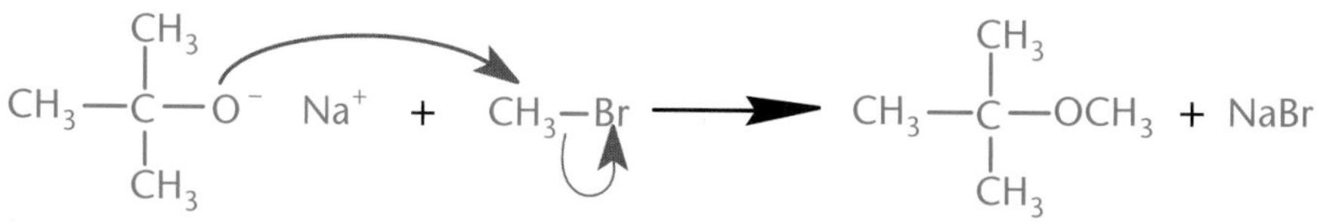

Figure 7.17

Remember that alkoxides will only attack nonhindered halides. Thus, to synthesize the methyl ether shown in Figure 7.17, an alkoxide must attack a methyl halide; the reaction *cannot* be accomplished with the methoxide ion attacking a bulky alkyl halide substrate.

The Williamson ether synthesis can also be applied to phenols (see Figure 7.18). Relatively mild reaction conditions are sufficient, owing to the acidity of phenols.

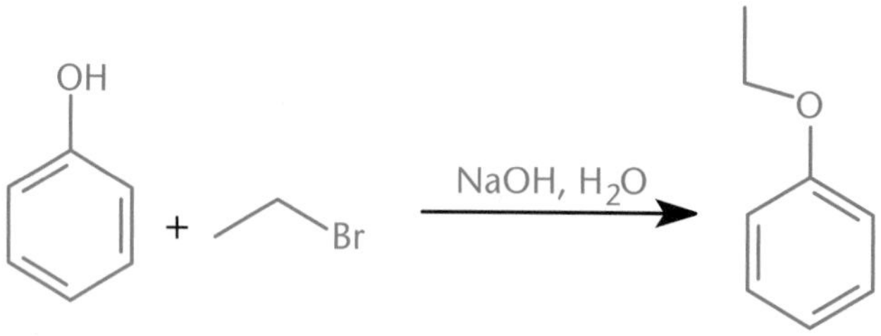

Figure 7.18

Cyclic ethers can be prepared in a number of ways, but you are likely to see it via internal S_N2 displacement. Intramolecular reactions are favored because, as we know, the rate and equilibrium of the reaction are affected by the reagent concentrations. With intramolecular reactions, the reagents see fairly high concentrations of each other; they are basically tied together (see Figure 7.19).

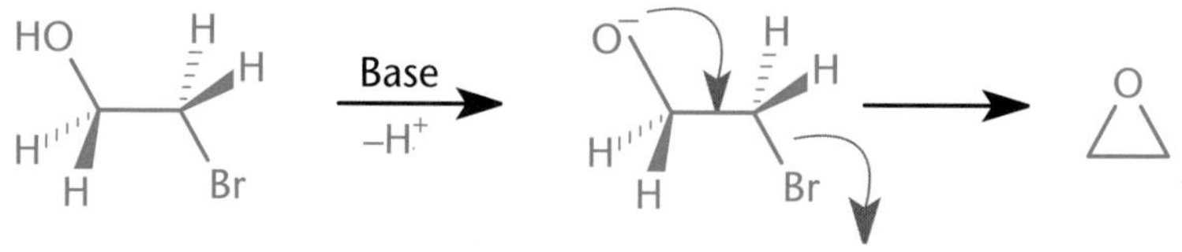

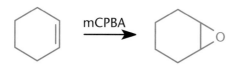

Figure 7.19

Key Concept

More S_N2! This time, however, it's intramolecular—the nucleophile and leaving group are part of the same molecule.

Another way to make cyclic ethers is by the oxidation of an alkene with a **peroxy acid** (general formula RCOOOH) such as mcpba (*m*-chloroperoxybenzoic acid). This reaction will also produce an epoxide or oxirane, as in Figure 7.20.

Figure 7.20

MCAT Expertise

Intramolecular reactions are often seen on the MCAT because they can be confusing to test takers. With every reaction on the MCAT, identify an electrophile (positive) and a nucleophile (negative) first, and you know that they will then come together—even if they are part of the same molecule.

REACTIONS

Peroxide Formation

Ethers react with the oxygen in air to form highly explosive compounds called **peroxides** (general formula ROOR). You don't need to worry about the mechanism of this formation, but you should know that the reaction is possible.

Cleavage

Cleavage of straight-chain ethers will take place only under vigorous conditions, usually at high temperatures in the presence of HBr or HI. Cleavage is initiated by protonation of the ether oxygen. The reaction then proceeds by an S_N1 or S_N2 mechanism, depending on the conditions and the structure of the ether (Figure 7.21). Although not shown here, the alcohol products usually react with a second molecule of hydrogen halide to produce an alkyl halide.

Key Concept

Remember, strong bases are poor leaving groups. Without protonation, the leaving group would be an alkoxide (strongly basic), and the reaction would be unlikely to proceed.

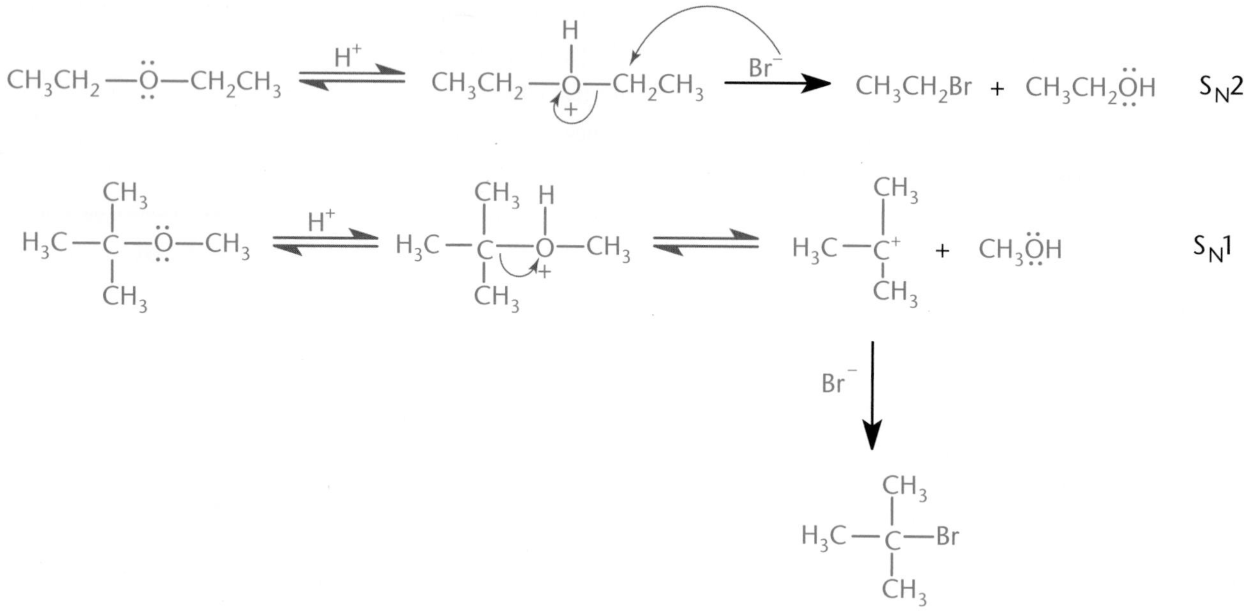

Figure 7.21

Key Concept

Cleavage of straight chain ethers is acid-catalyzed. Cleavage of epoxides can be acid-catalyzed (the nucleophile (e.g., H_2O, ROH) attacks the more substituted carbon of the epoxide) or base-induced (the nucleophile (e.g., RMgX, $LiAlH_4$, OH^-) attacks the least substituted carbon of the epoxide).

Because epoxides are highly strained cyclic ethers, they are ready to react and, thus, susceptible to S_N2 reactions. Unlike straight-chain ethers, these reactions can be catalyzed by acid or reacted with base (nucleophiles), as shown in Figure 7.22. In symmetrical epoxides, either carbon can be nucleophilically attacked. However, in asymmetrical epoxides, the *most* substituted carbon is nucleophilically attacked when catalyzed with acid, and the *least* substituted carbon is attacked with a nucleophile (basic conditions).

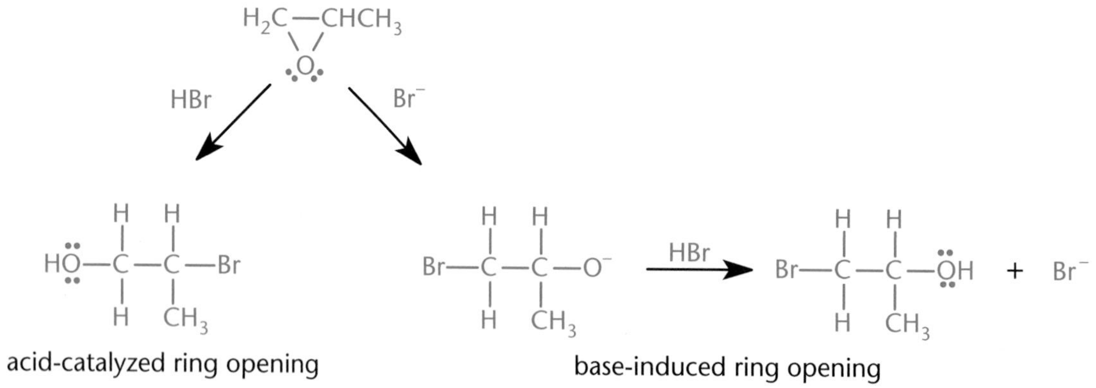

Figure 7.22

Base (nucleophile) induced cleavage has mostly S_N2 character, so it occurs at the least hindered (least substituted) carbon. Because the environment is basic, it provides a better nucleophile than an acidic environment.

In contrast, acid-catalyzed cleavage is thought to have some S_N1 character and some S_N2 character. The epoxide's oxygen is protonated, converting it to a better leaving group. As a result, the carbons share a bit of the positive charge. Because substitution stabilizes this charge (remember, 3° carbons make the best carbocations), the more substituted carbon becomes a good target for nucleophilic attack.

Conclusion

Alcohols and ethers may be popular among humans and animals, but they are a particular favorite of MCAT test makers. We get our first look at the unique properties that stem from hydrogen bonding: Remember that alcohols can form hydrogen bonds but ethers cannot. Know how alcohols and ethers are synthesized and understand the major reactions in which each participates. From this point forward, oxidation and reduction will be important reactions. Know that an oxidizing agent will have lots of oxygen, and a reducing agent will have lots of hydrogens. Don't let epoxides, ethers, or alcohols intimidate you; the same basic principles and reaction mechanisms that we've seen with more simple compounds apply here as well. Whenever you get a really complicated reaction, just take a step back, figure out what will act as the nucleophile and electrophile, and then go from there.

Key Concept

Base-induced cleavage has mostly S_N2 character, whereas acid-catalyzed cleavage seems to have some S_N1 character.

CONCEPTS TO REMEMBER

☐ Alcohol = ROH.

☐ Alcohols (and any other compound that has a hydrogen bonded to an O, N, or F) will undergo hydrogen bonding, leading to a relatively high boiling point.

☐ Whereas alkyl groups stabilize positive charges, they destabilize negative charges.

☐ Alcohols can be made by nucleophilic substitution, electrophilic addition to a double bond, or nucleophilic addition to a carbonyl.

☐ If a reactant has a lot of oxygen, it's an oxidizing agent; if it has a lot of hydrogen, it's a reducing agent.

☐ Terminal alcohols are oxidized to carboxylic acids, secondary alcohols are oxidized to ketones, and tertiary alcohols cannot be oxidized.

☐ PCC only oxidizes terminal (primary) alcohols to aldehydes.

☐ The oxygen of alcohols or ethers can be protonated to make them into better leaving groups.

☐ Cleavage of straight-chain ethers is acid catalyzed; cleavage of cyclic ethers (epoxides) can be carried out in acid or base.

☐ Base-induced epoxide cleavage has S_N2 character; acid-catalyzed cleavage has S_N1 and S_N2 character.

More specifically, the Wittig reaction forms carbon–carbon double bonds by converting aldehydes and ketones into alkenes (see Figure 8.15). The first step involves the formation of a phosphonium salt from the S_N2 reaction of an alkyl halide with the nucleophile triphenylphosphine, $(C_6H_5)_3P$. This compound is simply a phosphorus atom that has three aromatic phenyl groups attached to it. With its lone pairs and the added electron density from the phenyl groups, the phosphorus makes a great nucleophile and readily attacks the partially positive carbon on the alkyl halide. This phosphonium salt is then deprotonated (losing the proton α to the phosphorus) with a strong base, yielding a neutral compound called an **ylide** (pronounced "ill-id") or **phosphorane**. The ylide form is a **zwitterion** (a molecule with both positive and negative charges), and the phosphorane form has a double bond between carbon and phosphorus. (The phosphorus atom may be drawn as pentavalent, because it can use the low-lying $3d$ atomic orbitals.)

Key Concept

The term *salt* refers to any ionic compound that contains enough cations and anions to be electrically neutral. In Organic Chemistry, this will usually be a one-to-one relationship.

Figure 8.15

Key Concept

The ylide can act as a nucleophile and attack the carbonyl.

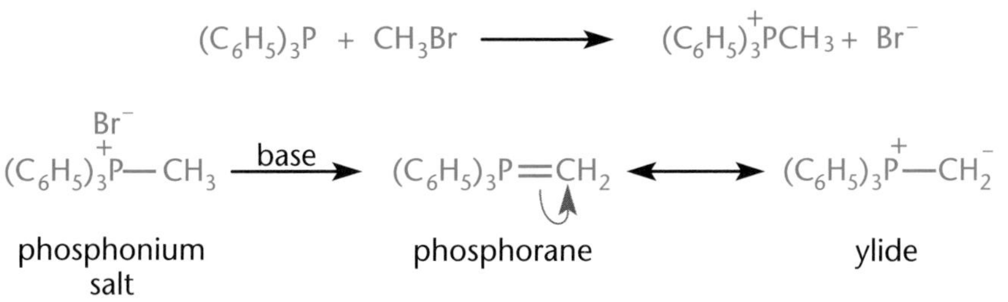

Notice that an ylide is a type of carbanion and, thus, has nucleophilic properties. When combined with an aldehyde or ketone, an ylide attacks the carbonyl carbon, giving an intermediate called a *betaine* (a specific kind of zwitterion), which forms a four-membered ring with an ionic bond between the oxygen and the phosphorus. This ringed intermediate is called an *oxaphosphetane,* and it decomposes to yield an alkene and triphenylphosphine oxide, as shown in Figure 8.16.

Key Concept

The Wittig reaction ultimately converts C=O to C=C (aldehydes/ketones to alkenes).

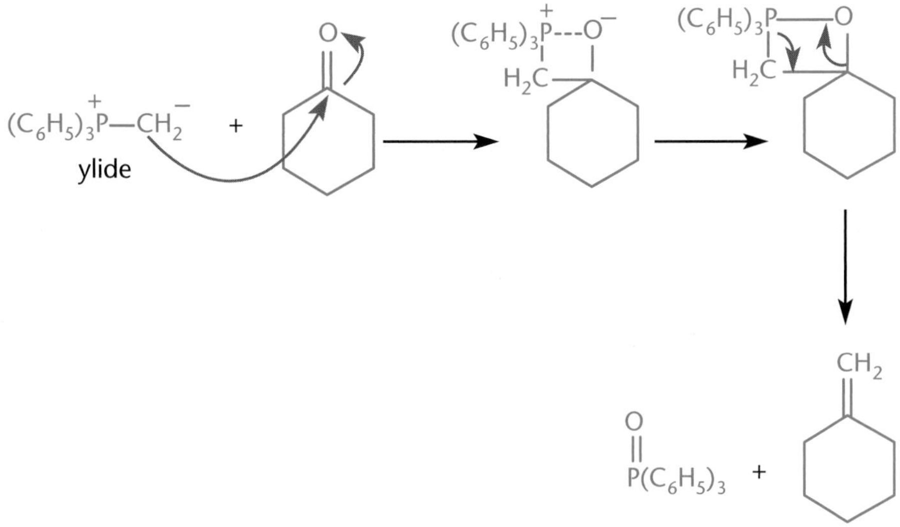

Figure 8.16

This decomposition reaction is driven by the strength of the phosphorus–oxygen bond that is formed.

OXIDATION AND REDUCTION

MCAT Expertise

As mentioned earlier, oxidation and reduction are important reactions of aldehydes and ketones, because aldehydes are midway between alcohols and carboxylic acids on the oxidation spectrum and ketones are maximally oxidized. Also, although knowledge of these mechanisms is not required for the MCAT, it should not be surprising that the carbonyl carbon acts as an electrophile.

Aldehydes occupy the middle of the oxidation–reduction spectrum; they are more oxidized than alcohols but less oxidized than carboxylic acids. Ketones, on the other hand, are as oxidized as secondary carbons can get.

Pretty much any oxidizing agent (except PCC) can oxidize aldehydes into carboxylic acids; some examples are $KMnO_4$, CrO_3, Ag_2O, and H_2O_2.

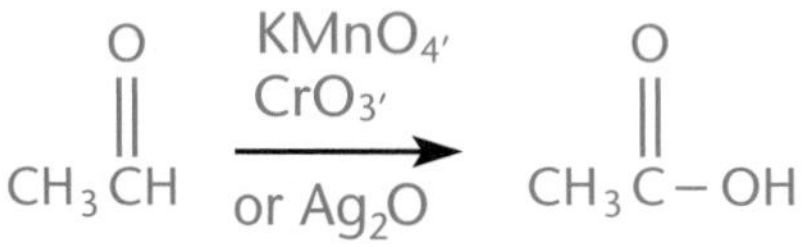

Figure 8.17

A number of different reagents will reduce aldehydes and ketones to alcohols. The most common ones seen on the MCAT, shown in Figure 8.18, are lithium aluminum hydride (LAH) and sodium borohydride ($NaBH_4$), which is often used when milder conditions are needed.

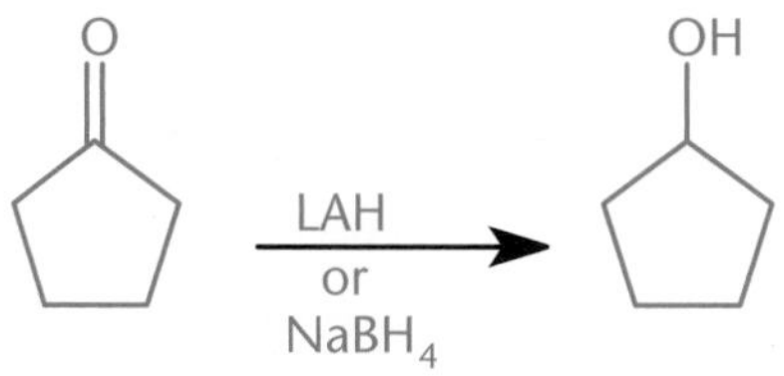

Figure 8.18

If we want to get more extreme, there are two ways to reduce aldehydes and ketones all the way to alkanes. In the **Wolff-Kishner reduction** (Figure 8.19), the carbonyl is first converted to hydrazone (we discussed this reaction earlier in this chapter, under the section on condensation reactions with ammonia derivatives). The hydrazone then releases molecular nitrogen (N_2) when it is heated with a base, forming an alkane. Note that the Wolff-Kishner reaction is useful only when the product is stable under basic conditions.

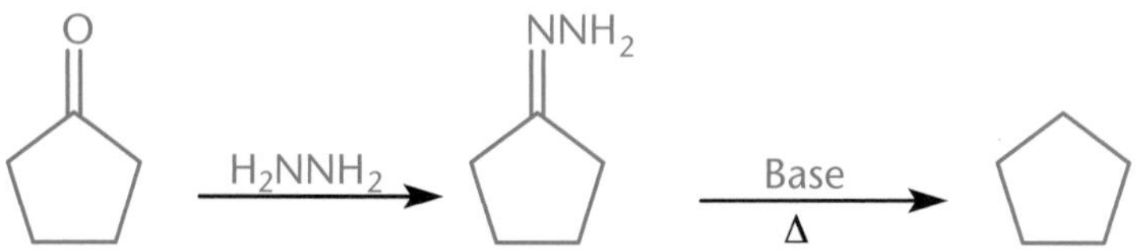

Figure 8.19

An alternative reduction that is not subject to this restriction is the **Clemmensen reduction** (Figure 8.20). In this reaction, an aldehyde or ketone is heated with amalgamated zinc in hydrochloric acid.

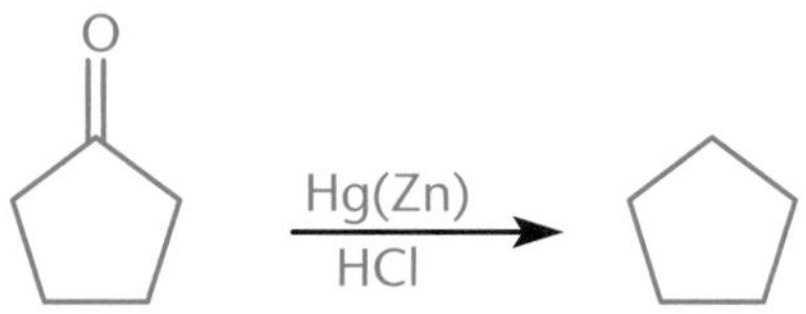

Figure 8.20

Key Concept

Both aldehydes and ketones can be fully reduced to alkanes by:

– Wolff-Kishner (H_2NNH_2, Base (KOH), Ethylene glycol (a high boiling solvent))

—Clemmensen [Hg(Zn), HCl]

Conclusion

We hope we have demonstrated in our review of aldehyde and ketone chemistry that the Organic Chemistry on the MCAT is going to be a lot different from that in your college courses. As the compounds we discuss become more and more reactive, it might feel as if the amount of information you need to learn is growing exponentially. It's true that we now have to be aware of several different synthesis routes and a lot more possible reactions. But remember that we don't need to memorize all the different reactions that take place; what we really need to do is understand the trends that govern every reaction. For instance, we learned that most of the reactions of aldehydes and ketones proceed through a mechanism in which a nucleophile attacks the carbonyl carbon. This electrophilicity and vulnerability to attack are hallmarks of the carbonyl group, as we'll see when we examine its role in other compounds, continuing in Chapter 10 with carboxylic acids.

CONCEPTS TO REMEMBER

☐ In a carbonyl, the carbon is partially positive, and the oxygen is partially negative.

☐ Aldehydes are terminal functional groups; ketones are midchain functional groups.

☐ Aldehydes can be synthesized from primary alcohols with PCC.

☐ Aldehydes can be oxidized to carboxylic acids or reduced to primary alcohols.

☐ Ketones cannot be further oxidized, but they can be reduced to secondary alcohols.

☐ The enol form is significant because it can act as a nucleophile, but it is not prevalent in solution.

☐ Many nucleophiles will add to the electropositive carbonyl carbon.

☐ Ammonia deriviatives often add in condensation reactions, removing water and forming a C=N.

☐ The Wittig reaction swaps out a C=O for a C=C.

☐ The Wolf-Kishner reduction and the Clemmensen reduction reduce ketones or aldehydes to alkanes.

Practice Questions

1.

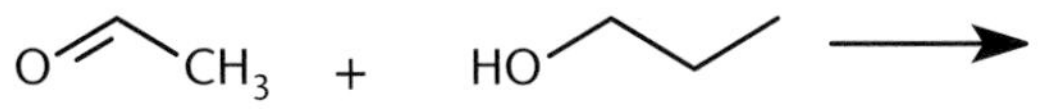

What is the product of the above reaction?

A.

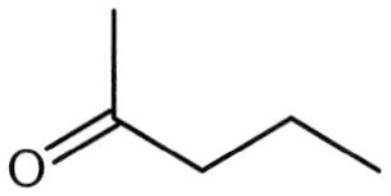

B.

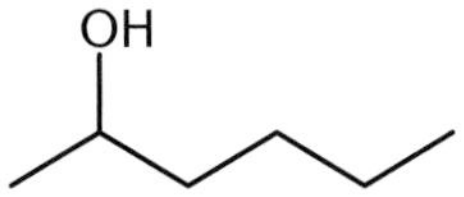

C.

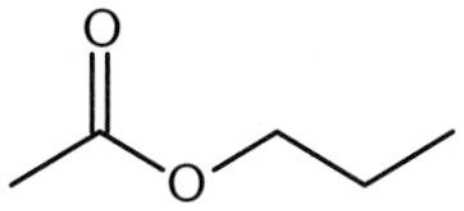

D.

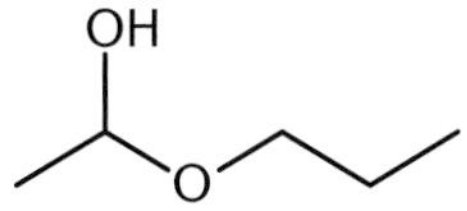

2.

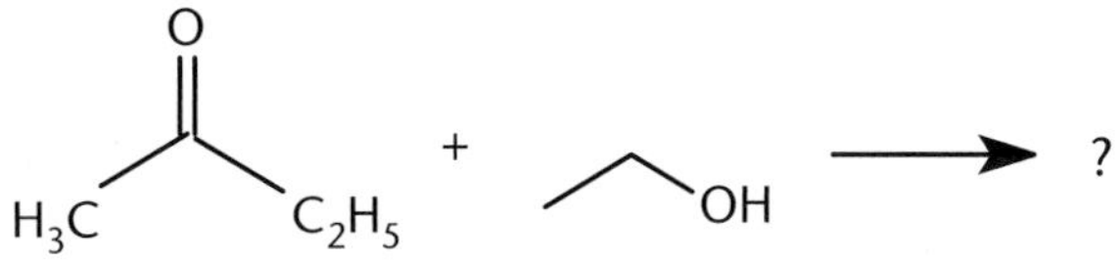

What is the major product of the above reaction?

A. 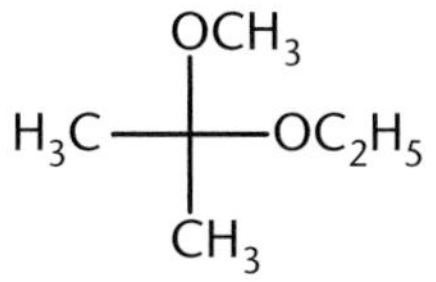 H_3C—$\overset{\displaystyle OCH_3}{\underset{\displaystyle CH_3}{|}}$—$OC_2H_5$

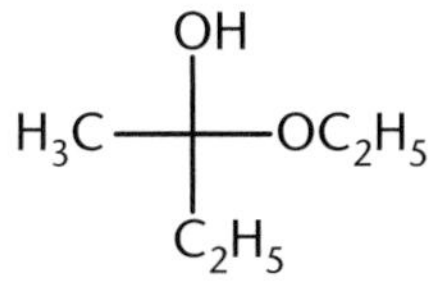

B.

C. H_3C—$\overset{\displaystyle OH}{\underset{\displaystyle C_2H_5}{|}}$—$OC_2H_5$

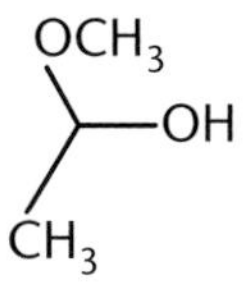

D.

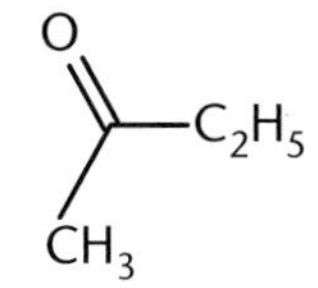

3.

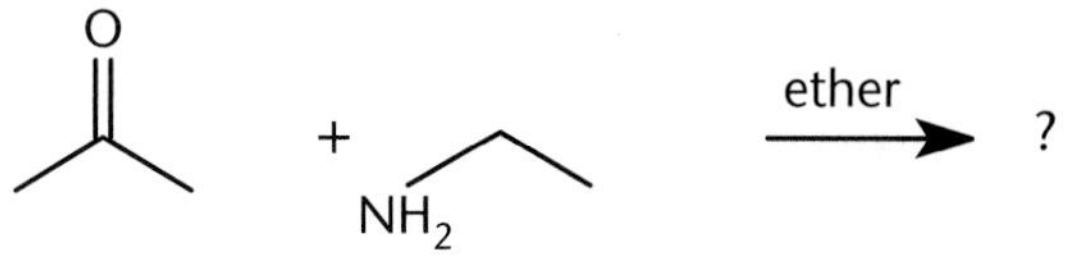

What is the product of the above reaction?

A.

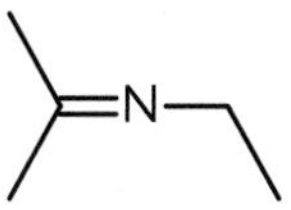

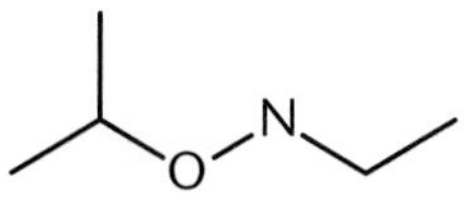

B.

C.

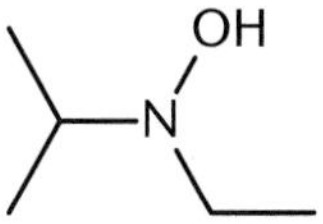

D.

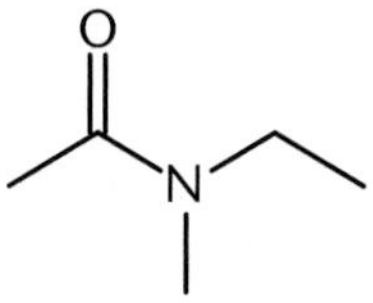

4. All of the following properties are responsible for the reactivity of the carbonyl bond in propanone EXCEPT the fact that

A. the carbonyl carbon is electrophilic.
B. the carbonyl oxygen is electron withdrawing.
C. a resonance structure of the compound places a positive charge on the carbonyl carbon.
D. the π electrons are mobile and are pulled toward the carbonyl carbon.

5.

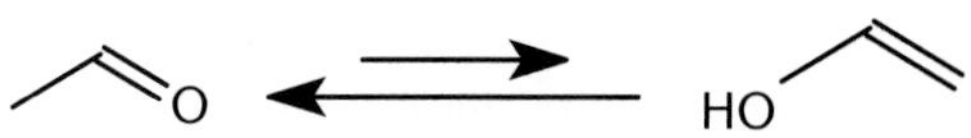

The above reaction is an example of

A. esterification.
B. tautomerization.
C. elimination.
D. dehydration.

6.

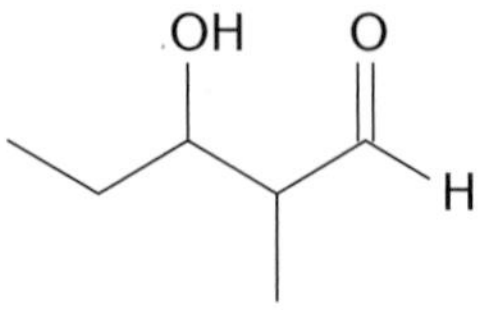

Which of the following reactions produces the above compound?

A. $CH_3CHO + CH_3CH_2CH_2CHO \rightarrow$
B. $CH_3COCH_3 + CH_3CH_2CH_2CHO \rightarrow$
C. $CH_3CH_2COCH_3 + CH_3CHO \rightarrow$
D. $CH_3CH_2CHO + CH_3CH_2CHO \rightarrow$

7.

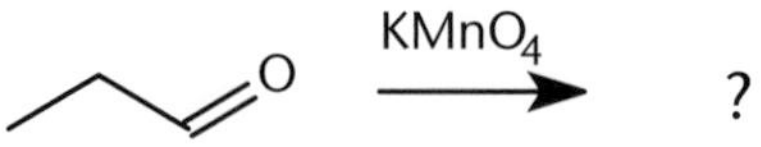

What is the product of the above reaction?

A. C_3H_7OH
B. C_2H_5COOH
C. C_3H_7CHO
D. CH_3COOH

8. Heating an aldehyde with Zn in HCl produces

A. a ketone.
B. an alkane.
C. an alcohol.
D. a carboxylic acid.

9.

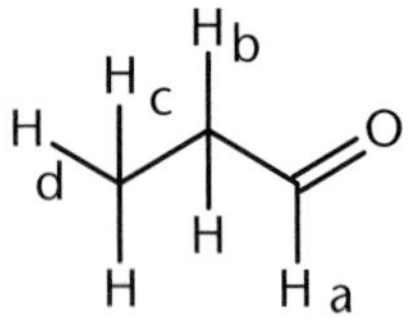

Which hydrogen atom in the above compound is the most acidic?

A. a
B. b
C. c
D. d

10.

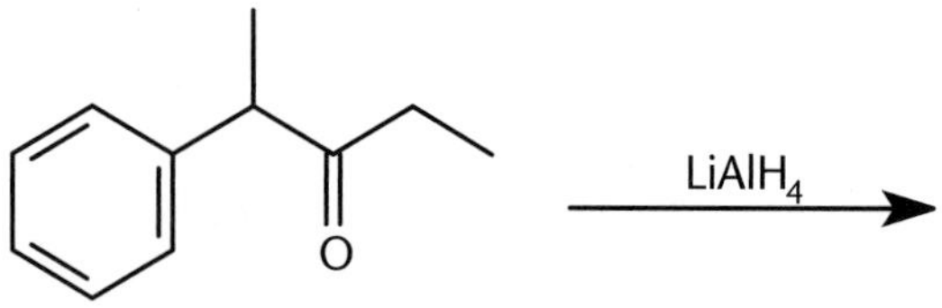

What product is obtained in the above reaction?

A.

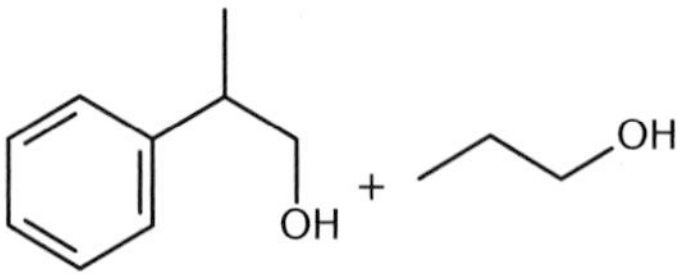

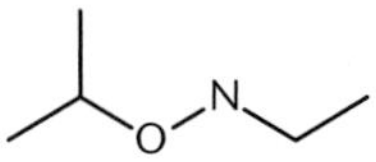

B.

C.

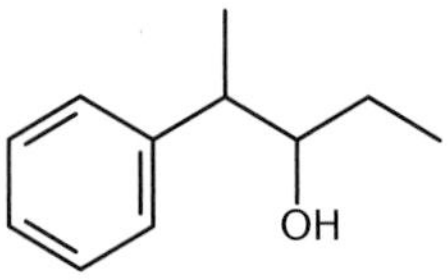

D.

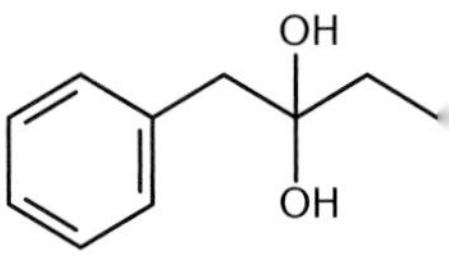

11. What is the product of the reaction between benzaldehyde and an excess of ethanol (C_2H_5OH) in the presence of anhydrous HCl?

A.

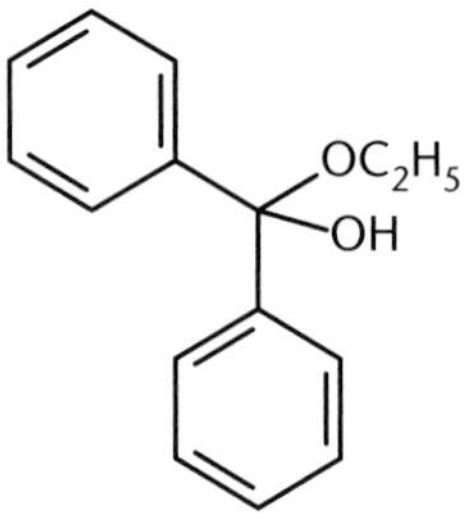

B.

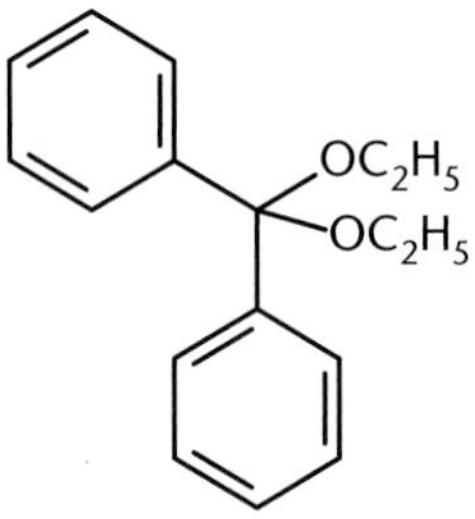

C.

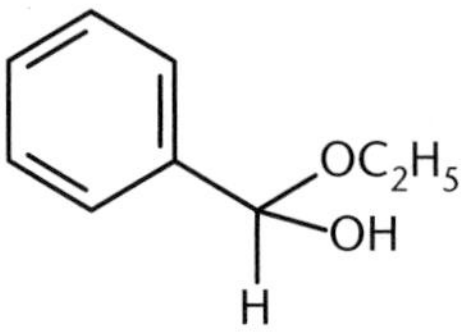

D.

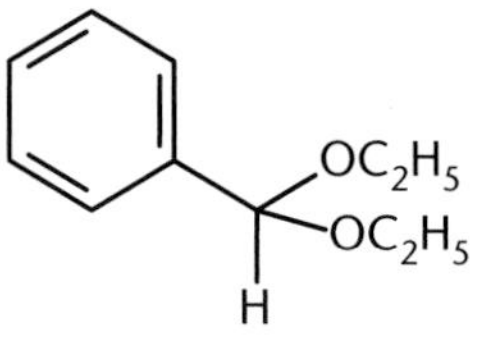

then attacks the carbonyl groups of the other aldehyde molecule, CH_3CH_2CHO, forming the above aldol. The correct choice is (D).

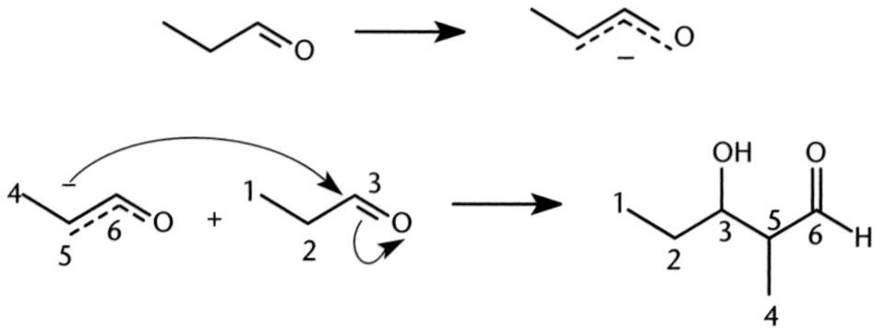

7. B

Aldehydes are easily oxidized to the corresponding carboxylic acids by $KMnO_4$. The –CHO group is converted to –COOH. In this reaction, therefore, C_2H_5CHO is oxidized to C_2H_5COOH, which is choice (B). In choice (A), the aldehyde has been reduced to an alcohol. In choice (C), a –CH$_2$ group has been added. Thus, choices (A) and (C) are incorrect. In choice (D), the –CHO group has been oxidized to –COOH, but a –CH$_2$ group has been removed, so choice (D) is incorrect.

8. B

Heating an aldehyde or a ketone with amalgamated Zn/HCl converts it to the corresponding alkane; this reaction is called the Clemmensen reduction. Note that aldehydes and ketones can also be converted to alkanes under basic conditions by reaction with hydrazine (the Wolff-Kishner reduction).

9. B

The hydrogen alpha to the carbonyl group is the most acidic, because the resultant carbanion is resonance-stabilized:

10. B

$LiAlH_4$ reduces carboxylic acids, esters, and aldehydes to primary alcohols and ketones to secondary alcohols. In this reaction, therefore, the ketone is converted to a secondary alcohol. Thus, the correct answer is choice (B), $C_6H_5CH(CH_3)CHOHCH_2CH_3$.

11. D

This molecule corresponds to an acetal: two alkoxyl functionalities bonded to the same carbon. This question states that an excess of ethanol is present, so benzaldehyde will first be converted to a hemiacetal, having an alkoxyl and a hydroxyl functionality bonded to the same carbon, then an acetal. Choices (A) and (B) are wrong because they show the presence of two benzene rings in the final product. Choice (C) shows a hemiacetal, which is not the final product. Because the question indicates an excess of ethanol, we should expect a second reaction between the hemiacetal and ethanol.

12. D

Hydrazine is nucleophilic and attacks the carbonyl carbon of both molecules, forming a negatively charged oxide intermediate. However, for benzoyl chloride, the C=O double bond is re-formed, and chloride is displaced because it is a good leaving group. Therefore, answer (D) is correct since this is an example of a substitution reaction. Benzaldehyde, on the other hand, forms a hydrazone with hydrazine via nucleophilic addition and condensation (the carbonyl oxygen atom leaves as water). Answer (A) is incorrect because benzaldehyde and benzoyl chloride undergo different reactions, answer (B) is incorrect because the final products are clearly different, and answer (C) is incorrect because the reaction types have been transposed.

13. D

The structure of 3-ethylhept-6-en-3-ol is shown below:

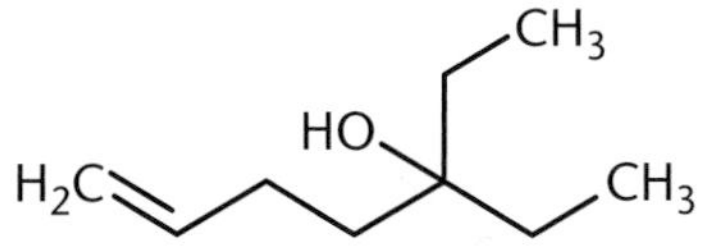

An anhydrous environment implies that Grignard reagents are being used. Because various Grignard reagents are present among the choices, all of them are feasible. Answers (A) and (B) both produce the product required; the only difference is the initial Grignard reagent. Answer (C) also produces the same product, because Grignard reagents will alkylate esters to completion, forming tertiary alcohols. Since answers (A), (B), and (C) all give 3-ethylhept-6-en-3-ol, answer (D) is correct.

Practice Questions

1. Which of these molecules could be classified as a soap?

   A. $CH_3(CH_2)_{17}CH_2COOH$
   B. CH_3COOH
   C. $CH_3(CH_2)_{19}CH_2COO^-Na^+$
   D. $CH_3COO^-Na^+$

2. Which of these compounds would be expected to decarboxylate when heated?

   A. 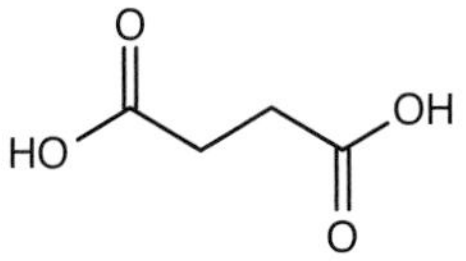
   C. 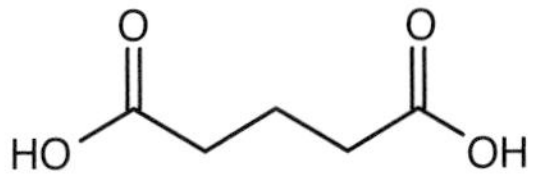
   B. 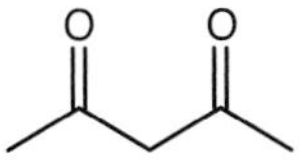
   D.

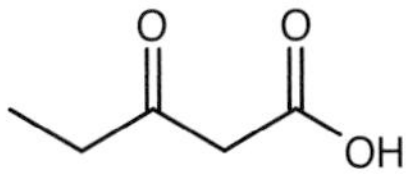

3. Oxidation of which of the following compounds is most likely to yield a carboxylic acid?

   A. Acetone
   B. Cyclohexanone
   C. 2-Propanol
   D. Methanol

4. Carboxylic acids have higher boiling points than the corresponding alcohols because

   A. molecular weight is increased by the additional carboxyl group.
   B. the pH of the compound in solution is lower.
   C. acid salts are soluble in water.
   D. hydrogen bonding is much stronger than in alcohols.

5. Which of the following carboxylic acids will be the most acidic?

   A. $CH_3CHClCH_2COOH$
   B. $CH_3CH_2CCl_2COOH$
   C. $CH_3CH_2CHClCOOH$
   D. $CH_3CH_2CH_2COOH$

6. Which of the following substituted benzoic acid compounds will be the least acidic?

   A. 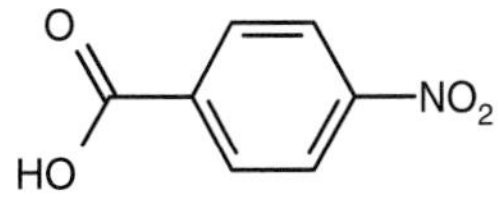
   C. 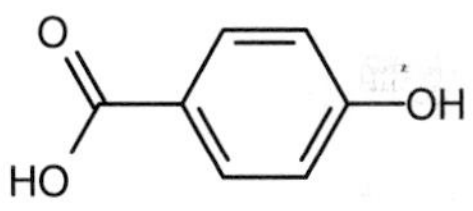
   B. 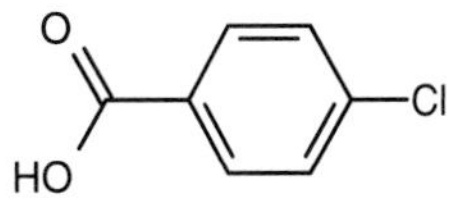
   D.

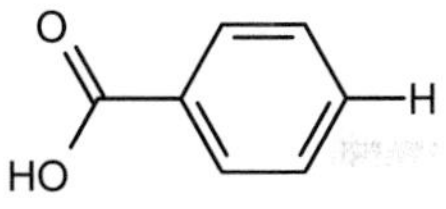

7. Predict the final product of the following reaction.

   $$CH_3(CH_2)_4CH_2OH \xrightarrow[\text{acetone}]{CrO_3,\ H_2SO_4} ?$$

   1-hexanol

   A. $CH_3(CH_2)_4CHO$
   B. $CH_3(CH_2)_4COOH$
   C. $CH_3(CH_2)_4CH_3$
   D. $HOOC(CH_2)_4COOH$

8. Carboxylic acids can be reacted in one step to form all of the following compounds EXCEPT

   A. acyl halides.
   B. amides.
   C. alkenes.
   D. alcohols.

9. The reduction of a carboxylic acid by lithium aluminum hydride will yield what final product?

    A. An aldehyde

    B. An ester

    C. A ketone

    D. An alcohol

10. Which of the following CANNOT be used to convert butanoic acid to butanoyl chloride?

    A. PCl_3

    B. PCl_5

    C. CCl_4

    D. $SOCl_2$

11. Which of the following reagents will reduce butanoic acid to butanol?

    A. $LiAlH_4$

    B. $LiAlH_4$, H_2O

    C. $NaBH_4$

    D. All of the above

12. In the presence of an acid catalyst, the major product of ethanoic acid and ethanol is

    A. acetic anhydride.

    B. butene.

    C. diethyl ether.

    D. ethyl acetate.

Small Group Questions

1. What is the difference between a carboxylate anion and an alkoxide anion?

2. Recall that the α-hydrogen on a carboxylic acid is especially acidic. Is it more or less acidic than the hydroxyl hydrogen?

Explanations to Practice Questions

1. C

A soap is a long-chain hydrocarbon with a highly polar end. Generally, this polar end, or head, is a salt of a carboxylic acid. Choice (C) fits these criteria and is the correct answer. The remaining choices all fail one or both of the criteria and are therefore wrong. Choice (A) is not a salt. Choice (B) is acetic acid, which is not a salt and does not possess a long chain. Choice (D) is sodium acetate, which is a salt but does not have a long hydrocarbon chain.

2. D

This compound is a β-keto acid: a keto functionality β to a carboxyl functionality. Decarboxylation occurs with β-keto acids and 1,3-diacids, because they can form a cyclic transition state that permits simultaneous hydrogen transfer and loss of carbon dioxide. Choice (B) is a diketone and does not have a single carboxyl group. Choices (A) and (C) are 1,4- and 1,5-diacids, respectively, and will decarboxylate but with more difficulty. The correct answer is choice (D).

3. D

Oxidation of methanol, choice (D), will yield first formaldehyde and then formic acid; this is the correct answer. Acetone, choice (A), cannot be oxidized further unless extremely harsh conditions are used. This is because the carbonyl carbon is bonded to two alkyl groups and further oxidation would necessitate cleavage of a carbon–carbon bond. Choice (B), cyclohexanone, is likewise limited in its options for further oxidation. Choice (C), 2-propanol, can be oxidized to acetone but no further without harsh conditions.

4. D

The boiling points of compounds depend on the strength of the attractive forces between molecules. In both alcohols and carboxylic acids, the major form of intermolecular attraction is hydrogen bonding; however, the hydrogen bonds of carboxylic acids are much stronger than those of alcohols, because the acids are much more polar. This makes the boiling points of carboxylic acids higher than those of the corresponding alcohols, so choice (D) is correct. Boiling points also depend on molecular weight, choice (A), but in this case, the difference in molecular weight has a smaller influence than the effect of hydrogen bonding. Therefore, choice (A) is wrong. Choice (B) is a correct statement but does not sufficiently explain the difference in boiling points. Choice (C) discusses the behavior of an acid's salt in solution, which is wrong for the same reason.

5. B

The acidity of carboxylic acids is significantly increased by the presence of highly electronegative functional groups. Their electron-withdrawing effect upon the carboxyl group increases the stability of the carboxylate anion, favoring proton dissociation. This effect increases as the number of electronegative groups on the chain increases, and it also increases as the distance between the acid, functionality and electronegative group decreases. Among the carboxylic acids listed, choice (D) is the only unsubstituted acid, and therefore, must have the lowest acidity. Choice (A) is β-halogenated, whereas choices (B) and (C) are α-halogenated, so we can reject (A). Finally, choice (B) contains two α-halogens and choice (C) includes only one, so the electron-withdrawing effect in choice (B) is stronger, and (B) is the correct answer.

6. C

The effects of different substituents upon the acidity of benzoic acid compounds are correlated with their effects on the reactivity of the benzene ring (see Chapter 6). Activating substituents donate electron density into the benzene ring, and the ring in turn donates electron density to the carboxyl group, destabilizing the benzoate ion formed and therefore decreasing a compound's acidity. Deactivating substituents have the opposite effect: They withdraw electrons from the ring, which in turn withdraws negative charge from the carboxyl group, thus stabilizing the carboxylate anion and increasing the compound's acidity. Choice (A) contains a nitro group attached to the ring, and choice (B) has a chloride; both of these substituents have deactivating effects, so these choices can be eliminated. Choice (D) is unsubstituted benzoic acid, whereas choice (C) has a strongly activating hydroxyl substituent. Thus, choice (C) will be the least acidic and is the correct answer.

7. B

Jones's reagent (chromium trioxide in aqueous sulfuric acid) oxidizes primary alcohols directly to monocarboxylic acids, so choice (B) is correct. This reagent is too strong an oxidizing agent to give an aldehyde as the final product (an aldehyde will be formed but will immediately be oxidized further), so choice (A) is wrong. Choice (D), a dicarboxylic acid, cannot form because there is no functional group handle on the other end of the molecule for the reagent to attack and it cannot attack the inert alkane. Nor will it reduce an alkane such as choice (C), so this is also wrong.

8. C

Carboxylic acids cannot be converted into alkenes in one step. Acyl halides (A) are formed with thionyl chloride. Amides (B) are formed by reaction with ammonia. Alcohols (D) may be formed using a variety of reducing agents. To form alkenes (C), carboxylic acids may be reduced to alcohols, which can then be transformed into alkenes by elimination.

9. D

Lithium aluminum hydride (LAH) is a strong reducing agent. LAH can completely reduce carboxylic acids to primary alcohols, choice (D). Aldehydes are intermediate

products of this reaction; therefore, choice (A) is wrong. Esters are formed from carboxylic acids by reaction with alcohols, so choice (B) is wrong. Ketones are formed by the Friedel-Crafts acylation of the acyl chloride derivatives of acids, so choice (C) is wrong.

10. C

PCl_3 (A), PCl_5 (B), and $SOCl_2$ (D) are all reactive enough to donate a chloride to a carboxylic acid to form the acyl chloride. Carbon tetrachloride is more often used as a solvent than as a reagent, because its C–Cl bond is stable and is not a good source of Cl^- nucleophiles.

11. A

Lithium aluminum hydride ($LiAlH_4$) is an effective reducing agent for carboxylic acids. It is also reactive with water, so performing the reaction as it is listed in choice (B) does not work. Although sodium tetrahydroborate (C) is a reducing agent, it is not strong enough to dissolve two carbon-oxygen bonds.

12. D

The reaction described is a Fischer esterification, in which the –OH group of ethanoic acid is first protonated to form water, which is a good leaving group. The nucleophilic oxygen atom of ethanol then attacks the electrophilic carbonyl carbon of ethanoic acid, ultimately displacing water to form ethyl acetate. The acid catalyst is regenerated from ethanol's released proton. Although acetic anhydride can form via the coupling of two acetic acid molecules, it would not be a major product given the conditions listed in the question, so answer (A) is incorrect. Ethers and alkenes do not form under these conditions, either, so answers (B) and (C) are incorrect.

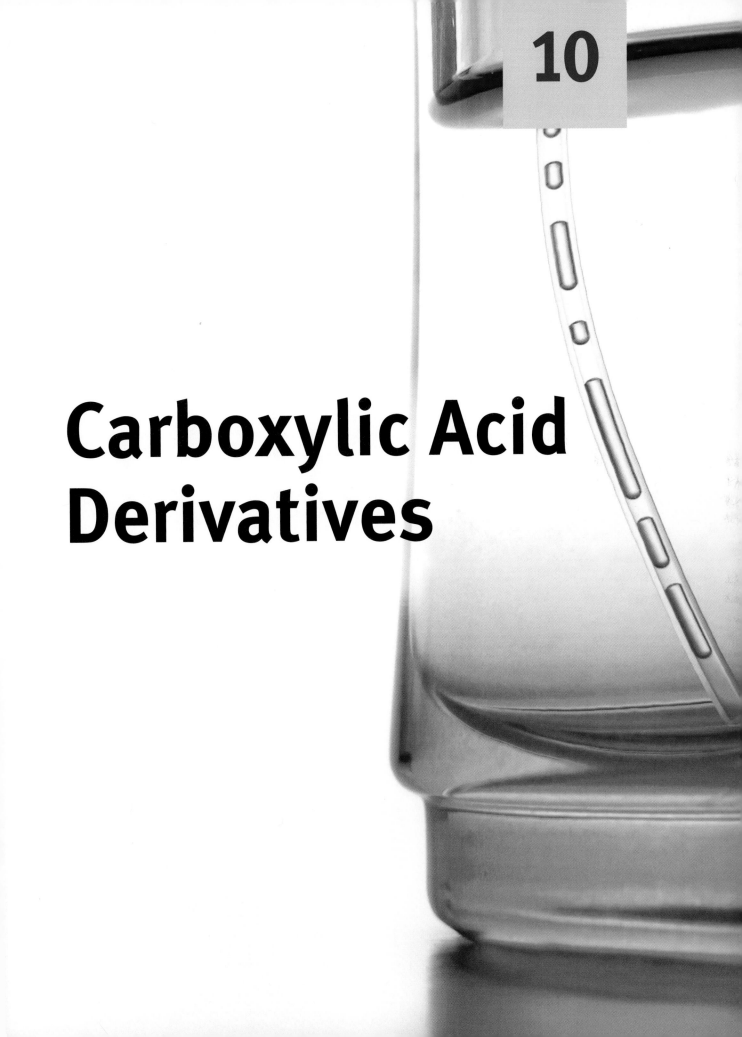

Carboxylic Acid Derivatives

If you're one of those poor souls who still doesn't believe carboxylic acids are all that thrilling, we can't blame you. They don't always seem too exciting, at least to the human eye. But if you were a molecule with free electrons, you'd probably think that carboxylic acids were a party. It's true: carboxylic acids have many of the same characteristics as parties. First, they provide a place where all nucleophiles are welcome. We saw this in the last chapter, where the carbonyl is susceptible to attack by everything from water to amines to other carbonyls (in the enol form). In addition, it's just like a party where the guests keep coming and going; some guests stay for a while (amines), and others just pop in and out to make an appearance (halides). Throughout this chapter, we will discuss this party and the different names the carboxylic acid derivative carries, depending on the guests that are present. The big ones on which we will focus are **acyl halides**, **anhydrides**, **amides**, and **esters**. Each of these molecules replaces the –OH on the carboxyl group with **–X**, **–OCOR**, **–NH$_2$**, or **–OR**, respectively. The nice thing about this party is that, similar to parties with humans, everyone comes in the same way. Some people drive and some take cabs, but everyone must walk through the same front door. We will notice a common mechanism with all of the following reactions.

Acyl Halides ★★★★★☆

NOMENCLATURE

Acyl halides are also called **acid** or **alkanoyl halides**. (Remember that the acyl group is RCO–.) Acyl halides are the most reactive of the carboxylic acid derivatives. They are named in the IUPAC system by changing the –oic acid ending of the carboxylic acid to **–oyl halide**. Some typical examples, shown in Figure 10.1, are ethanoyl chloride (also called acetyl chloride), benzoyl chloride, and *n*-butanoyl bromide.

> **MCAT Expertise**
>
> Order of carboxylic acid derivative reactivity: acyl halides > anhydrides > esters = carboxylic acids > amides.

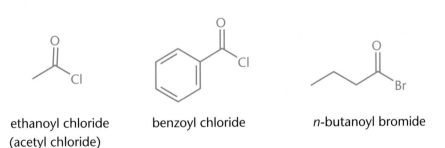

| ethanoyl chloride (acetyl chloride) | benzoyl chloride | *n*-butanoyl bromide |

Figure 10.1

SYNTHESIS

The most common acyl halides are acid chlorides, although you may occasionally encounter acid bromides and iodides. Acid chlorides are prepared by reacting a carboxylic acid with thionyl chloride, SOCl$_2$. SO$_2$ and HCl are the other products, and the evolution of SO_2 drives this reaction (see Figure 10.2). Alternatively, PCl_3 or PCl_5 (or PBr_3, to make an acid bromide) will accomplish the same transformation.

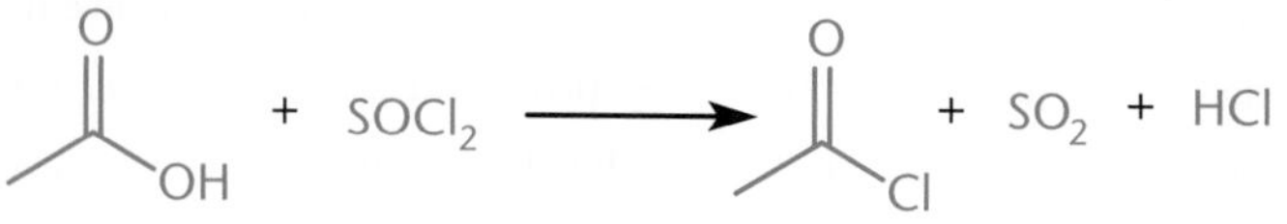

Figure 10.2

REACTIONS: NUCLEOPHILIC ACYL SUBSTITUTION

As we'd expect, all of the reactions of acyl halides occur via nucleophilic acyl substitution, as discussed in Chapter 9.

Hydrolysis

The simplest reaction we'll see is the conversion of an acid halide back into its corresponding carboxylic acid. Acid halides react rapidly with water to form their carboxylic acid and HCl (see Figure 10.3). This makes acid halides dangerous: If they are exposed to either your eyes or airways, they will react with the water in those spaces, forming HCl and carboxylic acid *on you*, a sensation you'd probably not wish to experience.

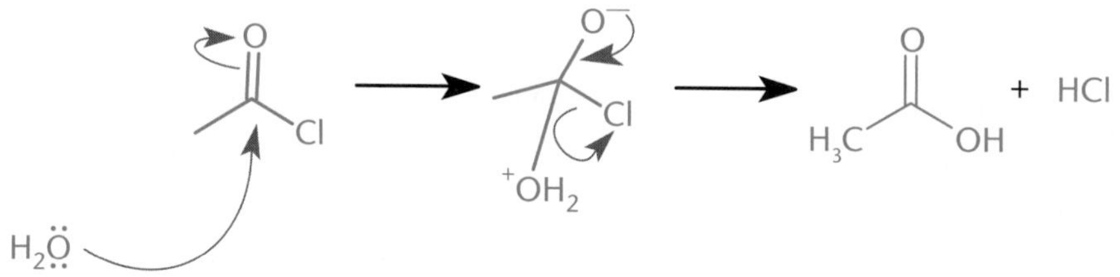

Figure 10.3

Conversion into Esters

Another similar reaction is the conversion of acyl halides into esters. The basic mechanism is the same as hydrolysis, once again proceeding through a tetrahedral intermediate. This time, though, we use *alcohol* as the nucleophile. The leaving group is still chlorine, which can pick up a hydrogen in solution, making HCl as a side product (see Figure 10.4).

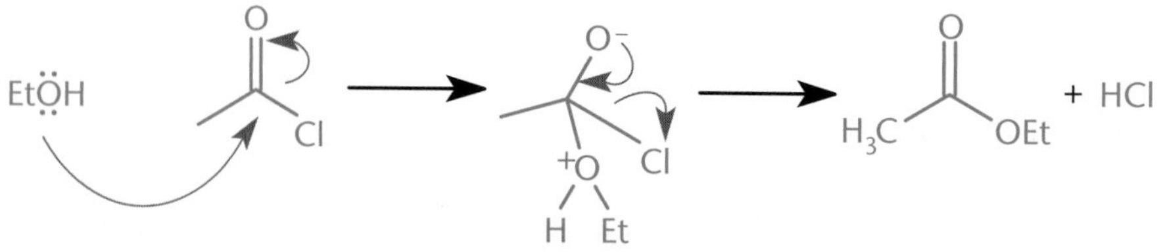

Figure 10.4

Key Concept

The steps are the same for all of these reactions. The carbonyl carbon acts as an electrophile and is attacked by a nucleophile. In the second step, the leaving group takes the extra electrons. Note: Aldehydes and ketones do not have a leaving group. That is why they undergo nucleophilic *additions*.

Mnemonic

Hydrolysis = *hydro* + *lysis*, or cleavage by water.

Conversion into Amides

Acyl halides can be converted into amides (compounds of the general formula $RCONR_2$) by an analogous reaction with amines. The lone pairs on nucleophilic amines, such as ammonia, attack the carbonyl group, displacing chloride. The side product is ammonium chloride (a salt—remember this means an ionic compound), formed from excess ammonia and HCl (see Figure 10.5).

Whereas *acyl halides* react with amines to form amides, if we were to react *ketones* with amines, the product would be an *imine* (discussed in Chapter 8).

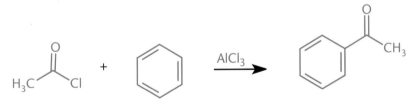

Figure 10.5

OTHER REACTIONS

Friedel-Crafts Acylation

Aromatic rings can be acylated in a Friedel-Crafts reaction (as discussed in Chapter 6), a type of electrophilic aromatic substitution. The nucleophile is the aromatic ring, and the electrophile, as we'd expect, is the carbonyl. However, when the acyl chloride attacks, its bond to chlorine is almost completely broken by the reaction with $AlCl_3$. The pi electrons of the aromatic system act as a nucleophile, attacking the electrophilic acyl cation or acylium ion (RCO^+). The product, as we can see in Figure 10.6, is an alkyl aryl ketone.

> **MCAT Expertise**
>
> This mechanism is a two-in-one for us! The electrophile, of course, is the carbonyl carbon and the nucleophile is the benzene ring. So, we have either a nucleophilic acyl substitution or an electrophilic aromatic substitution, depending on your perspective.

Figure 10.6

Reduction

Acid halides can be reduced to alcohols or selectively reduced to the intermediate aldehydes using a bulky hydride reagent that has only one hydride to transfer: $LiAlH(OC(CH_3)_3)_3$.

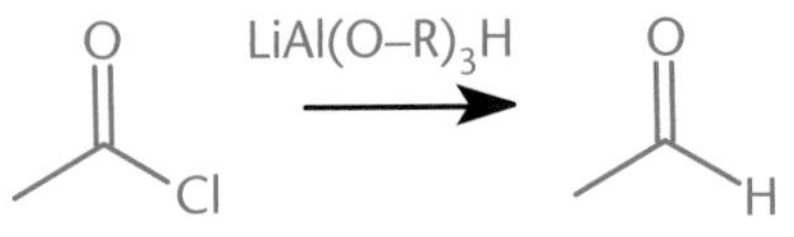

Figure 10.7

Key Concept

Anhydride means "without water." Anhydrides are formed from the condensation of two acid molecules (with loss of water).

Anhydrides ★★★★☆☆

NOMENCLATURE

Anhydrides, also called **acid anhydrides**, are the condensation dimers of carboxylic acids with the general formula RCOOCOR. They are named by substituting the word *anhydride* for the word *acid* in an alkanoic acid. The most common and important anhydride is **acetic anhydride**, the dimer of acetic acid. You should be able to recognize that succinic, maleic, and phthalic anhydrides, shown in Figure 10.8, are cyclic anhydrides arising from intramolecular condensation or dehydration of diacids, but you won't need to memorize their names.

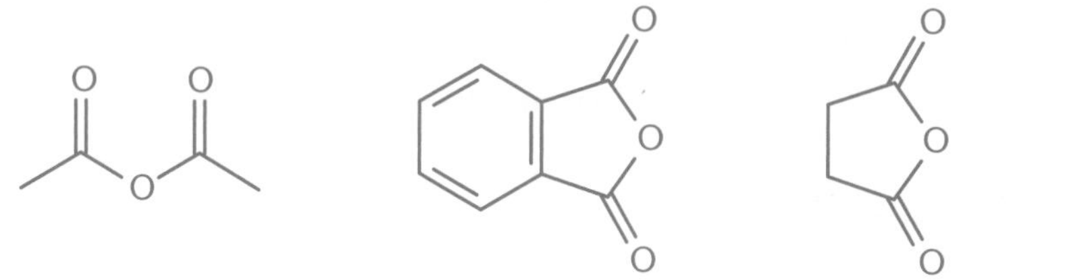

acetic anhydride (ethanoic anhydride) | phthalic anhydride | succinic anhydride

Figure 10.8

SYNTHESIS

As we just mentioned, anhydrides are the product of a condensation reaction between two carboxylic acids (see Figure 10.9). The mechanism is a combination of a few reactions we've already discussed. The hydroxide group of one acid acts as the nucleophile, and (of course) the carbonyl is the electrophile. One molecule is of water is lost in the condensation.

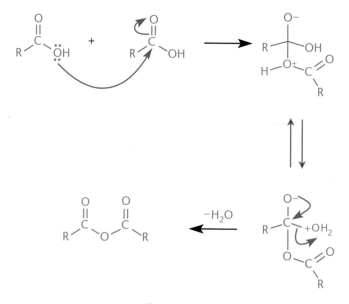

Figure 10.9

Anhydrides can also be synthesized by the reaction of an acid chloride and a carboxylate anion, as shown in Figure 10.10.

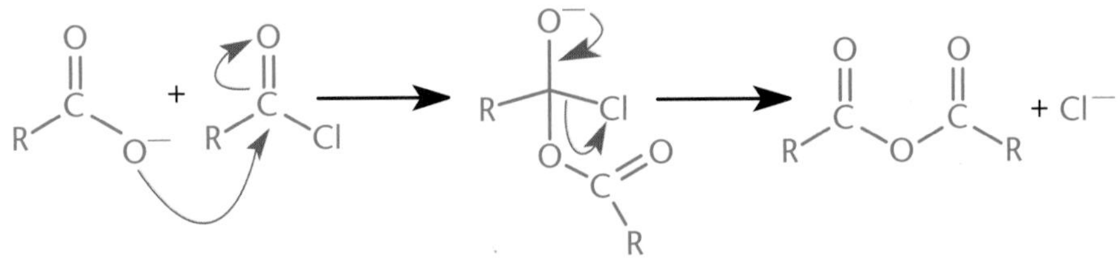

Figure 10.10

Certain cyclic anhydrides can be formed simply by heating carboxylic acids (see Figure 10.11). The reaction is driven forward by the increased stability of the newly formed ring; as such, only five- and six-membered ring anhydrides are easily made. In this reaction, the hydroxyl group of one –COOH acts as the nucleophile, attacking the carbonyl on the other –COOH.

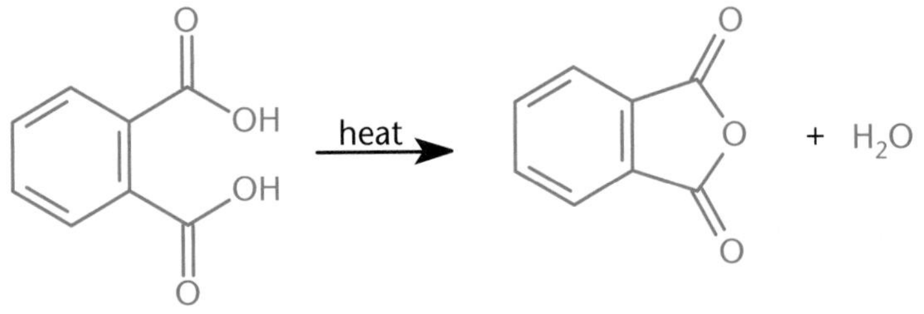

o-phtalic acid   phthalic anhydride

Figure 10.11

> **MCAT Expertise**
>
> Always remember that intramolecular reactions are more likely to occur than a reaction involving two separate molecules. Think about two people handcuffed together; they are much more likely to get into a fight than two random people passing each other on the street.

REACTIONS

Anhydrides react under the same conditions as acid chlorides, but because they are more stable, they are less reactive. The reactions are slower, and no matter what the nucleophile, they will produce a carboxylic acid side product (wasting all that carbon!) instead of the HCl produced by acid halides. Cyclic anhydrides are also subject to the following reactions, which cause ring opening at the anhydride group along with formation of the new functional groups.

Hydrolysis

We can break up anhydrides into two equivalents of carboxylic acids by exposing them to water. For these reactions to be useful, the anhydride must be symmetric.

Key Concept

The carbonyl compound is the electrophile, the nucleophile is water, and the leaving group is a carboxylic acid (which is not as good a leaving group as the halogens in the acyl halide reactions).

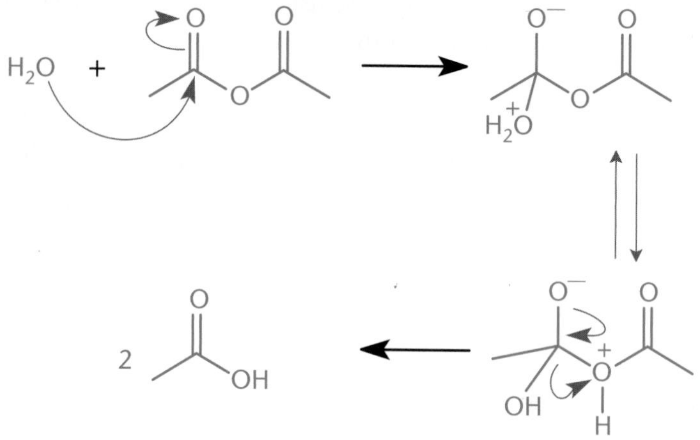

Figure 10.12

Key Concept

Reactions that convert compounds to amides only differ in the attacking nucleophile.

Note that in the reaction shown in Figure 10.12, the leaving group is actually a carboxylic acid.

Conversion into Amides

Anhydrides can also be cleaved by ammonia, producing amides and carboxylic acids (see Figure 10.13a).

There's a problem here, though. One of our products is a carboxylic acid, and we're carrying out the reaction in an environment filled with ammonia. That means we've now got an acid in a basic environment. The two will react, forming a salt, specifically **ammonium carboxylate** (see Figure 10.13b).

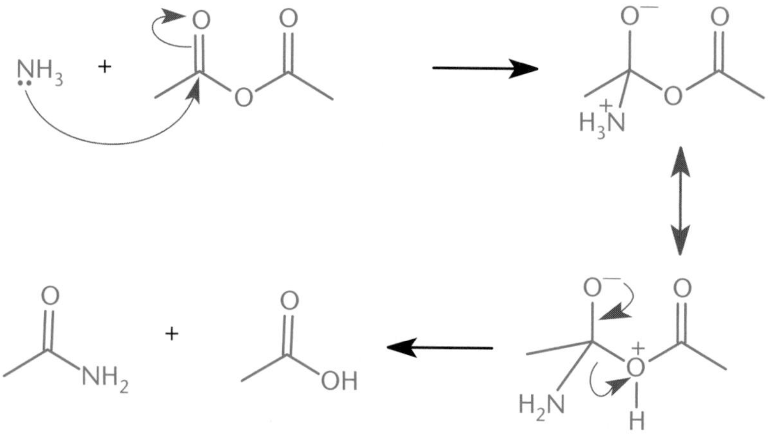

Figure 10.13a

Key Concept

Acid chlorides can be converted into any of the other derivatives, anhydrides can make any of the less reactive derivatives (esters and amides), and esters can be converted into amides.

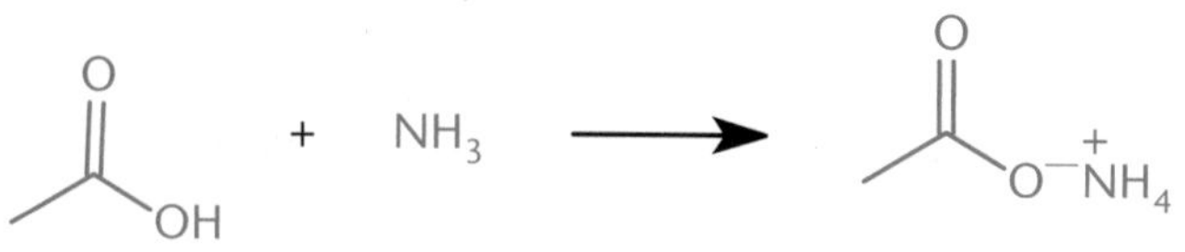

Figure 10.13b

So, even though the leaving group is actually a carboxylic acid, the final products will be an amide and the ammonium salt of a carboxylate anion.

Conversion into Esters and Carboxylic Acids

Another nucleophile we can plug into this formula is an alcohol; this reaction will form esters and carboxylic acids (see Figure 10.14).

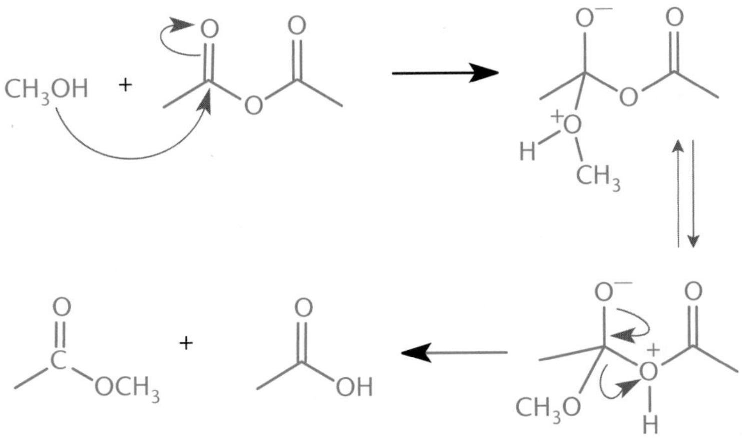

Figure 10.14

Acylation

Once again, we return to Friedel-Crafts acylation. When we add AlCl$_3$ or another Lewis acid catalyst (see Figure 10.15), the reaction will occur readily.

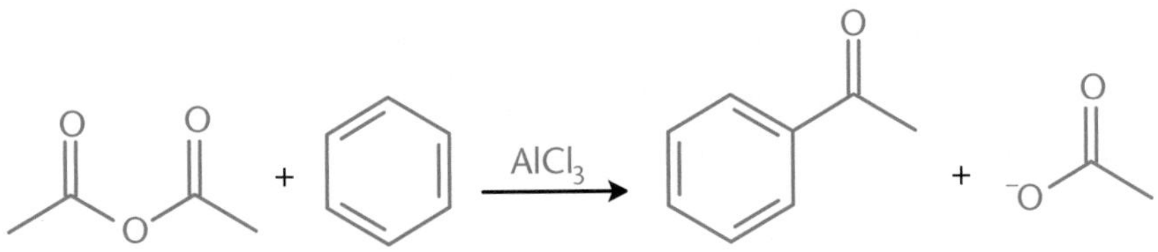

Figure 10.15

> **MCAT Expertise**
>
> This reaction is the same as the earlier two-in-one involving both EAS and nucleophilic acyl substitution.

Amides ★★★★★☆

NOMENCLATURE

Amides are compounds with the general formula RCONR$_2$. They are named by replacing the –oic acid ending with **–amide**. Alkyl substituents on the nitrogen atom are listed as prefixes, and their location is specified with the letter *N*. Figure 10.16 shows one example.

> **Bridge**
>
> The peptide bond is an amide linkage that possesses double-bond character from resonance and is the most stable carboxylic acid derivative.

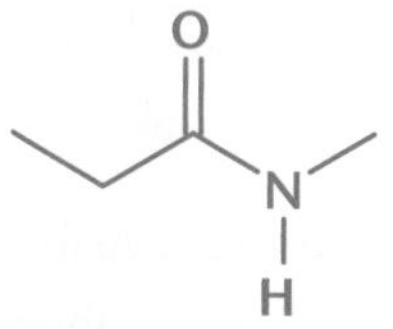

N-methylpropanamide

Figure 10.16

Key Concept

Only primary and secondary amines can be used to form amides.

SYNTHESIS

Amides are generally synthesized by the reaction of acid chlorides with amines or by the reaction of acid anhydrides with ammonia, as we just discussed. Note that loss of hydrogen is required for these reactions to take place. Thus, only primary and secondary amines will undergo this reaction.

REACTIONS

Amides are the most stable of the carboxylic acid derivatives, so once they're bound to the carbonyl, they're staying around for a while. They're like the guests at a party who're still around at 3 A.M. and just can't take the hint that we want them to leave. It takes extreme conditions to get them to leave; while faking a big argument with your significant other works well for unwanted human guests, acidic or basic conditions will do the trick at the molecular level.

Real World

Extreme conditions (e.g., strong acid) are necessary to hydrolyze an amide, which is why we have stomach acid: to help provide the catalysis necessary for proteases to break down proteins.

Hydrolysis

Amides can be hydrolyzed under acidic conditions via nucleophilic substitution. The acidic conditions allow the carbonyl oxygen to become protonated, making it more susceptible to nucleophilic attack by a water molecule. The product of this reaction is a carboxylic acid and ammonia, as shown in Figure 10.17.

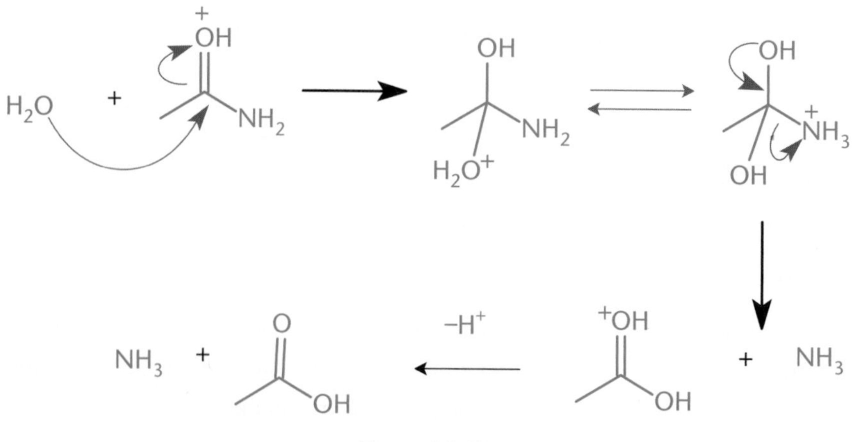

Figure 10.17

Hydrolysis can also occur if conditions are basic enough. The reaction is similar, except that the carbonyl oxygen is not protonated and the nucleophile is a hydroxide ion. The product of this reaction will be the carboxylate ion.

Hofmann Rearrangement

The Hofmann rearrangement converts amides to primary amines with the loss of the carbonyl carbon as CO_2. The initial reactants are bromine and sodium hydroxide, which react to form *sodium hypobromite* (as seen in Figure 10.18). The mechanism is fairly intense. As such, it is most important for you to focus on the reactants and products.

The mechanism involves the formation of a **nitrene**, the nitrogen analog of a *carbene*. This nitrene is attached to the carbonyl, and like a carbene, it only has six electrons; thus, it is an electrophile looking for more electrons. The electron deficiency is resolved by rearranging to form an **isocyanate**, which has a double bond on either side of the carbon, one to oxygen and one to nitrogen (hence, *iso–*, meaning *equal*). The isocyanate molecule is then hydrolyzed to form the amine, with CO_2 as a leaving group.

> **Key Concept**
>
> Hofmann rearrangement = amide ⟶ primary amine (with loss of a carbon, as CO_2).

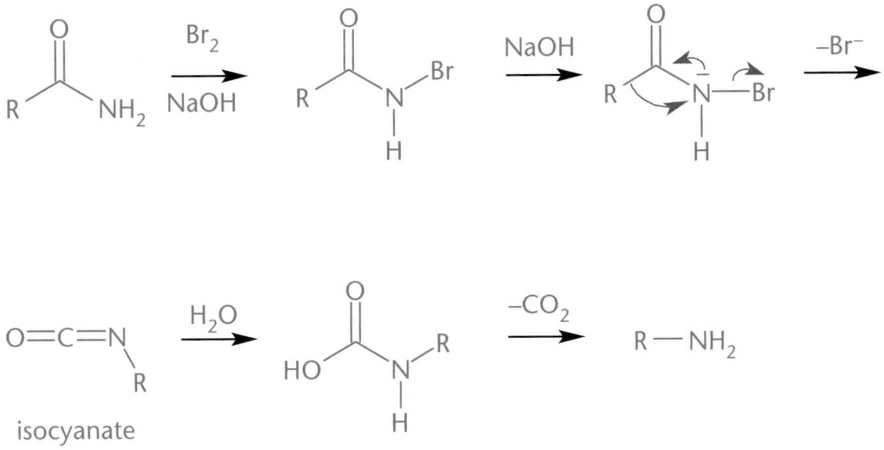

Figure 10.18

Reduction

Amides can be reduced with lithium aluminum hydride (LAH) to their corresponding amine (see Figure 10.19). Although this reaction also gives an amine product, it is different from the Hofmann rearrangement because there is no loss of carbon. LAH just does the good old-fashioned reduction we've seen before.

> **Key Concept**
>
> Reduction also produces amines, but no carbon is lost.

Figure 10.19

Esters

NOMENCLATURE

Esters, the dehydration products of carboxylic acids and alcohols, are found in many fruits and perfumes (items also commonly found at your Great Aunt Esther's house . . . coincidence?). They are named in the IUPAC system as **alkyl** or **aryl alkanoates**. As we mentioned in the last chapter, *ethyl acetate*, derived from the condensation of acetic acid and ethanol, is called *ethyl ethanoate* according to IUPAC nomenclature.

SYNTHESIS

Key Concept

Acid + alcohol = ester.

Under acidic conditions, mixtures of carboxylic acids and alcohols will condense (losing water) into esters. This is called Fischer esterification. Esters can also be obtained from reaction of acid chlorides or anhydrides with alcohols, as we saw in previous sections. Phenolic (aromatic) esters are produced in the same way, although the aromatic acid chlorides are less reactive than aliphatic (nonaromatic) acid chlorides, so we need to kick up the reaction conditions by adding a base as a catalyst (see Figure 10.20).

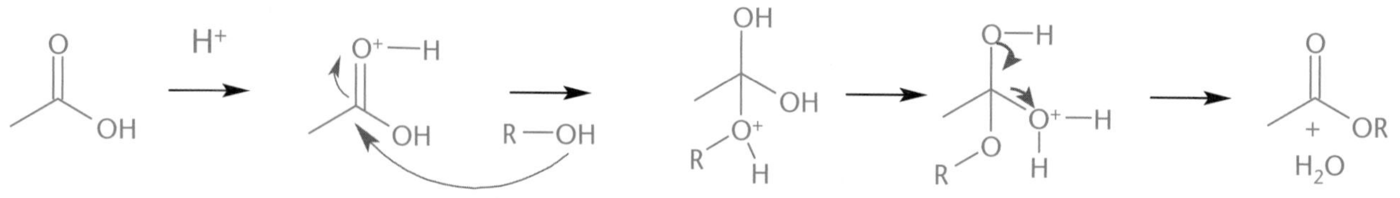

Figure 10.20

REACTIONS

MCAT Expertise

Hydrolysis, especially of esters, is a popular topic on the MCAT.

Hydrolysis

Esters, just like every other derivative of carboxylic acids, can be hydrolyzed. Hydrolysis of esters produces carboxylic acids and alcohols. Because esters and carboxylic acids (the products) are equally reactive, we can drive the reaction forward by using either acidic or basic conditions.

Under acidic conditions, the mechanism is as shown in Figure 10.21.

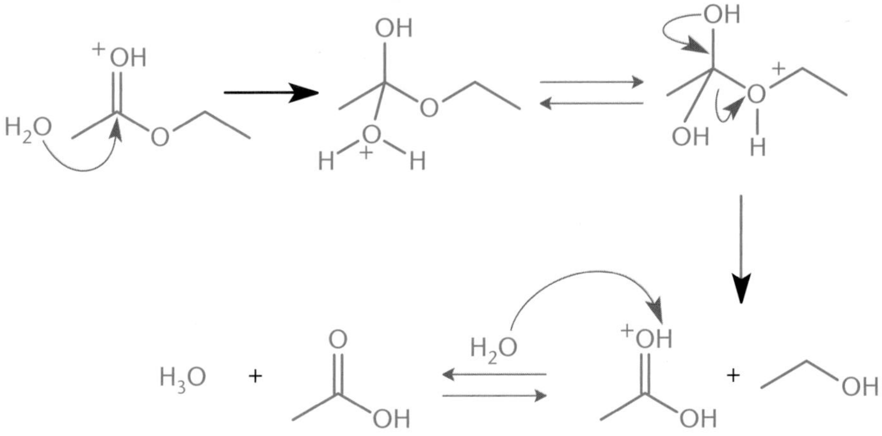

Figure 10.21

The reaction proceeds similarly under basic conditions, except that the oxygen on the C=O is not protonated and the nucleophile is OH⁻ instead of water.

Triacylglycerols, also called fats, are esters of long-chain carboxylic acids (fatty acids) and glycerol (1,2,3-propanetriol). **Saponification** is the process by which fats are hydrolyzed under basic conditions to produce soaps (see Figure 10.22). Alternatively, acidification of the soap regenerates triacylglycerol. This process is sometimes used on solutions of free fatty acids to increase the caloric content of animal feed, but we don't recommend trying it with your hand soap—it tastes pretty bad, as anyone who has had his mouth washed out with soap can attest.

Bridge

Triacylglycerols are actually esters, with glycerol as the alcohol (ROH) and free fatty acids as RCOOH.

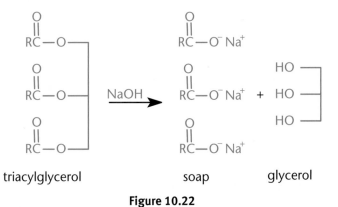

| triacylglycerol | soap | glycerol |

Figure 10.22

Conversion into Amides

As we saw before, nitrogen bases, such as ammonia, will attack the electron-deficient carbonyl carbon atom, displacing an alkoxide to yield an amide and an alcohol side product (see Figure 10.23). This reaction is not very common because it's much more effective to start with acid chloride.

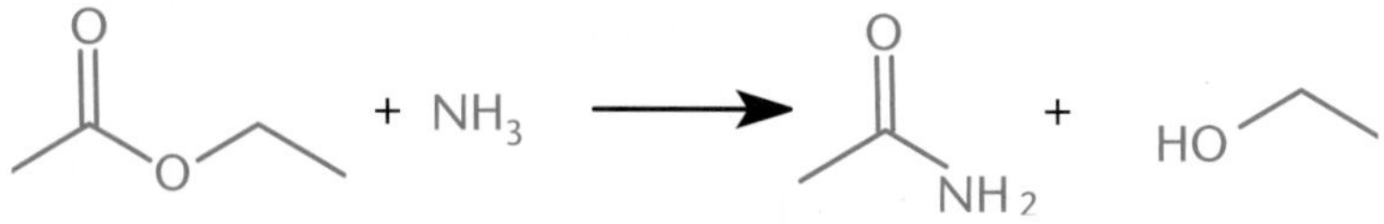

Figure 10.23

Transesterification

Other alcohols can act as nucleophiles and displace the alkoxy groups on esters. This process, which simply transforms one ester into another, is aptly named **transesterification** (see Figure 10.24).

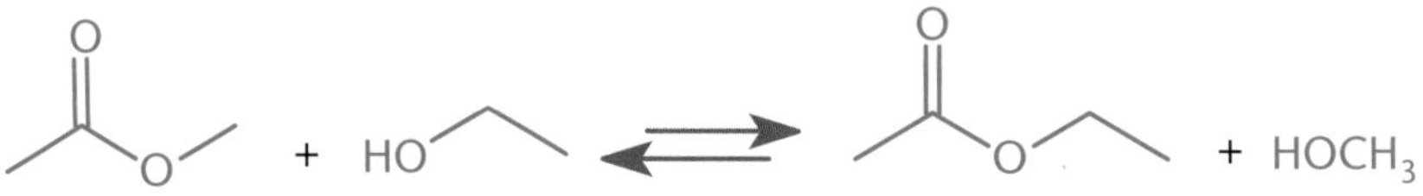

Figure 10.24

Grignard Addition

The negatively charged carbon of a Grignard reagent adds to the carbonyl group of esters. This reaction results in a ketone, as the carbonyl is re-formed and the alkoxy group is kicked off. There's a catch, though: The ketone product will be more reactive than the initial ester and, thus, readily attacked by more Grignard reagent. To get around this problem, two equivalents of Grignard reagent can be used to produce tertiary alcohols with good yield. (The intermediate ketone can be isolated only if the alkyl groups are sufficiently bulky to prevent further attack.) The first round of this reaction proceeds just like all the others in this chapter, as nucleophilic substitution, but the second round is nucleophilic addition, because the carbonyl is turned into an alcohol instead of being re-formed (see Figure 10.25).

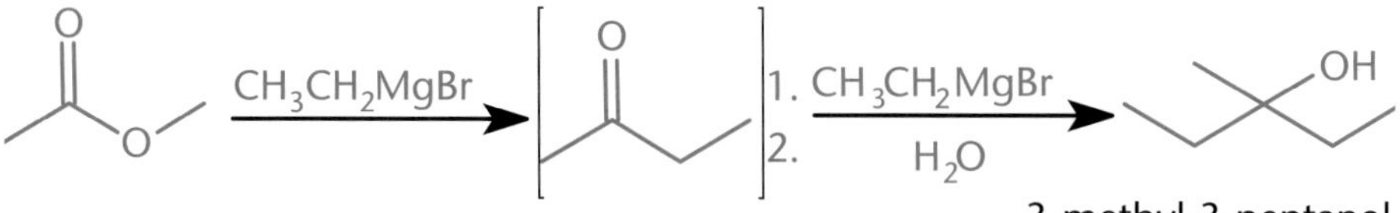

3-methyl-3-pentanol

Figure 10.25

Condensation Reactions

Another ester reaction you're likely to see on Test Day is the **Claisen condensation**. In the simplest case, two moles of ethyl acetate react under basic conditions to produce a β-keto-ester, specifically, *ethyl 3-oxobutanoate*, or *acetoacetic ester* by its common name. (The Claisen condensation is also called the *acetoacetic ester condensation*.) The reaction proceeds by addition of an enolate anion (created by the basic conditions) to the carbonyl group of another ester, followed by displacement of an ethoxide ion (see Figure 10.26). Don't worry if that all sounds confusing; this is the same mechanism we learned in Chapter 8 for aldol condensation, but now we're using esters, which have built-in leaving groups, as our reactants.

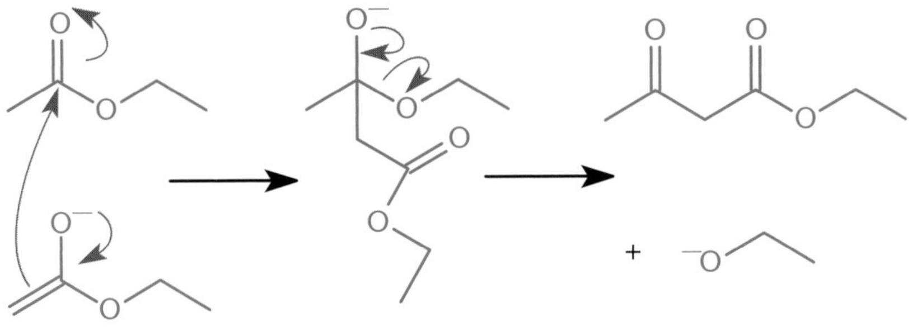

Figure 10.26

Bridge

The Claisen condensation is the mechanism by which the long hydrocarbon chains of lipids are synthesized in biological systems. Acetyl coenzyme A performs the function of ethyl acetate, and long chains are built up from units of two-carbon atoms. This is why long-chain compounds with 14, 16, and 18 carbon atoms are more common in living organisms than those with the odd chain lengths of 15 and 17.

Reduction

Esters can be reduced to primary alcohols with LAH but *not* with the weaker $NaBH_4$. This is a helpful trait for chemists, because it allows for selective reduction in molecules with multiple functional groups. Note in Figure 10.27 that the products are two alcohols.

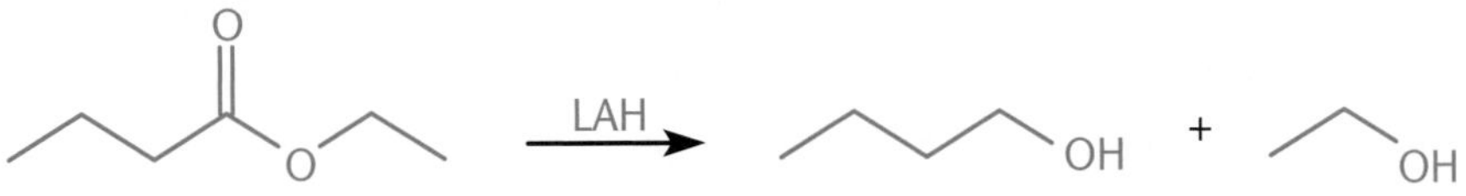

Figure 10.27

Key Concept

The more powerful LAH is necessary to reduce the ester. Remember that $NaBH_4$ is weaker and more selective (aldehydes and ketones) than $LiAlH_4$ but both are essentially equivalent to an H^- nucleophile.

PHOSPHATE ESTERS

Let's switch gears for a minute and talk about phosphate esters. Although phosphoric acid derivatives are not carboxylic acid derivatives, they do form esters similar to those that we've discussed so far.

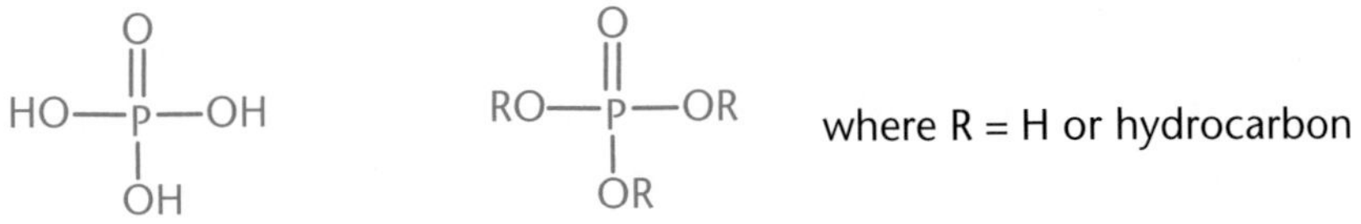

where R = H or hydrocarbon

phosphoric acid   phosphoric ester

Figure 10.28

Phosphoric acid and the mono- and diesters are acidic (more so than carboxylic acids), so they usually exist as anions. Like all esters, they can be cleaved under acidic conditions into the parent acid (in Figure 10.28, H_3PO_4) and alcohols.

Many living systems are literally covered in phosphate esters in the form of phospholipids (phosphoglycerides), shown in Figure 10.29, in which glycerol is attached to two carboxylic acids and one phosphoric acid.

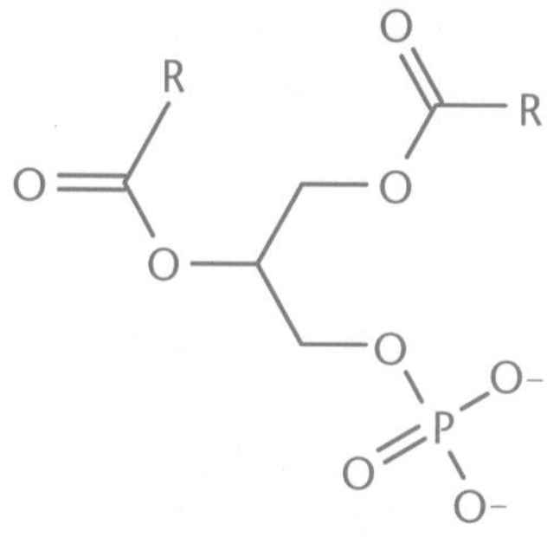

Bridge

Phosphodiester bonds should look familiar to you from your studies of molecular biology. They are responsible for holding the DNA backbone together, connecting nucleotides with covalent linkages.

phosphatidic acid
diacylglycerol phosphate
(a phosphoglyceride)

Figure 10.29

Phospholipids are the main component of cell membranes, and phospholipid/carbohydrate polymers form the backbone of nucleic acids, the hereditary material of life. The nucleic acid derivative adenosine triphosphate (ATP), the fuel that drives our cellular engines, can give up or regain one or more phosphate groups. ATP facilitates many biological reactions by releasing phosphate groups (via hydrolysis) to other compounds, thereby increasing their reactivity. This reaction is downhill in free energy, so it is thermodynamically favorable and drives many biological reactions.

Conclusion

That was a whole lot of information in only a handful of pages, but as we're sure you noticed, it's actually only a few reactions happening in a wide variety of contexts. The MCAT test makers don't want you to memorize all the possible reactions; they simply want you truly to understand the trends and the underlying reasons for these reactions. Make sure you know the order of reactivity of the derivative (from acyl halides, the restless party guest, to amides, the guest who just won't go home). Also, learn the general mechanism for nucleophilic substitutions and the special reactions of esters and amides. Your study of amides will pay off right away. The next chapter introduces nitrogen-containing compounds, and we will return to the *very* special case of amino acids in the final chapter.

CONCEPTS TO REMEMBER

The most important derivatives of carboxylic acids are acyl halides, anhydrides, esters, and amides. We decided to organize these derivatives from most reactive (least stable) to least reactive (most stable).

ACYL HALIDES

☐ Can be formed by adding $RCOOH + SOCl_2$, PCl_3 or PCl_5, or PBr_3.

☐ Undergo many different nucleophilic substitutions; H_2O yields carboxylic acid, ROH yields an ester, and NH_3 yields an amide.

☐ Can participate in Friedel-Crafts acylation to form an alkyl aryl ketone.

☐ Can be reduced to alcohols or, selectively, to aldehydes.

ANHYDRIDES

☐ Can be formed by $RCOOH + RCOOH$ (condensation) or $RCOO^- + RCOCl$ (substitution).

☐ Undergo many nucleophilic substitution reactions, forming products that include carboxylic acids, amides, and esters.

☐ Can participate in Friedel-Crafts acylation.

ESTERS

☐ Formed by $RCOOH + ROH$ or, even more easily, by acid chlorides or anhydrides + ROH.

☐ Hydrolyze to yield acids + alcohols; adding ammonia yields an amide.

☐ Reaction with Grignard reagent (2 moles) produces a tertiary alcohol.

☐ In the Claisen condensation, analogous to the aldol condensation, the ester acts both as nucleophile and electrophile—but note the product difference.

☐ Are very important in biological processes, particularly phosphate esters, which can be found in membranes, nucleic acids, and metabolic reactions.

AMIDES

☐ Can be formed by acid chlorides + amines or acid anhydrides + ammonia.

☐ Hydrolysis yields carboxylic acids or carboxylate anions.

☐ Can be transformed to primary amines via Hofmann rearrangement or reduction.

Practice Questions

1.

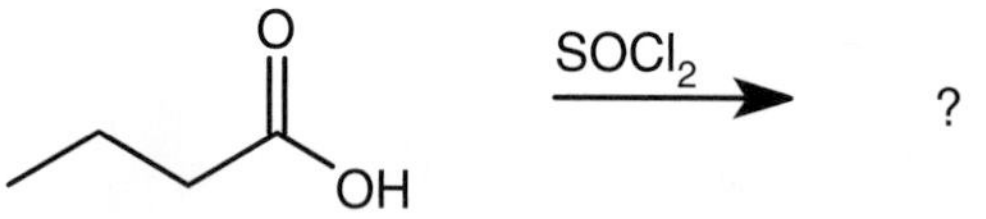

SOCl$_2$ → ?

What would be the product of the above reaction?

A.

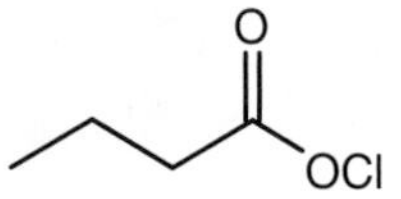

B.

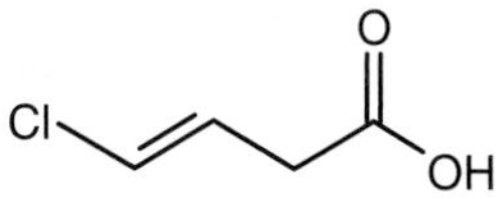

C.

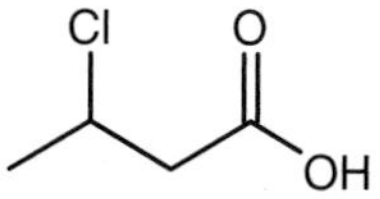

D.

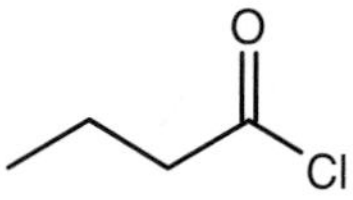

2. During the hydrolysis of an acid chloride, pyridine (a base) is usually added to the reaction vessel. This is done because

   A. the reaction leads to the production of hydroxide ions.

   B. the acyl chloride is unreactive.

   C. the hydrolysis reaction leads to the formation of HCl.

   D. the pyridine reacts in a side reaction with the carboxylic acid product.

3.

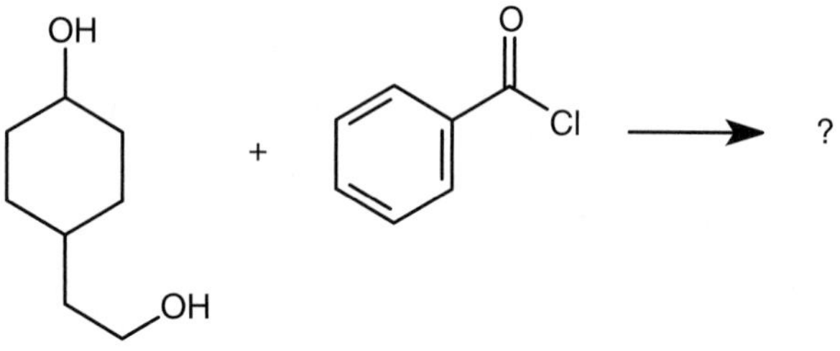

+ → ?

What would be the primary product of the above reaction?

A.

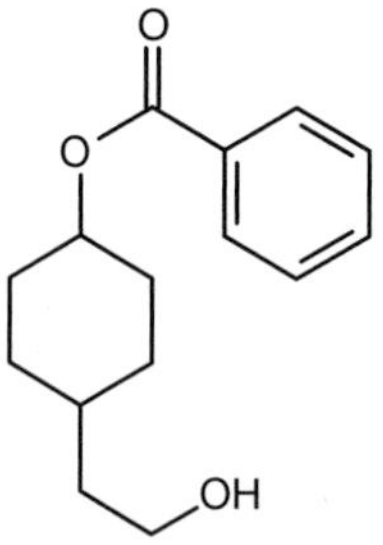

B.

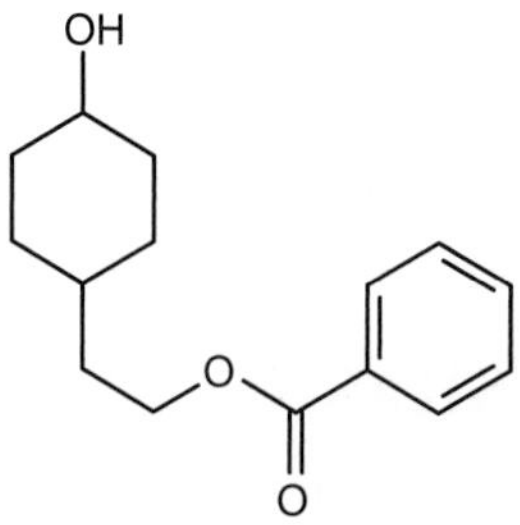

C.

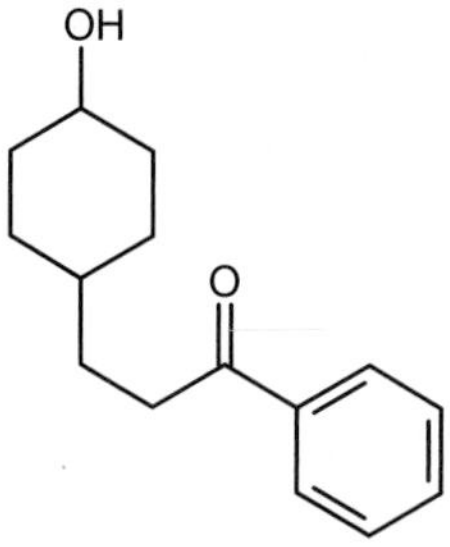

D.

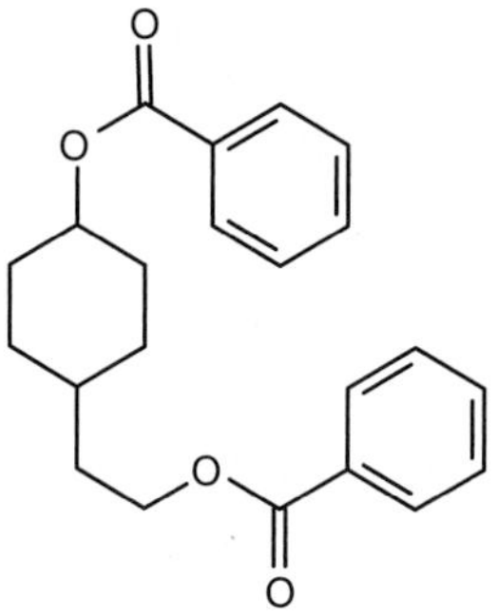

4. To produce a primary amide, an acid chloride should be treated with

   A. ammonia.

   B. an alcohol.

   C. a primary amine.

   D. a tertiary amine.

5. Which of the following would be the best method of producing methyl propanoate?

    A. Reacting propanoic acid and methanol in the presence of a mineral acid

    B. Reacting ethanol with propanoyl chloride in the presence of a base

    C. Reacting propanoyl chloride with an aqueous base

    D. Reacting propanoic acid with ethanol in the presence of a mineral acid

6.

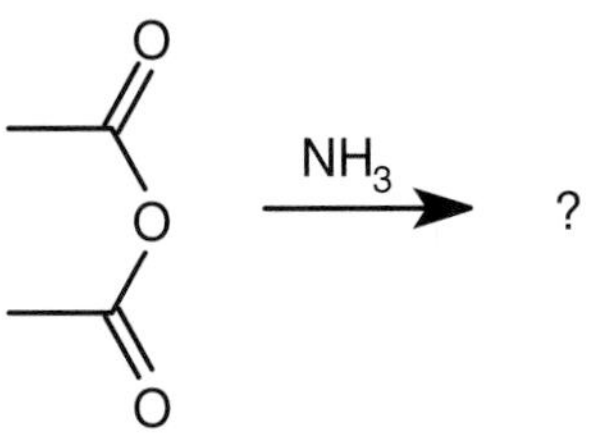

What would be the product(s) of the above reaction?

A.

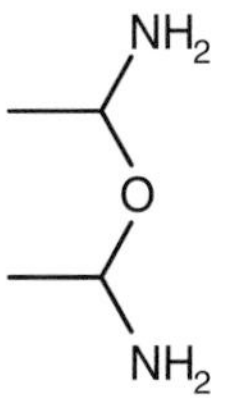

B. 2

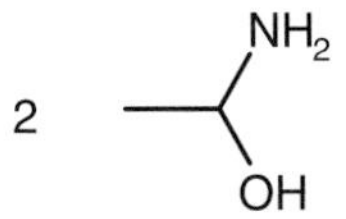

C.

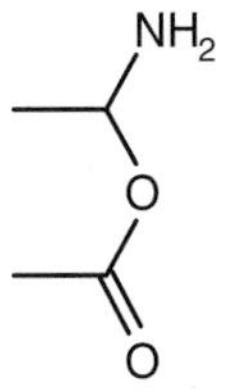

D.

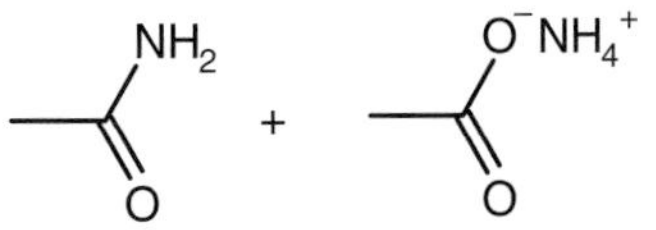

7.

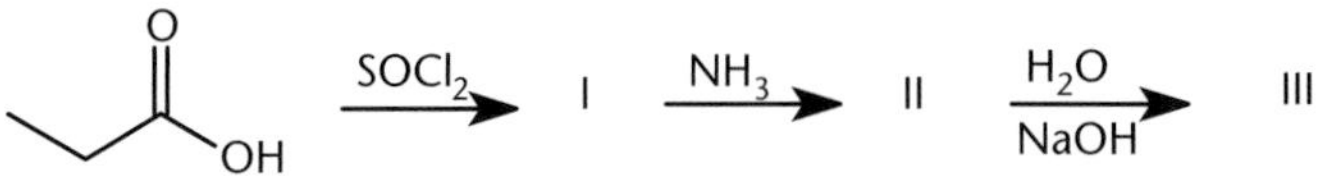

Which of the following correctly shows the intermediates and products of the reaction above?

A.

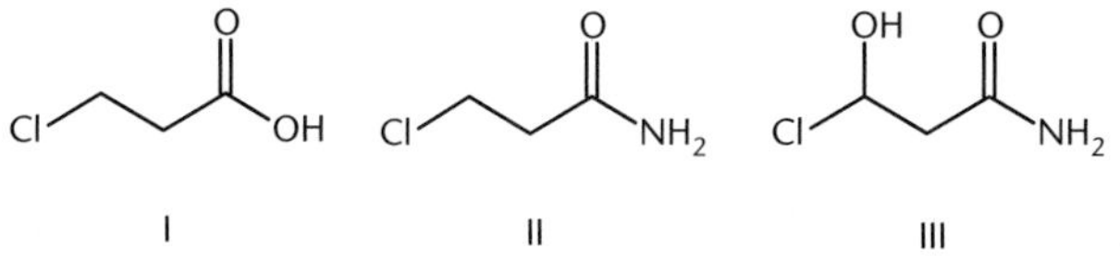

B.

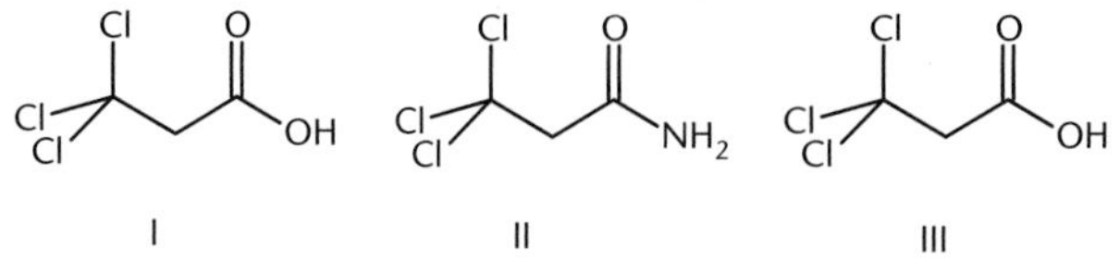

C.

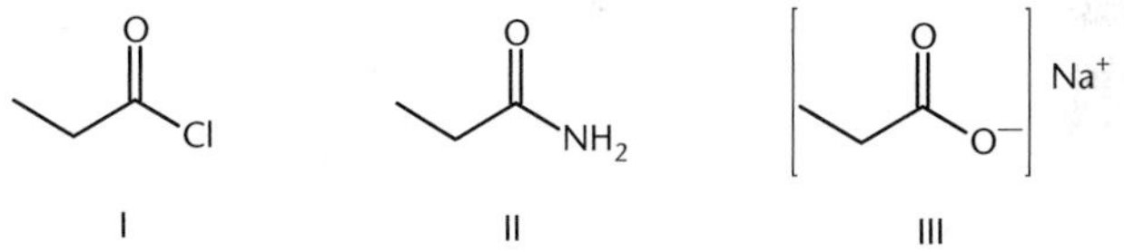

D.

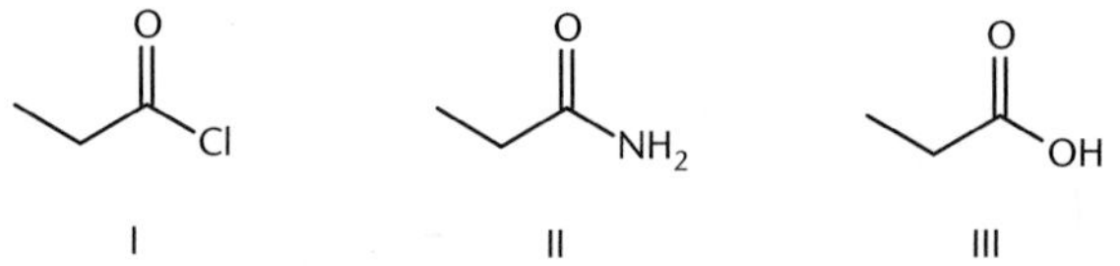

8. Which conversion between carboxylic acid derivatives is NOT possible by nucleophilic reaction?

    A. Acid chloride → ester

    B. Acid chloride → anhydride

    C. Anhydride → amide

    D. Ester → anhydride

9. Acyl halides make excellent reactants in carboxylic acid derivative synthesis because

    A. halides are amenable to nucleophilic attack.

    B. halides are amenable to electrophilic attack.

    C. halide ions are good leaving groups.

    D. there is a lack of rotation around the C=O bond.

10. Which of the following undergoes a Fischer esterification most rapidly?

A.

B.

C.

D.

Small Group Questions

1. We provided the mechanism for acid-catalyzed hydrolysis of esters. Draw out the mechanism for base-catalyzed hydrolysis and examine the similarities and differences between the mechanisms.

2. Why is the hydrolysis of esters (saponification) irreversible?

Explanations to Practice Questions

1. D

Treating a carboxylic acid with thionyl chloride results in the production of an acyl chloride. In this reaction, butanoic acid is converted to butanoyl chloride, which is choice (D).

2. C

Hydrolysis of an acid chloride results in the formation of a carboxylic acid and HCl. Therefore, basic pyridine serves to neutralize acidic HCl. The reaction does not result in the formation of hydroxide ions, so choice (A) is wrong. We can assume that pyridine does not neutralize carboxylic acid (D) because if it did, the reaction would be unsuccessful. No scientist would add a reagent that would consume the desired product! Thus, HCl must be the acid that pyridine neutralizes. Finally, choice (B) is incorrect because reactivity is characteristic of acyl chlorides. Again, the correct answer is choice (C).

3. B

In this question, an acid chloride is treated with an alcohol, and the product will be an ester. However, the esterification process is affected by the presence of bulky side chains on either reactant, as it is easier to esterify an unhindered alcohol than a hindered one. In this reaction, the primary hydroxyl group is less hindered and will react with benzoyl chloride more rapidly, so choice (B) is correct. Choice (A) is incorrect because the hydroxyl group is secondary and therefore more hindered and the reaction rate will be slower. Choice (C) is incorrect because it is not an ester. Choice (D) is prevented by the same steric issues that hold back choice (A).

4. A

Acid chlorides react with ammonia or other amines to form amides. These amines must have a hydrogen to give up so that they can form a bond with carbon; therefore, only ammonia and primary or secondary amines can undergo this reaction. A primary amide is one in which only one carbon substituent is bound to nitrogen, so it must be the carbonyl carbon. Therefore, nitrogen cannot come with any pre-existing bonds to other carbons. Ammonia, choice (A), must be used. The reaction of an alcohol with an acid chloride produces an ester, so choice (B) is incorrect. A primary amine reacting with an acid chloride would result in a secondary amide; thus, choice (C) is incorrect. Choice (D) is wrong because tertiary amines will not react with acid chlorides, as nitrogen has no leaving groups that it can release in exchange for new bonds.

5. A

Methyl propanoate is an ester; it can be synthesized by reacting a carboxylic acid with an alcohol in the presence of acid (A). Reacting ethanol with propanoyl chloride (B) will also result in the formation of an ester, but because ethanol is used, ethyl propanoate will be formed, not methyl propanoate. This is also the case for choice (D), because ethanol is used here as well. Choice (C) is incorrect because propanoyl chloride will not form an ester in the presence of base alone. Therefore, choice (A) is the correct response.

6. D

This question asks for the products when ammonia reacts with acetic anhydride. Recall from the notes that an amide and an ammonium carboxylate will be formed. The only choice showing such a pair is (D), acetamide and ammonium acetate.

7. C

This question gives a reaction scheme for the conversion of propanoic acid to various derivatives, and it asks what intermediate products are formed. The first reaction involves the formation of an acid chloride using thionyl chloride. Thus, choices (A) and (B), which depict intact carboxylic acid functionalities, can be eliminated. The second reaction is an ammonolysis of propanoyl chloride. The product should be propanamide, because ammonia will replace the chloride on the carbonyl carbon. This does not help us choose between (C) and (D), but it is an important concept to know for Test Day. The final reaction involves amide hydrolysis. Hydrolysis leads to carboxylic acid formation. Distinguishing between choices (C) and (D), which both have a carboxylic acid as the third product, involves understanding how carboxylic acids exist in acidic and basic conditions. In acidic solution, the carboxyl group will be protonated, whereas in basic solution, the carboxyl group will be deprotonated. This reaction involves hydrolysis in the presence of base; therefore, the resulting carboxylic acid will exist in solution as a carboxylate salt. Thus, choice (C) is the correct answer, because it has sodium propanoate as the product of the third reaction.

8. D

There is a hierarchy to the reactivity of carboxylic acid derivatives that dictates how reactive they are toward nucleophilic attack. This order, from highest to lowest, is acid chlorides > anhydrides > esters > amides. In practical terms, this means that derivatives of higher reactivity can form derivatives of lower activity but not vice versa. Acid chlorides are more reactive than anhydrides and esters; thus, answers (A) and (B) are incorrect. Anhydrides are more reactive than amides, making answer (C) incorrect. Nucleophilic attack of an ester cannot result in the corresponding anhydride. Esters can only be converted into amides. (D) is the correct answer.

9. C

Halide ions are excellent leaving groups, which make acyl halides reactive compounds (i.e., ready to kick off their halides in favor of substitution). The halides themselves are open to neither electrophilic nor nucleophilic attack, making (A) and (B) incorrect. Rotation about the carbonyl bond (D) is irrelevant because halides do not participate in that bond.

10. A

A Fischer esterification involves refluxing a carboxylic acid and a primary or secondary alcohol with an acid catalyst. Under these conditions, the carbonyl carbon is open to attack by the oxygen atom in the alcohol acting as a nucleophile. The rate of this reaction depends on the amount of steric hindrance around the carbonyl carbon, because there must be room for the alcohol to approach the carboxylic acid substrate. The molecule in choice (A) is the least sterically hindered; thus, the reaction will take place most rapidly and is the correct answer. Answers (B) through (D) have increasing amounts of steric crowding, which correlate with decreasing rates of esterification. As a result of having fewer alkyl groups, choice (A) also shows the least electron density being donated to the partially positive carbonyl carbon (in other words, choice (A) has the strongest carbonyl electrophile). Although this effect is minimal compared with the steric issues we discussed above, it does help us confirm that we chose the right answer.

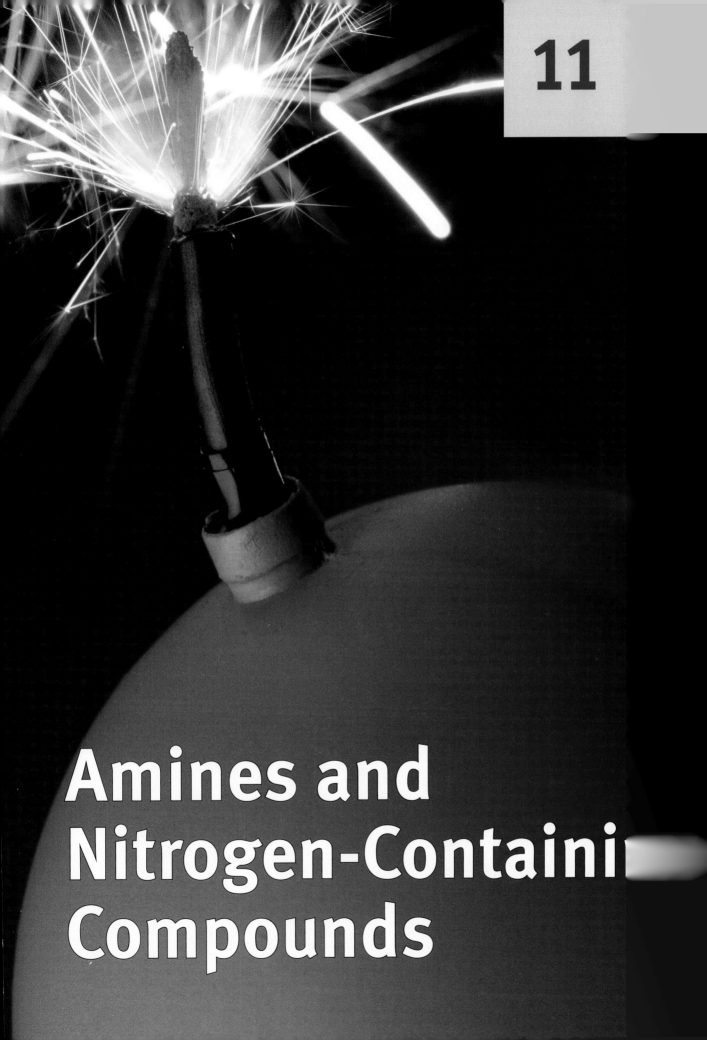

Amines and
Nitrogen-Containi
Compounds

Figure 11.10

Reactions

★★★☆☆

EXHAUSTIVE METHYLATION

Exhaustive methylation is also known as **Hofmann elimination**. In this process, an amine is converted to quaternary ammonium iodide by treatment with excess methyl iodide. In other words, the nitrogen now has methyl groups in all the positions where it used to have hydrogens or lone pairs. Treatment with silver oxide and water displaces the iodide ion and converts the molecule to ammonium hydroxide, which, when heated, undergoes elimination to form an alkene and an amine (see Figure 11.11). The predominant alkene formed is the least substituted, in contrast with normal elimination reactions, where the predominant alkene product is the most substituted. The least substituted alkene is formed because of the bulk of the quarternary ammonium salt leaving group.

> **Key Concept**
>
> Amines can be formed by the following:
>
> 1) S_N2 reactions:
>   - Ammonia reacting with alkyl halides
>   - Gabriel synthesis
> 2) Reduction of:
>   - Amides
>   - Aniline and its derivatives
>   - Nitriles
>   - Imines
>
> Amines can be converted to alkenes by exhaustive methylation followed by an E2 reaction forming the less-substituted alkene.

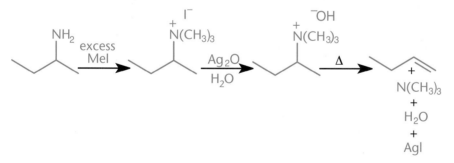

Figure 11.11

Conclusion

There are a lot of functional groups to remember in this chapter, and we urge you to learn them all. Once you've taken the time to learn the basics, make sure you take the time to *practice using them*. Look under the sink, flip through this book, or grab your old textbook from college—just pick some reactants and figure out what could happen. If you're not sure, ask a classmate; figure it out together. The best way to learn is to teach each other.

This isn't the last time you will see nitrogen-containing compounds in this book. Nitrogen returns in the final chapter in the form of amino acids (along with carbon, of course!), which combine to create the peptides and proteins that establish the structure and functions of every living thing. But once again, even as we deal with bigger and more complex molecules, the chemistry comes down to functional groups and general trends.

We hope this chapter has helped you realize that no matter what molecule the MCAT throws at you, as long as you know the characteristics of nitrogen-containing functional groups, you will be able to find the *best* answer. Even if that molecule is … melamine.

CONCEPTS TO REMEMBER

- ☐ The suffix *–amine* is used when the amine has the highest priority.

- ☐ The prefix *amino–* is used when the amine does not have the highest priority.

- ☐ Remember the nitrogen-containing functional groups: amides; carbamates = urethanes; isocyanates; enamines; imines; nitriles = cyanides; nitro; diazo; azide; carbene; nitrene.

- ☐ The boiling point of amines is between that of alcohols and alkanes.

- ☐ Certain amines can be optically active if inversion is inhibited by sterics.

- ☐ Amines have lone pairs, so they are bases/nucleophiles.

- ☐ A nitrogen double-bonded to carbon (imine) acts like an oxygen double-bonded to carbon (carbonyl).

- ☐ Addition of ammonia to an alkyl halide and the Gabriel synthesis are both S_N2 reactions.

- ☐ Many nitrogen-containing function groups are easily reduced to amines.

- ☐ Exhaustive methylation = Hofmann elimination. In this reaction, the nitrogen of an amine is released as trimethylamine, and the substituent is converted into the least substituted alkene.

Practice Questions

1. A compound with the general formula $R_4N^+X^-$ is classified as a

   A. secondary amine.
   B. quaternary ammonium salt.
   C. tertiary amine.
   D. primary amine.

2. Amines have lower boiling points than the corresponding alcohols because

   A. they have higher molecular weights.
   B. they form stronger hydrogen bonds.
   C. they form weaker hydrogen bonds.
   D. There is no systematic difference between the boiling points of amines and alcohols.

3. Which of the following would be formed if methyl bromide were reacted with phthalimide and followed by hydrolysis with aqueous base?

   A. $C_2H_5NH_2$
   B. CH_3NH_2
   C. $(C_2H_5)_3N$
   D. $(CH_3)_4N^+Br^-$

4. The reaction of benzamide with $LiAlH_4$ yields which of the following compounds?

   A. Benzoic acid
   B. Benzonitrile
   C. Benzylamine
   D. Ammonium benzoate

5. Which of the following amines has the highest boiling point?

   A. CH_3NH_2
   B. $CH_3(CH_2)_6NH_2$
   C. $CH_3(CH_2)_3NH_2$
   D. $(CH_3)_3CNH_2$

6. If 2-amino-3-methylbutane were treated with excess methyl iodide, silver oxide, and water, what would be the major reaction products?

   A. Ammonia and 2-methyl-2-butene
   B. Trimethylamine and 3-methyl-1-butene
   C. Trimethylamine and 2-methyl-2-butene
   D. Ammonia and 3-methyl-1-butene

7. Nylon, a polyamide, is produced from hexanediamine and a substance X. This substance X is most probably

   A. an amine.
   B. a carboxylic acid.
   C. a nitrile.
   D. an alcohol.

8. What is the IUPAC name for the compound shown below?

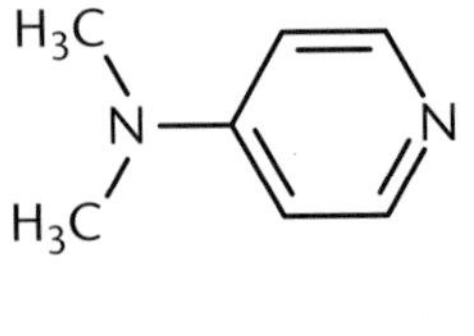

   A. 4-(*N*-dimethylamino)pyridine
   B. Dimethylaminopyridine
   C. 4-(*N*,*N*-dimethylamino)pyridine
   D. *N*,*N*-dimethylaminopyridine

9. Pyrrolidine is an excellent base with a pK_a of 11.27. In contrast, pyrrole, which has a similar structure, is a poor base with a pK_a of 0.4. Why is pyrrole such a poor base compared with pyrrolidine?

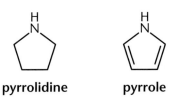

pyrrolidine   **pyrrole**

A. Pyrrole is aromatic.

B. Pyrrolidine is antiaromatic.

C. The nitrogen atom in pyrrole does not have any lone pairs.

D. The nitrogen in pyrrolidine contains an extra lone pair.

10. What product is formed from the following reaction?

$$\text{NH} \xrightarrow[\substack{\text{2. Ag}_2\text{O, H}_2\text{O} \\ \text{3. Heat}}]{\text{1. xs CH}_3\text{I}} \text{?}$$

A. NH_2

B. $N-$

C. $+ N(CH_3)_3$

D. $N(CH_3)_2$

Small Group Questions

1. Why is the C–N bond of an amide planar?

2. Does a protonated amide have resonance stabilization?

Explanations to Practice Questions

1. B

A quaternary ammonium salt has four substituents attached to the central nitrogen, resulting in a positive charge. As a result, this compound forms a salt, where X^- is usually a halide. Primary amines have the general formula RNH_2, secondary amines have the general formula R_2NH, and tertiary amines have the general formula R_3N. Therefore, choices (A), (C), and (D) are incorrect.

2. C

Amines form weaker hydrogen bonds than alcohols, because nitrogen has a lower electronegativity than oxygen. The molecules are not held together as tightly and are therefore more volatile.

3. B

The reaction between methyl bromide and phthalimide results in the formation of methyl phthalimide. Subsequent hydrolysis then yields methylamine, so choice (B) is the correct response. Therefore, the overall reaction is the conversion of a primary alkyl halide into a primary amine (known as the Gabriel synthesis). Choice (A) is wrong because it contains an ethyl group, not a methyl group. To form this compound, the initial reactant should be ethyl bromide. Choices (C) and (D) are incorrect because these are tertiary and quaternary nitrogen compounds, respectively, and the reaction only converts primary alkyl halides into primary amines.

4. C

Lithium aluminum hydride is a good reducing agent and is used to reduce amides to amines. Reduction of benzamide will result in the formation of benzylamine (C). Hydrolysis of benzamide would result in the formation of benzoic acid, so choice (A) is incorrect. Benzonitrile would be formed by amide dehydration, so choice (B) is also wrong. To form ammonium benzoate (D), benzamide would first have to be hydrolyzed and then reacted with ammonia, so this answer choice is also incorrect.

5. B

As the molecular weights of amines increase, so do their boiling points. Of the choices given, choice (B), heptylamine, has the highest molecular weight and therefore the highest boiling point, 142°C–144°C. For comparison's sake, choice (A), methylamine, has a boiling point of –6.3°C, butylamine, choice (C), has a boiling point of 77.5°C, and *t*-butylamine, choice (D), has a boiling point of 44.4°C.

6. B

Treatment of an amine with excess methyl iodide, silver oxide, and water is called exhaustive methylation or Hofmann elimination. A trisubstituted amine and an alkene are the products formed. 2-Amino-3-methylbutane is a primary amine; therefore, it will be able to pick up three methyl groups after separating from the alkyl chain. The trisubstituted amine produced will be trimethylamine. The predominant alkene product will be the least substituted alkene, because removal of a secondary hydrogen is sterically hindered. Therefore, this reaction will produce 3-methyl-1-butene, plus trimethylamine (B). Choices (A) and (D) are incorrect; ammonia cannot be a product of this reaction because the mechanism involves the addition of methyl groups. Choice (C) is incorrect because 2-methyl-2-butene, the more substituted alkene, would not be the predominant product.

7. B

An amide is formed from an amine and a carboxyl group or its acyl derivatives. In this question, an amine is already given; the compound to be identified must be an acyl compound. The only acyl compound among the choices given is a carboxylic acid, choice (B).

8. C

All groups (except hydrogen atoms) bonded to nitrogen need to be specified by the *N–* prefix, followed by the group. This prefix is repeated for each group. Answer (A) is incorrect because it fails to provide an *N–* prefix per methyl substituent, whereas answer (B) is incorrect because it lacks both a numerical position and *N–* prefixes. Answer (D) is incorrect because the position of the amino substituent is not specified.

9. A

The nitrogen atoms in pyrrolidine and pyrrole each have one lone pair (with three bond pairs) when neutral, so answers (C) and (D) are incorrect. An antiaromatic system has $4n$ electrons, where n is an integer. Because pyrrolidine lacks such a system, answer (B) is incorrect. Pyrrole is indeed aromatic, because it has six π electrons. Aromatic compounds have stable electron systems and prefer to remain undisturbed.

10. D

This is an exhaustive methylation reaction. The amine is not an individual product; rather, it is tethered to the alkene. Answer (B) shows an incomplete reaction, as there is no alkene present. Answer (A) is incorrect because the amine must be trisubstituted. Answer (C) is incorrect because the nitrogen can only pick up two methyl groups, based on the number of carbons to which it is already bound.

Purification and Separation

gas chromatography) through the stationary phase. This will displace **(elute)** the sample and carry it through the stationary phase. Depending on the substance and the polarity of the mobile phase, it will adhere to the stationary phase with different strengths, causing the different substances to migrate at different speeds. This is called partitioning, and it represents an equilibrium between the two phases. Different compounds will have different equilibrium constants and elute at different rates. This results in each compound separating within the stationary phase, allowing us to isolate them individually.

We can use a plethora of different media as our stationary phase, each one exploiting different properties that allow us to separate out our compound. Within this crowd, the property you will most likely see on the MCAT is polarity. For instance, **thin-layer chromatography (TLC)**, which we will soon discuss, uses silica gel, a highly polar substance, as its stationary phase. This means that any polar compound will adhere to the gel quite well and thus move (elute) slowly. In addition, when using **column chromatography**, size and charge both have a role in how quickly a compound moves through the stationary phase. Even strong interactions, such as antibody-ligand binding, are used in chromatography. The possibilities are virtually endless.

We've said that this whole analysis is based on the speed at which substances move through media, but we don't get out a radar gun to clock their speeds. In practice, we either measure how far each substance travels in a given amount of time (as in TLC), or we time how long it takes the substance to elute off the column (as in column or gas chromatography).

The four types of chromatography that we'll see on the MCAT are **TLC**, **column chromatography**, **gas chromatography (GC)**, and **high-pressure** (or **performance**) **liquid chromatography (HPLC)**.

THIN-LAYER CHROMATOGRAPHY

The adsorbent we use in TLC is either a piece of paper or a thin layer of silica gel or alumina adhered to an inert carrier sheet (glass or plastic). We then place the mixture that we want to separate onto the adsorbent itself; this is called **spotting** because we apply a small, well-defined spot of our mixture onto the plate. The TLC plate is then **developed**, which involves placing the adsorbent upright in a developing chamber (usually a beaker with a lid or a wide-mouthed jar) containing a shallow pool of **eluant** (solvent) at the bottom. We have to make sure that the initial spots on the plate are above the level of the solvent. If not, they'll simply elute off the plate and into the solvent, rather than moving up the plate. If everything's set up correctly, the solvent will creep up the plate via capillary action, carrying the different compounds with it at varying rates.

> ## Key Concept
>
> Chromatography separates compounds based on how strongly they adhere to the solid, or stationary, phase (or, in other words, how easily they come off into the mobile phase).

When the solvent front nears the top of the plate, the plate is removed from the chamber and allowed to dry.

As we mentioned before, TLC is often done with silica gel, which is polar and hydrophilic. The mobile phase on the other hand, is usually an organic solvent (often a mixture) of weak to moderate polarity, so it doesn't bind well to the gel. Because of this, nonpolar compounds hang out with the organic solvent and move quickly as the solvent moves up the plate, whereas the more polar molecules are stuck to the gel. **Reverse-phase chromatography** is the exact opposite. Here, the stationary phase is very nonpolar, so polar molecules move up the plate very quickly, whereas nonpolar molecules stick more tightly to the stationary phase.

The spots of individual compounds are usually white, which makes them difficult or impossible to see on the white TLC plate. To get around this problem, we can place the developed TLC plate under ultraviolet light, which will show any compounds that are ultraviolet sensitive (like forensic detectives searching a crime scene for DNA). Alternatively, we can use iodine, phosphomolybdic acid, or vanillin (yep, the kind that tastes good) to stain the spots. The problem with this is that the stain will destroy the compound (usually by oxidation), so we can't recover it.

Key Concept

If the sample travels farther, it is similar to the solvent.

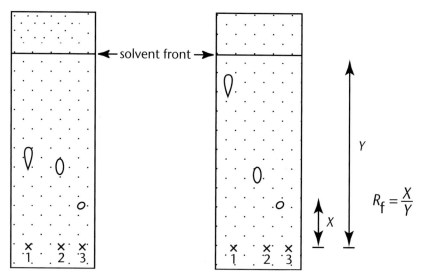

$$R_f = \frac{X}{Y}$$

Figure 12.7

Now let's get into the math behind TLC. We take the distance that the compound travels and divide it by the distance that the solvent travels (which will always be a larger number). This ratio is called the R_f **value** (see Figure 12.7). This is a relatively constant value for a particular compound in a given solvent, so we can use the R_f value to find the identity of an unknown compound.

Because we generally perform this technique on a small scale, TLC is frequently used only for qualitative identification (determining the identity of a compound). If we really wanted to, we could use TLC on a larger scale as a means of purification. **Preparative** or **prep TLC** uses a large TLC plate that has a big streak of a mixture on it. As the plate develops, the streak splits into bands of individual compounds, just as it did in the small-scale version. Because the streak is so large, we can scrape the bands off and rinse them with a polar solvent, recovering the pure compounds from the silica.

COLUMN CHROMATOGRAPHY

The principle behind column chromatography is the same as for TLC. The difference with column chromatography is that it uses a column filled with silica or alumina beads as an adsorbent, allowing for much greater separation (see Figure 12.8). In addition, TLC uses capillary action to move the solvent and compounds up the plate, whereas in column chromatography, solvent and compounds move down the column by gravity. To speed up the process, we can force the solvent through the column with nitrogen gas, a technique called **flash column chromatography**. In column chromatography, the solvent polarity can easily be changed to help elute our compound.

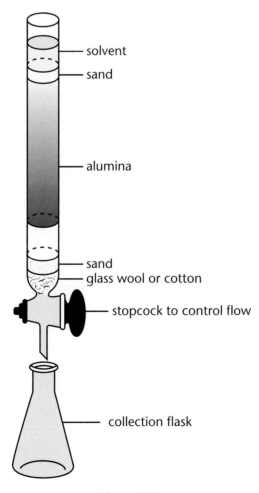

Figure 12.8

Eventually, the solvent drips out of the end of the column, and we can collect the different fractions that leave the column at varying times. Each fraction contains bands that correspond to different compounds. After collection, we can evaporate the solvent and isolate the compounds we want to keep. Column chromatography is particularly useful in biochemistry because it can be used to separate macromolecules such as proteins or nucleic acids. Several techniques can be used to isolate specific materials.

Ion Exchange Chromatography

In this method, the beads in the column are coated with charged substances, so they attract or bind compounds that have an opposite charge. For instance, a positively charged column will attract and hold the negatively charged backbone of DNA as it passes though the column, either increasing its retention time or retaining it completely. A salt gradient is used to elute the charged molecules that have stuck to the column.

Size-Exclusion Chromatography

In this method, the beads used in the column contain tiny pores of varying sizes. These tiny pores allow small compounds to enter the beads, thus slowing them down. Large compounds can't fit into the pores, so they will move around them and travel through the column faster. It is important to remember that in this type of chromatography, the small compounds are slowed down and retained longer. The size of the pores may be varied so that different molecular weight molecules may be fractionated. A common approach in protein purification is to use an ion exchange column followed by a size-exclusion column.

Affinity Chromatography

We can also customize columns to bind any substance of interest. For example, if we wanted to purify substance A, we could use a column of beads coated with something that binds A very tightly (hence the name *affinity* chromatography), such as a receptor for A, A's biological target, or even a specific antibody. This means that A will bind to the column very tightly and it will likely stay inside the column. Later, we can elute A by washing the column with a free receptor (or target or antibody), which will compete with the bead-bound receptor and ultimately free substance A from the column. The only drawback of the elution is that we now have our inhibitor or receptor bound to our biological target. This inhibitor can be difficult to remove if it binds tightly.

GAS CHROMATOGRAPHY

Gas chromatography (GC) is another method we have for qualitative separation. GC, also called **vapor-phase chromatography (VPC)**, is similar to all other types of chromatography that we've discussed (see Figure 12.9). The main difference, conceptually, is that the eluant is a gas (usually helium or nitrogen) instead of a liquid.

Key Concept

All chromatography is about how "like" the substance is to the mobile and stationary phases *except* for size-exclusion chromatography.

The adsorbent is inside a 30-foot column that is coiled and kept inside an oven to control its temperature. The mixture is then injected into the column and vaporized. The gaseous compounds travel through the column at different rates, because they adhere to the adsorbent to different degrees and will separate by the time they reach the end of the column. The requirement for the compounds that we inject is that they be volatile: low-melting-point, sublimable solids or liquids. The major difference in practice between GC and the other methods we have discussed is that in GC, we leave the analysis in the hands of computers. The compounds are registered by a detector, which records the presence of a compound as a peak on a chart. It is common to separate molecules using GC and then to inject the pure molecules into a mass spectrometer for molecular weight determination (GC-mass spec).

> ### Key Concept
> To identify a compound or distinguish two different compounds, look at their retention times—that is, how long it took for each to travel through the column.

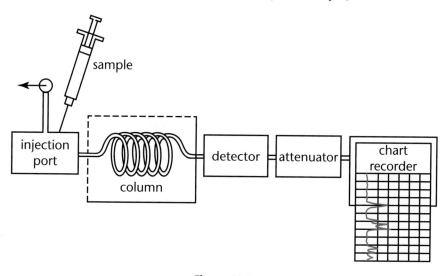

Figure 12.9

HPLC

HPLC stands for either **high-pressure** or **high-performance liquid chromatography**. As the name suggests, the eluant is a liquid, and it travels through a column of a defined composition. There are a variety of columns whose stationary phase is chosen depending on our target molecule and whose size is chosen depending on the quantity of material that needs to be purified. This is similar to a GC column, only a liquid is the eluent. In the past, very high pressures were used, but recent advances allow for much lower pressures, which is why the name changed from *high-pressure* to *high-performance*. In HPLC, a small sample is injected into the column, and separation occurs as it flows through. The compounds pass through a detector and are collected as the solvent flows out the end of the apparatus. It looks similar to GC, because computers do all the work for us, but we use liquid under pressure instead of gas. As the whole process is under computer control, sophisticated solvent gradients can be applied to the column to help resolve the various components in our mixture.

Electrophoresis

Another way we can separate a mixture of compounds that carry a charge is with **electrophoresis**. In molecular biology, this is one of the most important analytical techniques. This works by subjecting our compounds, usually macromolecules such as proteins or DNA, to an electric field, which moves them according to their charge and size. Negatively charged compounds (such as DNA) will migrate toward the positively charged anode, and positively charged compounds will migrate toward the negatively charged cathode. The velocity of this migration, known as the **migration velocity**, v, of a molecule, is directly proportional to the electric field strength, E, and to the net charge on the molecule, z, and is inversely proportional to a frictional coefficient, f, which depends on the mass and shape of the migrating molecules.

$$v = \frac{Ez}{f}$$

Generally speaking, the more charged the molecule or the stronger the electric field is, the faster it will migrate through the medium. Conversely, the bigger and more convoluted the molecule is, the slower it will migrate.

AGAROSE GEL ELECTROPHORESIS

There's a good possibility that once upon a time, in a college biology lab far, far away, you used **agarose gel electrophoresis** (see Figure 12.10) to separate pieces of nucleic acid (usually deoxyribonucleic acid [DNA] but sometimes ribonucleic acid [RNA]). The medium used in this type of electrophoresis is **agarose**, a plant gel derived from seaweed. Agarose is a great tool because it is nontoxic and easy to manipulate (unlike sodium dodecyl sulfate-polyacrylamide [SDS-PAGE]). Because every piece of nucleic acid is negatively charged (from its phosphate-sugar backbone), nucleic acids can be separated on the basis of size and shape alone (even without the charge-masking qualities of SDS, which we will soon discuss). It is also useful to stain agarose gels with a compound called *ethidium bromide*, which binds to nucleic acids and allows us to visualize our results by fluorescence under ultraviolet light. The staining process is toxic, however. Agarose gel electrophoresis can also be used to obtain our compound (preparatively) by cutting the desired band out of the gel and eluting out the nucleic acid.

SDS-PAGE

Sodium dodecyl sulfate-polyacrylamide gel electrophoresis is a useful tool because it separates proteins on the basis of mass alone; the procedure typically denatures the proteins. Polyacrylamide gel is the standard medium for electrophoresis and functions much in the same way as agarose gel. What makes it interesting is that SDS disrupts all noncovalent interactions. It binds to proteins and creates large chains with net negative charges, thereby neutralizing the protein's original charge. As the proteins move through the gel, the only variable affecting their velocity is f, the frictional coefficient, which depends on mass. After separation, we can stain the gel so the protein bands can be visualized and our results recorded. If you do not want to have your protein denatured, so-called "native" gels may be run.

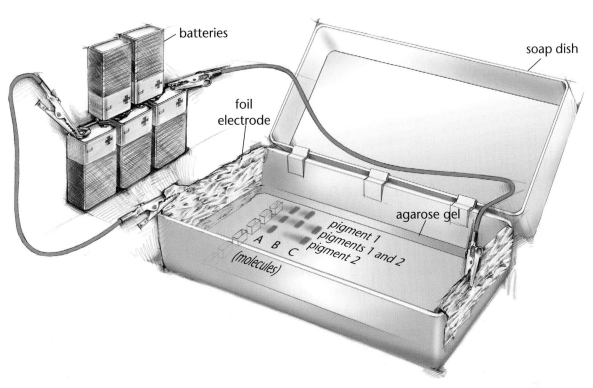

Figure 12.10

ISOELECTRIC FOCUSING

We also have a technique that exploits the acidic and basic properties of amino acids: **isoelectric focusing**. Each protein may be characterized by its **isoelectric point, pI**, which is the pH at which its net charge (the sum of all the charges on all of its amino acids) is zero (we will discuss this further in Chapter 15). If we take a mixture of proteins and place them in a electric field that exists across a gel with a pH gradient (acidic on one end, basic on the other, and neutral in the middle), the proteins will move until they reach the point that has a pH equal to their pI. At this pH, the protein's net charge is zero, so it will stop moving.

Let's go through an example to show how this works, as the concept behind this is essential for both Organic and General Chemistry. Let's say that we have protein with a pI of 9. As we know, this means that when the protein is in an environment

Key Concept

Because amino acids and proteins are organic molecules, the fundamental principle of acid-base chemistry apply to them as well.

- At a low pH, [H⁺] is relatively high. Thus, at a pH < pI, proteins will tend to be protonated and positively charged. As a result, they will migrate towards the cathode.

- At a relatively high (basic) pH, [H⁺] is lower and proteins will tend to be deprotonated and negatively charged. As a result, they will migrate towards the anode.

with a pH of 9, it will carry no charge; if it is at a pH that is higher or lower than 9, it will carry a charge. If we place this protein onto the gel at a pH of 7, there will be more protons around the protein (is more acidic than 9: thus, more protons in solution). These protons will attach to the available basic sites on the protein, creating a net positive charge on the molecule. This charge will then carry the protein toward the negatively charged cathode, which rests on the basic side of the gradient. As the protein moves closer to the cathode, there are fewer protons in the gel (the pH increases). Eventually, as the concentration of free protons drops and we near a pH of 9, the protons creating the positive charge will dissociate, and the protein will become neutral. A quick way to remember the charge of each end of the gel is to recall that we associate acids with protons, which carry a positive charge, and thus the anode is positively charged. We associate bases with the negatively charged hydroxide ion, which gives us the negatively charged cathode.

Conclusion

We hope that reading this chapter brought back loving memories of your Organic Chemistry lab, but if it didn't, don't worry—the MCAT doesn't care about your laboratory skills. As long as you understand the principles governing these techniques and when you should apply them, you'll be in great shape for the MCAT. Remember that purification and separation techniques exploit physical properties to obtain a purified product. The key factors are polarity, solubility, size and shape, boiling point, and charge. These factors can be traced back to the intermolecular forces or properties of the molecules themselves. Having a variety of tools and methods to separate and collect a purified product is essential in practical Organic Chemistry, but choosing the proper techniques often requires a great deal of knowledge and consideration of the product. In the next chapter, we'll take a look at some methods that will help identify, and sometimes separate out, an unknown product.

CONCEPTS TO REMEMBER

☐ Extraction separates dissolved substances based on differential solubility in aqueous versus organic solvents.

☐ Filtration separates solids from liquids.

☐ Recrystallization separates solids based on differential solubility; temperature is really important here.

☐ Sublimation separates solids based on their ability to sublime.

☐ Centrifugation separates large things (such as cells, organelles, and macromolecules) based on mass and density.

☐ Distillation separates liquids based on boiling point, which in turn depends on intermolecular forces.

☐ Chromatography uses a stationary phase and a mobile phase to separate compounds based on how tightly they adhere (generally due to polarity, size, or charge).

☐ Electrophoresis separates biological macromolecules (such as proteins or nucleic acids) based on size and sometimes charge.

Practice Questions

1. A mixture of sand, benzoic acid, and naphthalene in ether is best separated by

   B. filtration, followed by acidic extraction, followed by recrystallization.
   C. filtration, followed by basic extraction, followed by evaporation.
   D. extraction, followed by sublimation, followed by GC.
   E. filtration, followed by electrophoresis, followed by extraction.

2. Fractional distillation would most likely be used to separate which of the following compounds?

   A. Methylene chloride (boiling point of 41°C) and water (boiling point of 100°C)
   B. Ethyl acetate (boiling point of 77°C) and ethanol (boiling point of 80°C)
   C. Aniline (boiling point of 184°C) and benzyl alcohol (boiling point of 22°C).
   D. Aniline (boiling point of 184°C) and water (boiling point of 100°C).

3. Which of the following compounds would be the most effective in extracting benzoic acid from a diethyl ether solution?

   A. Tetrahydrofuran
   B. Aqueous hydrochloric acid
   C. Aqueous sodium hydroxide
   D. Water

4. Which of the following techniques would best separate red blood cells from blood plasma?

   A. Gel electrophoresis
   B. Centrifugation
   C. Isoelectric focusing
   D. HPLC

5. What would be the effect on the R_f values if the TLC described below were run with hexane rather than ether as the eluant?

Compound	Distance Travelled
benzyl alcohol	1.0 cm
benzyl acetate	2.6 cm
p-nitrophenol	2.3 cm
naphthalene	4.0 cm

   A. No effect
   B. Increase tenfold
   C. Double
   D. Decrease

6. If benzyl alcohol, benzyl acetate, p-nitrophenol, and naphthalene were separated by column chromatography with ether on silica gel, which compound would elute first?

   A. Benzyl alcohol
   B. Benzyl acetate
   C. p-nitrophenol
   D. Naphthalene

In the last chapter, we discussed various techniques for isolating, purifying, and identifying compounds. To use these methods, we usually have to have an idea about the identity of the compound we're trying to isolate. If the compound we are testing is completely unknown, we could use the previous chapter's techniques to determine many of its properties, and we could spend hours comparing its boiling point and melting point with literature values, hoping to find a match. However, there is a much more efficient way to identify a new unknown compound specifically and definitively. **Spectroscopy** measures the energy differences between the possible states of a molecular system by determining the frequencies of electromagnetic radiation (light) absorbed by the molecules. These possible states are quantized energy levels associated with different types of molecular motion, such as molecular rotation, vibration of bonds, nuclear spin transitions, and electron absorption. Different types of spectroscopy measure these different types of molecular properties, allowing us to identify the presence of specific functional groups and even to determine how they are connected.

One of the big advantages of spectroscopy is that only a small quantity of sample is needed. Also, the sample may be reused after a test is performed (except after mass spectroscopy). The downside of spectroscopy is that it's difficult to do in your kitchen (unlike finding boiling points). But, as long you have a chemistry lab available, these are some of the best techniques to identify compounds.

Infrared ★★★☆☆

BASIC THEORY

Infrared (IR) spectroscopy measures molecular vibrations, which can be seen as **bond stretching**, **bending**, or combinations of different vibrational modes. The useful absorptions of IR light occur at wavelengths of 3,000 to 30,000 nm, although when we represent IR on a graph, we use an analog of frequency called **wavenumber** (3,000 to 30,000 nm corresponds to 3,500 to 300 cm^{-1} in wavenumbers). When light of these frequencies/wavenumbers is absorbed, the molecules enter excited vibrational states. Bond stretching (which can be either symmetric or asymmetric) involves the largest change in energy and, thus, is observed in the higher frequency region of 4,000 to 1,500 cm^{-1}. Bending vibrations are observed in the lower frequency region of 1,500 to 400 cm^{-1}. The four types of vibration that can occur are shown in Figure 13.1.

MCAT Expertise

You will likely see a question or passage dealing with IR and/or ^{1}H-NMR on your exam. Pay attention to the tips on the following pages to be sure to get the high-yield information.

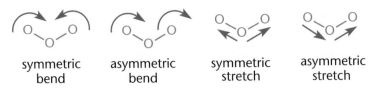

symmetric bend　　asymmetric bend　　symmetric stretch　　asymmetric stretch

Figure 13.1

In addition to these bending and stretching vibrations, there can be vibrations that incorporate a combination of bending, stretching, and rotating. Furthermore, even more complex vibration patterns, caused by the motion of the molecule as a whole, can be seen in the 1,500 to 400 cm^{-1} region. This is called the **fingerprint region**, as it is characteristic of each individual molecule. Spectroscopy experts can use this region to identify a substance, but you won't ever need to use it on the MCAT.

For an absorption to be recorded, the vibration must result in a change in the bond dipole moment. This means that molecules that do not experience a changing dipole moment, such as those composed of atoms with the same electronegativity or molecules that are symmetrical, do not exhibit absorption. For example, we cannot get an absorption from O_2 or Br_2, but we can from HCl or CO. Symmetric bonds will also be silent (the triple bond in acetylene, for example).

To get a spectrum, simply pass IR light (4,000 to 400 cm^{-1}) through a sample and record the absorption pattern. Percent transmittance is plotted versus frequency, where percent transmittance equals absorption minus one ($\%T = A - 1$); this means that maximum absorptions appear as the bottom of valleys on the spectrum.

CHARACTERISTIC ABSORPTIONS

For the MCAT, you only need to memorize a few absorptions. In fact, there are two that are more important than all the others. The first is alcohol (or anything else with an –OH group), which absorbs around 3,300 cm^{-1} with a broad peak, and the second is the carbonyl, which absorbs around 1,700 cm^{-1} with a sharp peak (compared with the –OH stretch). Fairly simply, huh? Don't get us wrong; it would be to your advantage to memorize all of Table 13.1, but unless you love memorizing numbers, we'd suggest spending your time on higher-yield concepts. One way to do this is to study the trends and differences in the table. Notice how the bond between any atom and hydrogen always has a relatively high frequency and how, as we add more bonds between carbon atoms, the frequency at which they will absorb increases. Or notice how N–H bonds are in the same region as O–H bonds, except they have a sharp peak instead of a broad one. This sort of information will be given to you in tables on the MCAT, so practice finding the trends now; it is an *essential* skill for Test Day.

Key Concept

Symmetric stretches do not show up in IR spectra because they involve no net change in dipole moment.

Key Concept

Wavenumbers (cm^{-1}) are an analog of frequency.

$f = \dfrac{c}{\lambda}$, whereas wavenumber $= \dfrac{1}{\lambda}$.

Table 13.1   Absorption Frequencies

Functional Group	Frequency (cm⁻¹)	Vibration
Alkanes	2,800–3,000	C–H
	1,200	C–C
Alkenes	3,080–3,140	=C–H
	1,645	C=C
Alkynes	2,200	C≡C
	3,300	≡C–H
Aromatic	2,900–3,100	C–H
	1,475–1,625	C–C
Alcohols	3,100–3,500	O–H (broad)
Ethers	1,050–1,150	C–O
Aldehydes	2,700–2,900	(O)C–H
	1,725–1,750	C=O
Ketones	1,700–1,750	C=O
Acids	1,700–1,750	C–O
	2,900–3,300	O–H (broad)
Amines	3,100–3,500	N–H (sharp)

APPLICATION

We can learn a great deal of information from an IR spectrum, and most of that information comes from the frequencies between 1,400 and 4,000 cm⁻¹; everything lower is out of scope for the MCAT.

MCAT Expertise

Infrared spectroscopy is best used for identification of functional groups. The most important peaks to know are those for the −OH (*broad* peak above 2,900 cm⁻¹) and the carbonyl peak (*sharp* peak near 1,700 cm⁻¹). If you know nothing else here, *know these!*

Frequency (cm⁻¹)

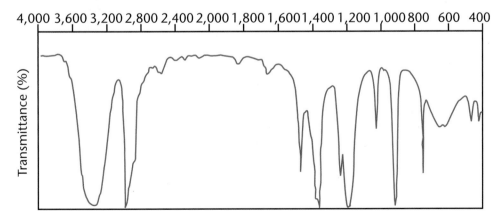

Figure 13.2

Figure 13.2 shows the IR spectrum for an aliphatic alcohol: The large broad peak at 3,300 cm⁻¹ is due to the presence of a hydroxyl group, whereas the sharper peak at 3,000 cm⁻¹ is due to the carbon–hydrogen bonds in the alkane portion of the molecule.

Nuclear Magnetic Resonance ★★★★★☆

BASIC THEORY

Nuclear magnetic resonance (NMR) spectroscopy is one of the most widely used spectroscopic tools in Organic Chemistry, and it's the most important technique to understand for the MCAT. NMR spectroscopy is based on the fact that certain nuclei have magnetic moments that are oriented at random. When such nuclei are placed in a magnetic field, their magnetic moments tend to align either with or against the direction of this applied field. Nuclei whose magnetic moments are aligned with the field are said to be in the **α-state** (lower energy), whereas those whose moments are aligned against the field are said to be in the **β-state** (higher energy). The nuclei can then be irradiated with radio frequency pulses that match the energy gap between the two states, which will excite some lower-energy nuclei into the β-state. The absorption of this radiation leads to excitation at different frequencies, depending on an atom's magnetic environment. In addition, the nuclear magnetic moments of each atom are affected by nearby atoms that also possess magnetic moments. Hence, a compound may contain many nuclei that resonate at different frequencies, producing a complex spectrum.

Real World

Magnetic resonance imaging (MRI) is a noninvasive medical diagnostic tool that uses proton NMR. Multiple cross-sectional scans of the patient's body are taken, and the various chemical shifts of absorbing protons are translated into specific colors. This produces a picture that shows the relative density of specific types of protons; for instance, a dark blue area on the MRI output screen indicates a high concentration of the types of protons giving rise to the range of resonances that correlate to dark blue. Comparison with normal MRI then allows the diagnostician to detect abnormalities in the scanned region.

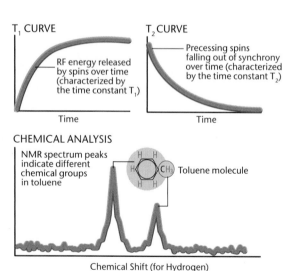

T_1 CURVE — RF energy released by spins over time (characterized by the time constant T_1)

T_2 CURVE — Precessing spins falling out of synchrony over time (characterized by the time constant T_2)

Time

Time

CHEMICAL ANALYSIS

NMR spectrum peaks indicate different chemical groups in toluene

Toluene molecule

Chemical Shift (for Hydrogen)

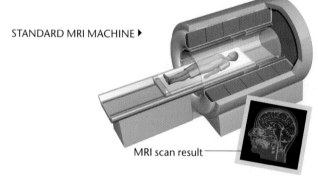

STANDARD MRI MACHINE ▶

MRI scan result

Results ▶

The computer registers the time it takes for each type of spin to release the absorbed radio energy (T_1 graph). The system can also monitor the precessing spins as they fall randomly out of sync (T_2 graph). At the same time, it records the precession frequency of the spins of different chemical groups, which are summarized by a value called the chemical shift. The shift forms the basis of NMR spectra plots that identify constituent chemical groups in a sample, such as those in the hydrocarbon molecule toluene (chemical analysis graph). MRI machines combine all these NMR data to produce views of internal body tissues, including images of the human brain (above right).

Figure 13.3

A typical NMR spectrum is a plot of frequency versus absorption of energy during resonance. Note that frequency decreases from left to right, just as it does for IR spectra. Alternatively, we can plot varying magnetic fields on the x-axis, increasing toward the right. Because different NMR spectrometers operate at different magnetic field strengths, a standardized method of plotting the NMR spectrum has been adopted. This standardized method, which is the only one seen on the MCAT, uses an arbitrary variable, called **chemical shift** (represented by the symbol δ), with units of **parts per million (ppm)** of spectrometer frequency. The chemical shift is plotted on the *x*-axis, and it increases toward the left (referred to as **downfield**). To make sure that we know just how far downfield compounds are, we use a reference peak to mark the location of 0 δ. TMS (tetramethylsilane) is the calibration standard and appears on every spectrum to mark 0 ppm.

Nuclear magnetic resonance is most commonly used to study ^1H nuclei (protons) and ^{13}C nuclei, although any atom possessing a nuclear spin (any nucleus with an odd atomic number or odd mass number) can be studied, such as ^{19}F, ^{17}O, ^5N, and ^{31}P.

^{1}H-NMR

Most ^1H nuclei come into resonance 0 to 10 ppm downfield from TMS. Each distinct set of nuclei gives rise to a separate peak. This means that if multiple nuclei are in relatively identical locations, they will give the same peak. For example, Figure 13.4 depicts the ^1H-NMR of dichloromethyl methyl ether which has two distinct sets of ^1H nuclei. The single proton attached to the dichloromethyl group is in a different magnetic environment from the three protons on the methyl group (which are all magnetically identical), so the two classes will resonate at different frequencies. The three protons on the methyl group are magnetically equivalent because this group rotates freely and, on average, each proton sees an identical environment. As a result, the three protons all resonate at the same frequency. Thus, as we can see in Figure 13.4, the spectrum for dichloromethyl methyl ether will have two separate peaks (the peak on the far right is TMS, not from our compound).

> **Bridge**
>
> Nuclei with odd mass or odd atomic numbers, or both, will have a magnetic moment when placed in a magnetic field. Not all nuclei have magnetic moments (^{12}C, for example).

> **Key Concept**
>
> TMS provides a reference peak. The signal for its H atoms is assigned $\delta = 0$.

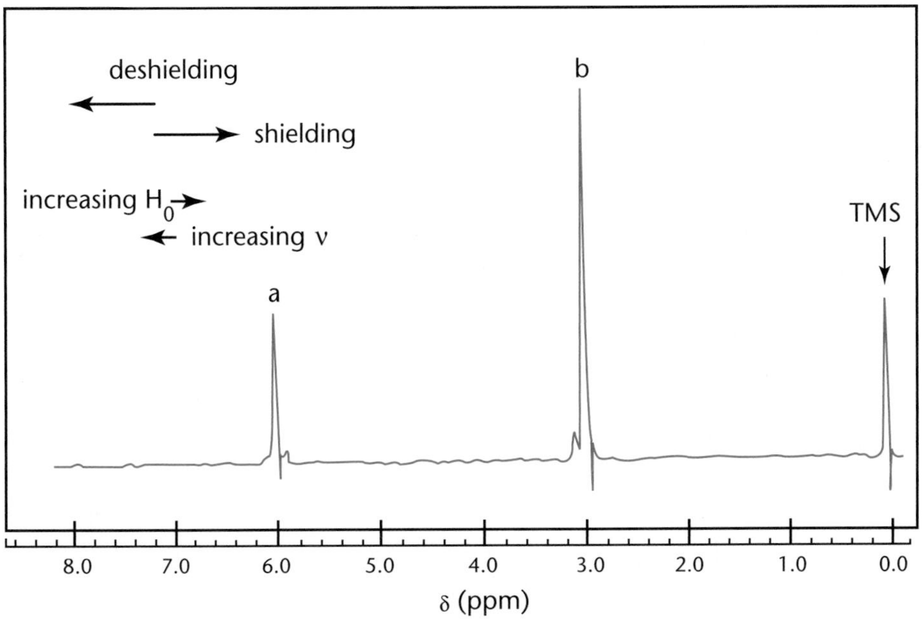

Figure 13.4

Key Concept

- Each resonance, which includes the group of peaks that are part of a multiplet, represents a single proton or a group of equivalent protons. (The number of resonances represents the number of groups of nonequivalent protons.)
- The relative area of each peak reflects the ratio of the protons producing each peak.
- The position of the peak (upfield or downfield) due to shielding or deshielding effects reflects the chemical environment of the protons.

Mnemonic

When dealing with ^{1}H-NMR on the MCAT, think of a proton being surrounded by a shield of electrons. As we add electronegative atoms or have resonance structures that pull electrons away from the proton, we Deshield and move Downfield.

The peak on the left (a) is from the single dichloromethyl proton, and the taller middle peak is from three methyl protons (b). The height difference isn't a coincidence; the taller peak represents the greater number of protons that caused it. Specifically, if we were to analyze the area under the peaks, we would find that the ratio of (b) to (a) is 3:1, corresponding exactly to the number of protons that produced each peak.

Now that we know which peak is which, let's talk about their respective positions on the graph. We can see that the peak for the single proton (a) is fairly far downfield compared with the other protons. This is because it is attached to a carbon with two electronegative groups (chlorine). These atoms pull electron density away from the surrounding atoms, thus **deshielding** the proton from its electron cloud. The more the proton's electron density is pulled away, the less it can shield itself from the applied magnetic field, resulting in a reading further downfield. With this same reasoning, we know that if we had an electron-donating group, such as the silica atom in TMS, it would help **shield** the ^{1}H nucleus and give it a position further upfield. That's why we use TMS as the reference peak, assigned to a value of zero; everything else will be more deshielded than TMS.

Now, let's make it a little more interesting. Consider a compound containing protons that are within three bonds of each other: in other words, a compound in which there are two adjacent atoms (generally C, N, or O) that each have protons attached. When we have two protons in such close proximity to each other, that are *not* magnetically identical, **coupling (splitting)** occurs. Let's use an example to illustrate the concept; see Figure 13.5.

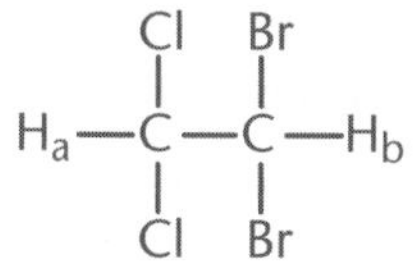

$$H_a - \underset{\underset{Cl}{|}}{\overset{\overset{Cl}{|}}{C}} - \underset{\underset{Br}{|}}{\overset{\overset{Br}{|}}{C}} - H_b$$

Figure 13.5

Notice the two protons, H_a and H_b, on 1,1-dibromo-2,2-dichloroethane. Because of their proximity, the magnetic environment of H_a can be affected by H_b, and vice versa. Thus, at any given time, H_a can experience two different magnetic environments, because H_b can be in either the α- or the β-state. The different states of H_b influence the nucleus of H_a (because the two H atoms are within three bonds of each other), causing slight upfield and downfield shifts. There is approximately a 50 percent chance that H_b will be in one of the two states, so the resulting absorption is a **doublet**, two peaks of identical intensity, equally spaced around the true chemical shift of H_a. H_a and H_b will both appear as doublets, because each one is coupled with one other hydrogen. To determine the number of peaks present (doublet, triplet, etc.), we use the $n + 1$ rule, where n is the number of protons that are three bonds away from our proton of interest. The magnitude of this splitting, measured in Hertz, is called the **coupling constant**, **J**.

Let's try a molecule that has even more coupled protons. In 1,1-dibromo-2-chloroethane (Figure 13.6), the H_a nucleus is affected by two nearby H_b nuclei and, thus, can experience four different states: αα, αβ, βα, or ββ.

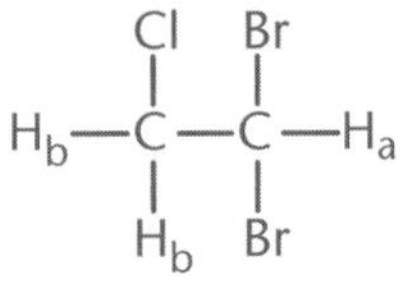

Figure 13.6

Although there are technically four different states, αβ has the same effect as βα (just as 3 × 4 is equal to 4 × 3), so both of these resonances occur at the same frequency. This means we will have three unique frequencies, αα, ββ, and αβ/βα. H_a will appear as three peaks (a **triplet**) centered on the true chemical shift, with an area ratio of 1:2:1.

Table 13.2 shows the area ratios for up to seven adjacent hydrogens, but it isn't necessary to know this table for the MCAT. Just remember that you simply add up the number of coupled hydrogens and add one (for our proton of interest itself) to determine the number of peaks. In addition, peaks that have more than four shifts will sometimes be referred to as a **multiplet**.

Now let's move on to H_b. Because both hydrogens are attached to the same carbon, they will be magnetically identical (this doesn't apply to alkenes, since they can't freely rotate around the double bond). These hydrogens are within three bonds of one other hydrogen, H_a. This means that they will appear as a doublet, but because there are two of them, the peak for H_b will be taller than the peak for H_a.

Table 13.2. Area Ratios for Adjacent Hydrogens

Number of Adjacent Hydrogens	Total Number of Peaks	Area Ratios
0	1	1
1	2	1:1
2	3	1:2:1
3	4	1:3:3:1
4	5	1:4:6:4:1
5	6	1:5:10:10:5:1
6	7	1:6:15:20:15:6:1
7	8	1:7:21:35:35:21:7:1

Table 13.3 indicates the chemical shift ranges of several different types of protons.

Key Concept

The splitting of the peak represents the number of adjacent hydrogens. A peak will be split into $n + 1$ peaks, where n is the number of adjacent hydrogens.

Key Concept

Proton NMR is good for

1. determining the relative number of protons and their relative chemical environments.
2. showing how many adjacent protons there are by splitting patterns.
3. showing certain functional groups.

Table 13.3. Proton Chemical Shift Ranges

Type of Proton	Approximate Chemical Shift δ (ppm) Downfield from TMS
RCH$_3$	0.9
RCH$_2$	1.25
R$_3$CH	1.5
2CH5CH	4.6–6.0
2C;CH	2.0–3.0
Ar2H	6.0–8.5
2CHX	2.0–4.5
2CHOH/2CHOR	3.4–4.0
RCHO	9.0–10.0
RCHCO2	2.0–2.5
2CHCOOH/2CHCOOR	2.0–2.6
2CHOH2CH$_2$OH	1.0–5.5
ArOH	4.0–12.0
2COOH	10.5–12.0
2NH$_2$	1.0–5.0

It would be to your advantage to memorize all of these values, but it's fairly low-yield information. The values that are useful to memorize are the outliers, the incredibly deshielded ones, like the aldehyde at 9 to 10 ppm, and the even more deshielded carboxylic acid between 10.5 and 12 ppm. Another popular peak on the MCAT is the hydrogen of an aromatic ring, which lies between 6.5 and 8.5 ppm. Once again, it's more helpful for you to learn to recognize trends than to memorize numbers. You already understand how electronegativity works, so just apply that concept here. The more electron density that is pulled away from the proton, the more deshielded it will be.

^{13}C-NMR

^{13}C-Nuclear magnetic resonance imaging is similar to ^{1}H-NMR, although there are a few key differences. First and foremost, it appears far less on the MCAT than ^{1}H-NMR, which means our main job is to know how it differs from ^{1}H-NMR. The most obvious difference is that ^{13}C-NMR signals occur 0 to 210 δ downfield from the carbon peak of TMS, quite a bit further than the 0 to 12 δ downfield that we saw with ^{1}H-NMR. We should also note that ^{13}C atoms are rare (although not as rare as the ^{14}C atoms used for carbon dating). In fact, ^{13}C atoms account for only 1.1 percent of all carbon atoms. This has two effects: First, a much larger sample is needed to run a ^{13}C spectrum (about 50 mg compared with 1 mg for ^{1}H-NMR), and second, coupling between carbon atoms is generally not observed (the probability of two ^{13}C atoms being adjacent is 0.011×0.011, or roughly 1 in 1,000).

However, coupling is observed between carbon atoms and the protons that are directly attached to them. This one-bond coupling works analogously to the three-bond coupling we saw in ^{1}H-NMR. For example, if a carbon atom is attached to two protons, it can experience three different states of those protons ($\alpha\alpha$, $\alpha\beta/\beta\alpha$, and $\beta\beta$), and the carbon signal is split into a triplet with the area ratio 1:2:1.

An additional feature of ^{13}C-NMR is the ability to record a spectrum without the coupling of adjacent protons. This is called **spin decoupling**, and it produces a spectrum of singlets, each corresponding to a separate, magnetically equivalent carbon atom. For example, compare the two following spectra of 1,1,2-trichloropropane. One (Figure 13.7) is a typical spin-decoupled spectrum, and the other (Figure 13.8) is spin-coupled. The number of ^{13}C resonances (except for symmetrically disposed atoms) will give us a carbon count in our molecule.

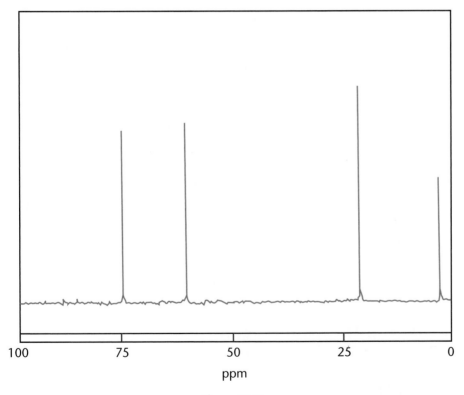

Figure 13.7

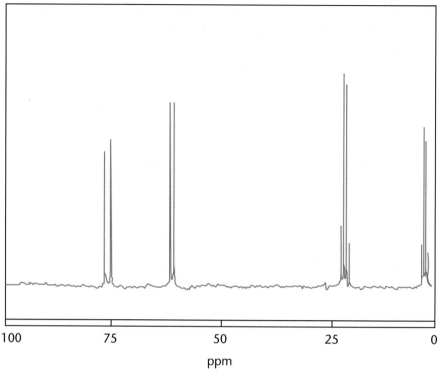

Figure 13.8

In general, we can use NMR spectroscopy to learn about the carbon skeleton of a compound, and we can get hints as to what the functional groups are. Specifically, NMR provides us with the following four types of information:

1. The number of nonequivalent nuclei, determined from the number of peaks

2. The magnetic environment of a nucleus, determined by the chemical shift

3. The relative numbers of nuclei, determined by integrating the peak areas in ^{1}H-NMR

4. The number of neighboring nuclei, determined by the splitting pattern observed (except for ^{13}C in the spin-decoupled mode)

Ultraviolet Spectroscopy ★★☆☆☆

BASIC THEORY

Although you will never have to interpret **ultraviolet (UV) spectroscopy** data on the MCAT, it is fair game to be discussed, so a basic understanding of how it works and when it is used will suffice. Ultraviolet spectra are obtained by passing ultraviolet light through a sample (usually dissolved in an inert, nonabsorbing solvent), and the absorbance is plotted against wavelength. The absorbance is caused by electronic transitions between orbitals. The biggest piece of information we get from

MCAT Expertise

Don't confuse ^{13}C-NMR and ^{1}H-NMR on the MCAT. Just pay attention to the *x*-axis.

MCAT Expertise

UV spectroscopy is most useful for studying compounds containing double bonds, and/or hetero atoms with lone pairs, that create conjugated systems. For the MCAT, that is all you need to know.

this technique is the wavelength of maximum absorbance, which tells us the extent of conjugation within conjugated systems, as well as other structural and compositional information. The take-home point here is that if you see UV spectroscopy on the MCAT, the compound being tested has conjugated bonds. The more conjugated, the lower the energy of the transition.

Mass Spectroscopy

BASIC THEORY

Mass spectrometry differs from most of the other methods we've discussed in this chapter, because it is actually not true spectroscopy (no absorption of electromagnetic radiation is involved) and because it is a destructive technique. Mass spectrometry destroys the compound, so we cannot reuse the sample once the analysis is complete. Most mass spectrometers use a high-speed beam of electrons to ionize the sample (eject an electron), a particle accelerator to put the charged particles in flight, a magnetic field to deflect the accelerated cationic fragments, and a detector that records the number of particles of each mass that exit the deflector area.

The initially formed ion is the molecular radical-cation (M^+), which results from a single electron being removed from a molecule of the sample. This unstable species usually decomposes rapidly into a cationic fragment and a radical fragment. Because there are many molecules in the sample and usually more than one way for the initially formed radical-cation to decompose into fragments, a typical mass spectrum is composed of many lines, each corresponding to a specific mass/charge ratio (m/z). The spectrum itself plots mass/charge on the horizontal axis and relative abundance of the various cationic fragments on the vertical axis (see Figure 13.9).

CHARACTERISTICS

The tallest peak (highest intensity) belongs to the most common ion, called the **base peak**, and is assigned the relative abundance value of 100 percent. The peak with the highest m/z ratio (the peak furthest to the right in Figure 13.9) is generally the **molecular ion peak (parent ion peak)** or simply M^+. Because this is the original compound with one electron missing, we can use it to find the molecular weight. Even further, because it has only lost one electron, the charge value is usually 1; hence, the m/z ratio can usually be read as the mass of the fragment itself.

APPLICATION

Fragmentation patterns can provide information that helps us identify or distinguish certain compounds. In particular, the fragmentation pattern provides clues to the compound's structure by way of molecular mass. For example, whereas IR spectroscopy

> ### MCAT Expertise
>
> Mass spectrometry is low-yield for the MCAT, but knowing that the M^+ (parent ion peak) tells us the molecular weight can be useful.

would be of little use in distinguishing between propionaldehyde and butyraldehyde, a mass spectrum would give us unambiguous data distinguishing the two.

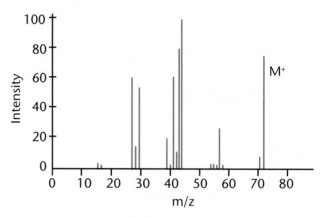

Figure 13.9

Figure 13.9 shows the mass spectrum of butyraldehyde. The peak at m/e = 72 corresponds to the molecular cation-radical M^+; this alone tells us that the compound has a molecular weight of 72 g/mol, meaning it must be butyraldehyde.

Looking further, we can see the base peak at m/e = 44, which corresponds to the cationic fragment resulting from the loss of a fragment weighing 28 g/mol (since $72 - 44 = 28$). Some quick math will show us that this is a C_2H_4 fragment, resulting from one of the most common rearrangements, the McLafferty rearrangement (an example of which is shown in Figure 13.10). Another peak to note is the one at 57 (which corresponds to the loss of a 15 g/mol fragment, a CH_3 radical).

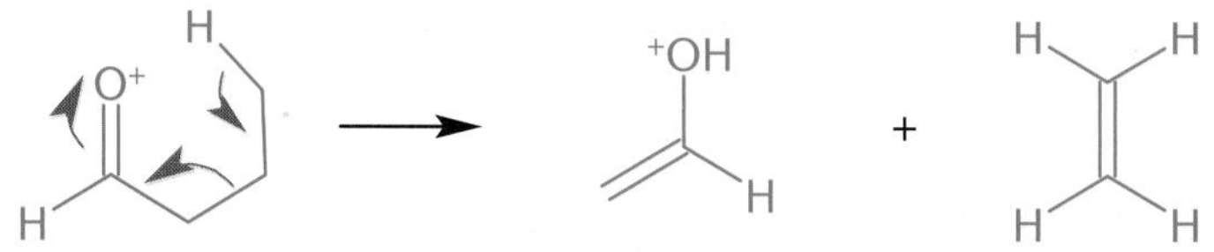

Figure 13.10

Mass spectroscopy is basically a math game, with each peak showing the weight of the molecule with a different fragment missing. Just remember that carbon is 12, hydrogen is +1, and oxygen is 16; then plug in the numbers and see what kinds of groups could have been fragmented off.

Conclusion

This chapter was full of numbers and values, but the most important thing to know about spectroscopy on the MCAT is that you don't need to know a lot of numbers. The numbers that you *do* need to know have already been stressed heavily in this chapter, but as always, your focus should be on the general mechanisms and principles. You should know the properties of molecules that each spectroscopy method exploits, and you should be able to make a rudimentary evaluation of each method's spectroscopic data. Know that IR is best for identifying the presence (or, more important, the absence) of functional groups and that NMR can help you figure out the configuration of these functional groups. Proton NMR will be much more common on the MCAT, but be aware that ^{13}C-NMR exists and that it measures chemical shift on a much higher scale. Know how to interpret the graphs—the chemical shift of deshielded protons will be downfield, or toward the left of the graph. Make sure that you can interpret split peaks (interference from neighboring hydrogens) and peak magnitude (number of magnetically identical hydrogens). A cursory understanding of UV spectroscopy (test for conjugation!) and mass spectroscopy (fragments based on mass) will suffice. In many MCAT passages, you will be given spectroscopic data, even though you will likely be able to solve the problems without even using it. If you *are* knowledgeable about spectroscopy, you'll be able simply to look at the data and circle the answer, saving yourself lots of time, a precious resource on the MCAT. Make sure that you have all the fundamental concepts in Organic Chemistry down first and then start perfecting your analysis of spectroscopic data.

CONCEPTS TO REMEMBER

- ☐ Infrared spectroscopy is used to find functional groups.

- ☐ Carbonyls = sharp peak at 1,700 cm^{-1}.

- ☐ Hydroxides = broad peak at 3,300 cm^{-1}.

- ☐ Amines = sharper peaks at 3,300 and 3,400 cm^{-1} for primary amines; secondary amines have one peak.

- ☐ ^{1}H-NMR is useful to find the structure of a compound and can also reveal the functional groups.

- ☐ ^{1}H-NMR measures how deshielded (how much electron density has been pulled away) protons are on a molecule. $\delta = 0$–12 ppm. The more deshielded the proton is, the further downfield it will be.

- ☐ In ^{1}H-NMR, protons three bonds apart experience coupling. If there is one proton three bonds away, it is a doublet; if there are two, it is a triplet; three, it is a quartet.

- ☐ ^{13}C-NMR is similar to ^{1}H-NMR, but $\delta = 0$–210 ppm.

- ☐ UV spectroscopy is useful for conjugated compounds.

- ☐ Mass spectroscopy can be used to find the mass of the compound and the masses of fragments of the compound.

Carbohydrates (or, as they are known colloquially, carbs) have experienced a tumultuous few decades in American culinary culture. Remember the food pyramid, which advised that we consume 6 to 11 servings of carbohydrates (in the form of bread, cereal, rice, and pasta) per day? Nowadays, we're inundated with no-carb or low-carb diets, but the truth is, carbohydrates still make up most of the food and drinks that fill our refrigerators and cupboards. It's a good thing, too, because carbohydrates are the most direct source of chemical energy for organisms ranging from protozoa to plants to people.

Carbohydrates are compounds that contain carbon, hydrogen, and oxygen in the form of polyhydroxylated aldehydes or ketones with the general formula $C_n(H_2O)_n$ (hence *carbo-hydrate*).

A single carbohydrate unit is called a **monosaccharide** (simple sugar) and, logically, a molecule with two sugars is called a **disaccharide**. **Oligosaccharides** are short carbohydrate chains (*oligos* is Greek for "a few"), whereas **polysaccharides** are long carbohydrate chains.

MCAT Expertise

The MCAT likes to take complicated molecules and test you on the most basic information about them. Therefore, when dealing with carbohydrates on the exam, look for the functional groups we have seen in all of the previous chapters and realize that they will always act the same.

Monosaccharides ★★★★☆

We classify monosaccharides the same way we classify most organic compounds: according to the number of carbons they possess. However, to name monosaccharides, we use the numerical prefix followed by the suffix *–ose* (think gluc*ose*). For example, **trioses**, **tetroses**, **pentoses**, and **hexoses** have three, four, five, and six carbons, respectively. The basic structure of monosaccharides is exemplified by the simplest of them all, glyceraldehyde, shown in Figure 14.1.

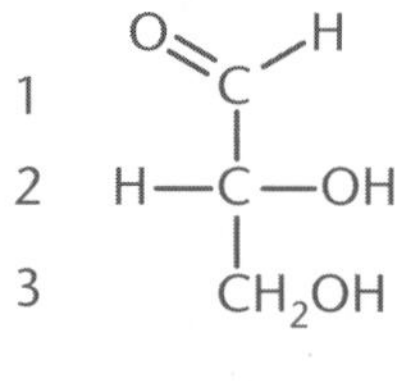

glyceraldehyde

Figure 14.1

Key Concept

Monosaccharides are the simplest units and are classified by the number of carbons.

Glyceraldehyde is a polyhydroxylated aldehyde, also known as an **aldose** (aldehyde sugar). The numbering of the carbon atoms in monosaccharides begins with the carbon closest to the carbonyl group. Thus, with aldoses, the aldehyde will always have the number C–1. Earlier we said that carbohydrates could be polyhydroxylated aldehydes or ketones, so let's go through the simplest ketone sugar, shown in Figure 14.2.

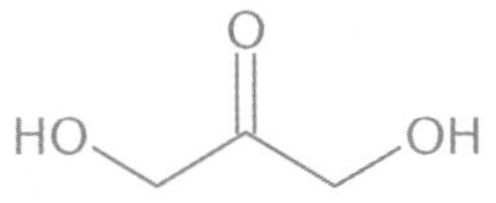

Figure 14.2

The simplest ketone sugar **(ketose)** is dihydroxyacetone. As we just mentioned, the ketone will receive the lowest possible number; in fact, every ketose that we will encounter on the MCAT will have the ketone group on C–2.

Notice that on every monosaccharide, every carbon *other* than the carbonyl will carry a hydroxyl group.

STEREOCHEMISTRY

Let's review the stereochemistry of monosaccharides by using Fischer projections to study the enantiomeric configurations of glyceraldehyde (see Figure 14.3).

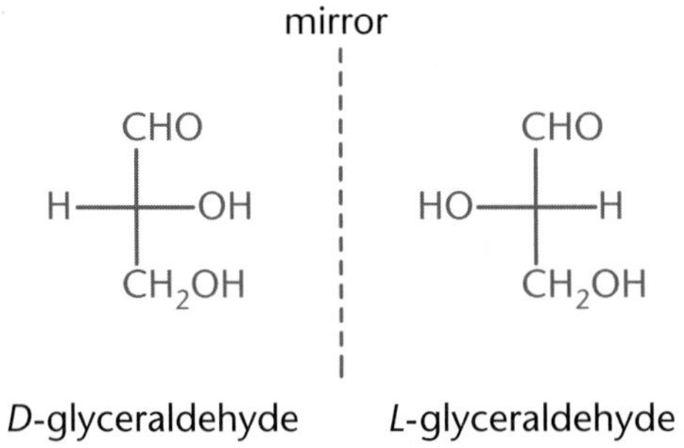

Figure 14.3

Key Concept

D and L are based on the stereochemistry of glyceraldehyde. These are not related to the + and − designations denoting optical rotation.

Early in the 20th century, scientists used glyceraldehyde to learn about the optical rotation of sugars. The results of this early study (which occurred before the *R* and *S* designations were used), led to the designation of **D** and **L** configurations. D-Glyceraldehyde was later determined to exhibit a positive rotation (designated as D-(+)-glyceraldehyde), and L-glyceraldehyde a negative rotation (designated as L-(−)-glyceraldehyde). On the MCAT, all other monosaccharides are assigned the D or L configuration based upon their relationship to glyceraldehyde. Therefore, if a molecule whose highest numbered chiral center (the chiral center farthest from the carbonyl) has the same configuration as D-(+)-glyceraldehyde, it is classified as a D sugar. A molecule that has its highest numbered chiral center in the same configuration as L-(−)-glyceraldehyde is classified as an L sugar. This is illustrated with glucose in Figure 14.4.

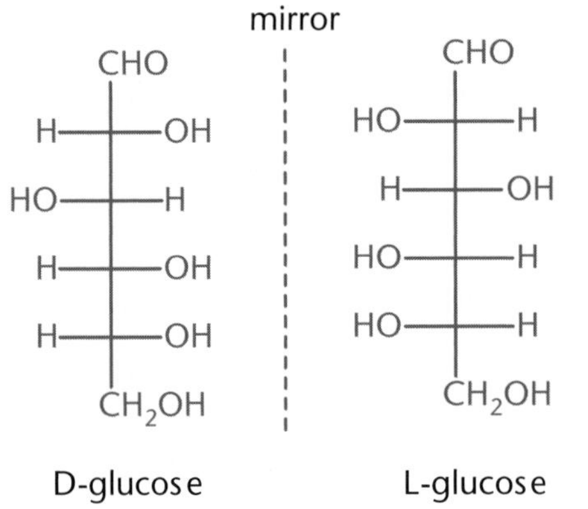

Figure 14.4

This serves as the basis of division for two optical families of sugars, the D family and the L family. All D sugars will have the hydroxide of their highest numbered chiral center on the right, and all L sugars will have that hydroxide on the left. Make sure that you are familiar with these three types of stereoisomers.

1. The same sugars, in different optical families, are enantiomers (such as D-glucose and L-glucose).

2. All nonidentical (nonmirror image) sugars within the same family (as long as both are ketoses/aldoses, and have the same number of carbons) are diastereomers.

3. Diastereomers that only differ at only one chiral center are known as **epimers** (such as D-ribose and D-arabinose, which only differ at C–2; see Figure 14.5).

Mnemonic

In a Fischer projection, if the *Lowest* −OH is on the *Left*, the molecule is *L*. If the −OH is on the *Right*, it's *D* (from the Latin root *dextro*, meaning "right").

Key Concept

Epimers differ in configuration at only one carbon.

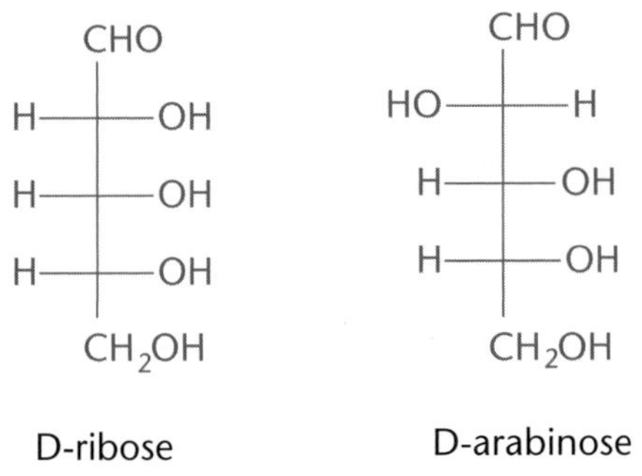

Figure 14.5

Some of the most important monosaccharides that you should memorize for the MCAT are shown in Figure 14.6.

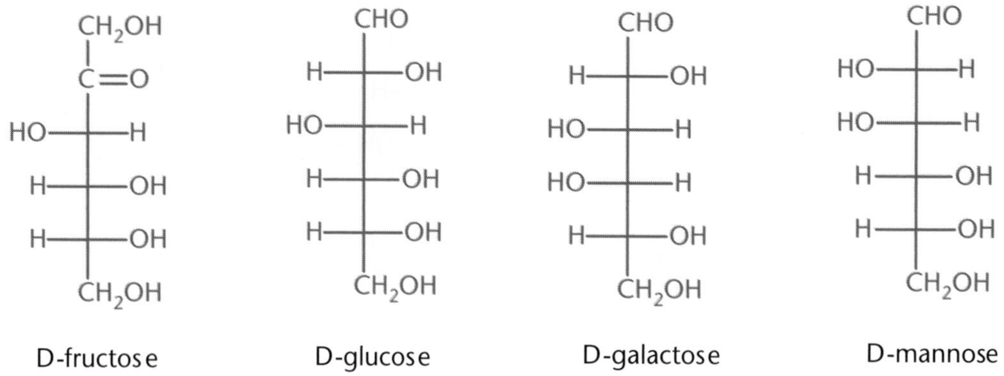

Figure 14.6

Note that in Figure 14.6, fructose is a ketose, whereas glucose, galactose, and mannose are all aldoses.

RING PROPERTIES

Because monosaccharides contain both a hydroxyl group (a nucleophile) and a carbonyl group (an electrophile), they can undergo intramolecular reactions to form cyclic hemiacetal (from aldoses) and hemiketals (from ketoses). Because of ring strain, the only cyclic molecules that are stable in solution are six-membered **pyranose** rings or five-membered **furanose** rings. Note that the hydroxide group is the nucleophile in the ring formation, so oxygen becomes a member of the ring structure.

Like cyclohexane, the pyranose rings adopt a chairlike configuration, and the substituents assume axial or equatorial positions to minimize steric hindrance. When we convert the monosaccharide from its straight-chain Fischer projection to the Haworth projection (shown in Figure 14.7), any group on the right of the Fischer projection will point down, and any group on the left side of the Fischer projection will point up. The reaction scheme in Figure 14.7 depicts the formation of a cyclic hemiacetal from D-glucose.

Key Concept

Note that the carbonyl carbon is (as always) a good electrophile and the many –OH groups can act as nucleophiles. What do you think will happen when these two groups are handcuffed together in the same molecule? Well, of course, an intramolecular nucleophilic acyl substitution!

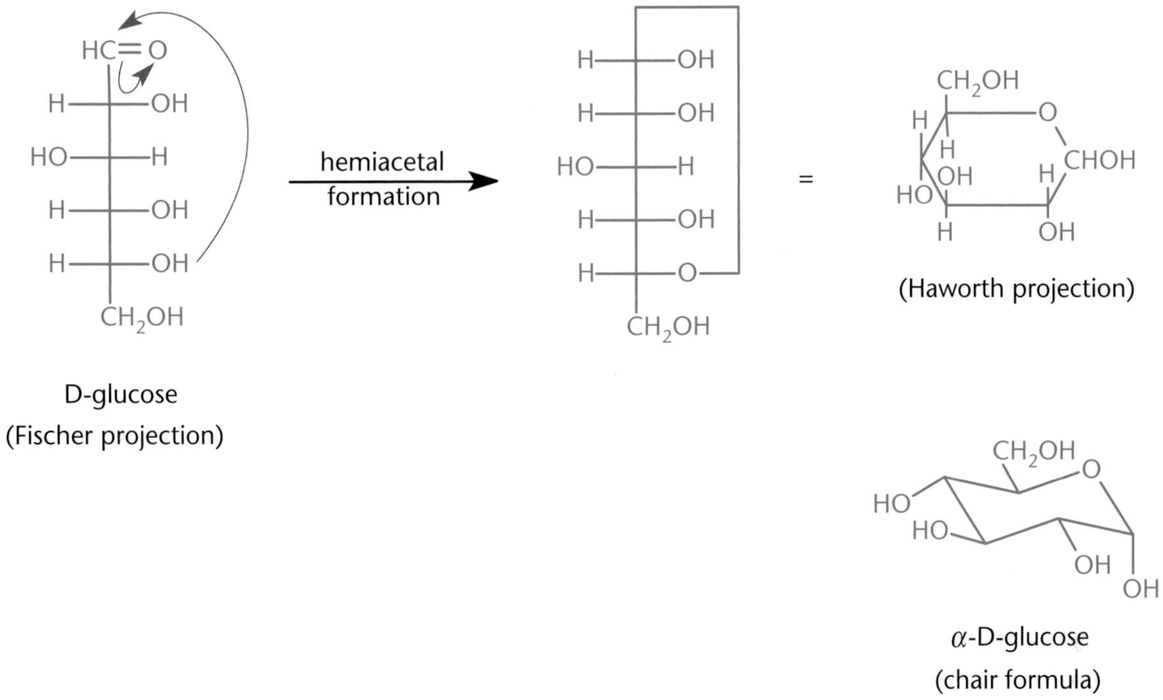

D-glucose
(Fischer projection)

(Haworth projection)

α-D-glucose
(chair formula)

Figure 14.7

Because the oxygen of the hydroxide on the highest-numbered chiral group (the same one that determines whether it is D or L) functions as the nucleophile in ring formation, six-membered rings are formed from six carbon aldoses or seven carbon ketoses. Alternatively, five-membered rings are formed from five carbon aldoses or six carbon ketoses.

When we convert a straight-chain monosaccharide into its cyclic form, the carbonyl carbon (C–1 for glucose) becomes chiral. Cyclic stereoisomers that differ about the new chiral carbon are known as **anomers**. In fact, the carbon that becomes chiral is named for this characteristic, labeled the **anomeric carbon**. When a sugar is drawn in ring form, it is easy to identify the anomeric carbon: Simply find the carbon that is attached to both the oxygen in the ring and a hydroxide group. In glucose, the **alpha** (α) anomer has the –OH group of C–1 *trans* to the CH$_2$OH substituent (pointing down), whereas the **beta** (β) anomer has the –OH group of C–1 *cis* to the CH$_2$OH substituent (pointing up).

When we expose hemiacetal rings to water (see Figure 14.8), they will spontaneously open and re-form. Because the substituents on the single bond between C–1 and C–2 can rotate freely, either the α or β anomer can be formed. This spontaneous change of configuration about C–1 is known as **mutarotation**, and it occurs more rapidly when we catalyze it with an acid or base. Mutarotation results in a mixture that contains both anomers at their equilibrium concentrations (for glucose: 36% α, 64% β).

Key Concept

Anomers differ in configuration only at the newly formed chiral center, which is created by the attack of the alcohol on two different sides of the planar carbonyl carbon. α = *trans* to the –CH$_2$OH (down in glucose). β = *cis* to the –CH$_2$OH (up in glucose).

MCAT Expertise

Here is a clarification of often confusing terms:

Anomerization—the forming of one anomer or another from the straight-chain sugar

Mutarotation—the process of one anomer changing into the other anomer by opening and reclosing

The α configuration is less favored because the hydroxyl group of the anomeric carbon is axial, adding to the steric strain of the molecule.

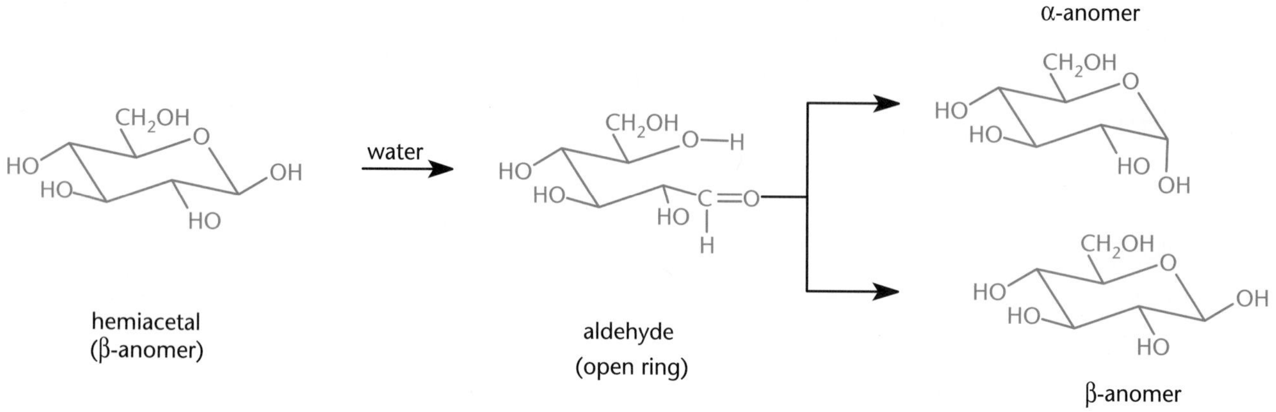

Figure 14.8

MONOSACCHARIDE REACTIONS

Ester Formation

The MCAT test makers love to test on compounds such as monosaccharides, because even though they look confusing at first, their component parts still react the same as they would in a smaller molecule. Because monosaccharides contain hydroxyl groups, they undergo many of the same reactions as simple alcohols. Specifically, we can convert monosaccharides to esters, using acid anhydride and a base. In this reaction, all of the hydroxyl groups will be esterified. The reaction in Figure 14.9 is an example of glucose esterification.

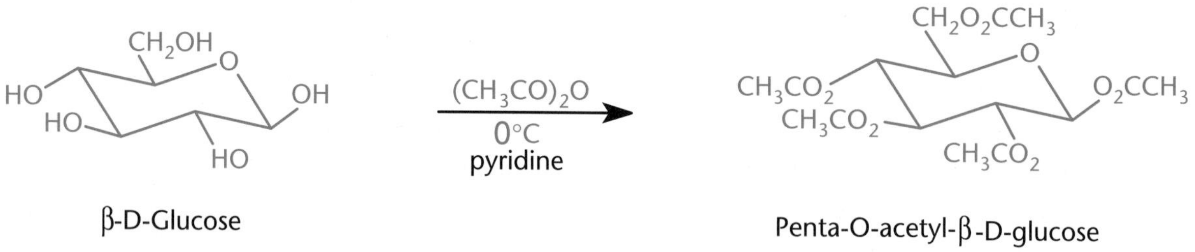

> **Key Concept**
>
> Reaction types are determined by the functional groups present. Think of alcohols and carbonyls.

Figure 14.9

Oxidation of Monosaccharides

As monosaccharides switch between anomeric configurations, the hemiacetal rings spend a short period of time in the open-chain aldehyde form. Just like other aldehydes, they can be oxidized to carboxylic acids; these oxidized aldoses are called **aldonic acids**. Because aldoses can be oxidized, they are considered reducing agents. Therefore, any monosaccharide with a hemiacetal ring (–OH on C–1) is considered a **reducing sugar**. Both Tollens's reagent and Benedict's reagent can be used to detect the presence of reducing sugars. A positive Tollens's test involves the reduction of Ag^+ to form metallic silver. When Benedict's reagent is used, a red precipitate of Cu_2O indicates the presence of a reducing sugar (see Figure 14.10).

An interesting phenomenon to be aware of is that ketose sugars are also reducing sugars and give positive Tollens's and Benedict's tests. Although ketones cannot be oxidized to carboxylic acids, they can isomerize to aldoses via keto-enol shifts. While in the aldose form, they can react with Tollens's or Benedict's reagents to form the carboxylic acid. A more powerful oxidizing agent, such as dilute nitric acid will oxidize both the aldehyde and the primary alcohol (C–6) to carboxylic acids.

> **Real World**
>
> Benedict's test can be used to detect glucose in the urine of diabetics.

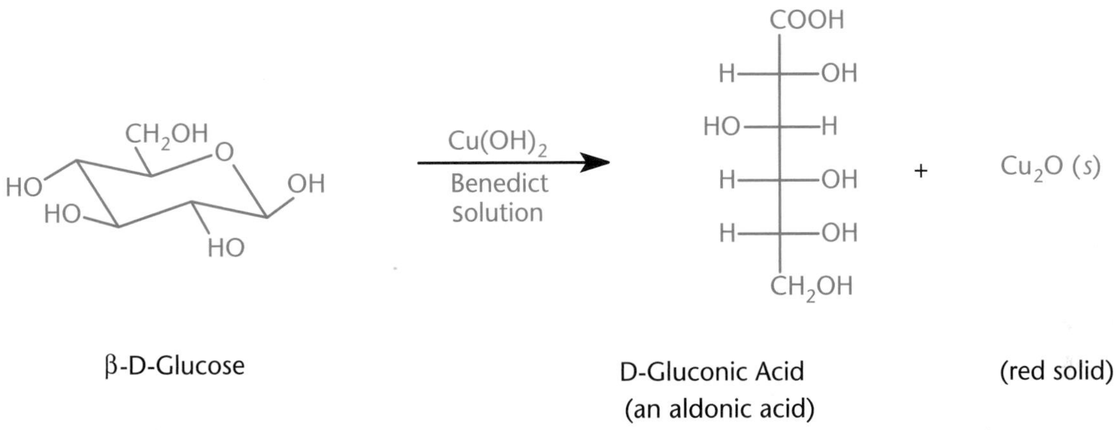

β-D-Glucose   D-Gluconic Acid   (red solid)
(an aldonic acid)

Figure 14.10

Glycosidic Reactions

As we remember from Chapter 8, hemiacetals will react with alcohol to form acetals. True to form, hemiacetal monosaccharides will react with alcohol under acidic conditions. The anomeric hydroxyl group is transformed into an alkoxy group, yielding a mixture of the α- and β-acetals (with water as a leaving group). The resulting C–O bond is called a **glycosidic linkage**, and the acetal is known as a **glycoside**. An example is the reaction of glucose with ethanol shown in Figure 14.11.

> **Key Concept**
>
> This reaction is not new to us, either; it is really just a dressed-up S_N2 reaction with the sugar acting as the nucleophile.

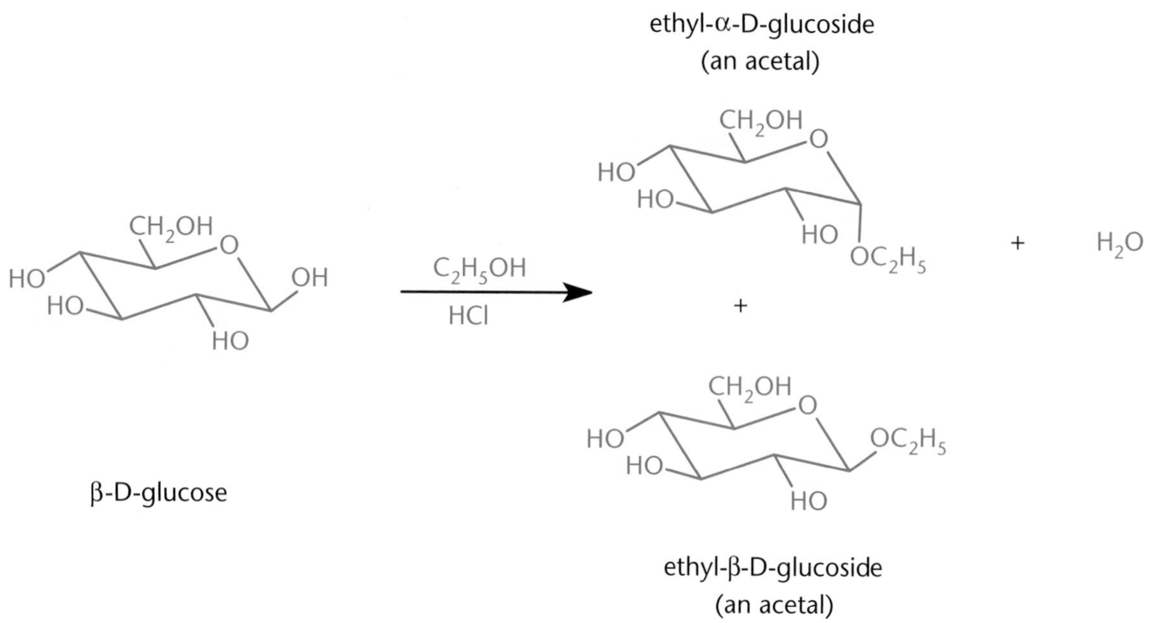

ethyl-α-D-glucoside
(an acetal)

β-D-glucose

C_2H_5OH

HCl

+ H_2O

+

ethyl-β-D-glucoside
(an acetal)

Figure 14.11

Disaccharides

★★★★☆☆

As discussed previously, a monosaccharide may react with alcohols to give acetals. Notice that monosaccharides also have hydroxide groups, so they, too, can function as the alcohol in reactions with other monosaccharides. When two monosaccharides react in this way, the product is called a **disaccharide**. The formation of a disaccharide is shown in Figure 14.12.

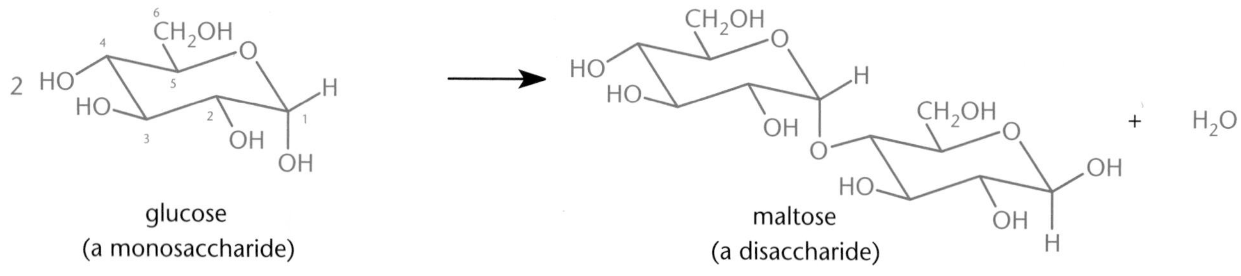

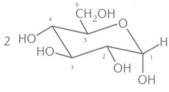

2

glucose
(a monosaccharide)

maltose
(a disaccharide)

+ H_2O

Figure 14.12

The most common glycosidic linkage occurs between C–1 of the first sugar and C–4 of the second, designated as a 1,4′ linkage; it is the one you will most likely see on the MCAT. 1,6′ and 1,2′ bonds are also observed. The glycosidic bonds may be either α or β, depending on the orientation of the hydroxyl group on the anomeric carbon. In Figure 14.13, the product has a 1,4′-α linkage (maltose). Two glucose monosaccharides joined by a 1,4′-β linkage yield cellobiose.

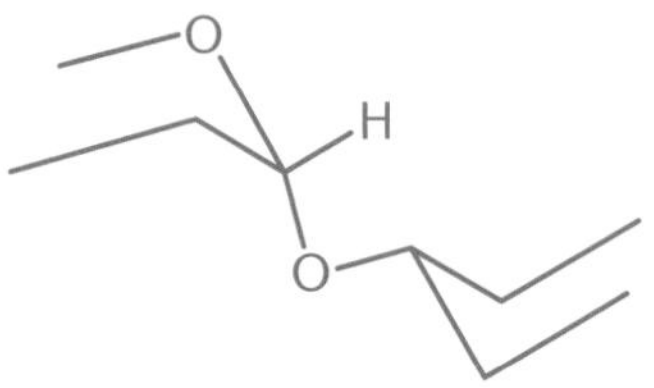

α-glycosidic linkage β-glycosidic linkage

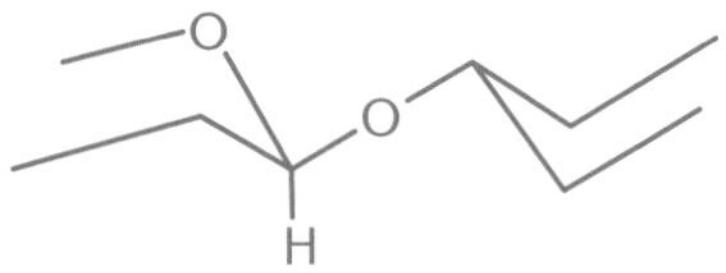

Figure 14.13

Real World

In lactose intolerance, a person is missing the enzyme lactase, which breaks the disaccharide lactose into glucose and galactose molecules.

Glycosidic linkages are often cleaved in the presence of aqueous acid. For example, we can cleave the glycosidic linkage of the disaccharide maltose into two molecules of glucose.

Polysaccharides   ★★★★☆☆

Polysaccharides are large chains of monosaccharides linked together by glycosidic bonds. The three most important biological polysaccharides are cellulose, starch, and glycogen. Although these three polysaccharides have different functions, they are all composed of the same monosaccharide, D-glucose. In cellulose, the chain of glucose molecules is linked by 1,4'-β-glycosidic bonds. Cellulose is the structural component of plants and is not digestible (think fiber), at least by humans. Cows on the other hand, can't get enough of the stuff. Starch is a polysaccharide that is more digestible by humans. Plants store energy as starch molecules by linking glucose molecules primarily in 1,4'-α-glycosidic bonds, although occasional 1,6'-α-glycosidic bonds form branches off the chain. Animals, on the other hand, store their excess glucose as glycogen. Glycogen is similar to starch, except that it has more 1,6'-α-glycosidic bonds (approximately 1 for every 12 glucose molecules), which makes it a highly branched compound (dendrimer). All three polysaccharides are composed of glucose subunits, but they differ in their configuration about the anomeric carbon and the position of glycosidic bonds, resulting in notable biological differences (see Figure 14.14).

Bridge

Key biological polysaccharides are cellulose (1,4'-β), starch, and glycogen (mostly 1,4'-α, although some are 1,6'-α).

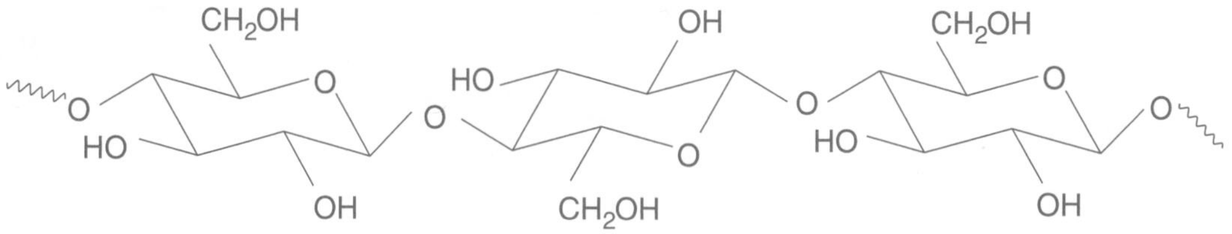

cellulose, a 1,4′-β-D-glucose polymer

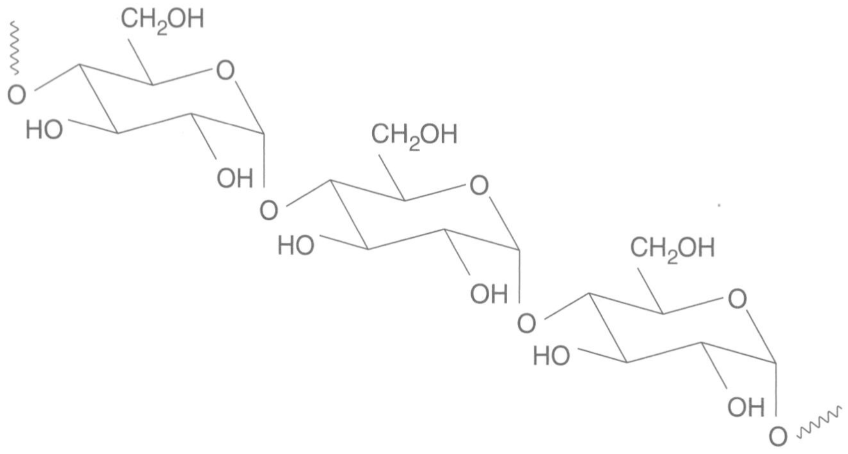

starch, a 1,4′-α-D-glucose polymer

Figure 14.14

Conclusion

This chapter was an introduction to the world of macromolecules, and as such, we began with the smallest of them all, simple carbohydrates. Although macromolecules are likely to appear on the MCAT, it's important to realize that no matter how big the molecule is, it will still follow the same rules that govern the smallest of molecules. In all of Organic Chemistry, our focus should be on nucleophiles and electrophiles. The only difference with macromolecules is that the nucleophile and electrophile may be on the same molecule. Keep this in mind, because things are going to get much bigger as we enter the last chapter of this text and begin our discussion of the nitrogen-containing macromolecules: proteins.

CONCEPTS TO REMEMBER

☐ Carbohydrates have the general formula $C_n(H_2O)_n$.

☐ Aldoses are sugars with aldehydes at the C–1 position; ketoses are sugars with ketones at the C–2 position.

☐ L-sugars have the highest-numbered chiral hydroxyl group on the left side of the sugar; D-sugars have the highest-numbered chiral hydroxyl group on the right (in a Fischer projection).

☐ D-glucose and L-glucose are enantiomers (nonsuperimposable mirror images).

☐ Any sugars that differ at only one chiral center are known as epimers.

☐ Sugars can undergo intramolecular reactions that form rings. Pyranose rings are six-membered sugar rings; furanose rings are five-membered rings.

☐ C–1 becomes chiral when a ring is formed; this newly chiral atom is known as the anomeric carbon. For glucose, the anomeric carbon can either be α (down) or β (up).

☐ Changing back and forth between the α and β position is known as mutarotation.

☐ The key reactions of monosaccharides are ester formation, oxidation, and glycosidic reactions.

☐ Polysaccharides: Cellulose is a chain of glucose with 1,4′-β-glycosidic bonds; starch and glycogen are mostly 1,4′-α-glycosidic bonds (with some 1,6′-β-glycosidic bonds that form branches off the chain).

Practice Questions

1. When glucose is in a straight-chain formation, it

   A. is an aldoketose.
   B. is a pentose.
   C. has five chiral carbons.
   D. is 1 of 16 stereoisomers.

2. All of the following are true of epimers EXCEPT

   A. they differ in configuration about only one carbon.
   B. they usually have slightly different chemical and physical properties.
   C. they are diastereomers (with the exception of glyceraldehyde).
   D. they always have equal but opposite optical activities.

3.

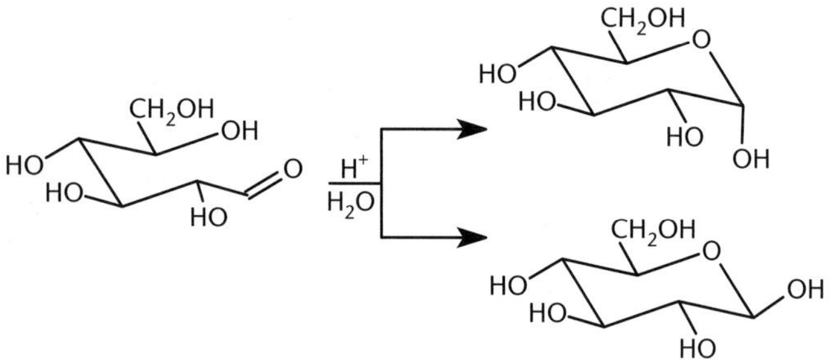

   The above reaction is an example of one step in

   A. aldehyde formation.
   B. hemiketal formation.
   C. mutarotation.
   D. glycosidic bond cleavage.

4. What is the product of the following reaction?

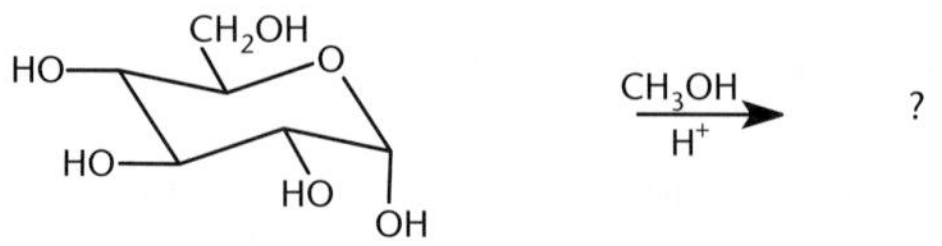

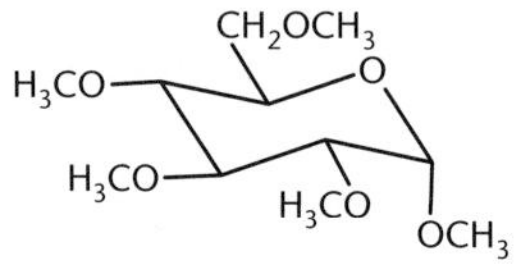

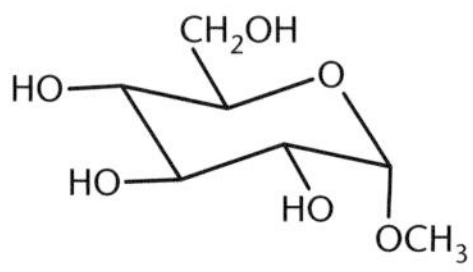

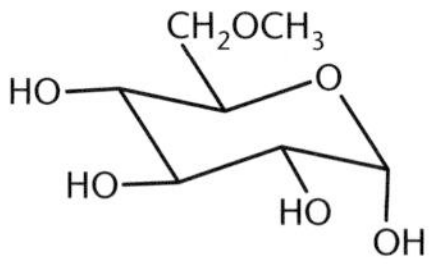

5. Which of the following compounds is not a monosaccharide?

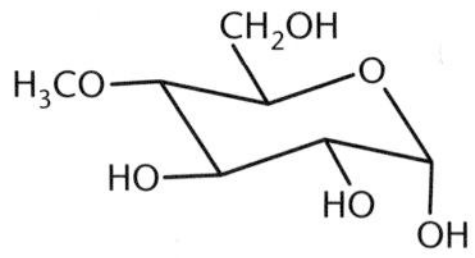

   A. Deoxyribose
   B. Fructose
   C. Glucose
   D. Maltose

6. The cyclic forms of monosaccharides are

   I. Hemiacetals
   II. Hemiketals
   III. Acetals

   A. I only
   B. III only
   C. I and II only
   D. I, II, and III

7. When the following straight-chain Fischer projection is converted to a chair or ring conformation, what will be its structure?

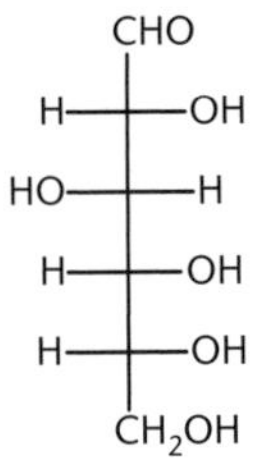

CHO
H——OH
HO——H
H——OH
H——OH
CH₂OH

A.

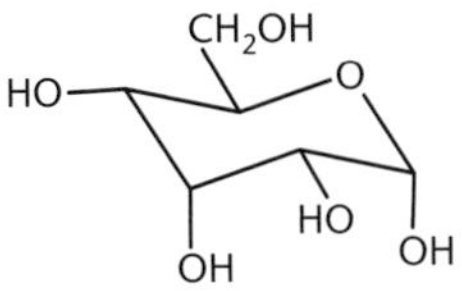

B.

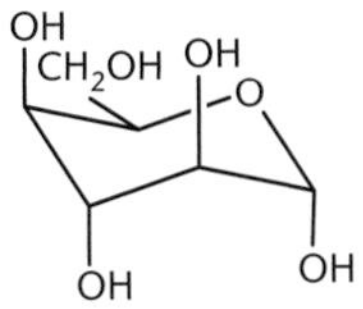

C.

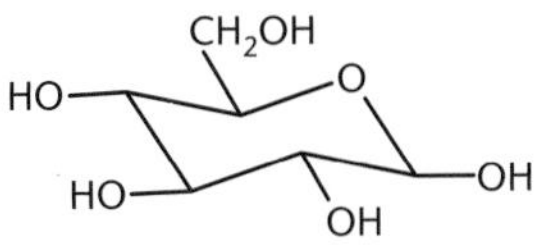

D.

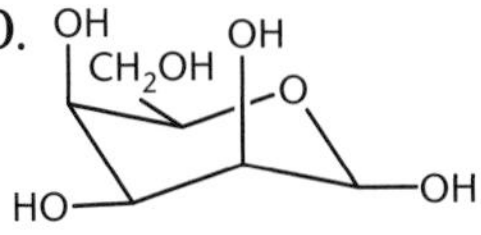

8. What would be the product of the following reaction?

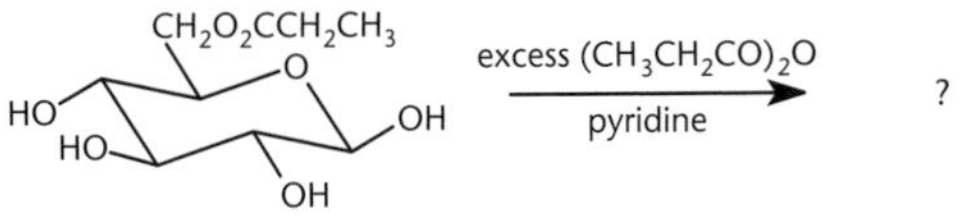

excess $(CH_3CH_2CO)_2O$
pyridine
?

A.

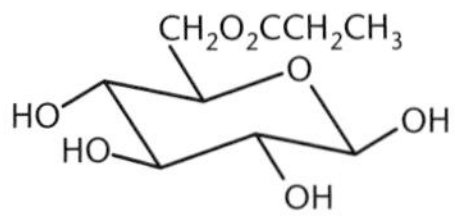

B.

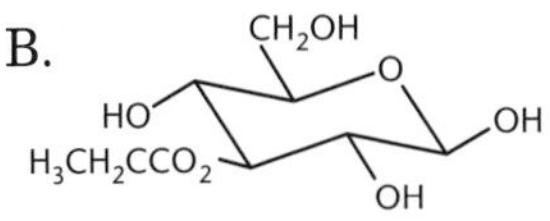

C.

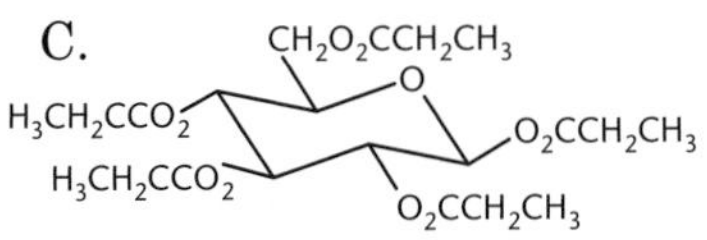

D.

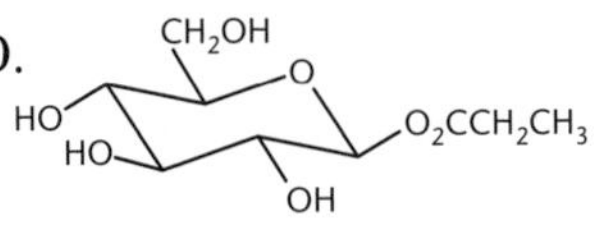

9. Which of the following are reducing sugars?

A. Fructose
B. Galactose
C. Glucose
D. All of the above

10. What description best fits the pair of sugars shown below?

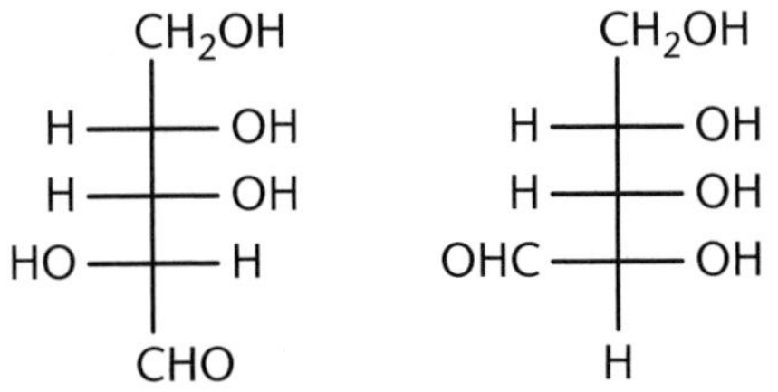

CH₂OH
H——OH
H——OH
HO——H
CHO

CH₂OH
H——OH
H——OH
OHC——OH
H

A. They are enantiomers.
B. They are diastereomers.
C. They are meso compounds.
D. They are identical.

11. Galactose is the C–4 epimer of glucose. Which structure below is galactose?

A.
CHO
H——OH
HO——H
HO——H
H——OH
CH₂OH

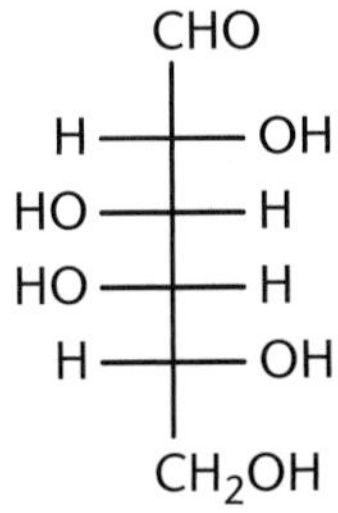

B.
CHO
H——OH
H——OH
H——OH
H——OH
CH₂OH

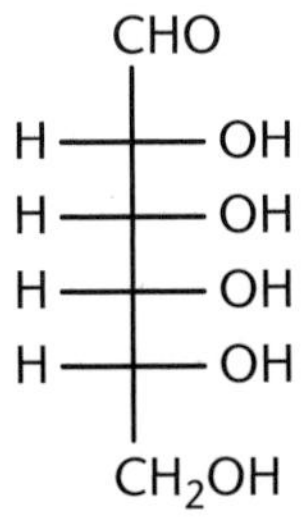

C.
CHO
HO——H
HO——H
H——OH
H——OH
CH₂OH

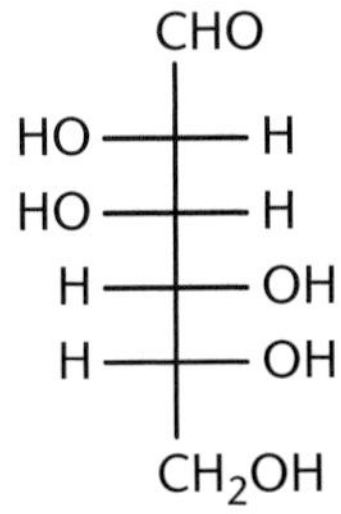

D.
CHO
H——OH
HO——H
H——OH
HO——H
CH₂OH

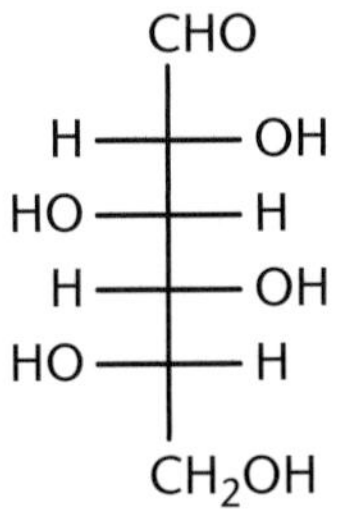

12. Under strongly acidic conditions, aldoses become oxidized to dicarboxylic acids called *aldaric acids*. An unknown pentose X, which is optically active, produces an optically inactive aldaric acid upon treatment with HNO_3. What is the structure of pentose X?

A.
```
        CHO
   H ——— OH
  HO ——— H
  HO ——— H
       CH₂OH
```

B.
```
        CHO
  HO ——— H
  HO ——— H
   H ——— OH
       CH₂OH
```

C.
```
       CH₂OH
  HO ——— H
  HO ——— H
   H ——— OH
        CHO
```

D.
```
        CHO
   H ——— OH
   H ——— OH
   H ——— OH
       CH₂OH
```

Small Group Questions

1. How many possible aldotetroses are there?

2. How do you convert from a Fischer projection to a chair conformation?

Explanations to Practice Questions

1. D

Glucose is an aldohexose, meaning that it has one aldehyde group and six carbons. Given this information, choices (A) and (B) can be eliminated. In aldose sugars, each nonterminal carbon is chiral. Therefore, glucose has four chiral centers, not five (C). The number of stereoisomers possible for a chiral molecule is 2^n, where n is the number of chiral carbons. Because glucose has four chiral centers, there are $2^4 = 16$ stereoisomers possible. Thus, choice (D) is correct.

2. D

Epimers are monosaccharide diastereomers that differ in their configuration about only one carbon (A). As with all diastereomers (C), epimers have different chemical and physical properties (B), and their optical activities have no relation to each other. Enantiomers have equal but opposite optical activities. Therefore, choice (D) is the only statement that does not apply to epimers.

3. C

In solution, the hemiacetal ring of glucose will break open spontaneously and then re-form. When the ring is broken, bond rotation occurs between C–1 and C–2 to produce either the α- or the β-anomer. The reaction given in this question depicts the mutarotation of glucose, corresponding to (C). Choice (A) is incorrect because the reactant is an aldehyde, not the product. Choice (B) is incorrect because a hemiketal has an –OH group and an –OR group. In addition, hemiketals are formed from ketones, and our starting product is an aldehyde. Finally, choice (D) is incorrect because there is no glycosidic bond in the starting product.

4. B

When glucose is reacted with ethanol under acid catalysis, the hemiacetal is converted to an acetal via replacement of the anomeric hydroxyl group with an alkoxy group. The result is a type of acetal known as a glycoside. This corresponds with choice (B). (A) is incorrect because the –OH on the C–6 carbon would not be converted to $-OCH_3$.

5. D

Maltose is a disaccharide made of two glucoses, making choice (D) the correct answer. All the other choices are monosaccharides.

6. C

Monosaccharides can exist as hemiacetals (I) or hemiketals (II), depending on whether they are aldoses (monosaccharides that contain an aldehyde functionality in their open-chain forms) or ketoses (monosaccharides that contain a ketone functionality in their open-chain forms). When a monosaccharide is in its cyclic form, the anomeric carbon is attached to the oxygen in the ring (which constitutes the acetal or ketal group) and is also attached to a hydroxyl functionality (hence, it is only a hemiacetal or hemiketal, since a full acetal or ketal would involve the conversion of this functionality to an alkoxy group). Therefore, choices I and II are true, making choice (C) the correct response.

7. C

Start by drawing out the Haworth projection. Recall that all the groups on the right in the Fischer projection will go on the bottom of the Haworth projection, and all the groups on the left will go on the top. Next, draw the chair structure, with the oxygen in the back right vertex. Label the carbons in the ring, 1 through 5, moving clockwise around the ring from the oxygen. Now, draw in the lines for all the axial substituents, alternating above and below the ring. Remember to start on the anomeric C–1 carbon, where the axial substituent points down. Now start filling in the substituents. The substituent can be in either position on the anomeric carbon, so skip that one for now. Look back to C–2 on the Haworth; the –OH is below the ring. That means that we'll put it in the equatorial position on the ring, because the axial position is pointing up. The –OH on C–3 is above the ring in the Haworth, so it should also go in the equatorial position on the ring, because the axial position points down. The –OH on C–4 is below the ring in the Haworth and will also end up in the equatorial position on the ring, because the axial position points up. Finally, the –CH$_2$OH group is above the ring in the Haworth, so it will go in the equatorial position in the ring (as the axial position points down). The only possible answer choice, therefore, is (C), which represents the β-anomer.

8. C

Glucose, because it has hydroxyl groups, can react like any alcohol and be converted to an ester. Therefore, the reaction of glucose with an anhydride in the presence of base, shown in this question, creates an ester group at each hydroxyl position. Choice (C) is the only answer that shows every hydroxyl group esterified.

9. D

All aldose sugars are considered reducing sugars, since they are easily oxidized to carboxylic acids by such reagents as Tollens's and Benedict's solutions. Galactose (B) and glucose (C) are aldoses; thus, they are reducing sugars. Although fructose (A) is not an aldose, it can be oxidized because it can isomerize to an aldose via a few keto-enol shifts in a basic solution. Therefore, all three monosaccharides are reducing sugars, and choice (D) is correct.

10. D

The easiest way to answer this question is to determine the stereochemistry of C–2 (counting from the aldehyde), which for both sugars is R. Since the other chiral carbons for both sugars are the same, they are identical; (A) and (B) are incorrect. (C) is incorrect because there is no internal plane of symmetry.

11. A

Galactose is a diastereomer of glucose, with the stereochemistry at C–4 (counting from the aldehyde) reversed. Being able to identify C–4 is enough to answer this question, even if you do not remember what glucose looks like. Since (B), (C), and (D) have identical stereochemistry at C–4, they are incorrect.

12. D

To answer this question, replace the ends of each sugar with carboxylic acids and then find the *meso* sugar. (B) is incorrect, since the aldaric acid remains optically active (no internal mirror plane), while (A) and (C) are identical (one is the 180° flip of the other.)

Amino Acids, Peptides, and Proteins

Congratulations! Welcome to the last chapter of this book, in which everything we've learned so far is put together. This chapter continues our discussion of macromolecules, although we will make things a bit more complicated than the carbohydrates in the previous chapter. Not only will, we be discussing C, O, and H, we will throw N into the mix as well via the building blocks of proteins, amino acids. To really understand amino acids, we need to know all about nucleophilicity, electrophilicity, acidity, basicity, resonance, intermolecular forces—basically the trends that we've discussed throughout this book. This extra complexity isn't surprising, because proteins have many more functions in our bodies than petroleum has uses in our commercial world. Proteins do everything from providing structure (keratin) to communicating signals (peptide hormones) to catalyzing reactions (enzymes). Proteins are the largest compounds that you will need to know for Organic Chemistry on Test Day, but they will still behave in the same way as other compounds containing the same functional groups. Go in with confidence; you already know how all these molecules work.

MCAT Expertise

Many of the Organic Chemistry topics we have already encountered can be tested with amino acids and proteins: carboxylic acid derivatives (peptide bond = amide linkage), hydrogen bonding, electrophoresis, stereochemistry, and acid-base properties. Expect to be tested on the basics, even when dealing with more complicated molecules.

Amino Acids ★★★★☆☆

Amino acids contain an amine group and a carboxyl group attached to a single carbon atom (the α-carbon). The other two substituents of the α-carbon are a hydrogen atom and a variable side chain referred to as the **R-group**. It is helpful to think of the α-carbon as the central atom of the amino acid, because it is the atom that has all of the different functional groups attached to it (see Figure 15.1).

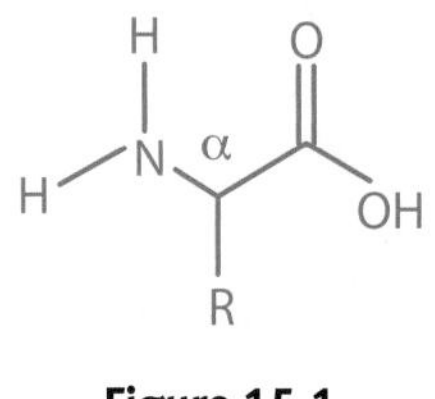

Figure 15.1

The α-carbon, with its four different groups, is a chiral (stereogenic) center (except in **glycine**, the simplest amino acid, where R = H and it only has three different groups attached to it), so all amino acids (except for glycine) are optically active. Naturally occurring amino acids (of which there are 20) are all L-enantiomers (as discussed in Chapters 2 and 14). Therefore, by convention, the Fischer projection for an amino acid is drawn with the amino group on the left (L = left). L-Amino acids have *S* configurations, except for cysteine, which is *R* because of the change in priority caused by the sulfur.

Key Concept

With the exception of glycine, all amino acids are chiral.

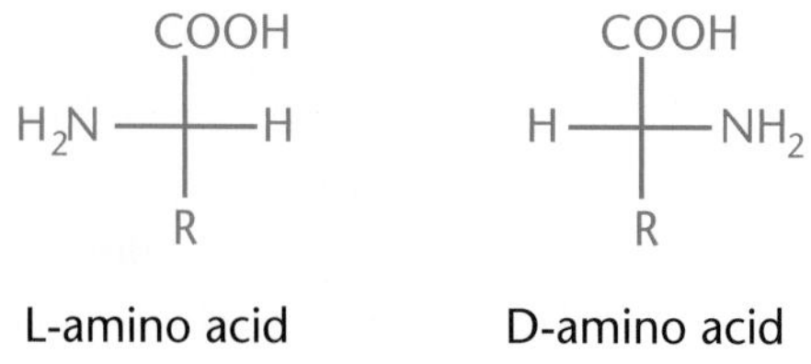

L-amino acid   D-amino acid

Figure 15.2

ACID-BASE CHARACTERISTICS

Acid-base chemistry just doesn't get any more interesting than amino acids, because they have both a basic amino group *and* an acidic carboxyl group. Species that can act as both acids and bases are described as **amphoteric** (water is also an amphoteric species). You can think of amino acids as double agents: They can play either role, depending on the terms and conditions. Whereas double agents will switch sides for money or protection, amino acids function as either acids or bases depending on the pH of their environment. This means that if there are lots of protons in solution (acidic, low pH), the amino acid will pick up a proton, thus functioning as a base. On the other hand, if there are few protons in solution (basic, high pH), the amino acid will donate a proton, thus functioning as an acid. Remember that science is all about equilibrium; if conditions go too extreme in one direction, something will occur to try to bring the system back to normal. Amino acids are a great example of this, and whether they are put into a highly acidic or highly basic environment, they will function to bring the system back toward neutral.

Now that we've discussed the theory behind amino acids, let get into how we are likely to see them on Test Day. Recall from previous chapters that amino groups take on positive charges when protonated and carboxyl groups take on negative charges when deprotonated. This means that when an amino acid is put into solution, as shown in Figure 15.3, it will take on both of these charges, forming a dipolar ion, or **zwitterion** (from German *zwitter*, or "hybrid"). The two oppositely charged halves of the molecule neutralize each other, so at a neutral pH, amino acids exist in the form of internal salts.

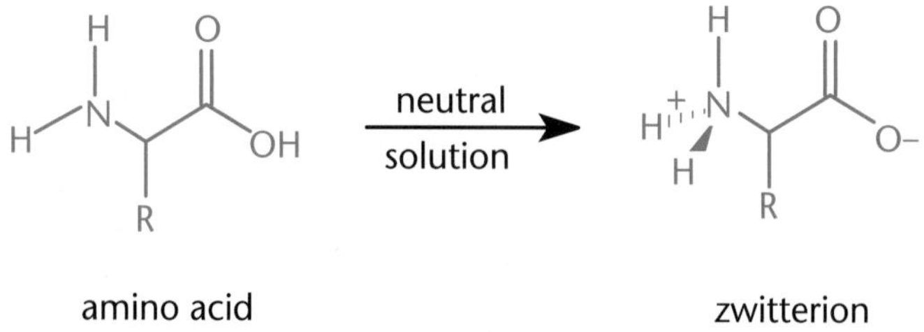

amino acid   zwitterion

Figure 15.3

Because there are two different locations that can either be protonated or deprotonated, amino acids have at least two different dissociation constants, K_{a1} and K_{a2} relative to the pH, or K_{b1} and K_{b2} relative to the pOH.

If we put a neutral amino acid into an acidic solution, as shown in Figure 15.4, it will become fully protonated. The amino group is protonated fairly easily (because it is protonated even at neutral pH), but it takes a fairly acidic environment to protonate the carboxyl group.

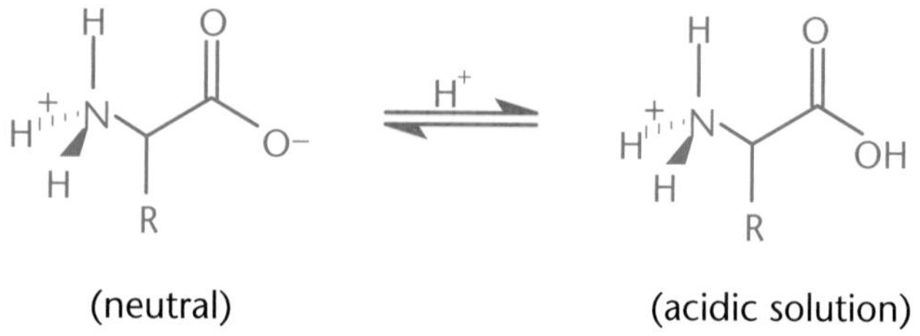

(neutral)   (acidic solution)

Figure 15.4

If we were to take a neutral amino acid and drop it into a basic solution, as shown in Figure 15.5, the opposite would occur, and the amino acid would become fully deprotonated. Here, the carboxyl group is easy to deprotonate (because it is deprotonated even at neutral pH), but it takes a more alkaline environment to deprotonate the amino group.

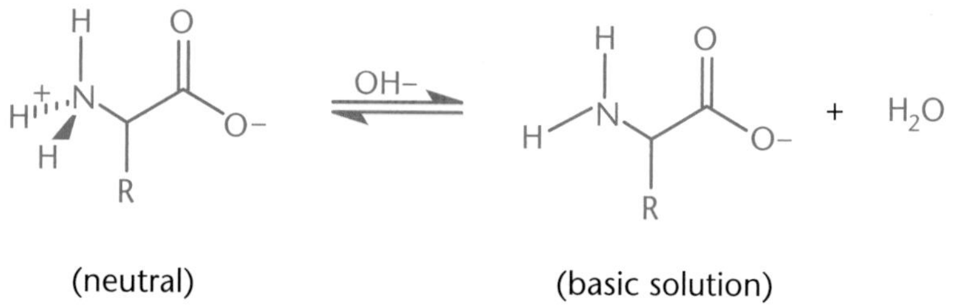

(neutral)   (basic solution)

Figure 15.5

This means that at a low pH, the amino acid will carry an excess positive charge and at a high pH, it will carry an excess negative charge. The intermediate pH, at which the amino acid exists as a zwitterion, is known as the **isoelectric point (pI)**, or **isoelectric pH**, of the amino acid.

This isoelectric pH must lie between pK_{a1} and pK_{a2}. Remember that pK_a is simply the pH at which dissociation occurs. As we should remember, p(anything) implies an inverse relationship. This means that a high K_a will have a low pK_a, just as a high proton concentration [H^+] will have a low pH.

TITRATION OF AMINO ACIDS

Because amino acids have acidic and basic properties, they are great candidates for titration. The titration of each proton occurs as a distinct step, resembling that of a simple monoprotic acid. Thus, the titration curve ends up looking like a combination of two or three monoprotic acids (three if the amino acid has an acidic or basic R-group) all tied together. Figure 15.6 shows the titration curve for glycine.

> **Key Concept**
>
> At its isoelectric point, an amino acid is uncharged.

Similar to acidic amino acids, the titration curve of basic amino acids is modified by the additional amino group that must be neutralized. These amino acids also have three dissociation constants, and the neutralization curves for the two amino groups overlap somewhat. The isoelectric point is shifted toward an alkaline pH and can be found by averaging the two basic pK_as together. Once again, three moles of acid are needed to neutralize one mole of a basic amino acid.

Understanding titration curves and isoelectric points helps us to predict the charge of any particular amino acid at a given pH. For example, in a mixture of glycine, glutamic acid, and lysine at pH 6, glycine will be neutral, glutamic acid will be negatively charged, and lysine will be positively charged.

Peptides

Peptides are composed of amino acid subunits, sometimes called **residues** (see Figure 15.11). We know that amino acids have a carboxyl group on one end and an amino group on the other, so when two amino acids with these groups combine, a **peptide bond**, which is simply an amide bond, forms between them. Peptides are basically small proteins (the distinction between a peptide and protein is vague, but it is generally accepted that peptides contain fewer than about 50 residues). Two amino acids joined together form a **dipeptide**, three form a **tripeptide**, and many amino acids linked together form a **polypeptide**.

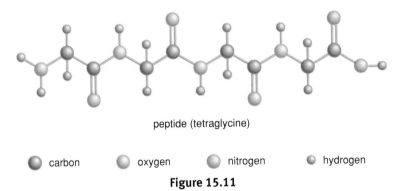

peptide (tetraglycine)

● carbon   ○ oxygen   ○ nitrogen   ○ hydrogen

Figure 15.11

REACTIONS

As we mentioned, amino acids are joined by peptide bonds (amide bonds) between the carboxyl group of one amino acid and the amino group of another. To form this bond, a condensation reaction occurs (water is lost). The reverse reaction, hydrolysis (cleavage by adding water) of the peptide bond, is catalyzed by an acid or base, as we saw earlier (see Figure 15.12).

In addition, certain enzymes digest the chain at specific peptide linkages. For example, trypsin cleaves at the carboxyl end of arginine and lysine, and chymotrypsin cleaves at the carboxyl end of phenylalanine, tyrosine, and tryptophan. Although you don't need to memorize where these enzymes cleave amino acids, they will often be described in a passage on the MCAT, so you should be comfortable identifying the location of peptide bonds within a peptide.

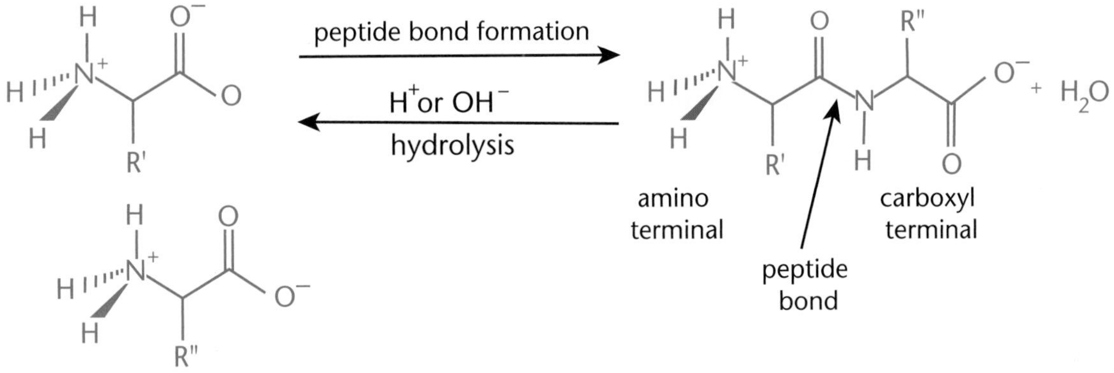

Figure 15.12

PROPERTIES

The terminal amino acid with a free α-amino group is known as the **amino-terminal** or **N-terminal** residue, whereas the terminal residue with a free carboxyl group is called the **carboxy-terminal** or **C-terminal** residue. By convention, peptides are drawn with the N-terminal end on the left and the C-terminal end on the right.

As we remember from previous chapters, amides have two resonance structures, so the true structure is a hybrid with partial double-bond character between the nitrogen and the carbonyl carbon (see Figure 15.13). This double-bond character leads to an important property: Rotation about the C–N bond is restricted. This restriction adds to the rigidity and stability of the backbone of proteins. The bonds on either side of the peptide unit, on the other hand, can rotate however they like, because they are only single bonds.

> **Key Concept**
>
> Rotation is limited around the peptide bond because resonance gives the C–N bond partial double-bond character.

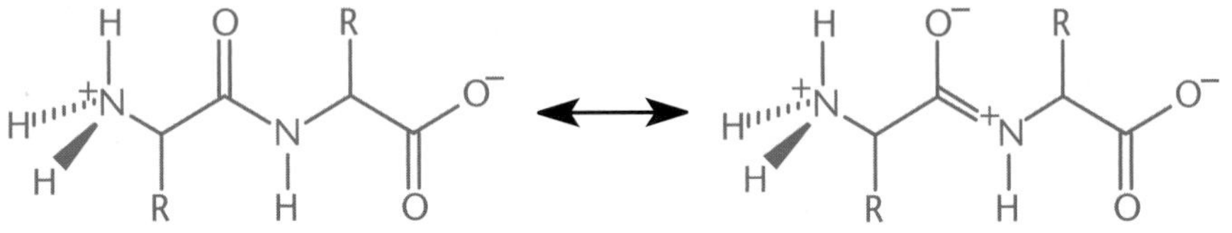

Figure 15.13

Proteins

Proteins are polypeptides that range from only a few to more than a thousand amino acids in length. They serve a vast array of functions in biological systems, acting as enzymes, hormones, membrane pores, receptors, and elements of cell structure. Proteins are the main actors of biological systems; after all, our genetic code is simply a grocery list of different protein codes. There are four levels of protein structure—**primary**, **secondary**, **tertiary**, and **quaternary**.

PRIMARY STRUCTURE

The primary structure of proteins is the structure that is coded into the DNA of the organism. It is the sequence of amino acids, listed from the N-terminus to the C-terminus, each linked by peptide bonds.

This is the most fundamental structure of the protein; it is the sequence that determines all higher levels of protein structure. In other words, a protein will assume whatever secondary, tertiary, and quaternary structures are the most energetically favorable for the given primary structure and the environment. This primary structure can be determined in a laboratory using a procedure called **sequencing**. This is most easily done on the DNA (the gene) that produced the protein.

SECONDARY STRUCTURE

The secondary structure is the local structure of neighboring amino acids. The most important thing to remember about secondary structure is that it is primarily the result of hydrogen bonding between nearby amino acids. Also, know that the two most common types of secondary structure are the **α-helix** and the **β-pleated sheet** (sometimes simply called **β-sheet**). β-sheets may be parallel or antiparallel. Some turns are also considered elements of secondary structure.

α-Helix

The α-helix is a rodlike structure in which the peptide chain coils clockwise about a central axis. This helix is stabilized by the intramolecular hydrogen bonds between carbonyl oxygen atoms and amide hydrogen atoms four residues away from each other ($n + 4$ hydrogen bond). The side chains of these amino acids point away from the helix's core, interacting with the cellular environment. A typical protein with this structure is **keratin**, a fibrous structural protein that is found in our hair and fingernails.

β-Pleated Sheet

In β-pleated sheets, the peptide chains lie alongside each other, forming rows. As we said before, these chains are held together by intramolecular hydrogen bonds between the carbonyl oxygen atoms on one peptide chain and the amine hydrogen atoms on another. To accommodate the greatest possible number of hydrogen bonds, the β-pleated sheet assumes a rippled, or pleated, shape (see Figure 15.14). The R-groups of amino residues point above and below the plane of the β-pleated sheet. Silk fibers are composed of β-pleated sheets.

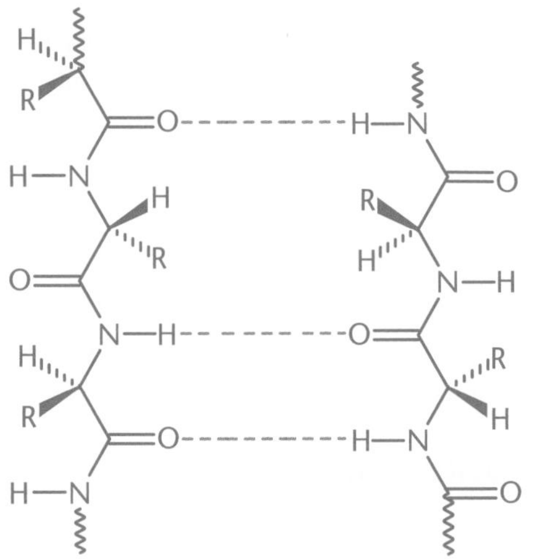

Figure 15.14

TERTIARY STRUCTURE

Tertiary structure refers to the three-dimensional shape of the protein. It is mostly determined by hydrophilic and hydrophobic interactions between the R-groups of amino acids. This three-dimensional structure is also determined by the distribution of disulfide bonds. A disulfide bond results when two **cysteine** molecules become oxidized to form **cystine** as shown in Figure 15.15. Disulfide bonds create loops in the protein chain. Disulfide bonds determine how wavy or curly our hair is; in fact, as many people learned in the 1980s, you can add more disulfide bonds to your hair—it's called a perm.

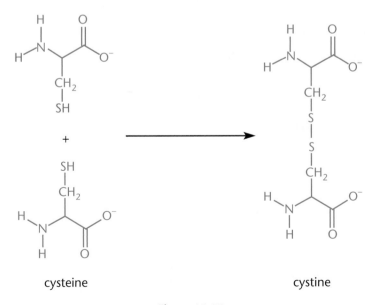

cysteine   cystine

Figure 15.15

Key Concept

- Primary structure consists of the amino acid sequence and covalent bonds.
- Secondary structure refers to the local structure of a protein as determined by hydrogen bond interactions.
- Tertiary structure is the three-dimensional shape of the protein.
- Quaternary structure is the arrangement of polypeptide subunits.
- Conjugated proteins have prosthetic groups.

Bridge

Recall from Biology that as a consequence of its quaternary structure, hemoglobin binds oxygen cooperatively. That is, it is easier to bind the second molecule of oxygen than the first, the third is easier than the second, and the fourth is the easiest to bind.

Amino acids other than cysteine can have significant effects on tertiary structures as well. For instance, proline, because of its ring shape, cannot fit into every location in an α-helix, so it causes a kink in the chain.

Amino acids with hydrophilic (polar or charged) R-groups tend to arrange themselves toward the outside of the protein, where they interact with the aqueous cellular environment. Amino acids with hydrophobic R-groups tend to be found close together, and they protect themselves from the aqueous environment by burying themselves in the middle of the protein.

Proteins are divided into two major classifications on the basis of their tertiary structure. **Fibrous proteins**, such as **collagen**, are found as sheets or long strands, whereas **globular proteins** (think *globe*), such as myoglobin, are spherical.

QUARTERNARY STRUCTURE

A protein can have quaternary structure only if it contains more than one polypeptide subunit. The quaternary structure refers to the way these subunits arrange themselves to yield a functional protein. The classic example of quaternary structure is **hemoglobin**, the oxygen-transporting machines that fill our red blood cells. Hemoglobin is composed of four different globular protein subunits.

CONJUGATED PROTEINS

Conjugated proteins derive part of their function from covalently attached molecules called **prosthetic groups**. These prosthetic groups can be organic molecules, such as vitamins, or even metal ions, such as iron. Proteins with lipid, carbohydrate, and nucleic acid prosthetic groups are referred to as **lipoproteins**, **glycoproteins**, and **nucleoproteins**, respectively. These prosthetic groups have major roles in determining the function of their respective proteins. For example, each of hemoglobin's subunits (as well as myoglobin) contains a prosthetic group known as the **heme group**. This heme group is composed of an organic porphyrin ring with an iron atom bound in the center. The heme group itself binds to and carries oxygen; as such, hemoglobin would be inactive without the heme group.

DENATURATION OF PROTEINS

Denaturation, or **melting**, is the process by which proteins lose their three-dimensional structure and revert to a **random-coil** state. Because this process destroys the protein's tertiary structure, it renders it completely functionless. There are several methods we can use to denature a protein—with a detergent, change in pH, temperature, or even solute concentration. The weak intermolecular forces that keep the protein stable and functional can be disrupted by any of these factors. When a protein denatures, the damage is usually permanent. However, certain gentle denaturing agents (such as urea) do not permanently disrupt the protein. Removing the reagent might allow the protein to **renature** (regain its structure and function). That is, the denaturation is reversible.

Conclusion

It's pretty amazing to examine the vastly different functions that are derived from various combinations of the same 20 amino acids. Even more interesting is that the same 20 amino acids comprising all of the proteins in our bodies are the same 20 amino acids that make the proteins of almost every single form of life on this planet, from *Escherichia coli* to aspen trees.

Many Organic Chemistry textbooks open with the sweeping claim that Orgo is the "chemistry of life"; we'd like to end with it. It's undeniably true that the molecules and reactions we study in Orgo are essential to the functions we use as qualifications for life: the ability to self-replicate and use energy from the environment. However, in the years since the term was coined, *organic chemistry* has come to include a great deal more than life processes. In fact, you've been using Orgo from just about the moment you woke up this morning: the gas in your car (Alkanes—Chapter 4), the plastic shopping bag lining your trash can (Alkenes and Alkynes—Chapter 5), the flowery scent of your perfume (Aromatic Compounds—Chapter 6), the aerosol propellant that allowed you to spritz on your perfume (Alcohols and Ethers—Chapter 7), the spearmint flavor of your toothpaste (Aldehydes and Ketones—Chapter 8), the preservative that keeps your toothpaste fresh (Carboxylic Acids—Chapter 9), the nail polish remover you used to clean off your chipped toenails (Carboxylic Acid Derivatives—Chapter 10) . . . all the way down to the carpet fibers that cushioned your toes as you stepped out of bed (Amines and Nitrogen-Containing Compounds—Chapter 11). Undoubtedly, extraction, filtration, or distillation was used to prepare the food and drink that you will consume today (Purification and Separation—Chapter 12), and odds are that someday (we hope not today!) you will need an MRI scan to assess or diagnose an injury or illness (Spectroscopy—Chapter 13). Of course, Organic Chemistry still includes the "chemistry of life": The bagel that you ate for breakfast (Carbohydrates—Chapter 14) is broken down into energy, which your body uses to build proteins, giving rise to every structure and function in your body (Amino Acids, Peptides, and Proteins—Chapter 15).

Despite the subject's compelling relevance to everyday life, college Organic Chemistry still manages to terrify and alienate its students, as we noted in the beginning of this book. The MCAT, on the other hand, doesn't ask you to memorize tables of reactants or regurgitate hundreds of named reactions from scratch. Instead, the

Real World

Denaturation is the loss of three-dimensional structure. Permanent denaturation occurs when cooking egg whites. They denature and form a solid, rubbery mass that cannot be transformed back to its clear liquid form.

MCAT asks you to look at the bigger picture, to know trends, to participate. We hope that studying for the MCAT has given you a chance to start over with Orgo—to focus on the *how* and the *why* instead of the *what*. Organic Chemistry, like the MCAT as a whole, should be seen not as an obstacle but as an opportunity. So work hard, have some fun along the way, and keep thinking about where you're heading . . . you can almost feel that white (polyester!) coat.

CONCEPTS TO REMEMBER

- ☐ Amino acids contain a carboxyl group, an amino group, a hydrogen, and an R-group attached to a central α-carbon.

- ☐ There are 20 naturally occurring amino acids, all of which are L-enantiomers, except for glycine which is achiral.

- ☐ Amino acids are amphoteric species (they can function as acids or bases).

- ☐ In a neutral solution, nonpolar and polar amino acids exist as zwitterions, acidic amino acids exist as negatively charged ions, and basic amino acids exist as positive ions.

- ☐ All amino acids have at least two pK_a's, and the isoelectric point (pI) is between the two pK_a's. For acidic amino acids with three pK_a's, the pI is between the two largest pK_a's; for basic amino acids with three pK_a's, the pI is between the two lowest pK_a's.

- ☐ During titration, when $pH = pK_a$, concentration of the protonated species is equal to that of the deprotonated species. This region is known as the buffer zone, and pH changes very little during this region (appears as a horizontal line).

- ☐ During titration, when $pH = pI$, all of the species have been deprotonated, and pH changes drastically (appears as a somewhat vertical line).

- ☐ Nonpolar amino acids are hydrophobic, so they are often found buried within protein molecules.

- ☐ Polar, acid, and basic amino acids are hydrophilic and are often found on the surface of proteins.

- ☐ Primary structure is determined by the amino acid sequence (N → C); secondary structure is determined by local hydrogen bonding; tertiary structure (the three-dimensional shape) is determined largely by hydrophobic and hydrophilic interactions but also by disulfide bonds; quaternary structure is from the aggregation of more than one polypeptide subunits.

- ☐ Conjugated proteins derive part of their function from prosthetic groups (which can be either organic molecules or metal ions).

Practice Questions

1. If a mixture of alanine (pI = 6) and aspartic acid (pI = 3) is subjected to electrophoresis at pH 3, which of the following would you expect to occur?

   A. Alanine will migrate to the cathode, while aspartic acid migrates to the anode.
   B. Alanine will not move, while aspartic acid migrates to the cathode.
   C. Aspartic acid will not move, while alanine migrates to the cathode.
   D. Alanine will migrate to the anode, while aspartic acid migrates to the cathode.

2. In a neutral solution, most amino acids exist as

   A. positively charged compounds.
   B. zwitterions.
   C. negatively charged compounds.
   D. hydrophobic molecules.

3. What would be the charge of glutamic acid at pH 7?

   A. Neutral
   B. Negative
   C. Positive
   D. None of the above

4. If an amino acid (pI = 9.74) in acidic solution is completely titrated with sodium hydroxide, what will be its charge at pH 3, 7, and 11, respectively?

   A. Positive, neutral, negative
   B. Negative, neutral, positive
   C. Neutral, positive, positive
   D. Positive, positive, negative

5. Amino acids with nonpolar R-groups have which of the following characteristics in aqueous solution?

   A. They are hydrophilic and found buried within proteins.
   B. They are hydrophobic and found buried within proteins.
   C. They are hydrophobic and found on protein surfaces.
   D. They are hydrophilic and found on protein surfaces.

6. All of the following statements concerning peptide bonds are true EXCEPT

   A. their formation involves a reaction between an amine group and a carboxyl group.
   B. they are the primary bonds found in proteins.
   C. they have partial double-bond character.
   D. their formation involves hydration reactions.

7. How many different tripeptides can be formed that contain one valine, one alanine, and one leucine?

   A. 5
   B. 6
   C. 7
   D. 8

8. Beside peptide bonds, what other covalent bonds are commonly found in peptides?

   A. Hydrogen
   B. Ether
   C. Disulfide
   D. Hydrophobic

9. α-helices are secondary structures characterized by

A. intramolecular hydrogen bonds.
B. disulfide bonds.
C. a rippled effect.
D. intermolecular hydrogen bonds.

10. Denaturation involves the loss of what type(s) of structure?

A. Primary
B. Secondary
C. Tertiary
D. Both (B) and (C)

Small Group Questions

1. Amino acids naturally exist as L-enantiomers. What specific effect might a mutation that causes production of D-enantiomers have on a eukaryotic cell?

2. Can amino acids with multiple charges be used in buffer systems?

Explanations to Practice Questions

1. C

At pH 6, alanine will exist as a neutral, dipolar ion: The amino group will be protonated, whereas the carboxyl group will be deprotonated. At a pH of 3, there will be excess hydrogen ions in solution, which will protonate the carboxyl group, and the molecule will assume an overall positive charge. Alanine will therefore migrate to the cathode. On the other hand, aspartic acid will exist as a neutral dipolar ion at a pH of 3 because this is equivalent to its isoelectric point. Therefore, when it is subjected to electrophoresis, it will not move. In summary, alanine will migrate to the cathode, while aspartic acid will not move, making choice (C) the correct response.

2. B

Most amino acids (with the exception of the acidic and basic amino acids) have two sites for protonation, the carboxylic acid and the amine group. At a neutral pH, the carboxylic acid will be deprotonated (negatively charged), and the amine group will remain protonated (positively charged). This dipolar ion is called a zwitterion; therefore, (B) is the correct answer.

3. B

The amino acid in question is glutamic acid, which is an acidic amino acid because it contains an extra carboxyl group. At neutral pH, both of the carboxyl groups are ionized, so there are two negative charges on the molecule. Only one of the charges is neutralized by the positive charge on the amino group, so the molecule has an overall negative charge. Thus, the answer is choice (B).

4. D

With a pI = 9.74, the amino acid must have two basic groups. At pH 3, the two amine groups and the carboxyl group will be protonated to give a net positive charge. As the pH rises to 7, the proton will first dissociate from the carboxyl, but both amine groups will still be fully protonated, so the charge will still be positive. At pH 11, the molecule is above its isoelectric point and will be fully deprotonated, resulting in two neutral amine groups and a negatively charged carboxylate group, so the charge at pH 11 will be negative. Therefore, the correct sequence of charges is positive, positive, negative, corresponding to choice (D).

5. B

Nonpolar molecules or groups are those whose negative and positive centers of charge coincide. They are not soluble in water and are thus hydrophobic. Amino acids with hydrophobic R-groups tend to be found buried within protein molecules, where they do not have to interact with the aqueous cellular environment. This makes choice (B) the correct answer. Choices (A) and (D) are incorrect because nonpolar R-groups cannot be hydrophilic. Choice (C) is incorrect because nonpolar molecules are seldom located on the surface of proteins, where they would interact unfavorably with the aqueous cellular environment.

6. D

Formation of a peptide bond, which is the primary covalent bond found in proteins (B), involves a condensation reaction between the amine group of one amino acid and the carboxyl group of an adjacent amino acid (A). As a result of the carbonyl group present at the bond, the double bond resonates between C=O and C=N. This resonance gives the peptide bond a partial double-bond character (C) and limits rotation about the bond.

From this information, it can be seen that choices (A), (B), and (C) are all characteristics of the peptide bond.

Choice (D) is false because the formation of the peptide bond is a condensation reaction, involving the loss of water, rather than a hydration reaction, which involves the addition of water.

7. B

The six tripeptides that can be formed are these:

Val-Ala-Leu, Val-Leu-Ala,

Ala-Val-Leu, Ala-Leu-Val,

Leu-Val-Ala, Leu-Ala-Val

8. C

The key word in this question is *covalent*. Although hydrogen bonds (A) and hydrophobic bonds (D) are involved in peptide structure, they are not considered covalent bonds, because they do not involve sharing electrons. Therefore, choices (A) and (D) are incorrect. Ether bonds (B) are covalent bonds, but they are not found in peptides. The correct answer is disulfide bonds, choice (C). Disulfide bonds are covalent bonds forming between the sulfur-bearing R-groups of cysteines. The resulting cystine molecule constitutes a disulfide bridge and often causes a loop in the peptide chain.

9. A

When discussing secondary structure, the most important bond is the hydrogen bond. The rigid α-helices are held together by hydrogen bonds between the carbonyl oxygen of one peptide bond and the amine hydrogen of a peptide bond four residues removed. This hydrogen bond is intramolecular, so choice (A) is correct. Disulfide bonds are covalent bonds usually associated with primary and tertiary structure; therefore, choice (B) is incorrect. Choices (C) and (D) are incorrect because the rippled effect and intermolecular hydrogen bonds are both characteristic of β-pleated sheets.

10. D

Protein denaturation involves the loss of three-dimensional structure and function. Because the three-dimensional shape of a protein is conferred by secondary and tertiary structures, denaturation disrupts these structures. Therefore, both choices (B) and (C) are correct. Denaturation does not cause a loss of primary structure because it does not cause peptide bonds to break; thus, choice (A) is incorrect.

High-Yield Problem Solving Guide for Organic Chemistry

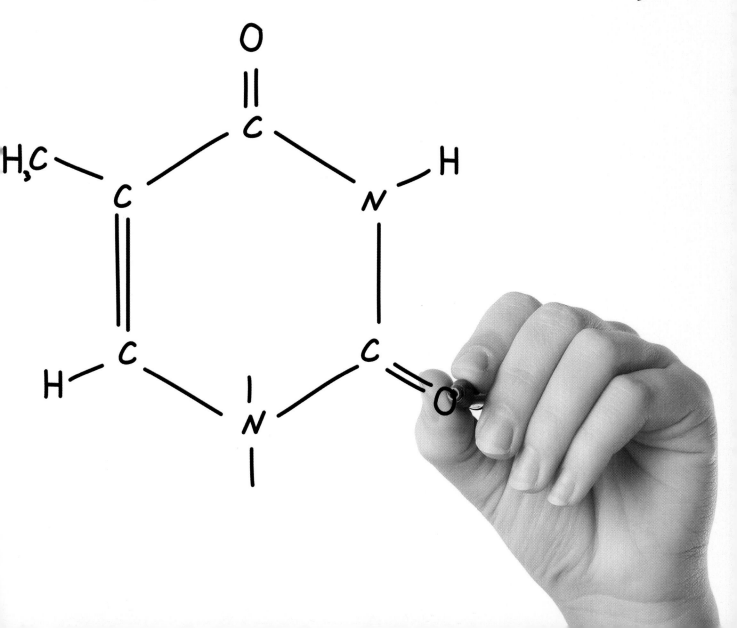

High-Yield MCAT Review

This is a **High-Yield Questions section**. These questions tackle the most frequently tested topics found on the MCAT. For each type of problem, you will be provided with a stepwise technique for solving the question and key directional points on how to solve for the MCAT specifically.

For each topic, you will find a "Takeaways" box, which gives a concise summary of the problem-solving approach, and a "Things to Watch Out For" box, which points out any caveats to the approach discussed above that usually lead to wrong answer choices. Finally, there is a "Similar Questions" box at the end so you can test your ability to apply the stepwise technique to analogous questions.

We're confident that this guide can help you achieve your goals of MCAT success and admission into medical school!

Good luck!

Key Concepts

Chapter 1

Nomenclature

Functional group priority

Nomenclature

What is the IUPAC name for the following compound?

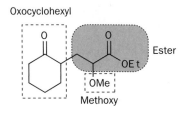

1) Identify the highest-priority functional group.

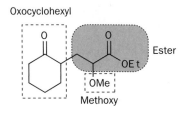

In this case, the highest-priority functional group is the ester. Therefore, we will name everything attached to the ester as a substituent, including the cyclohexyl ring on the left.

Takeaways

The key to the nomenclature problems is to be as systematic as possible. Don't try to do everything at once, or you risk confusing yourself.

2) Determine the longest continuous carbon chain attached to the highest-priority functional group and number them accordingly.

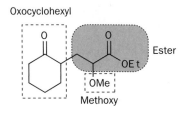

In this case, the longest continuous chain is three carbons, with carbon 1 being the carbonyl carbon (because the ester is the highest-priority functional group). Because the ester has three carbons, it will be a propanoate ester.

Things to Watch Out For

Don't forget to include parentheses if a substituent is further substituted so that you don't confuse the two numbering systems.

3) Locate the substituents on the carbon chain identified in step 2 and name and number them.

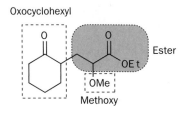

The first substituent is the ethyl group on the ester, which we will name by placing the word *ethyl* in front of the ester name.

Next, there is a methyl group attached to an oxygen at carbon 2, which will be named as a methoxy group.

Finally, how do we handle the ring attached to carbon 3? If there were nothing attached to the ring, we would name the ring as a cyclohexyl substituent. However, there is a ketone on the ring. When aldehydes or ketones are named as substituents recall that they are named as "oxo" groups. The numbering works by assigning the carbon attached to the ester carbon chain as carbon 1 as shown.

Therefore, the ketone on the ring will be at carbon 2. We'll name the whole ring as a (2-oxocyclohexyl) substituent and put it in parentheses so that we don't confuse the two numbering systems.

---

4) Put it all together.
The name of our compound will therefore be this:

ethyl 2–methoxy–3–(2–oxocyclohexyl)propanoate

Similar Questions

1) How would the name be altered if the alkyl group attached to the ester oxygen contained substituents?

2) Upon reduction with sodium borohydride, followed by dilute acid workup, the molecule below gave two products in unequal yield. Draw them and provide the correct IUPAC name for each.

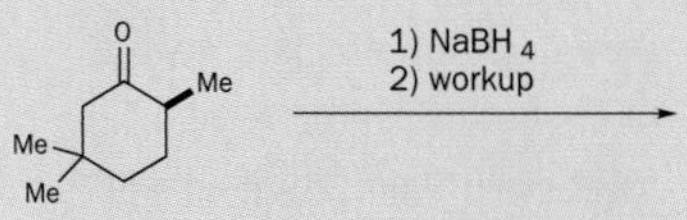

1) NaBH$_4$
2) workup

3) What are the two possible products of the reaction shown below? Draw and provide IUPAC names for both.

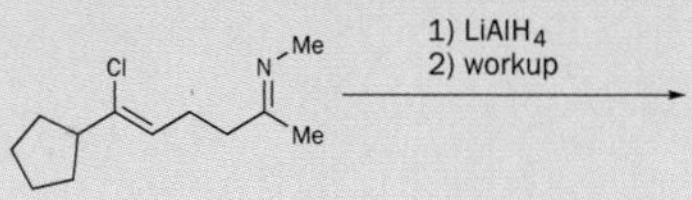

1) LiAlH$_4$
2) workup

Key Concepts

Chapter 2

Isomers

Enantiomers

Diastereomers

Isomers

The reagent *meta*-chloroperoxybenzoic acid (mCPBA) is often used to convert alkenes to epoxides. If the alkene shown below is treated with mCPBA, two products result. Draw these products and determine their isomeric relationship.

Takeaways

Be as systematic as possible in assigning isomeric relationships in order to avoid making mistakes and missing easy points on Test Day!

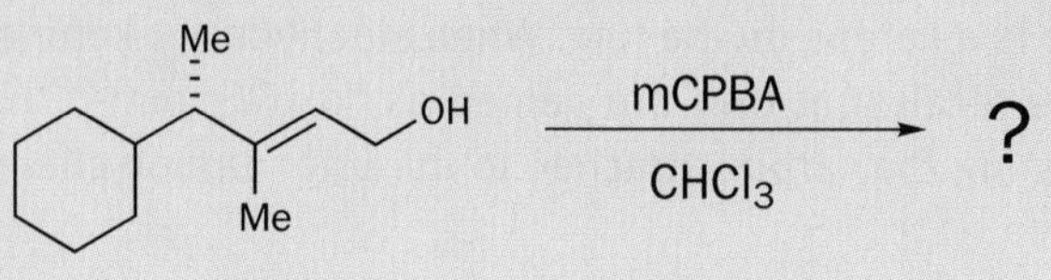

1) Draw the product(s) and note the major differences between them.

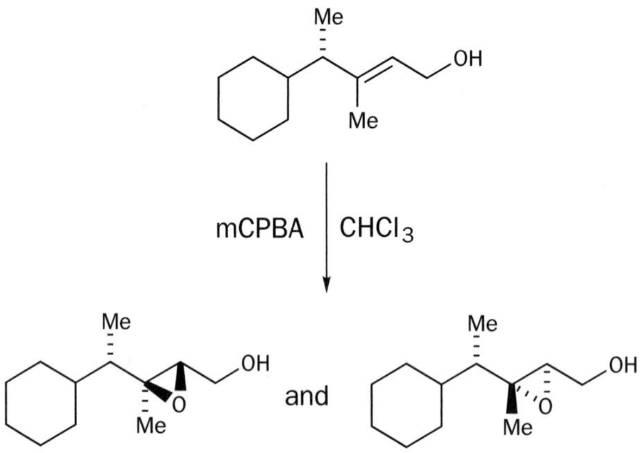

Recall that alkenes are flat due to both carbons being *sp²* hybridized. Therefore, the epoxide can form on either face of the alkene, giving rise to two possible products.

Notice that each isomer differs only in the stereochemical sense.

Things to Watch Out For

Avoid confusing *enantiomers* and *diastereomers*. This is where a great many mistakes are made on MCAT questions. Remember that if two molecules are nonsuperimposable mirror images, they are enantiomers. Provided that you have determined that the molecules are configurational isomers without a plane of symmetry, *any other molecules are diastereomers.*

2) Determine the isomeric relationship.

The first question you should ask yourself is whether or not the molecules have the same connectivity. Here they do, because they differ only in the orientation of two stereocenters, so they are not structural isomers.

Next, you need to figure out whether bond breaking would be required to interconvert them. Here, that is definitely true because to convert the top isomer to the bottom one, you would have to break both epoxide carbon–oxygen bonds and reassemble them on the opposite face of the molecule. Therefore, our molecules are configurational isomers.

Then, you will want to see if the molecules are nonsuperimposable mirror images of one another.

The molecules are not nonsuperimposable mirror images of one another because the stereocenter adjacent to the cyclohexyl ring has the same orientation in both products. (Note that the carbon where the ring is joined to the acyclic portion of the molecule is *not* a stereocenter. Why?) Therefore, our two molecules are *diastereomers*.

You can confirm this by assigning *R/S* designations to each stereocenter and then seeing that some of the stereocenters have the same orientation and some are different. For our two molecules to be *enantiomers,* each stereocenter would have to have the opposite orientation in each product.

Similar Questions

1) Alkynes can be reduced to alkenes selectively by manipulating the reaction conditions. Examine the reaction scheme below and determine the relationship between the two products.

2) If the alkenes in question 1 were reduced with Pd/H_2, would the isomeric relationship change?

3) Would the physical properties of the alkenes in question 1 be the same or different? What about when the alkenes were reduced?

Key Concepts

Chapter 2

Stereochemistry

Fischer projections

Oxidation/reduction

meso compounds

meso Compounds

A student wanted to prepare chiral polyols by taking sugars and reacting them with sodium borohydride. She took D-xylose, shown below, and treated it with sodium borohydride, followed by a dilute aqueous acid workup. On purifying and isolating the product, she found that it did not rotate plane-polarized light. What was the structure of the product, and why did it not rotate light?

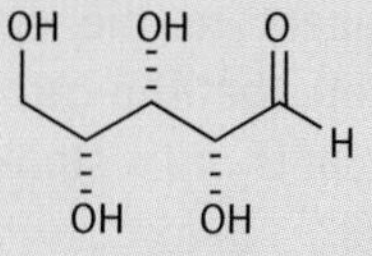

D-xylose

Takeaways

Anytime a molecule with stereocenters behaves as an achiral molecule, there must be a plane of symmetry somewhere in the molecule.

1) Convert the molecule from standard projection to Fischer projection.

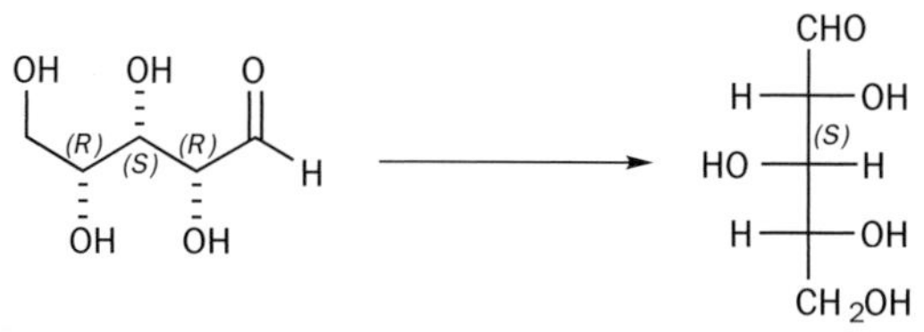

This will enable you to see stereochemical relationships much more clearly.

Things to Watch Out For

With molecules with multiple stereocenters, be sure to draw them as Fischer projections to be able to spot the symmetry planes easily.

2) Draw the product of the initial reaction.

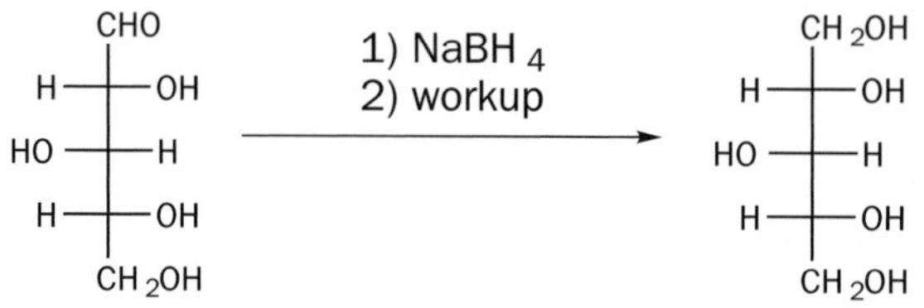

In this case, sodium borohydride reduces the aldehyde to an alcohol.

3) Look for planes of symmetry in the product.

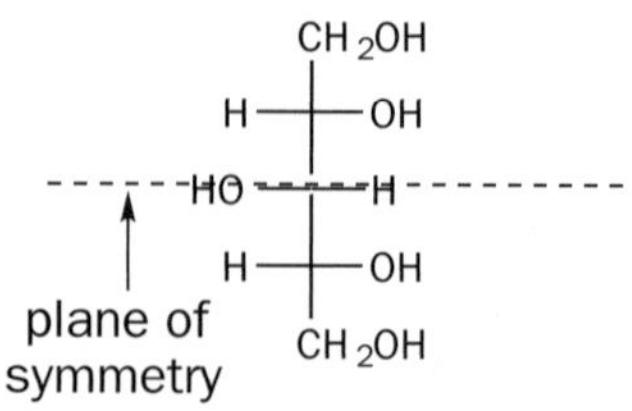

plane of symmetry

The fact that a molecule possesses stereocenters but is achiral is a dead giveaway that the molecule must be a *meso* compound. This would be caused by a plane of symmetry in the molecule. The plane of symmetry runs right through C3 in this case.

Similar Questions

1) Which of the remaining three D-aldopentoses (shown below) would result in achiral polyols when subjected to borohydride reduction?

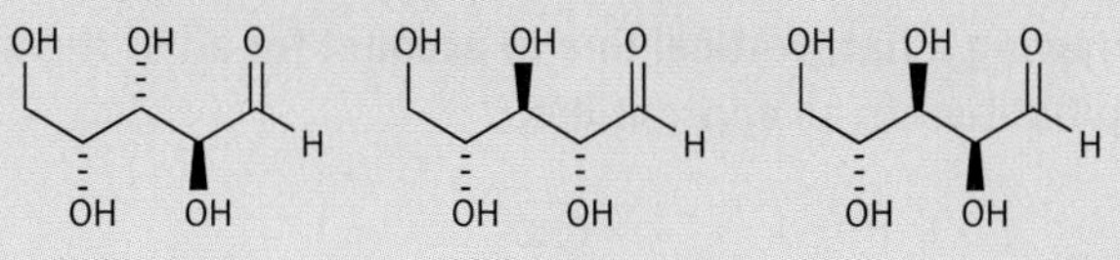

Key Concepts

Chapter 2

Stereochemistry

Fischer projections

Stereocenter

Fischer Projections

Redraw the following molecule in a Fischer projection:

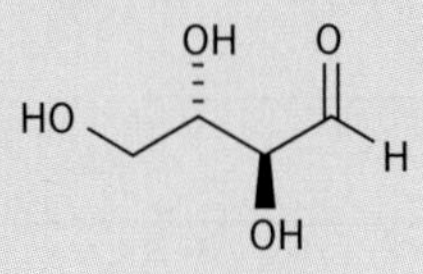

1) Begin by drawing a flat, vertical line to account for all of the stereocenters. Draw in end substituents as appropriate.

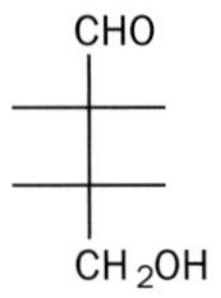

2) Determine the stereochemical orientation of the stereocenters in the original molecule by assigning *R/S* to each.

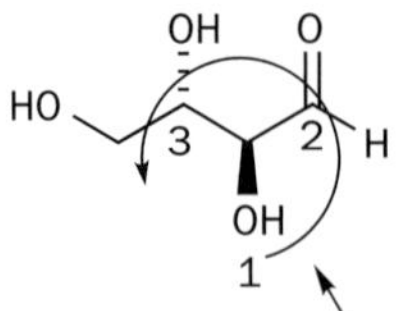

Going from 1 to 2 to 3 means turning to the left.

For the stereocenter adjacent to the aldehyde, the alcohol is the highest-priority substituent, followed by the aldehyde, then the carbon with the other stereocenter, and finally the hydrogen. Because the hydrogen is already oriented away from us, we can go ahead and assign the stereocenter to be *S*, because we "turn the wheel" to the left.

Applying the same methodology to the other stereocenter gives an *S* stereocenter as well.

MCAT Pitfall: *Be careful with assigning the second stereocenter because the hydrogen is coming out of the page at you.*

Takeaways

Assigning priorities is based on atomic number and is done one atom at a time. When you "turn" from the highest-priority to the lowest-priority substituent, think about the three highest-priority substituents as being on a steering wheel in a car, with the lowest-priority substituent as the steering column.

Things to Watch Out For

Don't forget that if a substituent is attached to a horizontal bond in a Fischer projection, that means that it is *coming out of the page at you.* If it is attached to a vertical bond, it is *going into the page away from you.*

3) Draw in the substituents in the Fischer projection and make sure that they match the original molecule.

$$
\begin{array}{c}
\text{CHO} \\
\text{HO} \!-\!\!|\!-\! \text{H} \\
\text{H} \!-\!\!|\!-\! \text{OH} \\
\text{CH}_2\text{OH}
\end{array}
$$

At this point, you can randomly insert the substituents and check to make sure that they match the original molecule. Assign priorities as before.

turn to right

$$
\begin{array}{c}
2 \\
\text{CHO} \\
1 \\
\text{HO} \!-\!\!|\!-\! \text{H} \\
3 \\
\text{H} \!-\!\!|\!-\! \text{OH} \\
\text{CH}_2\text{OH}
\end{array}
$$

$$
\begin{array}{c}
S \\
\text{CHO} \\
\text{HO} \!-\!\!|\!-\! \text{H} \\
\text{H} \!-\!\!|\!-\! \text{OH} \\
\text{CH}_2\text{OH} \\
R
\end{array}
$$

For the first stereocenter, we would turn to the right, meaning that you would think it would be *R*. However, note that the lowest-priority substituent, the hydrogen, is coming *out of the page* because it is attached to a horizontal line; we want the hydrogen to be going into the page. So we would flip the assignment from *R* to *S*. The first stereocenter then matches. Applying the same idea to the second stereocenter would give an *R* assignment.

$$
\begin{array}{c}
S \\
\text{CHO} \\
\text{HO} \!-\!\!|\!-\! \text{H} \\
\text{HO} \!-\!\!|\!-\! \text{H} \\
\text{CH}_2\text{OH} \\
S
\end{array}
$$

However, we need the *S, S* compound. We can do that by just exchanging the alcohol and the proton in the second stereocenter.

Similar Questions

1) Draw the Fischer projection of the enantiomer compound.

2) Draw the Fischer projection of all the diastereomers for the compound and the compound's enantiomer, diagramming the relationships between each.

3) Fumaric acid (trans-2-butenedioic acid) can undergo *syn* addition with D_2. Draw the Fischer projection of the product(s). If multiple products are produced, what is the relationship between them?

Key Concepts

Chapters 1–3

Acidity and basicity

Resonance

Induction

pK_a

Substituent effects

Acidity Trends

Place the following molecules in order of *decreasing* pK_a of the phenol proton:

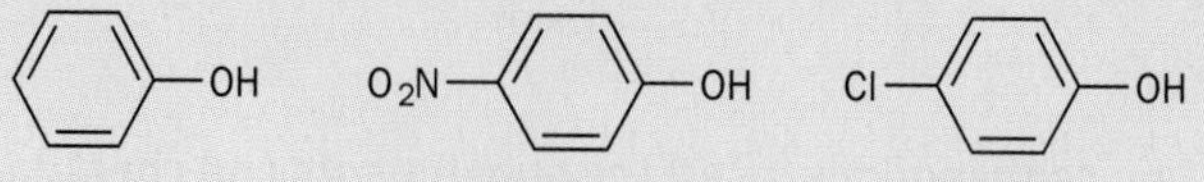

1　　　　　　**2**　　　　　　**3**

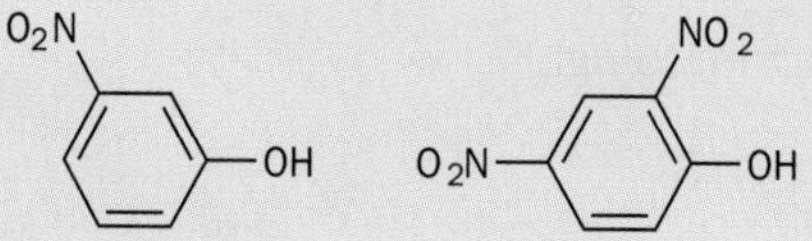

4　　　　　　**5**

1) Determine the potential stabilizing effects on each molecule.

All of the molecules possess the ability to have their conjugate base stabilized by resonance, but some have more resonance structures than others, as we'll see in a second.

*Remember: Decreasing pK_a means **increasing acidity** and **increasing stability** of a negative charge.*

*Remember: When it comes to charge stabilization, **resonance stabilization** is **always** more powerful than **inductive stabilization**.*

2) Look for resonance stabilization first.

You should zero in on molecule 5 right away as being the most acidic because it has the most electronegative substituent and the greatest number of electronegative substituents. That means that molecule 1 will have the least stable conjugate base and be the least acidic. When you remove the phenol proton, you can draw a total of six resonance structures:

Takeaways

Make sure to *draw* the anions resulting from deprotonation. This will get you thinking about stability and decrease the odds that you will miss some detail.

Things to Watch Out For

Don't confuse increasing *basicity* (least stabilized anion) with increasing *acidity* (most stabilized anion).

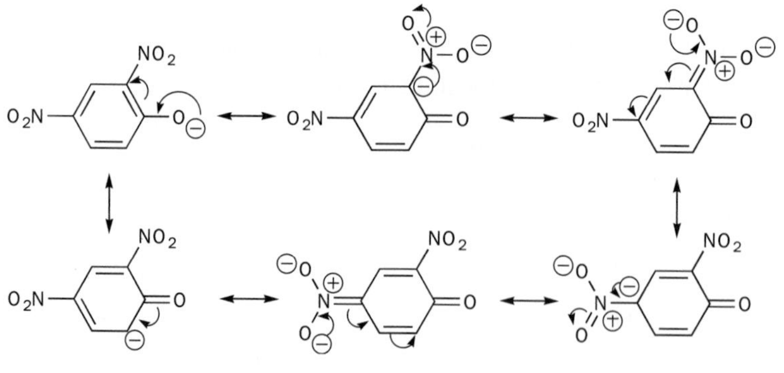

Notice that the negative charge only appears at the *ortho* and *para* positions on the ring (with respect to the alcohol). Thus, compound 4, with the nitro group in the *meta* position, can't benefit from the resonance stabilization of the negative charge into the nitro group.

Compound 2 has a nitro group at the *para* position, but its conjugate base won't be as stable because it only has one nitro group instead of two.

Remember: *The effects of electron withdrawing (or donating) substituents are additive.*

---

3) Look for inductive stabilization next.

Molecules 4 and 3 will benefit from inductive stabilization, and 4 will be more acidic than 3 because the nitro group is more electron withdrawing than a chloro group.

---

4) Place all of the molecules in order of their reactivity.

The unsubstituted phenol is the least acidic, followed by the compounds with only inductive stabilization, and finally the compounds that are resonance stabilized.

$1 < 3 < 4 < 2 < 5$

Similar Questions

1) How would you compare the acidity of the most acidic proton in each of the following molecules?

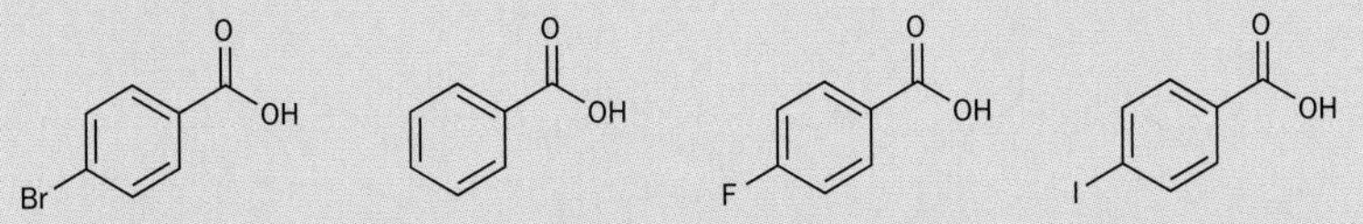

2) How would you compare the acidity of the most acidic proton in each of the following molecules?

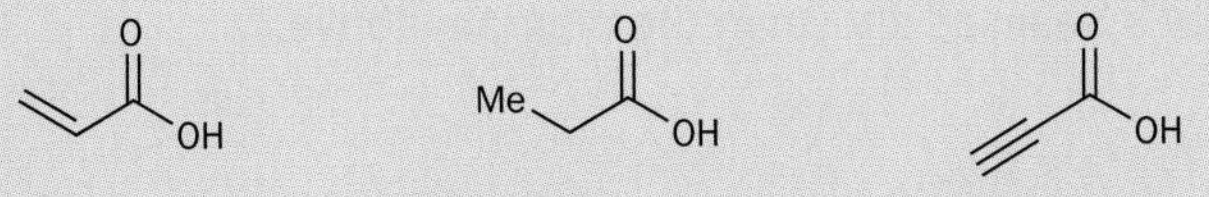

3) How would you compare the acidity of the most acidic proton in each of the following molecules?

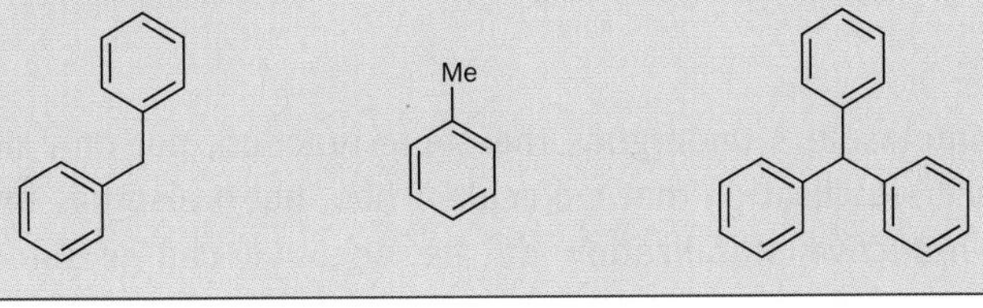

Key Concepts

Chapters 1–3

Acidity and basicity

Hybridization

Resonance

pK_a

Basicity Trends

Place the following molecules in order of *increasing* pK_a of the proton highlighted in bold:

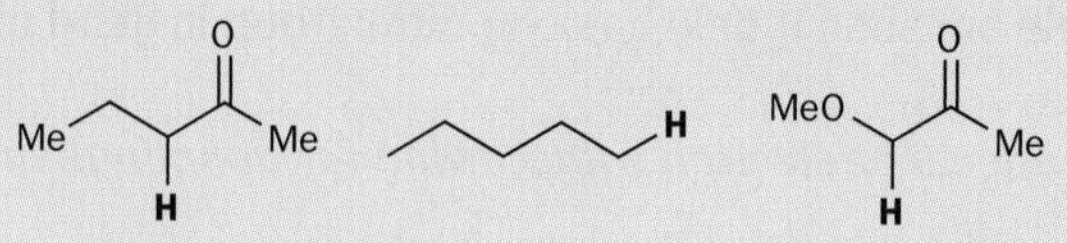

1) Determine the potential stabilizing effects on each molecule.

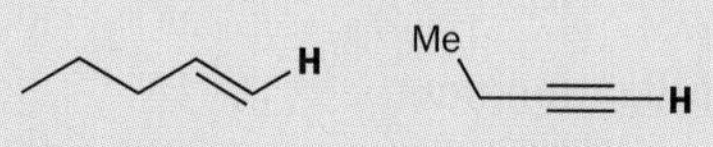

The only molecules that would possess resonance stabilization of the resulting anions if the bold proton were to be removed are 1 and 3, so these will be *less basic* than the others.

*Remember: Increasing pK_a means **increasing basicity** and **decreasing stability** of a negative charge.*

*Remember: When it comes to charge stabilization, **resonance stabilization** is always more powerful than **inductive stabilization**.*

Takeaways

Make sure to *draw* the anions resulting from deprotonation. This will get you thinking about stability and decrease the odds that you will miss some detail.

2) Look for resonance stabilization first.

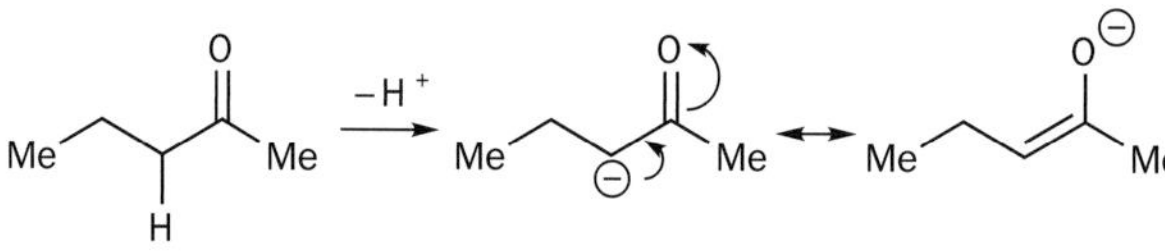

Molecule 1 clearly would have a resonance structure were the α-proton to be abstracted by a base, as shown in the diagram above.

Things to Watch Out For

Don't confuse increasing *basicity* (least stabilized anion) with increasing *acidity* (most stabilized anion).

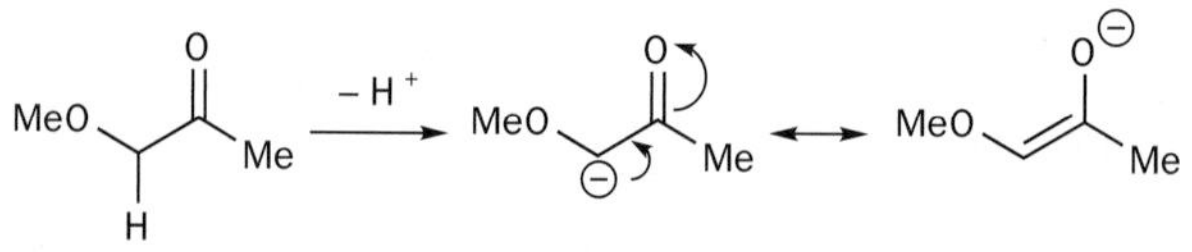

However, if molecule 3 undergoes the same reaction, not only does it have the resonance stabilization that molecule 1 has, but it also has an additional amount of *inductive* stabilization of the negative charge (in the middle resonance structure). The adjacent oxygen will help to stabilize the negative charge due to its electronegativity. Thus, molecule 3 is more stable and therefore *less basic* than 1.

3) Look for inductive stabilization next.
The only significant difference between the remaining molecules is the *hybridization of the carbon* attached to the bold proton. Notice that we have an *sp*-hybridized carbon (5), an *sp²*-hybridized carbon (4), and an *sp³*-hybridized carbon (2).

In this case, the carbon with the *sp* hybridization has the greatest "*s* character" because it is approximately 50 percent *s* and 50 percent *p*. Increasing *s* character helps stabilize a negative charge more. Remember that the charge distribution of an *s* orbital is spherical, with the electron closer to the nucleus (and therefore more stable) than an electron in a *p* orbital (recall that a *p* orbital has a nodal plane at the nucleus, meaning there is zero probability that an electron can be located there).

Thus, the anion generated from molecule 5 will be more stable than that generated from molecule 4, and finally the anion resulting from deprotonation of molecule 2 will be the least stable and most basic.

4) Place all of the molecules in order of their reactivity.
The final order in increasing basicity is thus the following:

$3 < 1 < 5 < 4 < 2$

Similar Questions

1) How would you compare the basicity of the protons highlighted in bold of the following molecules?

2) How would you compare the basicity of the protons highlighted in bold of the following molecules?

3) How would you compare the basicity of the protons highlighted in bold of the following molecules?

Key Concepts

Chapters 1–3

Polarity

Intermolecular forces

Solubility

Solubility Trends

Place the following molecules in order of *increasing* solubility in *dichloromethane*:

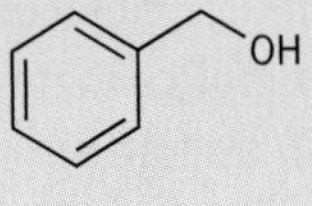

1

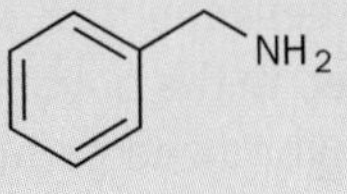

2

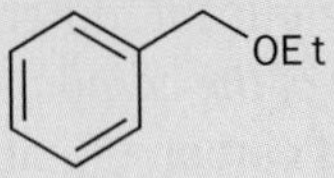

3

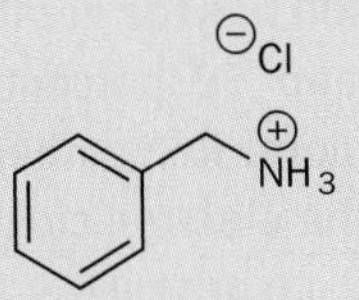

4

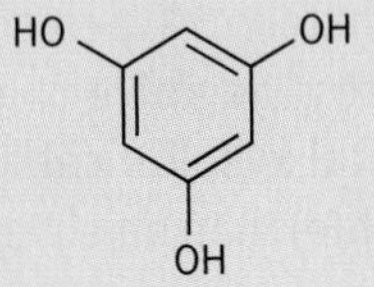

5

Takeaways

Remember that the principle that determines solubility is "*like dissolves like.*" Therefore, polar molecules will be more soluble in polar solvents, and nonpolar molecules will be more soluble in nonpolar solvents.

1) Determine the nature of the solvent.

In this case, we are concerned about the solubility of these molecules in dichloromethane, which is an organic, *nonpolar* solvent. Thus, the molecules that are most nonpolar will be most soluble in dichloromethane.

Remember: *The key principle with solubility is* ***"like dissolves like."***

---

2) Place the molecules in order of increasing solubility in the solvent of choice.

Here, we want to order the molecules from most polar to least polar.

This means that molecule 4 will be the most polar because it is a salt and bears a formal charge. Next will be molecule 5 because it has three hydroxyl groups (and can make three hydrogen bonds). It should also be clear that molecule 3 will be the least polar (and therefore the most soluble) because as an ether, it has no functional groups that would allow hydrogen bonding.

That leaves molecules 1 and 2. Molecule 1 would be more polar because oxygen is more electronegative than nitrogen.

Things to Watch Out For

Be sure to verify the nature of the solvent before ordering the molecules! Don't ever assume that the solvent is always water.

3) Place all of the molecules in order of their reactivity.

The final order in increasing solubility is thus the following:

4 < 5 < 1 < 2 < 3

Similar Questions

1) How would you compare the water solubility of the following molecules?

2) How would you compare the solubility of the following molecules in ether?

3) How would you compare the solubility of the following molecules in an aqueous solution at pH 1?

Nucleophilicity Trends

> Rank the following compounds in order of *increasing nucleophilicity* toward the same electrophile in a *polar, protic* solvent:
>
> CH_3OH Et_3N $H_3C-CO_2^{\ominus}$ Et_3P $CH_3O^{\ominus}$

1) Separate out nucleophiles with the same attacking atom and rank them first.
Look at the oxygen nucleophiles first. Here the methoxide anion is more basic than the acetate anion ($CH_3CO_2^{-}$), which in turn is more basic than methanol. Therefore, the methoxide anion will be the most nucleophilic of the three oxygen-containing molecules.

With the methoxide anion, the lone pair on oxygen is "stuck" on the oxygen atom, whereas with acetate, the negative charge can be delocalized through resonance; this makes methoxide more basic. Both molecules are more basic than methanol, because methanol lacks a negative charge.

Remember: When the attacking atom of different nucleophiles is the same, nucleophilicity and basicity are **directly proportional**. Recall that **basicity** is proportional to how **localized a lone pair** is.

2) Look next for nucleophiles where the attacking atom is in the same group.
Because phosphorus is directly below nitrogen in the periodic table, triethylphosphine is more nucleophilic. This is where the nature of the solvent makes a big difference. The more basic molecules are better hydrogen bond *acceptors*, meaning that they will be surrounded by solvent molecules and therefore less available to attack the substrate. The differences in basicity are *less pronounced* when molecules are in the same period, so this effect is only noticeable when the attacking atoms are in the same group.

If the solvent were *polar aprotic*, then the trend would be *exactly the opposite*. Here, the hydrogen bonding effect is removed, so the molecules with the most localized charge density—the most basic—will also be the most nucleophilic.

Comparing the basicity of triethylphosphine and triethylamine is a bit more complicated. The key to determining basicity is remembering that in triethylphosphine, the lone pair on phosphorus is contained in an sp^3 hybrid orbital that is made up of one s- and three $3p$-orbitals. Contrast this with triethylamine, where the nitrogen lone pair is in an sp^3 hybrid composed of one s- and three $2p$-orbitals. This means that the electrons in the phosphorus lone pair are in a larger hybrid orbital, as $3p$-orbitals are larger than $2p$-orbitals.

This, in turn, means that the electrons in the phosphorus lone pair are more stable, because they probably have more volume to exist in. If the phosphorus lone pair is *more stable,* then the lone pair is *less reactive* and *less basic* (less likely to want to reach out and grab a proton).

---

3) Look for relationships between nucleophiles in the same period.

Now the question is between the two groups we have ordered separately. Which one is more nucleophilic? In most cases, this question is answered by realizing that for different nucleophiles where the attacking atoms are in the *same period, nucleophilicity roughly parallels basicity.* That being the case, triethylamine is more basic than the acetate anion.

$CH_3OH < CH_3CO_2^- < CH_3O^- < Et_3N < Et_3P$ (polar, protic solvent)

This trend is borne out experimentally. The relative reactivities of each nucleophile toward CH_3I in CH_3OH as solvent are as follows:

Nucleophile	Relative Rate
CH_3OH	1
$CH_3CO_2^-$	20,000
CH_3O^-	1,900,000
Et_3N	4,600,000
Et_3P	520,000,000

In a *polar, aprotic* solvent, the order of nucleophilicity would parallel basicity:

$CH_3OH < Et_3P < CH_3CO_2^- < Et_3N < CH_3O^-$ (polar, aprotic solvent)

Similar Questions

1) Place the following molecules in order of increasing nucleophilicity: pyridine (benzene with one of the carbons in the ring replaced by a nitrogen), triethylamine, acetonitrile (CH_3CN), and DMAP (4-dimethylaminopyridine). (Note that the solvent doesn't impact nucleophilicity here, because the same atom is nucleophilic in all four compounds.) Which of the two nitrogens in DMAP is more nucleophilic, and why?

2) How would the nucleophilicity of fluoride, chloride, bromide, and iodide rank in an S_N2 reaction with methyl iodide in methanol? In dimethyl sulfoxide?

3) How would you order the nucleophilicity of the following molecules in methanol: Et_3N, Ph_3P, Et_3P, Ph_3N, and Et_3As? Provide a rationale for your ordering. (*Hint*: What about their structures makes all of the molecules above both basic *and* nucleophilic?)

Key Concepts

Chapter 4

Reaction mechanisms

Carbocation stability

Aromaticity

Solvolytic conditions

Hückel's rule

Substrate Reactivity: S_N1 Reactions

Place the following molecules in order of *increasing* reactivity towards methanol under solvolytic conditions:

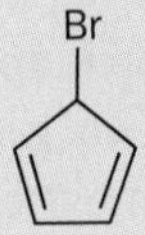

Takeaways

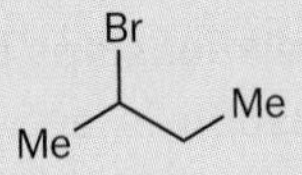

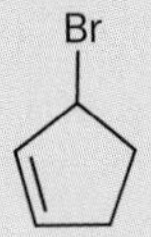

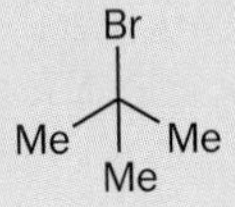

Reactivity in the S_N1 reaction is determined by carbocation stability because carbocation formation is the rate-limiting step.

1) Determine the potential stabilizing effects on each molecule.
"Solvolytic conditions" is code for an S_N1 reaction. With that in mind, the question is essentially asking you to place the molecules in order of increasing carbocation stability.

Molecules 2 and 4 would benefit from resonance stabilization, so at first glance they will be more stable carbocations than the others.

*Remember: When it comes to charge stabilization, **resonance stabilization** is **always** more powerful than **inductive stabilization**.*

---

2) Look for resonance stabilization first.
Molecule 4 clearly would have a resonance structure were the bromide to leave and form a cation:

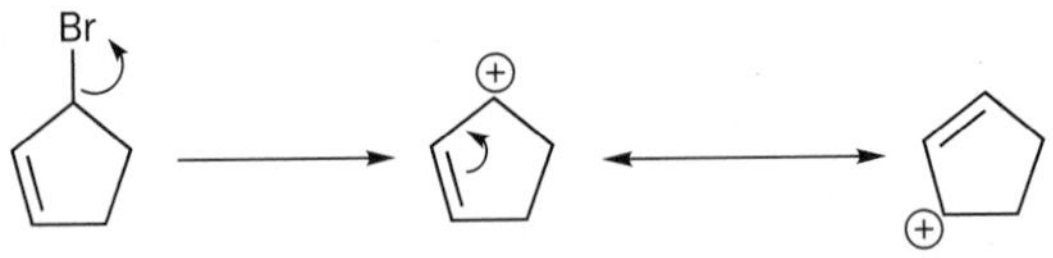

Things to Watch Out For

Don't forget that charged molecules can be aromatic as well!

You might think that if one alkene helps stabilize the carbocation, then *two* alkenes would do it better. Be careful with this, though: Take a look at the carbocation generated from 2:

Even though the carbocation at the right could have five resonance structures, notice that it is *antiaromatic*: It is cyclic, planar, and with conjugated alkenes, but it does not fit Hückel's rule. Therefore, this carbocation will be the *least stable* of all five molecules.

---

3) Look for inductive stabilization next.

Now we will look at the remaining molecules to determine their carbocation stability. If you draw the carbocations resulting from each bromide, you get the following:

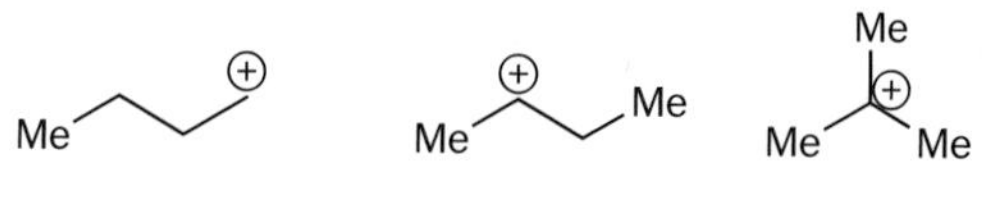

1   **3**   **5**

Because the stability of a carbocation is proportional to its substitution, 5 (tertiary) will be more stable than 3 (secondary) and finally 1 (primary).

---

4) Place all of the molecules in order of their reactivity.

The final order in increasing reactivity is thus as follows:
2 < 1 < 3 < 5 < 4

Similar Questions

1) 1–Chlorocycloheptatriene is dramatically more reactive in S_N1 reactions than is 1–bromocyclohexadiene. Why is this the case?

2) If 1–bromobutane (molecule **1**) were forced to become a carbocation, what product(s) would be isolated from the solvolytic reaction with methanol?

3) Compare the reactivity of 1–iodocyclopropene to 1–iodocyclopropane in a solvolysis reaction with ethanol, and provide an explanation for your comparison.

Key Concepts

Chapters 4–6

Nucleophilic addition

Oxidation and reduction

Substitution and elimination

Spectroscopy

Takeaways

Again, the key here is to move one step at a time so as not to get overwhelmed. Interpret each clue as you read through the passage and make notes on the reaction scheme, if necessary.

Things to Watch Out For

Be careful with the identities of **A** and **B**. They must be isomeric because they have the same molecular formula and give the same product when exposed to the same reaction conditions.

Identifying Structure of Unknown Hydrocarbon

For every mole of the mixture of **A** and **B** that was reacted, two moles of **C** were obtained. Compound **D** was reacted with a large excess of methyl iodide and potassium *tert*-butoxide in *t*-butanol as solvent. Kinetic studies were performed, and this reaction was found to be second order overall, with the reaction being first order with respect to **D** and potassium *tert*-butoxide. This reaction was heated and the product, 1-butene, was distilled off *in situ*.

Given this information, provide the structures of compounds **A**, **B**, **C**, and **D**.

1) Work through the problem one step at a time—backward in this case, because we are given the structure of the final product.

You should immediately suspect that some sort of elimination is going on to furnish 1-pentene. There are a myriad of clues suggesting this: the fact that an alkene is the product; that there is a strong, bulky base present in the reaction; and that the kinetic data specifically tells you that this reaction is an E2 reaction. This probably means that compound **D** is some sort of amine, but which amine is it? Also, amines are poor leaving groups, so how could an elimination occur?

There must be something about adding methyl iodide to the amine that is converting it to a good leaving group. This is exactly analogous to protonating an alcohol to turn it into a good leaving group. Thus, compound **D** must be *N,N*-dimethylbutylamine, given the fact that **C** is reacted with dimethylamine.

2) Determine the relationship between C and D.

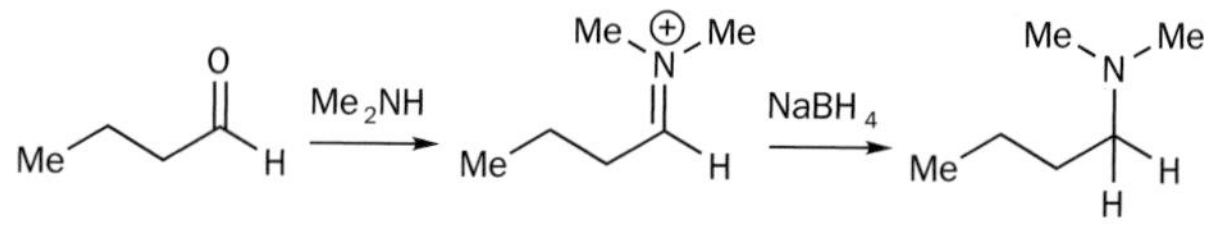

C

C_4H_8O

D

$C_6H_{15}N$

Because you are going from an aldehyde (note the diagnostic aldehyde peak for **C** in the NMR), this must be a reductive amination. Recall that when a carbonyl reacts with a primary amine, an *imine* is formed, but when a secondary amine is used, an *iminium ion* is the key intermediate.

3) Identify compounds A and B.

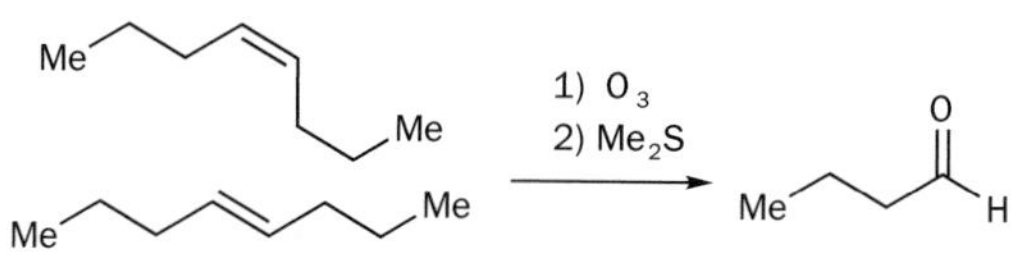

A + B

C_8H_{16}

C

C_4H_8O

The use of ozone should be a tip-off that **A** and **B** are going to be alkenes, and it must be a symmetrical alkene because one mole of the alkene mixture gives two moles of aldehyde. As for the fact that **A** and **B** give the same aldehyde, this should tell you that **A** and **B** must be geometric isomers—the only isomers that could react in the same way to give the same product.

Similar Questions

1) What would happen to compound **C** if it were exposed to sodium borohydride before the amine instead of after?

2) What alkene would you need to start with if 3-methylpentene were the alkene isolated at the end of the process?

3) Compound **C** could be reacted with methyl amine instead of dimethylamine to give the same alkene at the end because there is an excess of methyl iodide in the E2 elimination. However, a stronger reducing agent than $NaBH_4$ would be necessary to give the amine. Why do you think this is the case?

Key Concepts

Chapters 4–6

Substitution vs. elimination

Isomerism

Reaction mechanisms

S_N2

E2

Takeaways

When trying to decide between substitution and elimination, use the following decision pathway:

1) First, consider the structure of the substrate. If it is primary, you know that either S_N2 or E2 must be occurring. If it is tertiary, S_N2 cannot occur.

2) Next, consider the nature of the nucleophile/base. Is it a strong, bulky base? Then elimination is preferred. Is it smaller but still a strong base? Then substitution is preferred.

3) Finally, consider the solvent. Remember that S_N1/E1 reactions require polar, protic solvents, whereas S_N2 reactions require polar, aprotic solvents.

Identifying Reaction Mechanisms

When the trimethylammonium salt shown below is treated with a strong bulky base, only demethylation is observed.

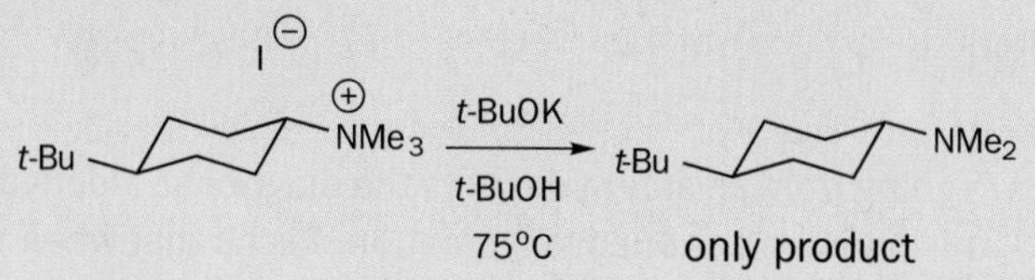

When the isomeric salt shown below is subjected to the same conditions, the product distribution below is obtained.

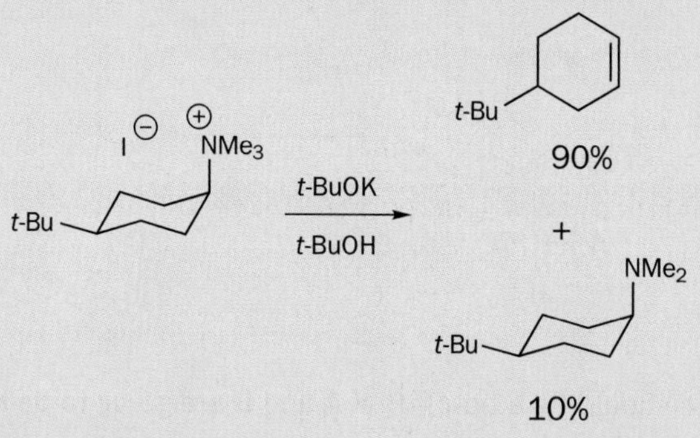

When the *tert*-butyl group is removed, the product distribution shifts back to favor demethylation.

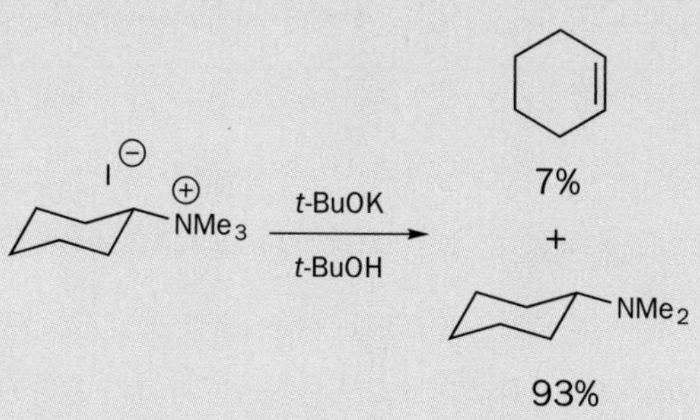

Provide explanations for the results of these reactions.

1) Identify the reactions taking place in each reaction.
   Reaction 1: S_N2

For the first reaction, the reaction appears to be an S_N2 reaction with a primary substrate, a good leaving group, and a good nucleophile (*t*–BuOK).

Reaction 2: E2

The second reaction seems to be going mainly through an E2 mechanism because the substrate is secondary and a strong, bulky base is present.

Reaction 3: S_N2

In the third reaction, the major product is again that of an S_N2 reaction (primary substrate, good leaving group, good nucleophile).

---

2) Given the preferences of each reaction and the properties of the substrate, explain the reaction outcome.

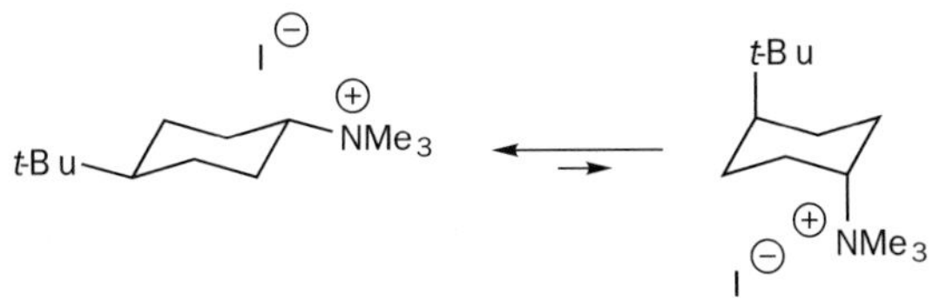

Recall that E2 reactions require antiperiplanar geometry of the substrate. Because the conformation shown above is that of the ring and cannot change without getting the diaxial isomer, substitution is the only path available.

In the first reaction, the ring is essentially locked in the conformation shown because a "ring flip" would generate the diaxial isomer, which is strongly disfavored energetically.

In the second reaction, the molecule starts with the leaving group in an axial position, which is properly aligned for E2 elimination. Elimination is favored over substitution because we have a strong, bulky base.

In the third reaction, the preferred conformer of the molecule is the one shown. This is because the trimethylammonium substituent is essentially the same as a *tert*-butyl group, meaning that the equatorial conformer is preferred. The Newman projection is then similar to that in the first reaction, leading to substitution being preferred.

Remember: *The bulkiest substituent on a cyclohexane ring always goes to the equatorial position.*

Things to Watch Out For

Be sure to take into account all of the factors listed above. Often one small change can completely change the preferred mechanism of a reaction.

Similar Questions

1) Predict the product if the following substituted cyclohexane were subjected to the same conditions as reaction 1 above.

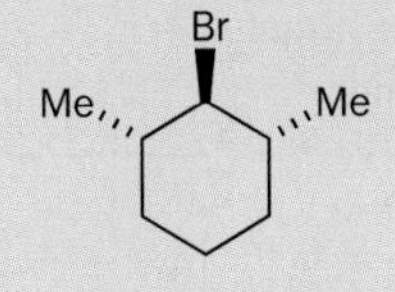

2) Why does neopentyl bromide (2,2-dimethyl-1-bromopropane) not undergo S_N2 substitution, even though it is a primary alkyl halide?

3) Explain why the enantiomerically pure molecule below undergoes racemization when dissolved by itself in a polar, protic solvent.

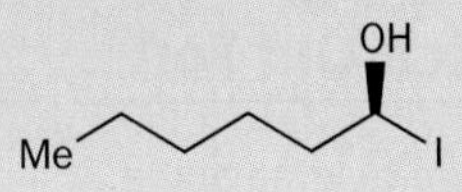

Key Concepts

Chapter 6

Aromaticity

Electrophilic aromatic substitution

Electrophilic Aromatic Substitution

Show how you might prepare *p*-bromobenzoic acid starting from benzene.

1) Identify the substituents on the ring and their regiochemical preferences. Work backward, if necessary.

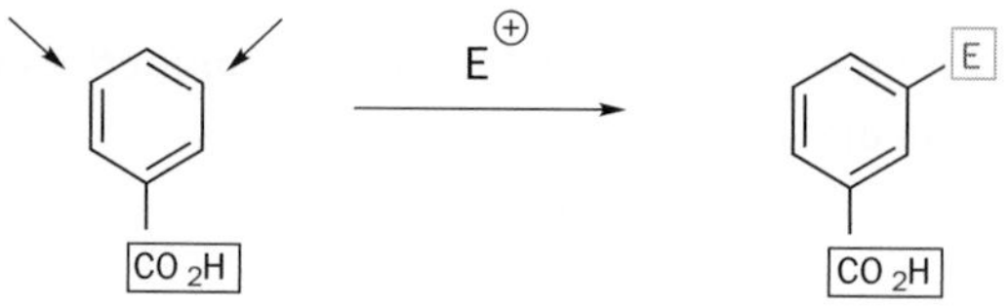

Clearly, we can't put both substituents on the ring at the same time. So we'll have to put one substituent on at a time.

If the intermediate before the last step is the carboxylic acid, when this molecule is substituted, the electrophile will go to the *meta* position, giving the incorrect regiochemistry.

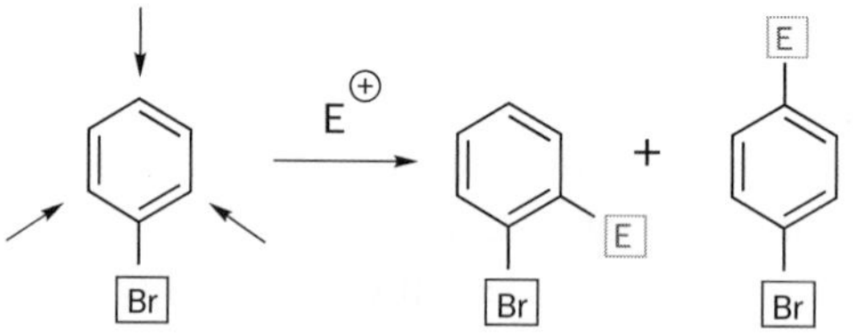

If bromobenzene is substituted, the electrophile will go to the *ortho* and *para* positions. We can then separate the isomers to give the desired *para* isomer.

Remember: *The carboxylic acid is a* meta-*director because it is resonance electron withdrawing. The bromo group is an* ortho, para-*director because it is resonance electron donating.*

Takeaways

Identify the regiochemical preferences of each substituent on an aromatic ring before thinking about specific reactions.

2) Establish reaction conditions to get to the desired product.

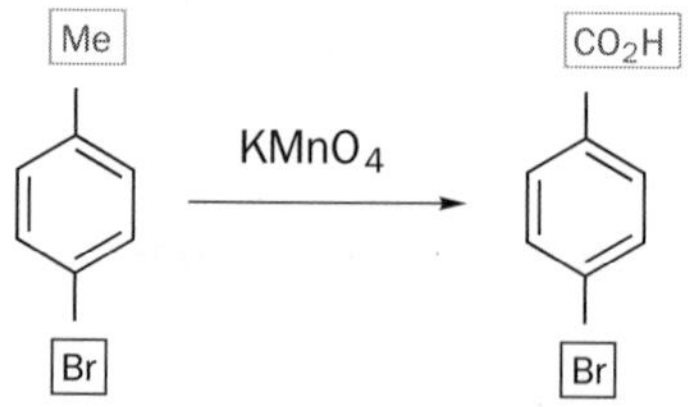

Now that we've decided to brominate first, we have to figure out which electrophile we will place on bromobenzene to get to the carboxylic acid.

Things to Watch Out For

Be sure to arrange the synthetic steps in the correct order!

The most straightforward way to do this is to place a methyl group on bromobenzene and then oxidize the methyl group to the carboxylic acid.

---

3) Write down the complete synthetic scheme in the forward direction.

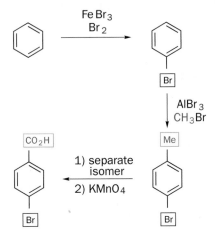

Similar Questions

1) How might *para*-bromobenzoic acid be prepared from *para*-dibromobenzene?

2) If 3-bromomethoxybenzene were nitrated once, where do you expect that the nitro group would appear in the product?

3) Show how triphenylmethane could be prepared from excess benzene and chloroform.

Identifying Structure of Unknown Aromatic

Given the diagram and the ^{1}H-NMR spectra shown below, determine the structures of molecules **A** through **H**.

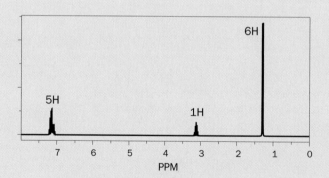

^{1}H-NMR of compound **A**

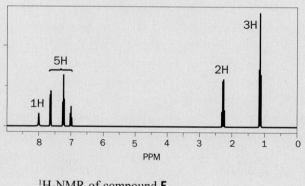

^{1}H-NMR of compound **E**

1) Determine the type of reaction.

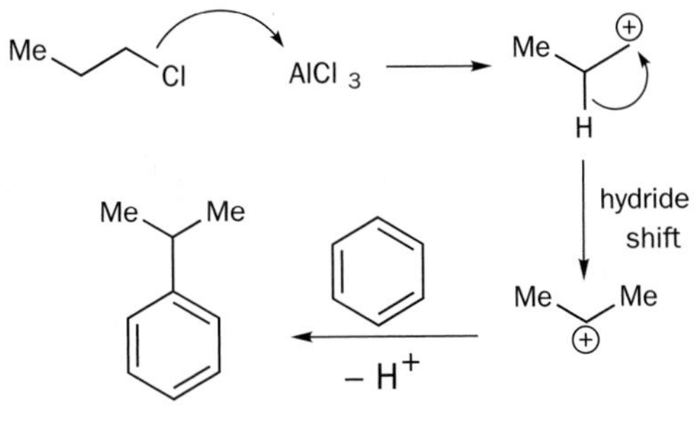

A

For the reaction to form product **A**, you should immediately recognize these conditions as that of a Friedel-Crafts alkylation. However, note from the NMR that the product is not simply propylbenzene because there are only two aliphatic signals in the NMR, not three. Therefore, the product must be isopropylbenzene.

---

2) Identify product B.
Product **B** is the product of a Friedel-Crafts *acylation*, giving a carbonyl.

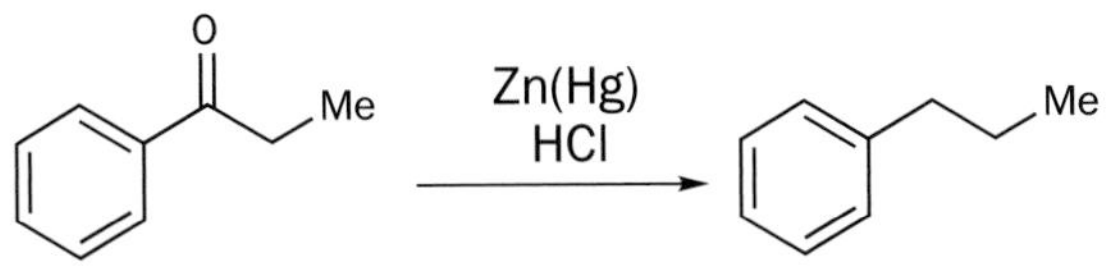

$C_9H_{10}O$ C_9H_{12}

B   **C**

Even if you didn't remember this, you should know that B contains a ketone from the stretch in the IR [the other stretches are for sp^3 C–H's (just to the *right* of 3,000 cm^{-1}) and the aromatic sp^2 C–H's (just to the *left* of 3,000 cm^{-1})]. In the next step, the carbonyl is removed and replaced with a methylene in the *Clemmensen reduction*.

---

3) Identify product D.

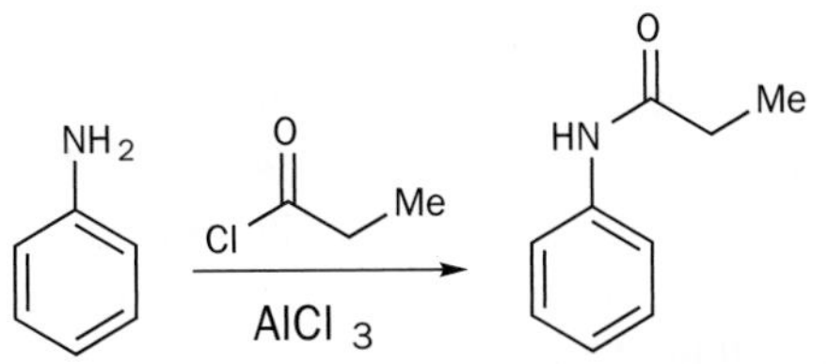

C_6H_7N $C_9H_{11}NO$

D   **E**

In the reaction to give molecule **D**, note that benzene is first *nitrate*, then the nitro group is reduced to an *amine*. Remember that if you see a nitrogen-bearing functional group followed by reductive conditions, an amine is almost certainly being generated. You should recognize the conditions to give **E** as another Friedel-Crafts acylation; however, note that in the NMR, there are still five aromatic protons. Therefore, the only other place that the acyl group can go is on the amine.

Remember: *The amino group is much more nucleophilic than the benzene ring, so with a Lewis acid in the reaction, the amine adds to the acid chloride carbonyl and then eliminates chloride to give the amide* **E**.

---

4) Rerun the reaction with molecule E.

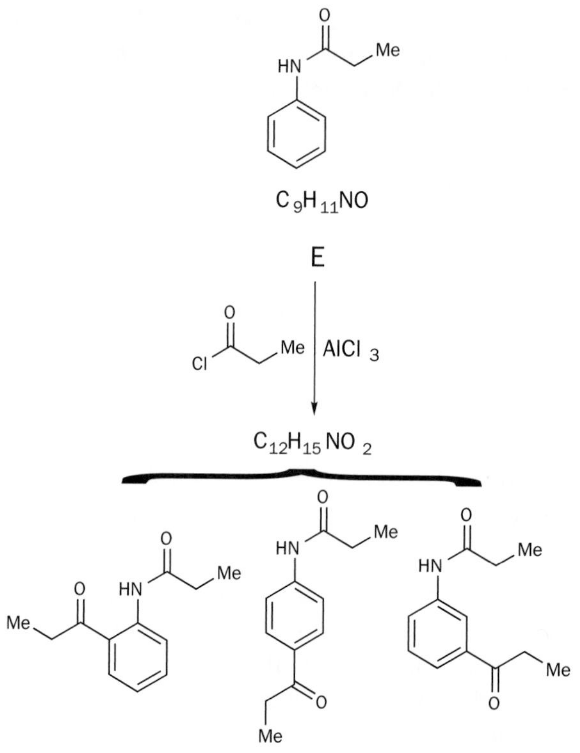

$C_9H_{11}NO$

E

$C_{12}H_{15}NO_2$

F   G   H

The third time seems to be the charm for this grad student. When he repeats the acylation reaction on **E**, this time the reaction works. You should suspect this not only from the molecular formula but from the fact that three products are formed in unequal yield-one of the telltale signs of electrophilic aromatic substitution. Because the nitrogen in **E** is still an *ortho-, para-* director, even with the adjacent carbonyl, the major products **F** and **G** will be the *ortho* and *para* isomers, and **H** will be the *meta* isomer.

High-Yield Problems continue on the next page

Key Concepts

Chapters 7–10

Nucleophilic addition

Resonance

Reaction rate

Takeaways

The rate at which a carbonyl compound reacts with a nucleophile is proportional to its electrophilicity—in other words, how much of a partial positive charge exists on the carbonyl carbon.

Things to Watch Out For

Don't forget to account for the fact that reactions may be possible other than just the reaction you've been asked about. In general, *acid-base reactions* (proton transfers) are faster than *intramolecular reactions,* which are faster than *intermolecular reactions*.

Substrate Reactivity: Nucleophilic Addition

Place the following molecules in order of *decreasing rate* of nucleophilic addition with lithium aluminum hydride:

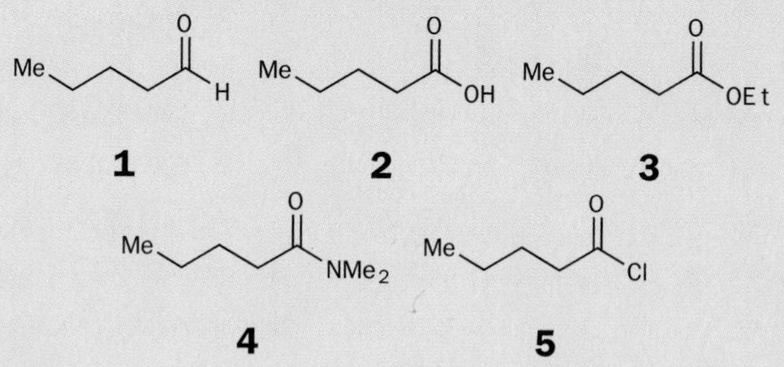

1) Determine the nature of the nucleophile.
Here, the nucleophile is coming from lithium aluminum hydride, which we can think about as being "H⁻."

2) Place the molecules in order of increasing electrophilicity.
Remember that molecules in which the carbonyl carbon is more electrophilic will react faster with nucleophiles. The electrophilicity of the carbonyl carbon is determined by the following resonance structure:

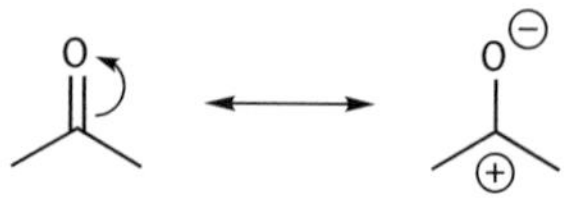

Molecules in which the resonance structure on the right is *more important* will have more electrophilic carbonyl carbons and therefore react the *fastest* with a nucleophile.

With that in mind, it should be clear that molecule 5 will react the fastest. Take a look at its analogous resonance structure:

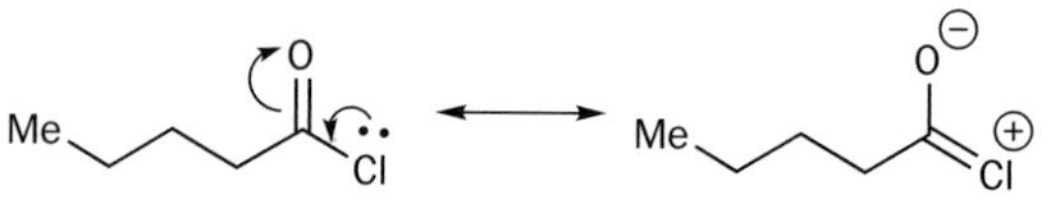

This resonance structure doesn't seem very reasonable because chlorine ends up having a positive charge on it. This means that the resonance structure with the positive charge on carbon is relatively more important, meaning that this molecule will react relatively quickly.

Hydrogen isn't quite as electronegative as chlorine, meaning that the aldehyde (molecule 1) will be the next most reactive.

High-Yield Problems

Between molecules 3 and 4, 3 will be more reactive. You can figure this out by examining the resonance structures below:

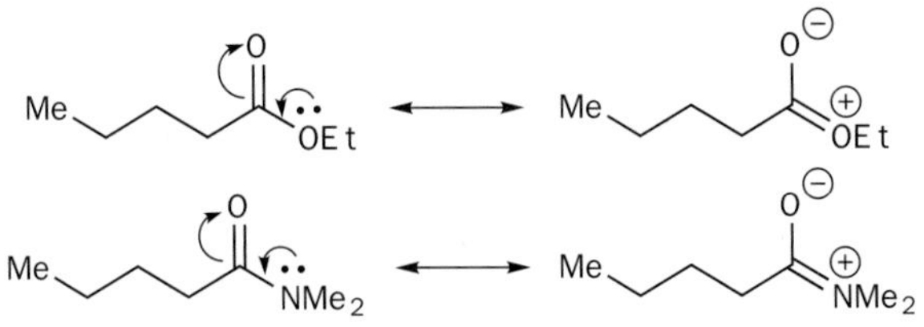

The nitrogen is more stable with a positive charge than oxygen due to its lower electronegativity. So it doesn't mind giving its lone pairs up to the carbonyl as much. When it does give up its lone pairs, though, it helps reduce the partial positive charge on carbon, and therefore the amide is less reactive toward nucleophiles than the ester.

Finally, how do we handle the carboxylic acid? As it turns out, this molecule is the least reactive toward nucleophilic addition, because an *acid–base reaction* occurs before any nucleophilic addition:

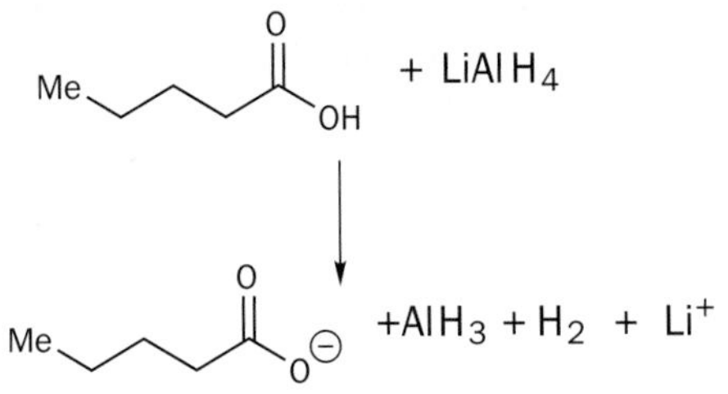

Whereas before, electron donation into the carbonyl occurred through a resonance structure with charge separation, here the carboxylate is already charged. So it can push its electron density into the carbonyl, resulting in a distribution of a negative charge:

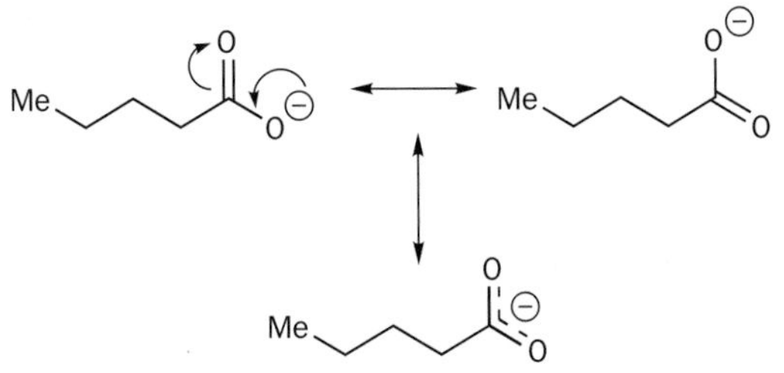

If there's a lot of negative charge floating around in the carbonyl, that's only going to repel the reagent, which is also negatively charged, making the carboxylic acid the least susceptible to attack.

---

3) Place all of the molecules in order of their reactivity.
The final order in decreasing rate of nucleophilic addition is as follows:

$5 > 1 > 3 > 4 > 2$

---

1) Nucleophilic substitutions can also occur with weak nucleophiles under acid catalysis. This requires that the carbonyl oxygen pick up a proton before the nucleophile adds. Rank the compounds above in order of *increasing basicity* of the carbonyl lone pair and explain your rankings.

2) How would you compare the reactivity of the following compounds towards methylmagnesium bromide:

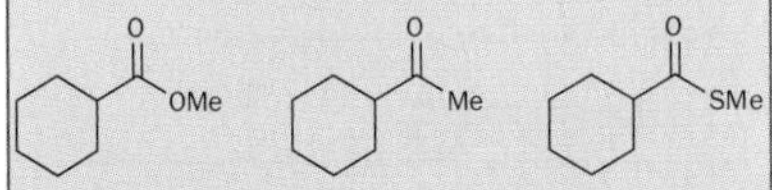

3) In the *haloform reaction*, methyl ketones are converted to their corresponding carboxylates. Provide a detailed, stepwise mechanism for the following haloform reaction:

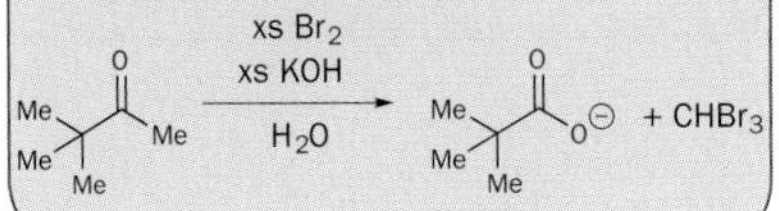

Key Concepts

Chapters 7–10

Oxidation/reduction

Isomerism

Identifying Structure of Unknown Oxy Compound

A student carried out the following series of transformations in the lab.

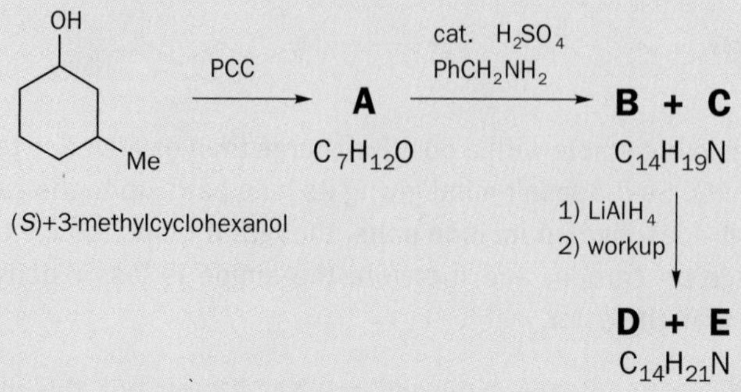

Upon A's reaction with catalytic acid and benzylamine, the student obtained a mixture of two products, B and C. The mixture of B and C is subjected to lithium aluminum hydride. Following a diluted aqueous workup and chromatographic separation, two more products, D and E, are obtained in unequal yield.

Identify the structures of compounds A through E, given their molecular formulas.

Takeaways

The key to these types of problems is identifying the nature of the reagents and then identifying how they would react with the starting materials for each step. Try to look for combinations of *electrophiles* and *nucleophiles*.

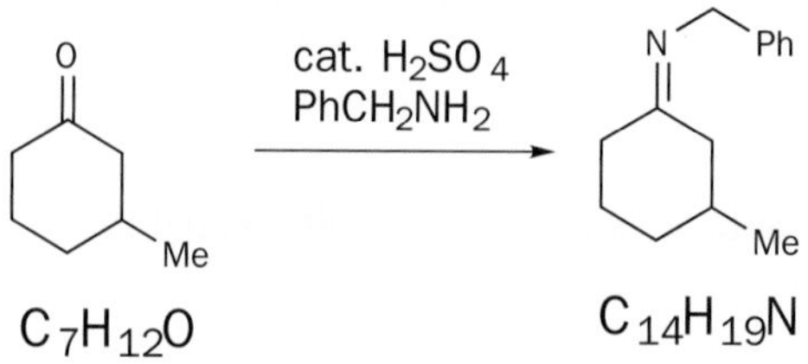

Things to Watch Out For

If the molecular formulas are supplied, be sure to check your structure against the given molecular formula.

1) React alcohol with PCC.

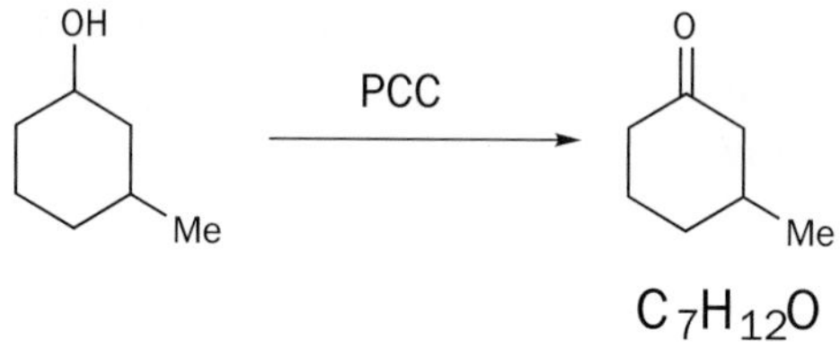

The first step of this process is to take the alcohol and subject it to PCC oxidation, which would give a ketone.

2) Subject ketone to an acid catalyst and benzylamine.

You should suspect that some sort of nucleophilic addition is going to take place. Recall that a ketone that reacts with a primary amine gives an *imine*.

3) Determine the other product of this reaction.

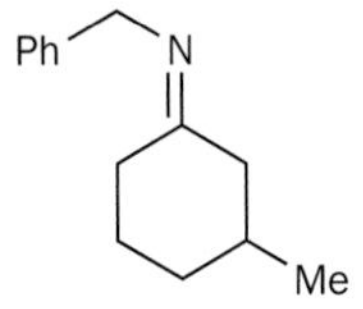

Recall that anytime there is a double bond, there exists the possibility of having *geometric isomers*. The double bond doesn't have to be a carbon–carbon double bond! So the other product must be the other geometric isomer.

4) React imine with LAH.

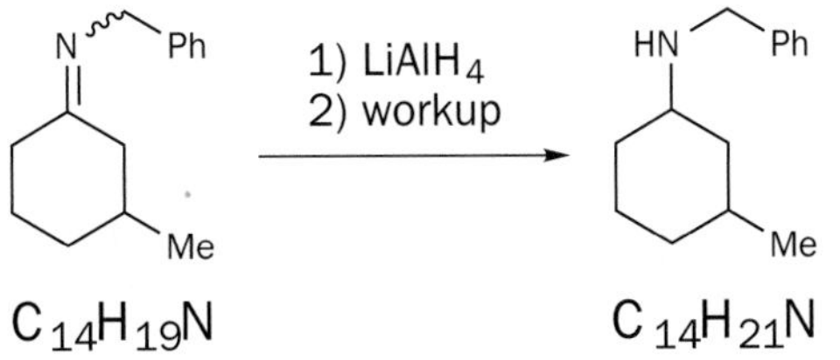

Reacting each of the imines with lithium aluminum hydride (LAH) will afford an amine. Note that you should be able to identify $LiAlH_4$ as a *reducing agent* because there are a lot of H's attached to either B or Al.

The student obtained two products in unequal yield. This suggests that the two products are *diastereomers*. In this case, there are two possible diastereomers:

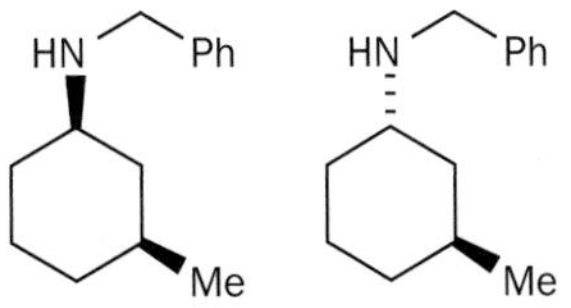

The methyl stereocenter has the same orientation for both molecules because it has been unchanged since the beginning. Therefore, the difference in stereochemistry must be at the nitrogen-bearing stereocenter.

Similar Questions

1) How many total stereoisomers are produced in the last reduction step? (*Hint:* How many stereocenters are there in the molecule?)
2) The final amine products were placed in a polarimeter and found not to rotate plane-polarized light. Why should this be the case?

Key Concepts

Chapter 10

Acids and bases

Enolate ion

Claisen condensation

Intramolecular reactions

Intramolecular Ring Closures

Provide a detailed, stepwise mechanism to account for the following transformation:

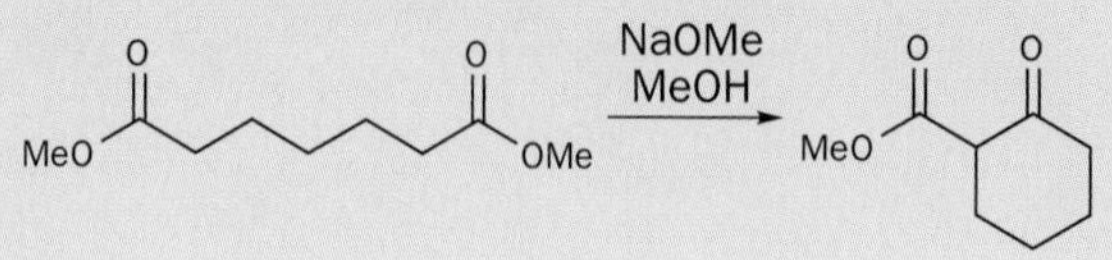

1) Examine the product for clues to the connectivity.

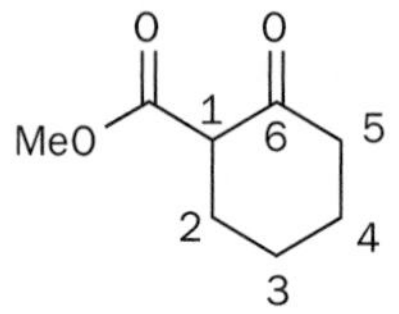

Anytime you see one molecule going to form a ring, you should suspect that there is an intramolecular reaction. Here, note that in the six-membered ring, the α-carbon of one ester is directly connected to a ketone. That, combined with the fact that there is a β-keto ester in the product, should tell you that what is going on is an intramolecular Claisen condensation.

Remember: *Intramolecular reactions are always faster than intermolecular reactions because the reactants are already close together.*

---

2) Start pushing electons.

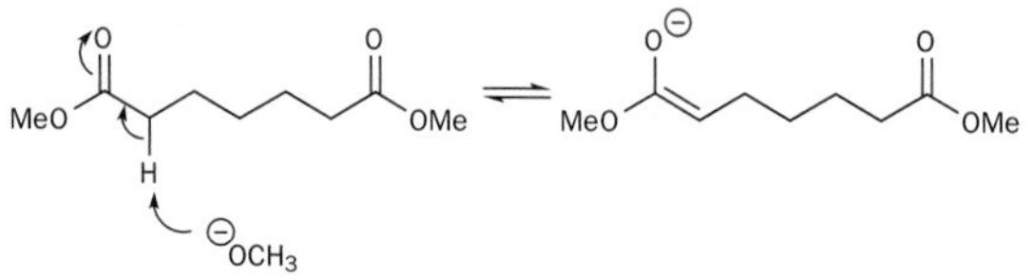

First, generate an enolate for the Claisen condensation, which must take place next to one of the esters.

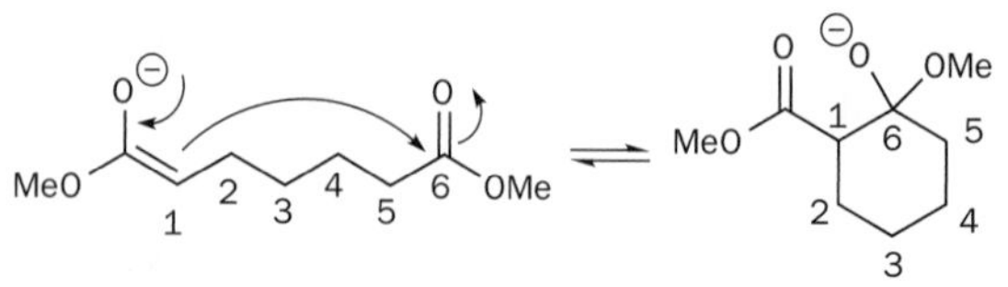

Then, the intramolecular reaction takes place. Numbering along the carbon chain and in the product is always a good idea. This will help you make sure that everything is in the right place.

Takeaways

Remember that with mechanism problems, you always want to get toward the specified products. Don't include steps that don't get you any closer to where you want to be.

Things to Watch Out For

Make sure that if charged intermediates are involved in your mechanism, they go away before you get to the product, unless the product is charged as well.

Also, be sure that your arrows are pointing in the right direction! The head of the arrow is pointing toward where the electrons are moving, not where they start from.

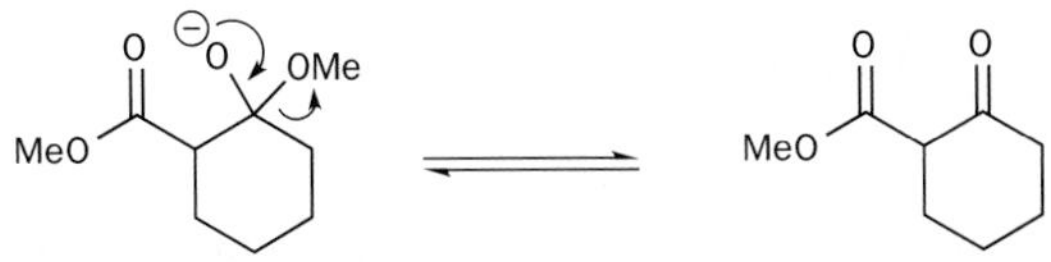

Here, finish the mechanism by generating the keto ester functionality that is in the product.

Similar Questions

1) Provide a detailed, stepwise mechanism for the following transformation:

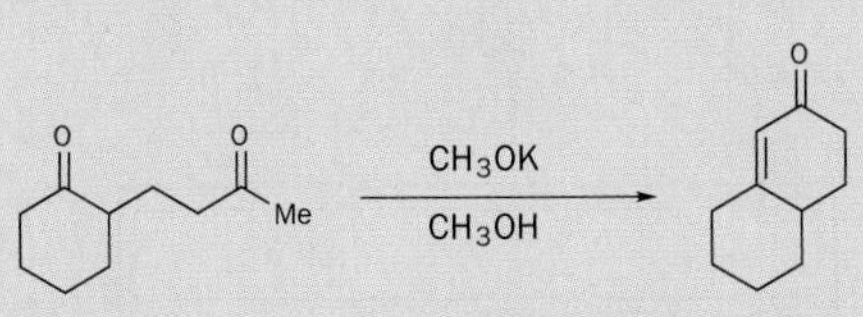

2) Provide a detailed, stepwise mechanism for the same reaction above, except run an *acid* instead of a *base*.

3) Provide a detailed, stepwise mechanism to account for the following reaction:

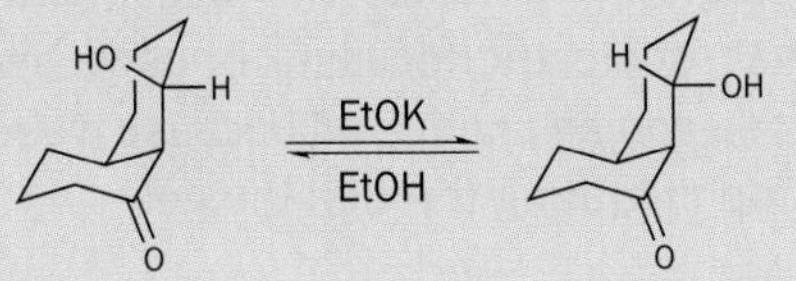

Key Concepts

Chapter 12

Isoelectric focusing

Determining isoelectric point

Electrolytic cell

Isoelectric Focusing

Suppose you are trying to separate glycine, glutamic acid, and lysine given the following information:

	pKa COOH	pKa NH$_3^+$	pKa R group
Glycine:	2.34	9.63	—
Glutamic acid:	2.19	9.67	4.25
Lysine:	2.18	8.95	10.53

Indicate in which region of the gel each amino acid will stop migrating.

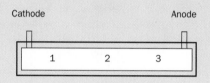

Takeaways

To solve isoelectric focusing questions, determine the pI of the samples being separated. Then, determine the orientation of the pH gradient on the gel. The samples will migrate toward their pI, isoelectric point.

1) Identify if it is an isoelectric focusing problem.

Whenever a question gives you the pK$_a$ of the substance being purified, think ion exchange chromatography or isoelectric focusing. In the above question, we can be certain that isoelectric focusing is used because the separatory apparatus has a cathode and an anode and because we're told that each amino acid will eventually stop migrating through the gel.

2) Determine the isoelectric points of the sample(s).

To find the pI for an amino acid, identify the deprotonation reaction that converts the amino acid with +1 overall charge into the zwitterion with 0 overall charge; also, identify the deprotonation reaction that converts the zwitterion into a form with −1 overall charge. The pI for the amino acid is the average of the pK$_a$'s for these two reactions.

For glycine, the sequence of deprotonation reactions is the following:

$$
\underset{\substack{|\\ H}}{\overset{\substack{R\\ |}}{NH_3^+ - C - COOH}} \underset{pK_{a1} = 2.34}{\rightleftharpoons} \underset{\substack{|\\ H}}{\overset{\substack{R\\ |}}{NH_3^+ - C - COO^-}} \underset{pK_{a2} = 9.63}{\rightleftharpoons} \underset{\substack{|\\ H}}{\overset{\substack{R\\ |}}{NH_2 - C - COO^-}}
$$

For glycine, the pKa's for the reactions leading to and from the zwitterion are pK$_{a1}$ and pK$_{a2}$. So the pI for glycine is the average of its pK$_{a1}$ and pK$_{a2}$.

$$
\text{pI of glycine} = \frac{(2.34 + 9.63)}{2} = 5.99
$$

Things to Watch Out For

Be careful in problems that ask you to separate proteins. Remember that the pI of a protein cannot be determined simply by averaging the pI of the individual amino acids. If the isoelectric point of a protein is not given, then another method must be used to separate the proteins.

For glutamic acid, the sequence of deprotonation reactions is this:

$$
\begin{array}{ccccccc}
& \text{RH} & \xrightleftharpoons{pK_{a1}=2.19} & \text{RH} & \xrightleftharpoons{pK_{a2}=4.25} & \text{R} & \xrightleftharpoons{pK_{a3}=9.67} & \text{R}^- \\
& | & & | & & | & & | \\
\text{NH}_3^+\!-\!\text{C}\!-\!\text{COOH} & & \text{NH}_3^+\!-\!\text{C}\!-\!\text{COO}^- & & \text{NH}_3^+\!-\!\text{C}\!-\!\text{COO}^- & & \text{NH}_2\!-\!\text{C}\!-\!\text{COO}^- \\
| & & | & & | & & | \\
\text{H} & & \text{H} & & \text{H} & & \text{H}
\end{array}
$$

(The side chain is acidic, so we need to include a reaction for its deprotonation. The conjugate base of an acidic side chain is negatively charged.) For glutamic acid, the pKa's for the reactions leading to and from the zwitterion are pK_{a1} and pK_{a2}. So the pI for glutamic acid is the average of its pK_{a1} and pK_{a2}.

$$
\text{pI of Glutamic acid} = \frac{(2.19 + 4.25)}{2} = 3.22
$$

For lysine the sequence of deprotonation reactions is this:

$$
\begin{array}{ccccccc}
& \text{RH}^+ & \xrightleftharpoons{pK_{a1}=2.18} & \text{RH}^+ & \xrightleftharpoons{pK_{a2}=8.95} & \text{RH}^+ & \xrightleftharpoons{pK_{a3}=10.53} & \text{R} \\
& | & & | & & | & & | \\
\text{NH}_3^+\!-\!\text{C}\!-\!\text{COOH} & & \text{NH}_3^+\!-\!\text{C}\!-\!\text{COO}^- & & \text{NH}_2\!-\!\text{C}\!-\!\text{COO}^- & & \text{NH}_2\!-\!\text{C}\!-\!\text{COO}^- \\
| & & | & & | & & | \\
\text{H} & & \text{H} & & \text{H} & & \text{H}
\end{array}
$$

For lysine, the pKa's for the reactions leading to and from the zwitterion are pK_{a2} and pK_{a3}. So the pI for glycine is the average of its pK_{a2} and pK_{a3}.

$$
\text{pI of lysine} = \frac{(8.95 + 10.53)}{2} = 9.74
$$

3) Determine the relative pH gradient of the gel.

Electrophoresis is always run on electrolytic cells. Recall that electrolytic cells require an outside source of energy. The negative terminal is connected to the cathode, and the positive end is connected to the anode. This means that the anode (acidic end of the gel) will attract negative anions and the cathode (basic end of the gel) will attract positive anions.

Therefore, we know that zone 1 is at a higher pH than zone 2, which is at a higher pH than zone 3.

4) Determine where the samples will migrate.

This means that proteins will migrate toward their pI. At the pI, the protein will not have a net charge (it will be in its zwitterion form) and thus will no longer be induced to migrate in the electric field.

In the above problem, glutamic acid will align itself in region 3, glycine will align itself in region 2, and lysine will align itself in region 1.

Remember: *Amino acids are amphoteric and thus will be positively charged at pH values below their pI and negatively charged above their pI.*

Similar Questions

1) If a segment of polypeptide with a pI of 6.7 is subjected to electrophoresis at pH 5, will the segment move toward the cathode or the anode?

2) What is the isoelectric point of aspartic acid?

3) In what form is an amino acid said to be when it reaches its isoelectric point?

Key Concepts

Chapter 12

Extraction (liquid-liquid separation)

Acid/base properties

Separation

Takeaways

In an extraction problem, each compound will either be dissolved in the aqueous layer or the organic layer. However, if a compound is acidic or basic, it is possible to transpose it to the aqueous layer by using basic or acidic washes, respectively.

Things to Watch Out For

Don't assume that the organic phase will be on top—this depends on the densities of the two phases. For example, dichloromethane (1.3 g mL^{-1}) is denser than water (1.0 g mL^{-1}); dichloromethane will sink to the bottom of the separatory funnel, with the water floating on top.

Extraction

A student wishes to separate methyl phenyl ketone, aniline, and phenol from a mixture. To perform the separation, the mixture is dissolved in a solution consisting of 500 ml of H_2O and 500 ml of dichloromethane. The solution is then washed with water three times, and the aqueous layer (A) is extracted. The remaining solution is then washed with 20 percent Na_2CO_3 three times and the aqueous layer (B) is collected. The remaining organic layer is finally washed with 10 percent HCl, and the aqueous layer (C) is once again collected, leaving behind the organic layer (D). What were the contents of samples A, B, C, and D?

1) Determine the difference between the molecules being separated.

Acetophenone, aniline, and phenol are all organic compounds. However, aniline is a weak base whereas phenol is a weak acid. Methyl phenyl ketone is the most hydrophobic of the three compounds because it doesn't possess any functional groups capable of making hydrogen bonds.

2) Determine into what phase each of the compounds will dissolve after the first set of washings.

All three compounds are uncharged organic compounds and as such will dissolve in the organic layer, in dichloromethane. Thus, the first set of washings will not aid in separating any of the three compounds.

3) Determine into what phase each of the compounds will dissolve after the second set of washings.

When the sample is washed with Na_2CO_3, phenol will be deprotonated to yield sodium phenoxide (the conjugate base of phenol). Because this molecule is charged, it will move into the aqueous layer. After the washing, the deprotonated phenol will move to the aqueous phase, whereas methyl phenyl ketone and aniline will remain in the organic layer.

Remember: *Washing a mixture with a base is an effective way to move acidic compounds from the organic layer into the aqueous layer.*

4) Determine into what phase each of the compounds will dissolve after the third set of washings.

At this point, the only remaining compounds in the organic layer are acetophenone and aniline.

When the sample is washed with HCl (a strong acid), aniline will be protonated to an anilinium ion. This positively charged molecule will move into the aqueous layer, whereas acetophenone will remain in the organic layer.

Remember: *Washing a mixture with an acid is an effective way to move basic compounds from the organic layer to the aqueous layer.*

Similar Questions

1) Design an extraction procedure to separate a mixture of phenol and benzoic acid dissolved in ether.

2) In order to extract *p*-nitrophenol from phenol in an ether solution, a student washes the organic layer with 10 ml of a 5 percent aqueous solution of NaOH. After the washing, what will be left in the organic layer?

Key Concepts

Chapter 12

Purification

Chromatography

Ion exchange

Separation

Column chromatography

Chromatography

In an effort to purify ATCase, a crude cell extract in a potassium phosphate buffer is run on a Q-Sepharose column (mono Q is an anion exchanger: $-CH_2-N(CH_3)_3^+$). What characteristic of ATCase allows it to be separated using an anion exchanger? Are any additives necessary to achieve a successful purification?

1) Determine the difference between the molecules being separated.

In the question stem, we are told that mono Q (the stationary phase in the column) is an anion exchanger. This means that it attracts anions and thus must have a positive charged group. Because we are trying to purify ATCase, it must bind to mono Q; if it doesn't, it will simply pass through the column along with the other positively charged proteins and thus not be purified. So we can conclude that ATCase is a negatively charged protein (an anionic protein), enabling it to be purified using an anion exchanger.

If an antibody or substrate for ATCase were available, affinity chromatography could have been used. Column chromatography could also be used to separate substances based on size.

Takeaways

All forms of chromatography have two phases, a stationary phase and a mobile phase. Separations of compounds take advantage of the different affinities that compounds have for the two different phases.

2) Determine which compound has a higher affinity for the stationary phase.

When the crude cell extract is run through the column, ATCase and other anionic proteins will stick to the stationary phase, whereas the rest of the extract will pass through the column relatively easily.

3) Determine which compound has a higher affinity for the eluent.

Now that the anionic proteins are bound to the Q-sepharose gel, they must be eluted based on their affinities (in this case the strength of their negative charge) for the stationary phase. For this purpose, NaCl is added in an increasing concentration gradient. The least negatively charged proteins will emerge from the column before the proteins with the greatest negative charge.

Things to Watch Out For

Be cautious not to assume that the desired product will attach to the stationary phase. You may be presented with a situation in which purification will be better accomplished if the desired product has a higher affinity for the mobile phase.

Similar Questions

1) Sample A (R_f value of 0.75) and sample B (R_f value of 0.50) were run on silica gel. What is the distance traveled by sample A if sample B traveled 2.0 cm?

2) If the pH of the buffer is increased from 7 to 9, how will the purification be affected?

3) If you want to separate two anionic proteins (protein A and protein B, where protein A is a tetramer of protein B) with the same anionic character, which type of chromatography will be most useful? Assume that the tetramer once formed in the cell does not dissociate and that the monomer cannot form the tetramer *in vitro*.

High-Yield Problems continue on the next page

NMR Spectroscopy

A grad student performed an electrophilic chlorination of phenol, as shown below.

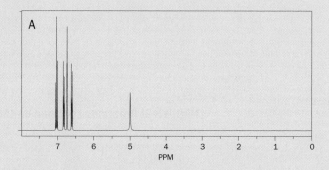

The grad student obtained three products, the *ortho*, *meta*, and *para* isomers, and separated all three. Unfortunately, he forgot to label which compound was which. ^{1}H-NMRs were taken of each product and are shown below. Match each spectrum to its corresponding product.

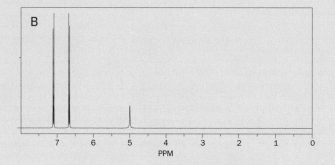

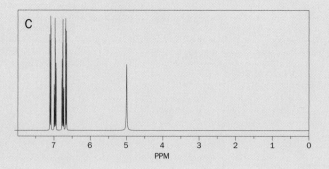

High-Yield Problems

1) Examine each spectrum for the number of signals.

In this case, spectrum **B** appears to be the most symmetric molecule because it has the least number of signals (3). Spectra **A** and **C** are the least symmetric, with five signals each.

The number of signals tells you a lot about the symmetry of a molecule. The fewer signals there are, the higher symmetry the molecule possesses.

---

2) Examine the structure of each product and try to start matching spectra based on your symmetry observations.

The three possible products are these:

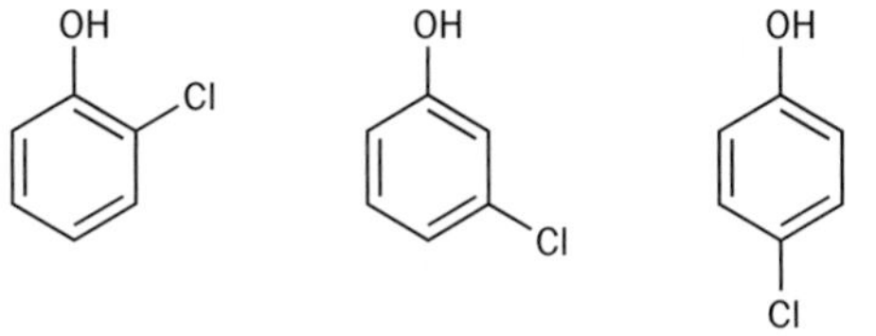

By inspection, the *para* isomer appears to be the most symmetric. Imagine jamming a pole down the middle of the ring, through the alcohol and chlorine. If you were to rotate the molecule 180 degrees around the pole, you would get the same molecule back. The proton adjacent to the alcohol will then account for one aromatic signal, and the protons adjacent to the chlorine another. Therefore, spectrum **B** must be that of the *para* isomer.

---

3) Take a closer look at each of the products to sort out the remaining spectra, if necessary.

Now we have to distinguish between the *ortho* and *meta* isomers. The main difference between them is that the *meta* isomer has one proton between the alcohol and the chlorine, whereas the *ortho* has none. In the *meta* isomer, this proton will give rise to a singlet in the NMR because there are no protons on the adjacent carbons. In the *ortho* isomer, each proton has at least one proton on the adjacent carbon, meaning no singlets.

Thus, spectrum **A** must correspond to the *meta* isomer because it is the only spectrum that has a singlet (near 6.75 ppm). By process of elimination, spectrum **C** must be the *ortho* isomer.

Similar Questions

1) Predict the splitting patterns resulting from all of the protons on the *ortho* and *meta* isomers.

2) Other than the chemical shift, how do you know that the signal around 5 ppm must be that of the alcohol proton? (*Hint:* Look at the *shape* of the signal.)

3) If the three isomers were of iodophenol instead of chlorophenol, how would the ¹H-NMR spectra be different from those displayed above?

Key Concepts

Chapter 13

Spectroscopy

IR spectroscopy

^{1}H-NMR spectroscopy

Combined Spectroscopy: IR and NMR

An unknown compound was discovered in an old, unused laboratory. Its molecular formula was determined to be $C_6H_9NO_2$ by high-resolution mass spectrometry. The following IR stretches were recorded: 3,300 (share), 2,890 (m), 2,220, 1,740 (s), 1,220, 984, 700, 650 cm^{-1}.

The ^{1}H-NMR spectrum of the compound is as follows:

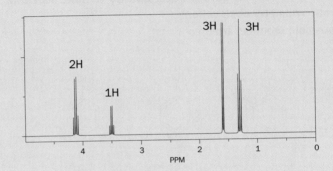

Given this information, determine the structure of the unknown compound.

Takeaways

With these combined structure problems, make sure to utilize all of the data at your disposal. The process is very much like taking the pieces of a jigsaw puzzle and putting them together.

1) Compute the number of sites of unsaturation.

$$U = \frac{(2n+2-m)}{2}$$

n = number of carbons; m = number of protons and/or halogens minus number of nitrogens. Ignore oxygen and sulfur.

Thus, $U = \frac{(2 \times 6 + 2 - 8)}{2} = \frac{6}{2} = 3$.

This means that the molecule has either three double bonds, one double bond and one triple bond, or some combination of rings and double or triple bonds.

Remember: If a molecule has four or more sites of unsaturation, you should immediately suspect that an aromatic ring is present.

Things to Watch Out For

Again, be sure not to overinterpret the IR data. There are only five or six functional groups whose presence can be conclusively indicated by the IR.

2) Look at the IR stretches to determine what functional groups are present.

Here, the stretch at 1,740 cm^{-1} indicates the presence of a carbonyl, and the stretch at 2,220 cm^{-1} indicates the presence of a triple bond (either an alkyne or a nitrile).

The one thing you do *not* want to do with the IR data is to try to interpret every single stretch. The IR is not nearly as informative as the NMR. Just look for the few stretches that are indicative of functional groups.

3) Do a little detective work to narrow down the structural possibilities. First let's think about the carbonyl. It can't be an aldehyde because there are no aldehyde signals in the NMR, and it can't be a carboxylic acid because there is no alcohol stretch in the IR. Because the stretch is closer to 1,740 than to 1,700, it is probably an ester rather than a ketone (you might also suspect this from the 1,220 stretch in the IR, which indicates a C–O stretch).

As for the triple-bond stretch, it is most likely a nitrile because there are no amine stretches in the IR.

---

4) Look more specifically at the information in the NMR to put the rest of the molecule together.
Look at the signal that's farthest downfield in the NMR. It comes from two protons that are adjacent to a methyl group (because the signal is a quartet). Because we suspect that the carbonyl is an ester, this signal must correspond to two protons that are right next to the ester oxygen. The fact that the signal is farthest downfield indicates that these protons are immediately adjacent to the oxygen, which is the most electronegative atom. We also know that this is an ethyl ester because these two protons are next to a methyl group.

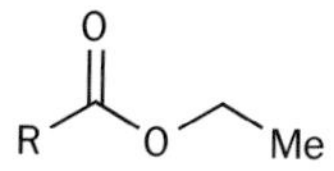

We've accounted for three carbons, two oxygens, and five hydrogens in the structure above, and we also know that the nitrile accounts for an additional carbon and nitrogen.

$$C_6H_9NO_2 - C_4H_5NO_2 = C_2H_4$$

We have two carbons and two hydrogens left to deal with. There can only be two possibilities, structurally:

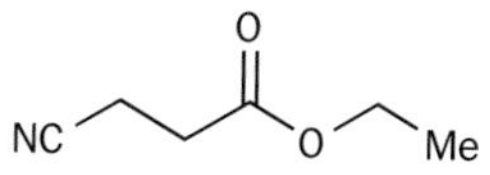

or

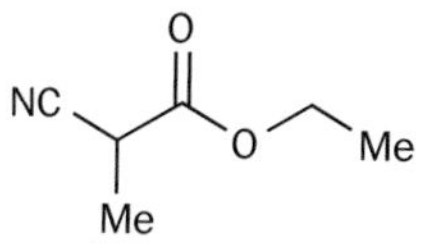

Note that the protons in the structure on the left would have to give rise to two triplets because each is adjacent to a carbon with two protons. However, the only signals we haven't accounted for in the NMR are a doublet integrating for three protons and a quartet integrating for one. These signals exactly match the structure on the right, so that must be the unknown.

Remember: *Once you have made a tentative structural assignment, check it against all of the data available to be sure you have the right molecule.*

Similar Questions

1) Why is it unlikely that the compound in the original question is cyclic (i.e., contains one or more rings)?
2) If the molecule were a methyl ketone rather than an ester (i.e., replace the ethoxy group with a methyl group), where do you expect that the carbonyl IR stretch would appear, and why?
3) Where would the signal for the methyl ketone protons in the compound described in question 2 show up in the NMR relative to the signal for the protons adjacent to the oxygen in the ester?

Art Credits for Organic Chemistry

Chapter 3 Cover—Image credited to Slim Films. From Proteins Rule by Carol Ezzell. Copyright © 2002 by Scientific American, Inc. All rights reserved.

Chapter 6 Cover—Image credited to Mark A. Reed. From Computing with Molecules by Mark A. Reed and James M. Tour. Copyright © 2000 by Scientific American, Inc. All rights reserved.

Chapter 9 Cover—Image credited to Ken Eward/BioGrafs. From Molecular Lego by Christian E. Schafmeister. Copyright © 2007 by Scientific American, Inc. All rights reserved.

Figure 9.11—Image credited to Bryan Christie. From Working Knowledge: Cleaning Agents by Louis A. Bloomfield. Copyright © 2000 by Scientific American, Inc. All rights reserved.

Figure 12.10—Image credited to Daniels and Daniels. From The Amateur Scientist: Sorting Molecules with Electricity by Shawn Carlson. Copyright © 1998 by Scientific American, Inc. All rights reserved.

Figure 13.3 (Graphs)—Image credited to Lucy Reading-Ikkanda. From The Incredible Shrinking Scanner by Bernhard Blümich. Copyright © 2004 by Scientific American, Inc. All rights reserved.

Figure 13.3 (MRI machine)—Image credited to George Retseck. From The Incredible Shrinking Scanner by Bernhard Blümich. Copyright © 2004 by Scientific American, Inc. All rights reserved.

Figure 13.3 (MRI image)—Image credited to Mehau Kulyk SPL/Photo Researchers, Inc. From The Incredible Shrinking Scanner by Bernhard Blümich. Copyright © 2004 by Scientific American, Inc. All rights reserved.

Glossary

Absolute configuration Three-dimensional orientation in space of the four substituents on a chiral center (i.e., the *R* or *S* configuration of a chiral carbon).

Acetals Stable compounds of the general formula $R_2C(OR')_2$, resulting from the nucleophilic addition of two moles of an alcohol to an aldehyde. Acetals are often used as a protecting group for aldehydes, because they are stable to basic and nucleophilic reagents but easily removed by acid hydrolysis.

Achiral A molecule that does not possess optical activity.

Activating group Activating groups make an aromatic ring more susceptible to electrophilic substitution. Activating groups, except for alkyl groups, have at least one pair of nonbonding electrons on the atom directly attached to the ring; these electrons stabilize the carbocation intermediate. Activating groups direct substituents to the *ortho* and *para* positions. Typical examples are $-NH_2$, $-OH$, $-CH_3$, and $-OCH_3$.

Activation energy Energy barrier that must be overcome in order for a reaction to occur. The activation energy required determines the rate of the reaction at a particular temperature.

Addition reaction Reaction in which an electrophile and then a nucleophile add to a pi bond, resulting in a more saturated compound.

Alcohols Compounds of the general formula ROH.

Aldehydes Compounds of the general formula RCHO.

Aldol condensation The nucleophilic addition of an enolate ion to a carbonyl compound to yield an aldol (a β-hydroxy aldehyde). The reaction is called a condensation because two molecules join to form one large molecule. This reaction can also be used for ketones but is less efficient.

Aliphatic compounds Nonaromatic hydrocarbons.

Alkanes The simplest organic molecules, consisting only of carbon and hydrogen and containing only single bonds. The general formula for alkanes is C_nH_{2n+2}. Also called paraffins.

Alkenes Hydrocarbons with at least one carbon–carbon double bond (C=C). Their general formula is C_nH_{2n}. Also called *olefins*.

Alkynes Hydrocarbons with at least one carbon–carbon triple bond (C≡C). Their general formula is C_nH_{2n-2}.

Allenes Dienes whose two C–C double bonds are adjacent (not separated by any single bonds). See *dienes*.

Allylic cation $RCH=CH-CH_2^+$: A carbocation with a positive charge adjacent to a double bond. This cation is more stable than a tertiary carbocation because of resonance stabilization from the *p*-orbital on the central carbon, which can overlap with the *p*-orbital on either carbon adjacent to it.

Alpha carbon A carbon adjacent to a carbon containing the functional group under consideration.

Alpha hydrogen The hydrogen bonded to an α carbon, which is usually affected by the nearby group. For instance, a hydrogen α to a carbonyl group is more acidic than other carbon-bonded hydrogens because of the resonance stabilization effect of the carbonyl on the resulting carbanion.

Amides Compounds of the general formula $RCONH_2$, RCONHR, or $RCONR_2$.

Amines Compounds of the general formula RNH_2 (primary), R_2NH (secondary), or R_3N (tertiary).

Amino acids Compounds of the general formula $NH_2CRHCOOH$. The 20 amino acids found in nature are the building blocks of proteins.

Angle strain Occurs in molecules when bond angles are forced from their ideal values.

Anhydrides Compounds of the general formula RCO_2COR. They are the dimeric products of two carboxylic acids, or acid derivatives, that have lost water or hydrogen halides.

Anion Negatively charged ion. Compare *cation*.

Anomeric carbon Hemiacetal or hemiketal carbon (the carbon attached to two oxygens) in a furanose or pyranose ring.

Anomers Diastereomers that differ in the configuration about the anomeric carbon (usually C-1 in hexoses). Anomers can be either α or β, depending on the orientation of the hydroxyl or alkoxy substitutent on the C-1 carbon.

***anti* addition** Addition in which two atoms or molecules add on opposite sides of a double bond. For instance, when Br_2 is added to an alkene, a bromonium ion intermediate is initially formed, and then Br^- attacks from the other side. See *syn addition*.

***Anti* conformation** The most stable conformation of straight-chain alkanes, in which the two largest R-groups are staggered by 180°.

Aromatic compounds (arenes) Cyclic compounds that fulfill the following criteria:

1) $4n + 2$ pi electrons (Hückel's rule)
2) Every atom of the ring is associated with at least one pi orbital.
3) Planar configuration
4) Pi electrons above and below the plane of the ring
5) Delocalized pi electrons

Aromatic compounds are unusually stable due to increased resonance. Examples are benzene, pyridine, and the cyclopentadiene carbanion.

Axial bonds Bonds perpendicular to the plane of a ring.

Base peak The most intense peak in a mass spectrum.

Beta carbon A carbon two carbons away from the functional group under consideration.

Boat conformation Transition-state conformation of cyclohexane, in which all hydrogens are eclipsed and the "flagpole" hydrogens repel each other because of their proximity. The boat conformation is less stable than the chair conformation because of steric hindrance.

Boiling point Temperature at which the vapor pressure of a liquid is equal to atmospheric pressure and the liquid and gas phases are in equilibrium.

Buffer solution Solution whose pH changes only slightly upon addition of either acid or base. The solution contains a conjugate acid-base pair that consumes any added base or acid.

Carbanion Carbon atom that possesses a formal negative charge (has an extra electron).

Carbocation Carbon atom that possesses a formal positive charge (lacks an electron).

Carbohydrates Compounds of the general formula $C_n(H_2O)_n$.

Carbonyl group C=O group found in aldehydes, ketones, and carboxylic acids, among others.

Carboxylic acids Compounds of the general formula RCOOH. The hydrogen is acidic due to resonance stabilization of the conjugate base.

Catalyst Any material that reduces the activation energy of a reaction and thus increases its forward and reverse reaction rates. Catalysts are neither altered nor consumed during a reaction.

Cation Positively charged ion. Compare *anion*.

Chain reaction A reaction involving several steps, each leading to a reactive substance that is necessary for the next step to occur. For example, in a free-radical reaction, each step after initiation of the radical produces a new radical that makes the reaction continue.

Chair conformation The most stable conformation of cyclohexane, in which all C–C bonds are 109.5° and all the substituents on alternating carbons are staggered.

Chiral center Atom, usually carbon, with four different substituents attached to it.

Chiral molecule A molecule not superimposable on its mirror image and that exhibits optical activity. A chiral center is usually but not necessarily present.

Chromatography Technique used to separate a complex mixture, based on the fact that different compounds will adhere to a particular adsorbent to a lesser or greater degree. A solvent elutes compounds in a mixture through the adsorbent at different rates, separating (resolving) them.

cis **isomers** Configuration about a double bond in which the two largest groups are on the same side of the molecule. See *geometric isomers*.

Condensation reaction Combination of two or more molecules, often with the loss of a small molecule such as water or alcohol (e.g., aldol condensation).

Conformation Orientation of atoms in a molecule that can be altered by rotation about a C–C single bond.

Conjugated dienes *Dienes* whose two C–C double bonds are separated by one single bond and are therefore subject to electron delocalization.

Covalent bonding Bonding in which the half-filled orbitals of two atoms

overlap such that both constituents share the resulting electron pair.

Cycloalkanes Saturated cyclic hydrocarbons of the formula C_nH_{2n}.

Deactivating groups Substituents that, when attached to benzene rings, make the ring less susceptible to electrophilic attack. These are compounds that withdraw electrons from the aromatic ring, destabilizing the carbocation intermediate. Examples include $-NO_2$, $-COOH$, $-CHO$, and halogens. Most are *meta* directors, except for the halogens, which are *ortho/para* directors.

Decarboxylation A reaction resulting in the loss of a molecule of CO_2. β-dicarboxylic and β-keto acids undergo decarboxylation easily.

Dehydration A reaction resulting in a net loss of H_2O, often observed in the elimination reactions of alcohols.

Dehydrohalogenation Reaction of alkyl halides resulting in the loss of HX and producing alkenes.

Delocalization of electrons Distribution of electron density over several atoms because of conjugation of pi bonds.

Denaturation Loss of secondary and tertiary structure of a protein, caused by an increase in temperature or a pH change. Denaturing agents disrupt hydrogen bonding, inactivating proteins.

Dextrorotatory Term used to describe the rotation of plane-polarized light by

an optically active molecule in a clockwise or positive (+) direction.

Diastereomers Stereoisomers that are not mirror images of each other (e.g., the *S*, *R* and *R*, *R* forms of tartaric acid).

Dicarboxylic acids Compounds of the general formula $HOOC(CH_2)_nCOOH$.

Dienes Compounds containing two double bonds. See *allenes*; *conjugated dienes*.

Diols Compounds with two alcohol groups. Geminal (gem) diols have the two –OH groups on the same carbon atom; vicinal (vic) diols, also known as glycols, have the two –OH groups on adjacent carbons.

Dipole moment Measure of the net polarity of a bond or molecule.

Eclipsed conformation The least stable conformation of a straight-chain alkane, in which the bulkiest R-groups are at an angle of 0° relative to an adjacent hydrogen atom.

Electron affinity Measurable energy change accompanying the addition of an electron to an atom.

Electronegativity Ability of an atom to attract electrons, resulting in polarized bonds.

Electrophiles Species that "love" electrons and therefore seek them out. They often are positively charged and seek electrons in order to fill their outer shells. Many typical electrophiles are Lewis acids.

Electrophilic addition Addition of an electrophile to an electron-rich species. A typical example is the addition of Br_2 to an alkene.

Electrophilic aromatic Substitution of an electrophile into the electron-rich pi system of an aromatic compound. Typically, a Lewis acid is used as a catalyst.

E1 (unimolecular elimination) Elimination reaction whose kinetics are first-order. The rate-limiting step is the departure of a leaving group, which produces a carbocation; a base then abstracts a proton to form a double bond.

E2 (bimolecular elimination) Elimination reaction whose kinetics are second-order. A base removes a proton, and the leaving group simultaneously departs, forming a double bond.

Enantiomers Stereoisomers that are nonsuperimposable mirror images of one another. For example, if there is one chiral center, then the *R* and *S* isomers are enantiomers.

Enols Compounds in which a hydroxyl group is located on the carbon atom of a double bond. They are tautomers of ketones, and an equilibrium exists between the two forms. The enol form is generally less stable than the keto form. (One exception is phenol, which is more stable in its enol form because of resonance stabilization.)

Epimers Stereoisomers of sugars that differ only in the configuration about the C-2 carbon atom.

Epoxides Compounds containing a three-membered cyclic ether.

Equatorial bonds Bonds lying in the plane of a ring.

Esterification The formation of an ester by reaction of an alcohol with an acid.

Esters Compounds of the general formula RCOOR.

Ethers Compounds of the general formula ROR.

Fatty acid Long-chain aliphatic carboxylic acids derived from the hydrolysis of fats.

First-order reaction Reaction whose rate depends on the concentration of only one reactant (rate = k [reactant]).

Fischer projection The representation of a three-dimensional chiral structure in two dimensions. The vertical lines indicate bonds that project into the plane of the paper, whereas the horizontal lines represent bonds that project out of the plane of the paper.

Formal charge The difference in the number of electrons possessed by an atom in a molecule and in its elemental state.

Free radical Highly reactive species possessing an unpaired electron.

Free radical substitution Chain reaction in which a radical abstracts a substituent from a molecule (usually hydrogen) and replaces it with another substituent, often a halogen, forming the product and a free radical. Free-radical substitutions are characterized by three steps: initiation, propagation, and termination.

Gauche **conformation** Conformation of straight-chain alkanes in which the largest R-groups are staggered by 60°.

Geminal (gem) Term describing compounds with two of the same functional groups attached to one carbon. See *vicinal*.

Geminal diol A compound that has two alcohol groups on the same carbon and is a hydrate of an aldehyde or ketone.

Geometric isomers Compounds that differ only in the geometry of the groups around a double bond (i.e., *cis* and *trans*).

Halogenation Reaction in which a halogen atom is incorporated into a substrate through an addition, free-radical, or substitution reaction.

Haworth projection Flat depiction of cyclic molecules. For sugars, the oxygen atom is always at the back, right corner of a Haworth projection, and the hemiacetal carbon is at the far right.

Heat of combustion Amount of heat released when a compound is burned.

For the combustion of a hydrocarbon:

$$C_nH_m + O_2 \rightarrow nCO_2 + \frac{m}{2}H_2O$$

Hemiacetal Unstable intermediate between aldehyde and acetal, containing one –OR group and one –OH group attached to the same carbon atom.

Hemiketal Unstable intermediate between ketone and ketal, containing one –OR group and one –OH group on the same carbon atom.

Hückel's rule Rule defining aromaticity, stating that cyclic conjugated molecules will exhibit unusual stability if they contain $4n + 2$ pi electrons.

Hydrocarbons Organic compounds containing only carbon and hydrogen.

Hydrogen bonding Weak electrostatic interaction between a hydrogen atom bonded to an electronegative atom, such as N, O, or F, and the lone pairs of other electronegative atoms.

Hydrogenation Reaction in which hydrogen is added to an unsaturated compound, usually performed with a catalyst.

Imines Compounds of the general formula $RCH = NC$ or $R_2C = NH$; the condensation products of aldehydes and amines.

Inductive effect An electron-withdrawing or electron-attracting effect transmitted through sigma bonds in response to a dipole.

Initiation reaction A reaction generating a free radical; for example,

$$Br_2 \rightarrow 2Br\bullet$$

Ion An atom or molecule with a net negative or positive charge. See *anion*; *cation*.

Ionic bond Bond between compounds with very different electron affinities, involving the transfer of an electron to the more electronegative atom (e.g., LiF).

Isoelectric point pH at which the number of positive charges and the number of negative charges on a compound (e.g., an amino acid) are equal.

Isomers Compounds with the same molecular formulas but different structures. See *geometric isomers*; *stereoisomers*; *structural isomers*.

IUPAC nomenclature Standardized system of nomenclature promoted by the International Union of Pure and Applied Chemistry.

Ketals Compounds of the general formula $R_2C(OR)_2$, formed from the reaction of a ketone and two alcohols and often used as protecting groups.

Ketones Compounds of the general formula RCOR.

Kinetic order of reaction Sum of the exponents of all the reactants present in a rate equation.

Leaving group Group that is replaced in a substitution reaction, which must be a weaker nucleophile than the species that will replace it. The best leaving groups form the most stable anions in solution.

Levorotatory Term used to describe the rotation of plane-polarized light by an optically active molecule in a counterclockwise or negative (−) direction.

Lewis acid Electron-pair acceptor (e.g., BF_3 or $AlCl_3$).

Lewis base Electron-pair donor (e.g., NH_3).

Lipids Triacylglycerols (1,2,3-triesters of glycerol) found in tissue and cells; classified as fats, terpenes, prostaglandins, or steroids.

Markovnikov's rule The rule stating that the addition of a protic acid (HX) to an alkene occurs such that the proton attaches to the carbon atom with the smallest number of alkyl groups, producing the most stable carbocation.

Mechanism Pathway by which a reaction occurs, describing all reactants, intermediates, and products and the conditions that must be present for the reaction to take place.

Melting point Temperature at which the solid and liquid phases of a compound are in equilibrium.

meso **compounds** Compounds with at least two chiral centers but with a plane of symmetry resulting in a mirror image that is superimposable on the original molecule.

Meta configuration In disubstituted benzene rings, the configuration in which the two functional groups are oriented in the 1,3 or 1,5 positions on the ring.

Micelles Clusters of molecules possessing hydrophilic ionic heads facing the surface of a sphere, where they can interact with water, and possessing hydrophobic hydrocarbon tails in the interior. Soap forms micelles, facilitating the dissolution of oils and fats.

Mobile phase Gaseous or liquid solvent used to move components through the adsorbent (stationary) phase in chromatography.

Monosaccharides Simple sugars that cannot be hydrolyzed to simpler compounds.

Mutarotation Exchange of position between the axial and equatorial substituents of the anomeric carbon of a cyclic sugar. Mutarotation is acid-catalyzed and results in a change in the direction of optical rotation.

Newman projection Representation of a molecule along a carbon-carbon axis, showing the different rotational conformers possible for the compound.

Nucleophile Species that is a "nucleus lover" and thus tends to donate an electron pair to an electrophile.

Olefins Another name for *alkenes*.

Optically active Term describing a compound that can rotate the plane of polarized light.

ortho **configuration** In disubstituted benzene rings, the configuration in which the two functional groups are oriented in the 1,2 or 1,6 positions on the ring.

Oxidation Loss of electrons. Compare *reduction*.

para **configuration** In disubstituted benzene rings, the configuration in which the two functional groups are oriented in the 1,4 positions on the ring.

Peptide bond Amide bond between the nitrogen of the amino group of one amino acid and the carbon of the carbonyl group of another amino acid. Characterized by partial double-bond character and thus imparts rigidity to peptide chains.

Peptides Molecules that consist of two or more amino acids linked to each other by peptide bonds.

Pi (π) bond Covalent bond formed by parallel overlap of two unhybridized atomic *p*-orbitals, as in a carbon–carbon double bond.

Polar covalent bond Bond formed by the sharing of electrons between two atoms of different electronegativities, resulting in the attraction of electrons toward the more electronegative atom.

Polarity Charge separation due to asymmetric distribution of electrons.

Polarized light Light in which all electric fields vibrate in one plane.

p-orbital: A dumbbell-shaped electron orbital centered on the nucleus. They exist for atomic numbers two and higher.

Primary amine An amine with two hydrogen and one hydrocarbon substituents (i.e., RNH_2).

Primary (1°) atom A carbon atom attached to only one other carbon atom, or a hydrogen atom or other group attached to such a carbon.

Primary structure The amino acid sequence of a protein.

Propagation Series of events immediately following initiation in a chain reaction. A reactive intermediate reacts with a stable molecule to form another reactive intermediate, thereby continuously regenerating the reacting species. This enables the reaction to continue until completion.

Proteins Long-chain polypeptides with high molecular weights.

Protonation Acceptance of a proton by an electron-pair donor.

Quaternary structure Interaction of protein subunits to form a large complex; the highest form of protein structure.

Racemic mixture A 50:50 mixture of the (+) and (−) enantiomers of an optically active substance.

Rate-determining step Slowest step in a multistep reaction. The rate of the reaction is dependent only on this step.

Reactive intermediates Reactive molecules or molecule pieces that are formed during a reaction and quickly proceed to subsequent steps of the reaction sequence.

Rearrangement Shifting of substituents with their electrons to a new location on the same molecule, leaving behind a more stable molecule (e.g., methyl and hydride shifts).

Reduction Gain of electrons. Compare *oxidation*.

Resonance Delocalization of electrons within a compound. Such compounds may be represented by various electron configurations and have a true electron configuration somewhere between the various possibilities. Because the electrons are spread out over the molecule, the structure gains added stability. See *tautomerism*.

Ring strain Tension experienced by cyclic compounds due to the bending and stretching of bonds in order to fulfill geometric (angular) and steric requirements.

Salts Positive and negative ions linked by electrostatic attraction. A salt is the neutralization product of an acid and a base.

Saponification Hydrolysis of an ester with a base, forming a carboxylic acid salt.

Saturated hydrocarbon A hydrocarbon with only single bonds.

Secondary amine An amine with one hydrogen and two hydrocarbon substituents (i.e., R_2NH).

Secondary atom A carbon atom attached to two other carbon atoms, or a hydrogen atom or other group attached to such a carbon.

Secondary structure Level of protein structure characterized by inter- and intramolecular hydrogen bonding. Examples of 2° structure are the α-helix and the β-pleated sheet.

Sigma (σ) bond Head-to-head overlap of hybridized or *s*-orbitals from separate atoms to form a bonding orbital.

S_N1 Unimolecular nucleophilic substitution. It is characterized by two steps: (1) dissociation of a molecule into a carbocation and a leaving group; (2) combination of a nucleophile with the carbocation. No inversion of configuration occurs, but a loss of stereochemistry does occur because of the formation of a planar intermediate.

S_N2 Bimolecular nucleophilic substitution. It occurs in one step, involving two principal reactants. A strong nucleophile pushes into a molecule, dislodging a leaving group. These reactions are characterized by an inversion of absolute configuration.

s-orbital A spherically symmetrical electron orbital centered on the nucleus.

Staggered conformation Arrangement of atoms about a carbon–carbon single bond such that the greatest spacing of adjacent groups is obtained. *Anti* and *gauche* conformations are special cases of staggered conformations.

Stationary phase Solid support used in chromatography to which compounds adsorb.

Stereoisomers Isomeric compounds that possess the same atomic connectivity but differ in their spatial orientation.

Steric hindrance Strain in a molecule produced by repulsion of groups adjacent or close to one another. Hindrance increases as size and bulk increase.

Structural isomers Compounds with the same molecular formula but different connections between atoms.

Sugars Carbohydrates; compounds containing the elements C, H, and O, with H and O in a 2:1 ratio. Simple sugars are called monosaccharides and can dimerize or polymerize into disaccharides and polysaccharides. Examples of mono-, di-, and polysaccharides, respectively, are glucose, maltose, and cellulose.

Syn addition Addition in which two atoms or molecules add to the same side of a double bond. See anti *addition*.

Tautomerism Equilibrium rearrangement in which a compound exists as two distinct structures differing in the position of both a proton and a double bond. See *resonance*, in which atoms retain their positions and electrons change location.

Termination The step in a chain reaction in which two reactive species join together to form a nonreactive species.

Tertiary atom A carbon atom attached to three other carbons, or a hydrogen atom or other group attached to such a carbon.

Tertiary amine An amine with three hydrocarbon substituents (i.e., R_3N).

Tertiary structure Level of protein structure dictated by hydrophobic and hydrophilic interactions, causing the molecule to fold into a complex shape.

Totally eclipsed conformation Eclipsed conformation in which the substituent pairs that eclipse each other are the same group or groups of equal priority.

Twist-boat conformation Intermediate between the two chair conformations in cyclohexane; similar to the *boat conformation* except it is more stable, because the twist relieves eclipsing.

Unsaturated compound Compound with double or triple bonds.

van der Waals forces Weak intermolecular interactions such as dipole–dipole interactions, hydrogen bonding, and London forces.

Vicinal (vic) Term describing compounds that have the same substituent on adjacent carbons. See *geminal*.

Vinylic Substituent on a double-bonded carbon atom (e.g., an enol is a vinylic alcohol).

Zwitterion Neutral dipolar molecule in which the charges are separated. Some amino acids are zwitterions.

Index

A

Absolute configuration, 30
Absorption frequencies, 236–37
Acet-, 158
Acetal formation, 140–41
Acetaldehyde, 13, 135
Acetic acid, 13
Acetic anhydride, 176
Acetoacetic ester condensation, 184–85
Acetone, 13
Acetylene, 9, 88
Acetylide ion, 89
Achiral, 29
Acid amino acids, 289
Acid anhydrides, 176–79
Acid halides, 173
Acid-base chemistry, 274
Acidic amino acids, 278, 280–81
Acidity, 117, 157, 159–60
Activators, 106, 108
Acyl halide, 16, 173, 187
  formation, 164
  nomenclature, 173
  reactions, 174–75
  synthesis, 173–74
Acylation, 105–6
  anhydrides, 179
Addition reactions
  alcohol, 119
  aldehydes, 139–43
  alkenes, 83–85
  alkynes, 90–91
Adsorbent, 218
Affinity chromatography, 222
Agarose, 224
Agarose gel electrophoresis, 224
-al, 135
Alcohol, 11, 16
  nomenclature, 115–16
  oxidation, 137–38
  physical properties, 116–17
  reaction mechanisms, 117–18

  reactions, 120–22
  synthesis, 118–19
Aldehydes, 13, 16, 18, 135, 148
  nomenclature, 135–36
  physical properties, 137
  reactions, 138–47
  synthesis, 137–38
Aldol condensation, 143–44, 184
Aldonic acids, 261
Aldose, 255, 265
Alipathic alcohols, 117
Alkanes
  nomenclature, 4–7, 61
  physical properties, 62, 72
  reactions, 62–65
Alkanoyl halides, 173
Alkene ozonolysis, 138
Alkenes, 94
  nomenclature, 8–9, 79–80
  physical properties, 80–81
  reactions, 83–88
  synthesis, 81–83
Alkoxy-, 12
Alkyl, 102
Alkyl alkanoates, 182
Alkyl groups, 128
Alkyl halides, 10
  substitution reactions, 65–69
Alkylation of ammonia, 198–99, 203
Alkynes
  nomenclature, 9–10, 88
  physical properties, 89
  reactions, 90–92
  synthesis, 89
Allyl, 9
  substituents, 159
α (alpha) anomer, 259, 260
α carbons, 14
α-helix structure, 284
α-state, 238
-amide, 179

Amides, 16, 173, 187, 195–96
  acyl halides conversion into, 175
  anhydrides conversion into, 178–79
  esters conversion into, 183–84
  nomenclature, 179–80
  reactions, 180–81
  reduction, 200–201
  synthesis, 180
-amine, 195, 203
Amines, 15, 16, 203
  ketones with, 175
  nomenclature, 195–96
  properties, 197–98
  reactions, 200
  synthesis, 198–200
Amino acids, 273–74, 289
  acid-base characteristics, 274–75
  Henderson-Hasselbalch equation, 277–78
  side chains, 278–82
  titration of, 275–77
Amino terminal residue, 283
Amino-, 15, 195, 203
Ammonia derivatives, 142–43, 148
Ammonium carboxylate, 178
Amphoteric species, 274
-ane, 4, 8, 9
Angle strain, 37
Anhydrides, 173, 187
  nomenclature, 176
  reactions, 177–79
  synthesis, 176–77
Anions, 224
Anomeric carbon, 259, 265
Anomerization, 259
Anomers, 259
Anti conformation, 36, 37
Antiaromatic compound, 101
Antibonding orbital, 48, 54

Anti-Markovnikov reaction, 85, 91, 94
Antioxidants, 63
Aprotic solvent, 66
Ar, 102
Arenes, 102
Aromatic alcohols, 116
Aromatic compound, 101
  nomenclature, 102–4
  properties, 104
  reactions, 104–7
Aryl alkanoates, 182
Aryl, 102
-ate, 158
Atomic orbitals, 47–48
Axial substituent, 38
Az, 196
Azide, 16, 196

B

Backbone chain, 4–5, 18
Backside attack, 68
Base peak, 245
Basic amino acids, 278, 281–82, 289
Basicity, 65, 66
Bending, 235
Benedict's test, 261
Benzene, 104, 108
Benzyl substituents, 159
β (beta) anomer, 259, 260
β state, 238
β carbons, 14
Betaine, 145
Beta-ketoacids, 160
Beta-pleated sheet, 284–85
Beta-sheet, 284
Bile salts, 162
Bimolecular elimination, 82–83
Bimolecular nucleophilic substitution, 68–69
Biological sciences, xii, xiii, xv, xx

Boat conformation, 37, 38
Boiling points, 197
Bond
  order, 53
  stretching, 235
Bonding orbital, 48, 54
Borane, 86
Branched-chain alkanes, 4–6
Brønsted-Lowry base, 65
Butyraldehyde, 135

C

-carbaldehyde, 136
Carbamates, 196
Carbenes, 196
Carbocation, 64, 66, 67
  intermediate, 81
Carbohydrates, 265
Carbons, 4
Carbonyl, 13, 148
  carbon, 139–42
Carboxyl acids
  nomenclature, 157–58
  physical properties, 158–60
  reactions, 161–165
  synthesis, 160–61
Carboxyl group, 157
Carboxylation of organometallic reagents, 161
Carboxylic acids, 14–15, 16, 18, 166
  conversion from anhydrides, 179
Carboxy-terminal residue, 283
Catalytic hydrogenation, 83
Catalytic reduction, 107
Cations, 224
Cellulose, 263, 264, 265
Centrifugation, 215–16, 227
Chain numbering, 18
Chair conformation, 37, 38, 40
Chemical properties, 25
Chemical shift, 239
Chiral centers, 28–29, 40
Chirality, 28–34
Chromatography, 218–23, 227
Cis, 27, 38, 79, 94
Cis-alkenes, 80
Claisen condensation, 184–85
Cleavage, 125–27, 128
Clemmensen reduction, 147, 148
C-NMR, 242–44
Cold finger, 214

Collagen, 286
Column chromatography, 219, 221–22
Combustion, alkanes, 62–63
Common names, 3–4
Computer-based testing strategies, xxi
Condensation
  aldol, 143–44
  with ammonia derivatives, 142–43
  esters, 184–85
Configuration, 30–31
Conformational isomerism, 35–39
Conformational isomers, 40
Conformers, 35–39
Conjugated proteins, 286, 289
Conjugation, 9
Constitutional isomers, 25–26
Coupling, 240
Coupling constant (J), 240
Covalent bonds, 47
Cracking, 64–65
C-terminal residue, 283
Cyanide, 16, 196
  hydrolysis, 161
Cyano-, 196
Cyanohydrins, 141
Cyclic conformations, 37–38
Cyclic ethers, 125
Cyclic halonium ion, 84
Cyclo-, 6
Cycloalkanes, 7
Cycloalkenes, 9
Cyclohexane, 38–39
Cysteine, 285
Cystine, 285

D

D-, 256–57, 265
Deactivators, 106, 108
Dec-, 4
Decarboxylation, 164–65, 166
Denaturation, 286–87
Deshielding, 240
Developed, 219
Di-, 5
Diastereomers, 34–35, 40
Diazo, 16, 196
Differences, 93
Dihalo, 84
-diol, 11
Diols, 11

Dipeptide, 282
Disaccharide, 255, 262–63
Disproportionation, 65
Distillation, 216–18, 227
Disubstituted cyclohexane, 38–39
Dodec-, 4
d-orbital, 48
Double bond, 49, 50, 54
Doublet, 240
Downfield, 239

E

(E), 28
E, 79
-e, 13, 15, 115
E1 elimination, 81–82, 94, 120
E2 elimination, 82–83, 94
Eclipsed molecule, 36
Electrophiles, 65, 84
Electrophilic addition
  alkenes, 83–84
  alkynes, 90
  to double bond, 118
Electrophilic aromatic substitution (EAS), 104–6, 108
Electrophilic carbonyl carbon, 157
Electrophoresis, 224–26, 227
Elimination reactions, 81, 120
Eluant, 219
Elute, 219
Enamines, 196
Enantiomers, 29, 40
Ene, 138
-ene, 8, 9
Enol, 138, 148
Enolization, 138
Entantiomers, 33
Epimers, 257, 265
Epoxides, 12, 126, 128
Equatorial substituent, 38
Esters, 16, 173, 187
  acyl halides conversion into, 174
  anhydrides conversion into, 179
  formation, 163–64, 260, 265
  nomenclature, 182
  reactions, 182–85
  synthesis, 182
Ethanal, 13
Ethenyl-, 9
Ether, 16, 12, 18

nomenclature, 123
physical properties, 124
reaction mechanisms, 117–18
reactions, 125–27
synthesis, 124–25
Ethyl alcohol, 11
Ethyl chloride, 10
Ethylene, 8, 79
  glycol, 11
Ethyne, 9
Exhaustive methylation, 201, 203
Extraction, 211–12, 227

F

Fibrous proteins, 286
Filtrate, 213
Filtration, 212–13, 227
Fingerprint region, 236
Fischer projections, 31–33, 256, 257
Flagpole interactions, 37
Flash column chromatography, 221
Form-, 158
Formaldehyde, 13, 135
Formic acid, 13
Formyl-, 136
Fractional distillation, 217–28
Free radical addition, 85
  alkynes, 91
Free-radical substitution, 63–64, 72
Friedel-Crafts acylation, 138, 175, 179
Friedel-Crafts reactions, 105–6
Functional groups, 15–16
Furanose rings, 258

G

Gabriel synthesis, 198–99, 203
Gas chromatography (GC), 219, 222–23
Gauche, 36
Geminal diols, 11
Geometric isomers, 27–28, 40
Globular proteins, 286
Glycine, 273
Glycogen, 263, 265
Glycols, 11
Glycoproteins, 286
Glycosidic linkage, 261
Gravity filtration, 213
Grignard reagents, 161, 184
Gycosidic reactions, 261–62, 265

H

H$_2$O addition, 85
Halide, 16, 159
Haloalkanes, 10–11, 18
Halogen, 10
Halogenation, 63–64, 104–5
Heme group, 286
Hemoglobin, 286
Henderson-Hasselbalch equation, 277–78
Hept-, 4
Hex-, 4
Hexoses, 255
High-pressure (-performance) liquid chromatography (HPLC), 219, 223
^{1}H-NMR, 239–42, 247
Hofmann elimination, 201
Hofmann rearrangement, 181, 196
Hückel's rule, 101, 103
HX addition, 84
Hybridization, 50–52
Hydrates, 11
Hydration, 140
Hydroboration, 86, 91–92
Hydrogen bonding, 116, 128, 158–59
Hydrogen cyanide (HCN) reactions, 141–46
Hydrolysis
    acyl halides, 174
    amides, 180–81
    anhydrides, 177–78
    esters, 182–83
    nitriles/cyanides, 161
Hydroxyl, 115

I

-ic acid, 158
Imine, 175, 196
Infrared (IR) spectroscopy, 235–37
Intermediate state, 69
Ion exchange chromatography, 222
Ionic bonds, 47
Iso-, 6
Isobutylene, 79
Isocyanate, 181, 196
Isoelectric focusing, 225–26
Isoelectric pH, 275

Isoelectric point (pI), 225, 275
Isomer, 18, 25
Isopropyl alcohol, 11

J

Jones's oxidation, 122

K

Ketal formation, 140–41
Keto, 138
Ketones, 13–14, 16, 18, 135, 148
    nomenclature, 136–37
    physical properties, 137
    reactions, 138–47
    synthesis, 137–38
Ketose, 256
Krebs cycle, 164

L

l, 47, 54
L-, 256–57, 265
Lactose intolerance, 263
Leaving groups, 66, 68, 72
Lewis acids/bases, 84, 86
Lindlar's catalyst, 90
Lipoproteins, 286

M

m, 47
m⁻, 102, 103
M⁺, 245
Macromolecule, 224
Markovnikov's rule, 84, 85, 94
Mass spectroscopy, 245–46
MCAT (Medical College Admissions Test)
    admissions role, xi
    mindset for, xvii
    planning for, x
    registration, xi
    scientific reasoning, xvi
    scoring, xiii–xv
    thinking skills, xv–xvi
    timed sections of, xii
Melting, 286–87
Meso compounds, 35, 40
Meta, 108
Meta-, 102, 103
Methanal, 13
Methoxy-, 12
Methoxyethane, 12

Methylene, 9
Micelles, 162
Michael additions, 139
Migration velocity, 224
Mobile phase, 218–19
Molecular ion peak (parent ion peak), 245
Molecular orbitals
    double, triple bonds, 49–50
    single bonds, 48–49
Monosaccharide, 255–62
    reactions, 260–62, 265
Monosubstituted cyclohexane, 38
Multiplet, 241
Mutarotation, 259, 265

N

N, 195
n, 47, 54
N-, 6, 15
N-, 179–80
Neo-, 6
Newman projection, 35–36
-NH2, 173
Ni (nickel), 83
Nitration, 105
Nitrene, 181, 196
Nitrile, 16, 196
    hydrolysis, 161
    reduction, 200
-nitrile, 196
Nitro, 16, 105
Nitro compound, 196
    reduction, 200
Nitrogen, 63
Nitrogen inversion, 197
Nitrogen oxides, 63
Nitrogen-containing compounds, 202, 203
    nomenclature, 195–96
    properties, 197–98
    reactions, 200
    synthesis, 198–200
Nitroglycerine, 198
Nitrous oxide, 198
Node, 47
Nomenclature, 3–4
Non-, 4
Nonbonded strain, 37
Nonpolar amino acids, 278–79, 289
N-terminal residue, 283
Nuclear magnetic resonance (NMR), 238–44

Nucleophiles, 65–66, 72
Nucleophilic acyl substitution, 162–64, 165, 166
Nucleophilic carbonyl addition, 8, 139–46
Nucleophilic substitution, 118, 142–43
Nucleophilicity, 65, 66
Nucleoproteins, 286

O

o-, 102, 103
Oct-, 4
Ol, 138
-OCOR, 173
-OH, 11, 18, 115
-oic acid, 157
-ol, 115
Olefins, 8–9, 79–80
Oligosaccharides, 255
-one, 13, 136
Optical activity, 33–34
-OR, 173
Orbitals, 47–50
Organometallic reagents, 161
Ortho, 106, 108
Ortho-, 102, 103
Oxaphosphetane, 145
Oxidation reactions
    alcohols, 122–23
    carboxylic acids, 160
Oxidation, 83
    aldehydes, 137, 138, 146
    alkenes, 86–88
    alkynes, 92
    ketones, 138, 146
    monosaccharides, 260–61, 265
Oxidizing agent, 128
Oxiranes, 12
Oxo-, 13, 136
-oyl halide, 173
Ozonolysis, 87, 138

P

p-, 102, 103
Para, 106, 108
Para-, 102, 103
Parent ion peak, 245
Parts per million (ppm), 239
Pauling, Linus, 50

PCC (pyridinium chlorochromate), 122, 128
Pd (palladium), 83
Pen-, 4
Pentacoordinate transition state, 68
Pentoses, 255
Peptide bond, 282
Peptides, 282
    properties, 283
    reactions, 282–83
    formation, 125
Peroxy acid, 125
Peroxycarboxylic acids, 87–88
Phase diagram, 214
Phenol
    reactions, 122
    synthesis, 119, 124
Phosphate esters, 185–86
Phosphodiester bonds, 186
Phosphorane, 145
Physical properties, 25
Physical sciences, xii, xiii, xiv, xx
Pi (π) bond, 49, 50, 88
Polar amino acids, 278, 279–80, 289
Polarity, 80, 212
Polarizers, 33
Polymerization, 88
Polypeptide, 282
Polysaccharides, 255, 263–64, 265
Polyurethanes, 196
p-orbital, 47, 48
Potassium permanganate, 86–87
Preparative (Prep) thin-layer chromatography, 221
Primary (1°) amine, 195
Primary (1°) carbon, 61, 62
Primary protein structure, 284, 289
Priority, 30
Propanal, 13
Propanoic acid, 13
Propenyl-, 2-, 9
Propionaldehyde, 13, 135
Propylene, 8, 79
Prosthetic groups, 286
Proteins
    conjugated, 286–87
    primary structure, 284
    quaternary structure, 286

    secondary structure, 284–85
    tertiary structure, 285–86
Protic solvent, 66
Pt (platinum), 83
Pyridine, 103–4
Pyrolysis, alkanes, 64–65
Pyrrole, 103–4

Q

Quaternary (4°) carbons, 61
Quaternary ammonium compound, 195
Quaternary protein structure, 286, 289
Quinones, 122

R

R, 31, 34
Racemic mixture, 34
Random-coil state, 286
Rate-limiting/rate-determining step, 67
Recrystallization, 214, 227
Reducing agent, 128
Reducing sugar, 26
Reduction, 83
    acyl halides, 175
    alcohols, 119
    aldehydes and ketones, 147
    alkynes, 90
    amides, 181
    amines, 199–201
    aromatic compounds, 107
    carboxylic acids, 163
    esters, 185
Relative configuration, 30
Residues, 282
Reverse-phase chromatography, 220
R_f value, 220
R-group, 273
Ring, 7
    flip, 38
    properties, 258–60
    strain, 37
    structures, 40

S

S, 31, 34
Salt, 145
Saponification, 183

Saturated hydrocarbons, 61
SDS-PAGE (sodium dodecyl sulfate-polyacrylamide gel electrophoresis), 224–25
Sec-, 6
Secondary (2°) amine, 195
Secondary (2°) carbons, 61, 62
Secondary alcohols, 128
Secondary protein structure, 284–85, 289
Second-order kinetics, 69
Sedimentation, 216
Separatory funnel, 211
Sequencing, 284
Shakespeare, 3
Sigma (σ) bond, 49
Similarities, 93
Simple distillation, 216
Single bond, 54
Size-exclusion chromatography, 222
S_N1 reactions, 66–72, 81–83, 94, 119, 127–28
S_N2 reactions, 68–72, 82–83, 94, 119–21, 124–28, 198–99, 203
Soap formation, 161–62, 165, 166
Solubility, 212
s-orbital, 47, 48
sp, 52
sp^2, 51–52, 80
sp^3, 50–51, 80
Spectroscopy, 235
Spin decoupling, 243
Splitting, 240
Spotting, 219
Staggered conformation, 36
Starch, 263, 264, 265
Stationary phase, 218
Stereochemistry, 256–58
Stereoisomerism, 26–27
    chiral compounds, 34–35
    chirality, 28–34
    conformational isomerism, 35–39
    geometric isomers, 27–28
Stereoisomers, 40
Stereospecific reactions, 83
Stinging nettles, 158
Straight-chain conformations, 36–37
Structural isomerism, 25–26
Structural isomers, 40

Sublimation, 214–15, 227
Substituent effects, 106
Substituents, 5, 18
Substituted alkanes, 10–15
Substitution reactions, 119, 120–22
Substrate, 66
Sulfide, 16
Sulfonation, 105
Syn addition, 83

T

T-, 6
Tale of Two Cities, A, 3
Tautomerization, 138
Tautomers, 138
Terminal alcohols, 128
Tert-, 6
Tertiary (3°) amine, 195
Tertiary (3°) carbons, 61, 62
Tertiary alcohols, 128
Tertiary protein structure, 285–86, 289
Test expertise
    answer elimination process, xix
    calm attitude, xix
    skipping around, xviii
    skipping questions, xix
    time management, xix
Test pacing, xx
Tetra-, 5
Tetroses, 255
Thinking skills, xv–xvi
Thin-layer chromatography (TLC), 219–21
Thiol, 16
Thionyl chloride, 164
Titration, amino acids, 275–77
Torsional strain, 37
Totally eclipsed molecule, 36
Trans, 27, 38, 79
Trans-alkenes, 80
Transesterification, 184
Tri-, 5
Triacylglycerols, 183
Trigonal bipyramidal transition, 69
Trioses, 255
Tripeptide, 282
Triple bond, 49, 54
Triplet, 241
Twist conformation, 37, 38

U

Ultraviolet light reactions, 64
Ultraviolet spectroscopy, 244–45
Undec-, 4
Unimolecular elimination, 81–82
Unimolecular nucleophilic
substitution, 66–68
Unsubstituted cyclohexane, 38
Urethanes, 196

V

Vacuum distillation, 217
Vacuum filtration, 213

Valeraldehyde, 135
Van der Waals forces, 37, 62
Vapor-phase chromatography
(VPC), 222
Verbal reasoning, xii, xiii, xiv, xx
Vicinal diols, 11
Vinegar, 157
Vinyl, 9

W

Wash, 212
Wave number, 235, 236
Williamson ether synthesis, 124
Wittig reaction, 144–46, 148

Wolff-Kishner reduction, 146,
147, 148
Writing sample, xii, xiii, xv, xx

X

-X, 173
X_2 addition, 84–85

Y

-yl, 5
Ylide, 145
-yne, 9, 88

Z

(Z), 28
Z, 79
Zwitterion, 145, 274